TITLE   Pankration
        in Ancient Greece
AUTHOR Spyros P. Loumanis
PUBLISHER'S SIERIES   History

Copyright© 2017   Spyros P. Loumanis

ISBN   978-960-93-9333-1

2nd Edition   Athens, July 2017

PANKRATION
IN ANCIENT GREECE

Translated into English and edited by Danae Seemann
Greek inscriptions translated by Stavros Koukoudakis
(used as the basis for the English translation, unless otherwise noted)

SPYROS P. LOUMANIS

PANKRATION
IN ANCIENT GREECE

*To all the pankratiasts
whose names were lost
in the mists of time*

ἐκ θεῶν γὰρ μαχαναὶ πᾶσαι βροτέαις ἀρεταῖς

(For from the gods come all the means for human achievements)

Pindar
Pythian 1.41

VIEW OF THE PALAESTRA AT ANCIENT OLYMPIA
(photo from the author's collection)

CONTENTS

PREFACE 15

Chapter 1, THE BEGINNING 19
Prehistory of competitive games 21
Athletics and religion 23
Athletics in time of war 26
Nudity 26
Creto-Mycenaean Era (2100 - 1200 BCE) 27
Homeric Age (1200 - 776 BCE) 29
Violence in ancient games 38

Chapter 2, PANKRATION 42
The technique 43
The rules 50
Ephedros and anephedros 51
'Dustless' victory - *akoniti* 51
Sacred draw 52
Training 52
Paidotribēs, gymnastēs and *aleiptēs* 55
Wages of the *paidotribēs* 58
Diet 59
Injuries 59
Medicinal treatment 59
Offenses 60
Sarapion 61
The palestrae 61

Chapter 3, THE GAMES 65
Sacred - panhellenic games 66
The sacred truce 67
The *Hellanodikēs* 71
The Olympic *prorrhesis* 72
Number of participants 74
The Olympian Games 76

The Isthmian Games 88
The Nemean Games 90
The Pythian Games 93

Chapter 4, THE ATHLETES 96
The Olympic Victors 99
The Isthmian Victors 162
The Nemean Victors 173
The Pythian Victors 186
The *Periodonikēs* 189
The *aph' Hēracleous* athletes 194

Chapter 5, HONORS FOR THE CHAMPIONS 196
Honors for winners at Olympia 196
Honors for winners returning home 197
Fame beyond the *palaestrae* 198
Professional associations – Guilds 199
Paradoxos 202
Money prizes for pankratiasts 203
Hero cults and deification of pankratiasts 210

Chapter 6, THE SOCIAL BACKGROUND OF THE CHAMPIONS 212
Limited to aristocrats 212
Restricted participation 213
Famous aristocrat pankratiasts 213
Pindar 214
The change in social class of the participants 242
Funding for athletes from lower classes 243
How the ruling class saw athletics 244

Chapter 7, PANKRATION IN EDUCATION 247
Organization of the education system 247
The institution of the *ephēbeia* 250
Spartan athletic festivals 257

Chapter 8, PANKRATION AFTER 393 CE 259
Olympism 259
The Roman period 259
Christianity 260

The internal breakdown of the games 261
Byzantium 262
Middle Ages - Renaissance 264

Chapter 9, PANKRATION IN THE EAST 265

EPILOGUE 268

BIBLIOGRAPHY 272

INDEX 279

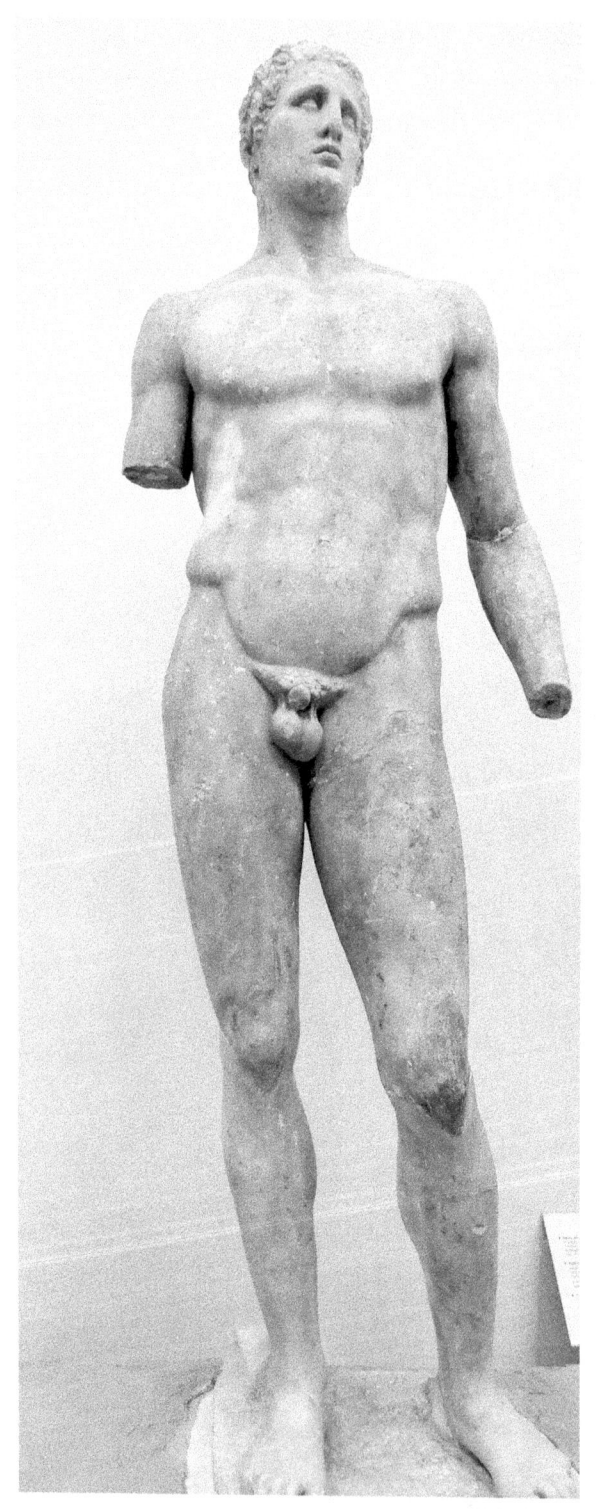

AGIAS, OLYMPIC PANKRATIAST AT THE 74th OLYMPIAD IN 484 BCE.
DELPHI MUSEUM
(photo from the author's collection)

PREFACE

This book is the result of my many years spent studying contact sports. Any attempt at understanding free fighting between two individuals inevitably leads to the source. The first historically complete form of fighting, called the *pankration*, was developed in Ancient Greece as a unique form of defense against a threat from humans. As an Olympic sport, it spread throughout the known world and influenced those that followed. It became part of Greek athletics and remained a singular phenomenon unrepeated in human history.

The space in which the match takes place brings the opponents together, as they ultimately communicate through their technique, regardless of what has motivated the conflict. Through combat, each one demonstrates his training and all of the cultural elements that it embodies. Thus, wherever pankration appeared, it transmitted elements of Greek civilization, functioning as an ambassador of the heritage that influenced the world as we now know it.

The history of pankration in particularly interesting to anyone who is involved in contact sports. It will be noted in this book that the answers to be found in connection with a particular sport are the same as those provided some 2,500 years ago, with astounding similarity. This may lead to further study and comparison between prevailing conditions in the two periods, while a better understanding of the present is gained along with ideas and inspiration to evolve as an athlete.

It will also be of interest to anyone seeking to learn more about Greek civilization in general since, in contrast with modern times, sports were closely linked to both religion and warfare. On the other hand, their interaction with politics and economics bears a great similarity to the present.

However, if we try to look at pankration in isolation, simply as a series of techniques performed between a pair of athletes, we would be no better off than trying to smell a flower in a photograph. For this reason, the book develops along two lines. The first is that it follows the historical unfolding of events. It was in ancient Greece that the concept of athletics was first developed and pankration embarked on its course at that time. The book follows its rise to glory and is there as it peaks. By following the course of the sport, we also observe the course of Greek civilization, since sports in the era under examination was a particularly complex phenomenon, reflecting events taking place beyond the *palaestrae* and *gymnasia*. The second line of this book follows a path from the general to the specific, wherein it describes a larger picture within which pankration is placed. Without this context, any description of the sport would seem piecemeal and even inexplicable in places. The context comprises three parameters: the religious environment, as it was shaped by the origins of physical competition; the athletic milieu, mainly manifested through the sacred Olympian, Isthmian, Nemean and Pythian games; and finally, the political and social climate. The influence of all three was very important because the games were primarily religious, filled with ancient symbolism, and taking part in them was an act of worship. They were also sporting events, though, as participants were engaged in an athletic competition which they sought to win. Everything that took place in Olympia and at the other sacred games were part of the experiential expression of the edifice we refer to as "ancient Greek civilization." Finally, the political and social environment could not be excluded, given that the impact of athletics on the people could be used to advantage.

If we focus on the sport, certain questions will emerge, such as: what was pankration; what rules were followed; was it violent; was it deadly; did it appeal to the public; what were the prevailing beliefs about pankratiasts; why did athletes take part in such a difficult and tough competition; was it reasonable to fight to the death for an olive branch or some other plant; what was the value of a victory at Olympia; from which social class did pankratiasts mostly originate; did they enjoy special honors; how did the political authority look upon the sport; what changed and what remained the same over time; was it just another sport; did it influence people or society beyond the actual arena? All of these questions can be answered once we are in a position to understand the context in which athletes were called upon to compete.

There are not many direct sources on pankration to be found in ancient texts. However, there is significant information embedded in other fields which either touch upon our topic or are pertinent to pankration because they refer to the period of time under study. We will attempt to highlight all of these aspects. The chapters of the book are linked to one another so that some references also apply to topics which have been developed elsewhere in the book.

The limited material certainly makes research more difficult, but it also presents an opportunity. In areas where information is lacking, the imagination can fill in the gaps. In this way, and depending on how knowledgeable one is about ancient Greece, the reader can create a more personal concept of pankration which can be expanded as deeper knowledge is acquired. This process could lead to, if not a necessarily more accurate, a more personal and intensely felt impression of the sport, of the people engaged in it and the period overall. Perhaps this will spur further research and a creative dialog - that can only be a good thing.

In any case, the book attempts to reflect a reality as it emerges from the use of sources. It does not aim to glorify the sport nor the athletes, nor the particular period in history. It focuses on describing what was happening at the time and to identify the links between the sport and its people, and everything that was going on inside and around themselves, in their soul and in their environment.

Our time defines us and in the period in question, this is apparent even if we look at it from a distance of 2,500 years. This is possible when the image is so powerful and brilliant, that it can travel through time, in the souls of people, and helps us to see what was happening then and how its effects have reached us in the present.

So, prepare yourselves: a journey of more than 1,000 years is about to begin. When does it end? By the end of the book, you will be able to provide your own answer.

Spyros Loumanis
Athens, 2016

THE PALAESTRA AT ANCIENT OLYMPIA
(photo from the author's collection)

Chapter 1

THE BEGINNING

Life is uniquely characterized by movement. The human body is defined by this functional need, whether it is voluntary or involuntary movement.[1] This need is dictated by nature itself and it is closely linked to the metabolic system, which is the chemical processes of the body involved in nutrition and whose function is essentially reliant on motion.[2] Nutrition has always been the most important bodily function and was related to the instinct of self-preservation. In order to find food, our ancestors had to run, jump or throw something in order to evade wild animals or other dangers. These activities contained running, jumping, throwing, climbing and lifting, among others. These prehistoric athletes engaged in these types of activities from an early age, guided exclusively by their instincts. This instinct, combined with the experience they acquired over time as they managed to survive by relying on their actions, naturally led to developing the most effective techniques for a particular terrain, the distance they had to run or the type of evasive jumping required, or how to strike an animal. What was happening to them is exactly what continues to happen to all animals that must learn to jump or swim most effectively without the aid of a teacher, but only guided by nature.[3]

At the same time, because of their need to be on the defense, humans were forced to be in a constant state of battle-readiness, maintaining peak physical strength and excellent conditioning. Thus, continual and painstaking

---

1 Georgios Papantoniou, "Oi epidraseis tēs ēthikēs stous Olympiakous agōnes tēs archaiotētas: apo tēn enarxē tōn agōnōn eōs to telos tēs klasikēs epochēs [The effects of ethics on the Olympic games of antiquity: from the beginning of the games to the late classical period] (776-336 BCE)" (PhD dissertation, University of Thessaly, Trikala, 2003), p. 18.
2 Evangelos P. Papakyriakou, *Philosophia physikēs agōgēs kai athlitismou* [Philosophy of physical education and sports], Thessaloniki 1985, p. 49.
3 Papakyriakou, *Philosophia physikēs*, p. 53.

physical activity was desirable and constituted the predominant characteristic of many societies.

Nevertheless, human movement was not only intended to respond to everyday needs. In times of peace, people were able to devote more time and engage in forms of movement that may have appeared to have no specific purpose, but which contributed to their recreation.[4] Thus, from formless and primitive, movement evolved and took form. Moreover, it developed in two directions: in the first case, the same movement was repeated in time and rhythm to create dance, and in the second, two or more individuals combined their movements to engage in actions dictated by convention and thus creating a game.[5]

In this way, movement evolved from the primitive to dance and play, both of which subconsciously served to nourish. But the drive to satisfy the biological need for movement did not stop there. Play could be considered instinctive or natural, and it should be seen as a source of every developed form of athletic movement. Therefore, athletics were the natural evolution of play.[6]

Despite its natural origins, this impulse to play developed, became reoriented and moved in other directions, ultimately toward the pursuit and attainment of a higher purpose.[7] In each game, the movements that arose from it were not repeated in a standardized and unchanging manner. Through experience and maturity, they became deliberate. That is how we arrived at organized play. In this regard, we believe that logic and sentiment are two key factors that helped to create it. Humans were already in a position to set goals and targets in their lives, but also in their thoughts and actions. Every beginning and end of a movement in every game acquired a specific purpose. In this way, it was possible to move beyond the purposeless motions and impose a specific form and rules on a game.[8] Through the game, it was possible to demonstrate one's true potential as a creator, an innovator and an active poet of the world.[9]

Over time, the tendency to display physical strength and skills led to the development of a noble competition, resulting in participants endeavoring to improve performance and overcome their opponents. Thus, free physical activity became a premeditated, competitive event that evolved into a contest. The aspiration to excellence and the desire for distinction led competitors to

---

4 Papantoniou, "Oi epidraseis," pp. 19, 20
5 Papakyriakou, *Philosophia physikēs*, p. 49.
6 Papakyriakou, *Philosophia physikēs*, p. 50.
7 Papakyriakou, *Philosophia physikēs*, p. 50.
8 Papakyriakou, *Philosophia physikēs*, p. 51.
9 Georgios Farantos, *Philosophia 1: Theōria tou ellēnikou Athlētismou* [Philosophy 1: Theory of Greek Athletics], Telethrion, Athens 1992, p. 35.

strive for improvement, with the result that they provided a spectacle that was increasingly more enjoyable, exciting and pleasing to spectators. And so certain activities developed through which one competitor achieving victory over another emerged as the main purpose. Thus, we conclude that movement, dance, play and competition are expressions dictated to human beings by their very nature. That is why the roots of physical activity are lost in the very distant past, since they appeared along with humans from their primitive period and evolved along with them.[10]

The game, as a sport, may be seen as the primary form of athletics. The components of the game, the rivalry and intense voluntary physical effort constitute the competitive aspect of competitive athletics.[11] The agonistic approach entails great effort and testing based on rules and conditions marked by purity, honor and precision.[12]

Prehistory of competitive games

The early forms of athletics can be traced to the peoples of the East. Many athletic games were known in Egypt during the third millennium BCE and more so in the second. But these games, as well as the similar games in the region, essentially have nothing in common with the Greek games beyond the natural inclination of a strong young body to exercise. The sole purpose of these demonstrations was to entertain the public and to serve some kind of ideal comparable to the subsequent Olympic idea.[13]

Crete was at the crossroads between the East on one side and Mycenaean Greece on the other. It is in Crete, then, that we find early indications of the subsequent athletic spirit. Here, the games we know from Egypt and the East slowly evolved into sports with rules which, in addition to displays of strength, were also associated with religious events.[14] With the passing of time, humans became more "civilized," marking the end of the instinctive "natural athlete."[15]

We see that the belief that competition and games are a Greek invention is not correct, since movement is dictated by nature itself. However, compet-

---

10 Papantoniou, "Oi epidraseis," pp. 20, 21
11 Papakyriakou, *Philosophia physikēs*, p. 52.
12 Farantos, *Philosophia 1*, pp. 38, 39.
13 G. Sakellarakis, M. Andronikos, N. Gialouris, K. Palaiologou and M. Pentazou, *Oi Olympiakoi Agōnes stēn archaia Ellada* [The Olympic Games in ancient Greece], Ekdotiki Athinon, Athens 1982, p. 13.
14 Sakellarakis et al., *Oi Olympiakoi*, p. 14.
15 Papakyriakou, *Philosophia physikēs*, p. 53.

itive games are a Greek institution and a creation of the Greek spirit. This is because the Greeks took the games, gave them the form of major celebrations, cherished them, deified them and established them as humanistic, ethical, social, religious, political, psychological and educational events. They were first in the world to show that benevolent competition contributes to the advancement of civilization.[16] From that great historical moment in time, human beings ceased to be invisible units, but became free entities and members of a political and social whole.[17]

Athletics in ancient Greece were incorporated into the social life of the people and were an integral part of their education. In the Greek sense, education had exceptional depth; it meant the cultivation of the whole person, where the body was not separate from the mind.[18]

The cultivation of the athletic spirit in ancient Greece was based on that very spiritual foundation upon which the other cultural values of Greek civilization rested. First among those was the liberation of the individual from despotism of any kind. The religious faith of Greeks did not deny them human freedom and therefore did not exempt them from human responsibility. Social discipline and compliance with the laws of the state comprised the obligation of free and responsible citizens. For ancient Greeks, the law was binding on both the gods and on humans, the rulers and the ruled. In order for the people to enjoy such responsible freedom, they needed to believe in themselves, in other words, in their body and spirit and in the supreme value of human life. The visible image of deity was man himself, since even the Greek gods had all of the human characteristics in their idealized form. For Greeks, physical perfection - beauty - was bearing a likeness to god.[19]

Besides the human factor, we are also defined by the environment. The magnificent landscape of Greece - the mountains, the sea, the air and the sun - can inspire nothing less than beauty and freedom.[20]

Religion was initially an assistant and a supporter of tradition and character; later on came the state, which had realized the benefits of athletics and helped to set an example and provided the means for their dissemination.[21]

Another important point of reference was the manner in which Doric severity (discipline, forbearance, terse speech) coupled with Ionic agility

---

16 Papakyriakou, *Philosophia physikēs*, p. 54.
17 Papakyriakou, *Philosophia physikēs*, p. 54.
18 Sakellarakis et al., *Oi Olympiakoi*, p. 8.
19 Sakellarakis et al., *Oi Olympiakoi*, p. 9.
20 Papakyriakou, *Philosophia physikēs*, p. 55.
21 Papakyriakou, *Philosophia physikēs*, p. 55.

(spirituality, realism, beauty) to create a cultural moral unity that was unique for that period.[22]

In antiquity, athletics represented reality; another form of religion that was not a transcendent but a purely human form of worship springing from a joy of life and its paramount goal - human perfection through beauty and truth - so that absolute good and happiness prevail and merge completely with the gods, as Plato believed.[23]

In antiquity, games were held for various reasons, usually to honor a dead hero, to select a groom or simply for entertainment. This tradition of occasionally holding games, as developed by the Greeks and evolved during the Archaic and classical period, would ultimately lead to the establishment of local and panhellenic competitions, finally elevating them to events of a unique social scale.[24]

Athletics and religion

Greek religion and athletic events have been closely linked for a very long time. Participation in these games was akin to a religious act. Athletes competed to honor the gods, as well as to win for their cities and for themselves.[25] Much later, from the Archaic period onward (after 800 BCE), though their association with religion did not cease, these games gradually were transformed into authentic sporting events. Nevertheless, the earlier function of the games was retained as part of worship traditions throughout antiquity, even when they acquired independent status.[26]

According to tradition, all of the major panhellenic events were established in honor of a dead hero or a divine action. The custom of honoring dead heroes with funerary games was maintained throughout antiquity. The connection between athletic competition and both funerary customs and religious feasts associated with fertility is due to the belief of the ancients that the relation between life and death is dialectical: new plants sprouts from the dead earth, the youth who engage in sports draw strength from dead heroes in whose honor they compete. A symbol of this ceaseless rebirth of hope, vi-

---

22 Papakyriakou, *Philosophia physikēs*, p. 55.
23 Papakyriakou, *Philosophia physikēs*, p. 56.
24 Konstantina Gogaki, *Oi antilēpseis tōn archaiōn Ellēnōn gia ton athlētismo* [The perceptions of the ancient Greeks about athletics] (Tipothito-Giorgos Dardanos, Athens, 2005), p. 31.
25 Donald Kyle, "Pan-Hellenism and Particularism: Herodotus on Sport, Greekness, Piety and War," The International Journal of the History of Sport 26, no. 2 (February 2009): p.189.
26 Sakellarakis et al., *Oi Olympiakoi*, p. 36.

tality and joy brought about by sports was the sacred flame of Olympia, which burned perpetually at the *Prytaneion* (home of the priests and magistrates). Remembrances of this earlier role of the games were preserved through religious agricultural celebrations in classical times.[27]

Primitive societies associated the life-giving power of the earth, manifested through the succession of the seasons and the cycle of growth and decay, with divine intervention. The cyclical fertility of the natural world led them to imagine a number of fertility gods who personified the forces of nature. Through formalized rituals, they hoped to appease them so the gods in turn would ensure abundance, wealth and prosperity. Beginning with the simple assumption that every birth must be the result of the conjoining of two forces - a man and a woman - it followed that they had to invent the existence of a male deity analogous to Mother Earth who they would consider as a symbol of strength on which the fertility of the earth depended. This union of divine power with the annual rebirth and growth of crops led to creating a religious cult in which athletic competition played an important role and which sought to demonstrate physical strength and endurance. Thus, physical activities and the demonstration of physical prowess became a part of the cult's rituals and the staging of games was incorporated into the ritual of religion. The winner in these games was considered a symbol of fertility and was honored with the victor's wreath, thus also symbolizing a divine presence. During the ceremony, the god would take a human form in the winner, who was not meant to receive a prize of any material value, but instead a symbol expressing the divine aspect of fertility. In this way, the fertility of nature was linked to the activities of humans, through which a winner would emerge.[28]

The idea that one individual would mediate between gods and humans came about gradually. It had to be perceived as the duty of the strongest, given that bodily strength was associated with healthier agricultural crops and plentiful harvests. Thus, the process of identifying the strongest individual through competition became an event of great importance for society and took on a religious dimension.[29]

However, the smooth development of these competitive activities presupposed the consistent prevalence of some form of religion. The revival of the Olympic games was the result of a religious compromise, on the one hand, and the dominance of the new religion of the Dorian conquerors. This compromise served as the basis for the development of a new type of society,

---

27 Sakellarakis et al., *Oi Olympiakoi*, p. 36.
28 G. Papantoniou, "Religiosity as a main element in the ancient Olympic Games," Sport in Society 11, no. 1 (January 2008): pp.32, 33.
29 Papantoniou, «Religiosity,» p. 41.

which acquired considerable energy and vigor with the creation of the new *polis*, or city-state.

Each new city could select a specific deity as a protector and patron, but two or more cities could worship the same one. Often, cities would decide together to establish ritual celebrations in honor of the same deity. Their citizens would get together regularly to organize sacred ceremonies and share extravagant meals accompanied by hymns, prayer and games. Each city sent its own official delegation of *theoreis*, or envoys, to take part in the sacrifices. The sacred games were major religious gatherings. A key characteristic of these events was that the people came together to celebrate the same cult and this connection linked initially a large number of cities, and ultimately the entire Greek world. This shared characteristic was a common religion. The foundation of the sacred games was mainly religious, not political. It is clear that the games in Olympia, which were revived as part of tradition, brought with them traces of their religious past and cult character. But they gradually emerged in their new form with the appearance and prevalence of the new city-state, marking in turn the dawn of what we know as ancient Greece. In mythology, we saw gods and heroes fighting for victory and the right to found their own games, and they were seen as patrons of specific events. Cronus, Zeus, Apollo, Hermes and Ares were the first to take part in games, followed by Idaean Heracles, Pelops, Oinomaeus, Heracles, the Dioskouroi and a whole line of kings and governors.[30]

In his epinicean odes, Pindar confesses that "nothing that the gods accomplish ever appears unbelievable." Therefore, the victories of heroes depended on the will of the gods, since they are the ones who endowed the victors with the necessary talents, which combined with their efforts to help them claim a victory. The entire ideological structure of the Olympic games was built on religious feeling. The victor was considered sacred and this explains the extravagant honors bestowed upon him, as he symbolized the god in whose honor the games were held. Any violation of the rules applied to the games was seen as an act of disrespect and punishment involved offerings to the offended gods. But as the Olympic games evolved during this period in history, they were often the object of religious intervention, as religion attempted to control them. It should be noted that such interventions would often hide financial or even political motives.[31]

---

30 Papantoniou, «Religiosity,» p. 39.
31 Papantoniou, "Religiosity," p. 40.

Athletics in time of war

Religiosity and militarism in ancient Greece were compatible concepts. The Greeks took part in religious duties, but the warlike Greek states were not disposed to risk a loss or a conquest simply for religious reasons. Their acceptance of the will of the gods was not absolute. Moreover, despite King Leonidas and the Battle of Thermopylae, the Spartans, being fully aware of their limited number of citizens, did not appreciate the reckless sacrifice of their soldiers. The Greeks had no idea about martyrdom or turning the other cheek, and meekly accepting catastrophe as the will of a just god and expecting judgment and resurrection. Their leaders regularly consulted the oracles and the soothsayers read all the omens, but they were realistic about their calculations with regard to waging wars. Political and military matters may well have taken precedence over the interpretations of divine will.

The Greeks had many contests throughout the year and the Persian campaign lasted a long time. Thus, certain games coincided with battles, raising tensions with regard to duty-bound obligations to the gods and the country, and calling on the political leadership to decide whether or not to fulfill its obligations to help other countries and defend Greece. Longtime enmities and self-interest were set aside to create a difficult and fragile alliance. For some, the games were convenient excuses used as tactics for distracting attention, delaying, creating divisiveness and facilitating desertion. The cities wished to be pious, but they were also aware of the risk of piety conflicting with the principle of justified self-defense.[32]

Nudity

Greek athletes in the prehistoric period appeared lightly dressed, but not nude. In Homer, athletes competing in wrestling and boxing wore a loincloth to cover their genitals, as the barbarians did.[33]

It is not known precisely when nude athletes first appeared at Olympia. At the *stadion* games in 724 BCE, Orsippus ran nude to improve his speed and won. Others believe it was the Athenians who first adopted nudity, while

---

32   Kyle, "Pan-Hellenism," pp.190, 191.
33   Evangelos Albanidis, *Istoria tēs athlēsēs ston archaio Ellēniko kosmo* (History of sport in the ancient Greek world), Salto, Thessaloniki 2004, p. 125.

others say it was the Spartans.³⁴ Plato said that the Cretans were first, followed by the Spartans. Once they overcame their initial embarrassment, they realized that aside from the benefits of exposing the entire body to the sun, they would also be unable to conceal any ugliness or imperfection due to lack of fitness. For the ancient Greeks, a beautiful body and beauty in general were to be admired.³⁵

Most studies now agree that nudity in physical exercise first appeared in Sparta, later spreading to Olympia and then to the rest of Greece. Starting in the sixth century BCE, nudity was established as a social indicator of free citizenship and Greek nationality,³⁶ while others believed nudity in athletic competitions was the ultimate symbol of egalitarianism - "equality before the law," and it overlooked social class altogether.³⁷

Creto-Mycenaean Era (2100 - 1200 BCE)

The athletic activity of the Cretans revolved around bull-leaping, foot races, Greek wrestling, boxing, pankration, dance, rolls, flips, hunting, archery, fencing, chariot racing and games. It was in Crete that athletics took firm root. It should be remembered that Zeus came to Olympia from Crete, thus launching the prehistoric-historic phenomenon of the Olympiads.³⁸

The Minoan civilization was deeply religious; the influence of religion on all aspects of social life was quite apparent, particularly in athletics and farming. With regard to athletics, one could say that during this period, the Cretans and Pelasgians enjoyed physical exercise for religious and cultural reasons, and indirectly for military purposes.³⁹

Already by about 2600 BCE, the Cretans had developed a noteworthy civilization whose course would continue over the ensuing fifteen hundred years, reaching its peak in the sixteenth century BCE. This civilization was mainly characterized by the construction of palaces in the largest cities on the island, which were later considered poles for political and religious power, and

---

34 Henri-Irénée Marrou, (2009). *Istoria tēs ekpaideusēs kata tēn archaiotētas: O ellēnikos kosmos* [A history of education in antiquity], trans. Valia Sereti (Daidalus I. Zacharopoulos, Athens 2009), p. 57.
35 Albanidis, *Istoria tēs athlēsēs*, p. 126.
36 Kyle, "Pan-Hellenism," pp.188, 189.
37 Thomas Hubbard, "Contemporary sport sociology and ancient Greek athletics," *Leisure Studies* 27, no. 4 (October 2008): p.381.
38 Papakyriakou, *Philosophia physikēs*, p. 58.
39 Papakyriakou, *Philosophia physikēs*, p. 59.

centers of the economic and cultural life of citizens. The Minoan people lived in a period of peace, security and prosperity that lasted centuries. Its naval supremacy kept the risk of war at bay and discouraged any would-be invaders. The cities and palaces always remained unfortified. In such an atmosphere of peaceful living, it was natural that physical activities did not focus on identifying tough, brave warriors. The ideal fighter, as the one developed among the people of the East after persistent physical exercise, had no place in Minoan society, where everything functioned smoothly, lawfully and justly and where its diffused civilization radiated brilliance, sensitivity, gentility and artistry.[40]

The decline of the Minoan civilization came on suddenly, probably as the result of the massive eruption of the Thera volcano. This event has been dated at between 1600 and 1500 BCE.[41] Between 1400 and 1100 BCE, Crete was part of the Mycenaean civilization and the Cretans and Achaeans were merged together. Then around 1100 BCE, the Dorians arrived in Crete.[42]

The Mycenaean centers developed their civilizations between 1600 and 1200 BCE, when they were destroyed. The cause of this destruction is not yet known. It seems that the last of the Achaeans took the secret of their destruction with them. The monuments found at Mycenaean centers indicate they were destroyed at their peak and that their ruin was complete. The period that followed their demise is known as the "Greek Dark Ages" (1100-800 BCE). No advancement was noted throughout this period; on the contrary, all of the arts declined and the Greek world fell into a darkness that endured for more than three centuries. During this time (about 1100 BCE), the Dorians reached the Peloponnese, not as conquerors but as a new wave of colonizers.[43]

The Mycenaeans were interested in weapons and were warlike. These were people with heroic leaders who were mostly warriors whose ultimate goal was to achieve glory and gain riches through war.[44] It is also generally believed that the Mycenaeans added a more competitive dimension to the Minoan athletic culture they had acquired.

Meanwhile, the brilliance of the Achaeans, the civilization marked by gold masks, famous burial offerings, a variety of bronze and ceramic vessels, and the impressive stone citadels, faded after a course of about five centuries.

---

40 Papantoniou, "Oi epidraseis," pp. 28, 29.
41 Papantoniou, "Oi epidraseis," p. 32.
42 Papakyriakou, *Philosophia physikēs*, p. 59.
43 Ioannis Mouratidis, *Istoria physikēs agōgēs me stoicheia philosophias* [The History of Physical Education (with Elements of Philosophy] (Christodoulidis, Thessaloniki 2009), p. 67.
44 Papantoniou, *Oi epidrasei*, p. 33.

What remained as their legacy was the heroic spirit of the era, the constant desire to subjugate and the games held in honor of their dead.[45]

The ability to overcome rules varied in proportion to human development and athletics means overcoming. As we saw previously, in the Mycenaean period, whoever overcame the limitations signified bravery, strength and the power of authority. In taking into account the fact that myth is the historical core of the past, Zeus came to Olympia during the Minoan period. Following a theomachy in the form of a wrestling match against his father, Cronus, Zeus won over the religious conscience of the people while also succeeding in establishing the new Olympian philosophy.[46]

Homeric Age (1200 - 776 BCE)

Worldwide athletics have their beginnings in this period. For the first time, the words came into use that would mark systematic physical development through the ensuing centuries and to the present day. Homer's epics describe athletic games for the first time. Homer's descriptions of the different sports are the source of information on the athletic practices of that period. The word "*athla*", meaning "arena," is first mentioned in *The Iliad*, while the word "*athlētēs*" (athlete) first occurs in *The Odyssey*. "*Athleō*," from which "*athlos*" is derived, refers to the competition, the labor, the great effort and achievement, while "*athlon*" is the prize for victory. The words for "best" (*aristos*) and "excellent" (*aristeuein*) also appear for the first time in Homer's epics and refer to brilliant success and dominance. These have remained unchanged, both as written and in meaning, to the present. "*Aristeuō*", the verb "to excel," in particular implies being first and earning distinction, while "*aristos, epi empsychon*" means the best person in skill, in bravery and in lineage. "*Epi apsychōn*" means the best, the most suitable, the most advantageous object. But "*aristeus*" in Homer also means the noblest, since excellence was the prerogative of the nobility.[47]

---

45 Papantoniou, *Oi epidraseis*, p. 36.
46 Sotiria Giannaki, Nikitas Nomikos and Thomas Yiannakis, "Ē ypervasē tōn koinōnikōn kai thrēskeutikōn oriōn ōs genesiourgos aitia tōn archaiōn Ellēnikōn Agōnōn [The transgression of social and religious norms as a trigger for the ancient Greek games," paper presented at 14th International Congress on Physical Education & Sport, May 19-21, 2006, Democritus University of Thrace, Department of Physical Education and Sports Science, Komotini, 2006, p. 13.
47 Gogaki, *Oi antilēpseis*, pp. 30, 31.

The Homeric physical culture was based on competition and the patriotic ideal.[48] The athletic events of that time included chariot racing, boxing, wrestling, foot races, armed combat, discus throwing, archery and javelin throwing.[49] There is no reference to pankration.

The purpose of competing was to develop physical and mental excellence in combat to serve the heroic spirit of the race, which would then help it to survive in the harsh living conditions of the time while also fulfilling the military needs of the state. That is why the Homeric Age and agonistic era were described as "heroic."[50]

The games were often part of the funerary rites, or took place to express human emotions relating to important events. During these games, the athletes competing around the tomb of the fallen hero on the one hand wanted to reenact and glorify the acts of the great men and their death to save their country. On the other, they could demonstrate that, as athletes, they possessed similar skills, strength and faith and were also willing to fight and to die gloriously, if need be, just as the dead they now honored with their athletic games had done.[51]

Homer's athlete was generally a robust competitor, someone who had the physical attributes to take part in games that were unplanned and held at random when opportunity presented itself, either to please the crowd or to pay respects to a beloved deceased after the funerary ritual. Competitors in the Homeric epics did not specialize in a particular event.[52]

According to Homer, excellence was manifested in a perfect physique and superior skills, in bravery and military prowess, physical vigor and muscular strength. The greatest glory for any man was derived from his physical strength, which was reinforced through agonistic activity. He was driven to demonstrate military valor and competitive vigor in order to be glorified in war and in the arena. Such courage and strength were considered the ultimate virtues and were morally binding on heroes in battle so that retreating was unthinkable and any such act would be humiliating. However, competitors were also encouraged to desire victory as they endeavored to avoid the shame of loss. The warriors commonly believed that death was the natural outcome of their actions, bringing honor to them and their descendants and ensuring

---

48　Papakyriakou, *Philosophia physikēs*, p. 61.
49　Papakyriakou, *Philosophia physikēs*, p. 62.
50　Papakyriakou, *Philosophia physikēs*, p. 62.
51　Papakyriakou, *Philosophia physikēs*, pp. 62, 63.
52　Papantoniou, "Oi epidraseis," p. 39.

eternal glory for the dead hero.⁵³ The ideal hero that emerges from the Homeric poems possessed physical and mental strength, intelligence and valor.⁵⁴

The Phaeacians believed that the most important thing a citizen could achieve - more important even than success in commerce and amassing wealth - is "what one can achieve with his own hands and legs," meaning athletic performance. This removed an individual from his daily routine and placed him in a sphere of high ideals. The first time that the word "athlete" is written, full of the meaning it expresses, was when Euryalus tells Odysseus, "You are no athlete." The latter was deeply insulted and set out to prove him wrong. In the Homeric world, there was no place for heroes who were not also athletes.⁵⁵

The moral value of athletic competition in the Homeric Age

The tradition of the Mycenaean concept of athletics not only continued but also evolved from the eleventh century BCE to the Archaic period, peaking in the sixth and fifth centuries BCE. The Homeric epics echo the customs of older times which were preserved in tradition, but also describe the contemporary conditions of the late Geometric period.⁵⁶

The domineering political structure in *The Iliad*, mainly based on faith in the king, remained robust and powerful. In *The Odyssey*, the scenario was very different. It depicted a society relieved from the anxiety of war in which its citizens enjoyed the benefits of peace and taking part in the joys of everyday life.⁵⁷ In *The Iliad*, the king bore all the responsibility, while in *The Odyssey*, the king was responsible for nothing. Perhaps that was due to the fact that history was approaching the eighth century BCE, the period during which the nobility took power.⁵⁸

The Homeric heroes were extremely well endowed with the virtues that everyone wished to possess: they were tall, handsome and well-built and indeed made up a separate world, since they were royals. Homer usually combined the idea of the skilled warrior with the idea of the king of noble descent. Ultimately, Homer believed that virtue requires even sacrificing one's life. In *The Iliad*, a showdown with the enemy, or an opponent in general, is undoubtedly a true test of a man's worth. *Aretē* did not mean a particular moral trait,

---

53 Papantoniou, "Oi epidraseis," pp. 45, 46.
54 Sakellarakis et al., *Oi Olympiakoi*, p. 31.
55 Sakellarakis et al., *Oi Olympiakoi*, p. 32.
56 Gogaki, *Oi antilēpseis*, p. 53.
57 Gogaki, *Oi antilēpseis*, p. 55.
58 Gogaki, *Oi antilēpseis*, p. 56.

but embodied qualities of excellence such as a noble heritage, good performance, success and prestige. A nobleman fulfilled the ideals of his class with this quality and it served to earn him distinction among its members. The contest's reward for excellence is honor and glory - values which are particularly encouraged by the aristocratic class. Its conscious acceptance of these values explains why the nobleman was prepared to sacrifice his life for them. It also explains the competitive manner in which these honorary, symbolic trophies were acquired, as the satisfaction of earning them had nothing to do with their actual material value. All this ultimately interprets the heroic character of the games and defines the subsequent course of Greek civilization, since the idea of competition moved from the context of physical strength to the more spiritual sphere; in other words, to achievements in poetry and theater.[59] A Greek could only achieve true happiness when he asserted his supremacy over his peers and was at the same recognized by the community as distinguished and superior.[60] Just as the late Middle Ages left us *The Imitation of Christ*, the Greek Dark Ages left to Classical Greece the imitation of the hero through Homer.[61]

As we have seen, the eighth century BCE marks the end of the "dark" era but also the start of the Archaic period, characterized by the appearance of written testimony as a tool in the hands of historians. The first period of Greek colonialism was seen a few hundred years earlier (fourteenth century BCE onward), which was the result of pressure by the excessive power of the Mycenaean people, and led to the Dorian invasion of the Peloponnese (twelfth century) and the annihilation of the Mycenaean world. After the collapse of Mycenaean civilization, the course of religion was stunted, implying the start of a transitional phase in post-Mycenaean religion. There is insufficient archaeological evidence to determine whether the same gods existed throughout the period, and it is impossible to know the location of places of worship. Perhaps they were inside homes or in smaller sanctuaries. Worship of the dead and of heroes was neglected throughout the period of the Dark Ages. At a time of great upheaval caused by the tempestuous currents of migration, the permanent settlement of the population was so uncertain and precarious that people avoided burying their dead and cremated them instead; it was more convenient to carry the ashes of their dead family member or local hero along with them to their destination. Thus, the heroes who were particularly influential among ordinary people because of their feats were no longer worshiped,

---

59 Gogaki, *Oi antilēpseis*, pp. 60, 61.
60 Marrou, *Istoria tēs ekpaideusēs*, p. 45.
61 Marrou, *Istoria tēs ekpaideusēs*, p. 49.

since their worship was closely tied to their place of burial and their strength was believed to derive from the remains preserved inside their tombs.

With the end of the Greek Dark Age and the beginning of the Archaic period, the political and social reorganization that followed was decisively important. The important phases of migration had already been completed and permanent settlement created the basis for social organization and economic development. However, this social stability and long-term survival in a particular location enabled the faithful who wished to exercise their religious duties to gradually move from the earlier system of having a single altar as a place of worship to constructing the first temples. The appearance of the temple as the residence of a deity is thought to have emerged in the eighth century BCE.

Nevertheless, from the ninth century onward, this new religious attitude was also expressed in the appearance of special places of worship just outside urban centers where the faithful would gather from neighboring settlements or even further afield to make their offerings (*anathēmata*) to the gods.[62] All of the main cults of classical Greece appeared during this period, in the space of one century.

The outlying places of worship, known as sanctuaries (*iera*), appeared alongside the rapid demographic development of the period. The population density in thinly populated areas increased and in many locations older settlements were revived and developed into urban centers. The role of these sanctuaries, removed from the cities, was important: they served as religious centers and determined the manner of worship, drawing area residents closer together. The result was a united community that worshiped the same deity as its protector, farmed the arable land in the region and functioned as a unified defensive force against any potential outside threat. Thus, the construction of a large regional sanctuary, often on the outskirts of the arable land, meant that a definitive step was taken to unify all of the communities in the area into a single unit: the *polis* (pl. *poleis*), or city-state, but essentially encompassed the body of citizens within that unit.

Along with the development of these places of worship came the revival of hero worship, the roots of which lay in the early Mycenaean period but which had faded during the Greek Dark Age. However, during the Archaic period, when the city-states were forming and becoming stronger, the presence of heroes was essential, since they functioned as protectors of the *poleis* when they came up against one another. During these conflicts, the citizens felt the need to call upon the gods for help. The problem, though, was that the major

---

62 An *anathēma* was an object intended to please a particular deity. It was an act of worship and honor.

gods of the Homeric pantheon, which had been passed down to the people as a joint legacy, could not be asked to support one city against the other, since they were worshiped in common. This justified the presence of the hero-protector of each *polis* in order to provide exclusivity of the divine cooperation in the hostilities between them. In this way, the citizens of Archaic society settled on their new land, feeling a sense of ownership and expressing their religiosity freely to their gods and their dead heroes. In retrospect, it is clear that these two developments determined the course of religious trends of the period and established the bases for forming *poleis*. And while the sanctuaries defined the territorial domination over a greater region, the worshiping of heroes concentrated people together within the marketplace of the new *polis*, where the hero's tomb was located.[63]

The Homeric epics had a major influence on the spread and adoption of the Olympian pantheon as a common religion for all Greeks. As such, it helped to unify the Hellenic world, with the political consequences this entailed.[64]

The Homeric world of the gods was formed on the basis of the needs and beliefs of the Ionic aristocracy and reflected the beauty and strength of the heroic-aristocratic protagonists of the epic. The moral foundation of the people was clearly built on religion. In other words, the dominant belief was that devotion to a divine imperative purifies humans and shapes morality. The heroes of the aristocracy lived in the shadow of divine justice, which influenced their fate and rewarded the pure of heart while punishing evil.[65]

Nevertheless, Homer's heroic society faded with the passing of the Archaic period. Finding themselves in a state of peaceful permanence and able to develop stable social structures, the people were in a position to turn to farming the land as the main means of their livelihood. Weary from the wars and hardships they had experienced in the preceding years, they finally found serenity. It was then natural that the ideals of Homer's hero-warriors would be set aside and be replaced by new principles based on peace, labor and justice.[66]

Through the prevailing religion and their everyday ethic, the Archaic Greeks had formulated a specific model that determined their attitude toward the gods, i.e. the respect and awe with which they were regarded, as well as their actions toward their fellow citizens, which were now based on dignity and the application of law. At the core of these beliefs were "fear of the gods" and "practical justice." The resulting morality imposed on society the idealized

---

63 Papantoniou, "Oi epidraseis," p. 60-65.
64 Papantoniou, «Oi epidraseis,» pp. 65, 66.
65 Papantoniou, «Oi epidraseis,» pp. 66, 67.
66 Papantoniou, «Oi epidraseis,» pp. 67, 68.

person, who was subject to the judgment of others through praise or reproach, respect or loathing, thus making it clear that morality was directly related to society's general opinion of the individual. Hence, people were motivated to do whatever drew them praise and respect and to avoid actions which were considered reprehensible and led to social rejection. In a society where the religious element was dominant and directed human actions, it was natural that the driving moral force was drawn from a belief in the gods.[67]

As for athletic games: in *The Iliad*, they were held in a Greek military camp in the lull between wars. These were games that took place at the tomb of the hero and were funerary games. These funerary games aimed at placating the soul of the dead hero to ensure the living were protected against evil. Such athletic games were held in honor of great men immediately after their death. They were a revival of an ancient rite of worship of the dead mentioned frequently by Homer, and their practice never waned.[68]

In *The Odyssey*, the games were part of festivals and were held along with other events at the peak of the ceremony. Contrary to *The Iliad*, the atmosphere in which these games were held was joyful and entertaining; this was their chief purpose. They were accompanied by music and artistic events, and lacked the military coarseness seen in *The Iliad*. These all had a celebratory character.[69]

The presence of the gods

In *The Iliad*, the presence of the gods during the games was strongly felt and continuous. The gods watched the games and clearly expressed their preferences and openly supported their favorites. Their presence and intervention were so intense that it seemed the gods themselves were competing, rather than mortals. The gods intervened in these games just as they did on the battle field.[70]

The presence of the gods in the games featured in *The Odyssey* continued, but was somewhat more discrete. The difference between *The Iliad* and *The Odyssey* was that in the former, the gods determined the outcome of the event, while in the latter, they played a supportive role for the hero. It is agreed

---

67 Papantoniou, «Oi epidraseis,» pp. 84, 85.
68 Gogaki, *Oi antilēpseis*, pp. 33, 34, 35.
69 Gogaki, *Oi antilēpseis*, p. 41.
70 Gogaki, *Oi antilēpseis*, p. 43.

in both epics, however, that any outstanding performance beyond normal limits had to be attributed to the gods.[71]

Participation in games

In *The Iliad*, the athletes taking part in games as a rule were heroes or royalty. Mainly, they were fighters who had distinguished themselves by their strength and military achievements. Courage in battle and military excellence were the characteristics of the predominant heroic prototype. So while it is known that ordinary soldiers in *The Iliad* trained to maintain their physical strength and for entertainment, they were unable to take part in the games that Homer described.

In *The Odyssey*, the lines separating social classes were less apparent and certainly less strict, since athletes who participated in the games were select young citizens and not just soldiers, meaning they were not necessarily military leaders and heroes.[72]

The techniques of the sporting events

The events described in *The Iliad* are: chariot racing, boxing, wrestling, foot races, armed combat, discus, archery and javelin. *The Odyssey* also refers to jumping. There was no particular specialization in a sport, since the athletes could take part in more than one.[73]

By the time of *The Odyssey*, there was already more specialization in athletics as they became more developed. The techniques used in the events described in *The Iliad*, where the description of the games was more detailed, were mainly combat-related. The athletes repeated the movements and practices they would have used in a military confrontation. The events were nothing more than the reenactment of battles between two actual opponents. The strikes were violent and sudden, causing injuries and serious trauma. The competitors were determined to overcome their opponent and demonstrate their physical courage, which was the same courage that made them heroes on the battlefield.[74]

---

71 Gogaki, *Oi antilēpseis*, p. 44.
72 Gogaki, *Oi antilēpseis*, p. 46.
73 Gogaki, *Oi antilēpseis*, p. 50.
74 Gogaki, *Oi antilēpseis*, p. 51.

As the city-state system took shape, athletics meant identifying athletes with the war heroes. Once the Olympic Pantheon was completed, the hero was the gods' chosen one.[75]

Victory was equivalent to a heroic feat and the rewards that followed were glory, happiness and honor. During this period, athletics came to be linked to the great moments of human inspiration through poetry. They were also associated the higher arts, such as sculpture, painting and statuary. The athletes and their movement were transformed into art through marble, gold, bronze and other metals.[76]

The agonistic spirit of the ancient Greeks

The religiosity of the Greeks in antiquity was more action-oriented than passive faith. Of all the activities engaged in by the Greeks that were dedicated to the gods, competitive festivals occupied a special place. They were able to demonstrate their piety with a number of sacrifices and processions. But aside from the expression of religious feeling, the games were also a way in which the participants could demonstrate their superiority over their peers and enjoy glory and honor. The term *agon* was used to describe an athletic contest, but it also meant a military conflict or battle. It was thus not just a matter of taking part in enjoyable activities, but rather a competition to be won at any cost. Toughness was the natural expression of the heroic ideal of the particular society and it should not be misinterpreted through misplaced comparisons using social criteria that define violence in the modern world.[77]

The agonistic spirit that Greeks shared seems to hark back to the roots of their history: to the Minoan and Mycenaean eras and to Homeric tradition. The Greek spirit of competition was also an integral part of Homeric narratives.[78]

---

75 Gogaki, *Oi antilēpseis*, p. 24.
76 Gogaki, *Oi antilēpseis*, p. 24.
77 Gogaki, *Oi antilēpseis*, p. 51.
78 Matthieu Boutet-Lanouette, «La vie agonistique dans les cites Grecques d'époque imperiale analyse de l' Αγών des Balbilleia d' Ephese (IER-IIIEsiecle p.C.)» (master's thesis, Quebec, 2007), p. 1.

Violence in ancient games

Bia, who according to mythology was born to Oceanus' daughter, Styx, and Pallas, and the sister of Zelus, Nike and Kratos, was the personification of force and violence. This force was the main characteristic of the universal cosmogonic myths of how the younger gods overcame the older ones. In other words, this conflict in cosmogonic myths is an essential structural component of competition to seize control of power or to establish a new order.[79]

The ferocity of the ancient games may be more easily understood if one considers that these events began as war games.[80]

From this perspective, "violence" in antiquity really means "obsession with victory." The latter was the challenge for the participant to prove his power, for the purpose of acquiring a good name for himself and his homeland, but was also an effort to approach the divine and to achieve cleansing. It also meant something else that was very important for the time: that through his glorification, his mortal nature achieved a little immortality.[81]

This theory protects us from falling into the trap of drawing wrongful conclusions about the relationship between Bia and the games. Here is what it says: The first theoretical approach is through western ethnocentrism, which means applying our own criteria to another society. This leads to incorrect conclusions and eliminates distinctions between diverse entities. Western ethnocentrism is what caused the disappearance of many Asian, African and American traditions which westerners believed should have evolved in the same way as their own, which they attempted to impose on other cultures.[82]

A second theoretical position is that research of a social phenomenon is incomplete if it is not linked to other structural characteristics of the society in which it occurs.[83]

Boxing, wrestling and pankration were the perhaps the most grievous sports. Philostratus claimed that pankratiasts were involved in a dangerous type of wrestling and they had to be skilled in various methods of strangulation. They bent ankles, twisted arms, threw punches and jumped onto their opponents. Contrary to the Spartans, the Eleans forbade biting or eye-gouging with the fingers in pankration, although they allowed strangulation.[84] Galen

---

79 Gogaki, *Oi antilēpseis*, p. 211.
80 Bruce Kidd, "The myth of the ancient Games," *Sport in Society* 16, no. 4 (2013): 416-424, p. 419.
81 Gogaki, *Oi antilēpseis*, p. 34.
82 Andreas Ioannidis, "Via kai athlēmata," *Archaiologia* (quarterly periodical) 1, no. 4, Athens, 1982, p. 51.
83 Ioannidis, "Via," p. 51.
84 Gogaki, *Oi antilēpseis*, p 225.

mocked pankration and boxing athletes for their excessive weight, as well as their brutality. As he observed, when they completely broke a limb or twisted it, or gouged out their eyes, then one could clearly see the beauty that their occupation had in store for them.[85]

Nevertheless, there was some impunity for champions. The law in classical Athens stated that there would be no prosecution if an athlete killed an opponent during athletic games. Even criminal behavior went unpunished.[86]

But let us attempt to define violence. Violence means exerting force by any means possible. Overcoming violence was always achieved with intervention into the dyadic structure of the violent act by a third entity, making it a triadic structure, namely opponent - referee - opponent.[87] In the case of pankration, it was opponent – *Hellanodikēs* - opponent. Thus, the *Hellanodikēs*, or Greek official, intervened to enforce the rules of competition. So up until this point, the actions of the pankratiasts were not perceived as violence.[88]

Military athletes

The epic tradition also influenced the development of the military elegy. Around the mid-seventh century BCE, Tyrtaeus claimed that the magnitude of a man's military prowess was determined by his sacrifice for his country, and therefore, physical exercise was beneficial only when it enhanced one's military skills. Later, Pindar equated the games with war and acknowledged that both warriors and athletes should receive the same honors.[89]

The theory that the purpose of physical training was to prepare good soldiers and make young men useful both in time of war and of peace gained popularity in the classical period. It was expressed by Solon, Plato and Aristotle, and even Philostratus, who lived during the Roman period.[90] Excessive physical training was the result of young men, practiced in the art of war, endeavoring to be of use to the city in a society where protecting one's fatherland was one of the highest ideals.[91]

---

85 Gogaki, *Oi antilēpseis*, p 225.
86 Evangelos Menenakos, Nicholas Alexakis, Emmanuel Leandros, Gerasimos Laskaratos, Nikolaos Nikiteas, John Bramis and Abe Fingerhut, "Fatal Chest Injury with Lung Evisceration During Athletic Games in Ancient Greece," *World Journal of Surgery* 29, no. 10, (2005): p. 1351.
87 Farantos, *Philosophia 1*, p. 56.
88 Nigel B. Crowther, "Athletics and Literature in the Roman Empire (review)," Mouseion: Journal of the Classical Association of Canada 7, no. 3 (2007): p. 268.
89 Gogaki, *Oi antilēpseis*, p. 218.
90 Gogaki, *Oi antilēpseis*, p. 220.
91 Gogaki, *Oi antilēpseis*, p 223.

The distinction of athletes into military and non-military was made later by Plato in *The Republic*, where in referring to the training of the guardians (*phylax*), he maintains that in their main mission to protect the *polis*, they functioned as athletes in the most crucial competition.[92]

In referring to military athletes, Plato believed that it was necessary for them to follow a different diet from that of other athletes, which he believed would make them sluggish and unhealthy. Athletes sleep throughout their lives and if they diverge even a little bit from their regular diet, they become very ill, he claimed, insisting that it was necessary to want to eat to the point of staying healthy and maintain the body in good condition.[93]

Alexander the Great was not very fond of athletics; though he established numerous artistic competitions and all sorts of hunting and stick fighting, he did not appear at all willing to institute a prize for either boxing or pankration.[94]

The belief in the superior value of military athletes would prevail throughout antiquity, as indicated in Pausanias' *Description of Greece: Elis* (second century CE). This conviction was based on the idea that the most courageous would be useful against an enemy. It would follow that an athlete's pugnacity would guarantee that he would exhibit the same characteristic in war from which his city had to be saved. And because a victory in games held in times of peace was a demonstration of the athlete's personal value in times of war, the honor that society bestowed upon an athlete was special.[95]

The social context of violence

What factors influenced the phenomena of violence in ancient athletics and how were they linked to other characteristics of ancient society?

First of all, the most important factor was war, which was the normal way of settling transnational affairs.[96] The result was the shaping of a military ideal which was reflected in all social events. Thus, even sports, influenced by the manner in which they were held and the techniques of war, possessed a warlike ethos and were closely linked to the activities of a militaristic aristocracy. The athlete was the extension of the warrior of the heroic period, as the

---

92 Gogaki, *Oi antilēpseis*, p. 254.
93 Gogaki, *Oi antilēpseis*, pp. 336, 337.
94 Gogaki, *Oi antilēpseis*, p. 259; Plutarch, *Alexander* 4.
95 Gogaki, *Oi antilēpseis*, pp. 263, 264.
96 Ioannidis, "Via," p. 52.

games were the unbroken continuation of the past. The further back we look, the most strongly held this belief was.[97]

Another reason was because it shaped the relationship between the individual and the societal whole. It was believed that the courageous warrior was beneficial to the *polis*. Therefore, triumph over an opponent was not merely the personal ambition of the athlete, but a prerequisite for his recognition by society. The games were not just a charming get-together; they involved battles during which the athlete lunged at his opponent as if he were the enemy he had to overcome.[98] Excessive training had the same goal. The more robust, the more useful athletes would be against the enemy.[99]

A third factor was the idealization that had emerged around "physical vigor," since the games in antiquity were defined by traditional customs and not by detailed regulations, as they are now.[100]

Yet another factor associating violence with sports was self-defense; in antiquity, the protection of the individual was not the exclusive responsibility of the state, as it is nowadays, but rather a matter that involved those closest to the individual.

There is a point, therefore, where war, self-defense, sport, and the social position of the athlete become linked together and explain why there was such a high degree of violence in athletic games.[101]

---

[97] Gogaki *Oi antilēpseis*, p. 230.
[98] Gogaki, *Oi antilēpseis*, p, 232.
[99] Gogaki, *Oi antilēpseis*, p, 233.
[100] Gogaki, *Oi antilēpseis*, p, 234.
[101] Gogaki, *Oi antilēpseis*, pp. 235, 236.

Chapter 2

PANKRATION

The ancients believed that pankration was created by the great hero and founder of Athenian democracy, Theseus, who combined wrestling with his fists to overcome the savage Minotaur in the Labyrinth. In reality, its origins have been lost in time.

The first historical reference to pankration appears in Argonautica by Apollonius of Rhodes. It describes one battle scene in particular where martial pankration[102] was used in a struggle between Castor and the Bebrycian giants, Itymoneus and Mimas[103]. Reference is made to kicking, which was only used in pankration, and strikes with the hand, though the word "fist" is not used. Here is the excerpt:

105 B
αὐτὸς δ᾽ Ἰτυμονῆα πελώριον ἠδὲ Μίμαντα,
τὸν μὲν ὑπὸ στέρνοιο θοῷ ποδί, λὰξ ἐπορούσας,
πλῆξε καὶ ἐν κονίῃσι βάλεν, τοῦ δ᾽ ἆσσον ἰόντος
δεξιτερῇ σκαιῆς ὑπὲρ ὀφρύος ἤλασε χειρί,
δρύψε δέ οἱ βλέφαρον, γυμνὴ δ᾽ ὑπελείπετ᾽ ὀπωπή.

Translated[104]:
[Polydeuces] slew huge Itymoneus and Mimas.
The one, with a sudden leap, he smote beneath the breast
with his swift foot and threw him in the dust; and as the other
   drew near

---

102 Lazaros E. Savidis, *Pankration: to olympiakon agōnisma* [Pankration: the Olympic sport], Eleftheri Skepsis, Athens, 2004, p. 48.
103 Apollonius of Rhodes, *Argonautica* 105 B
104 Apollonius of Rhodes, *Argonautica* 105 B, trans. R.C. Seaton, retrieved Sept. 29, 2016, http://www.theoi.com/Text/ApolloniusRhodius2.html.

> he struck him with his right hand above the left eyebrow, and tore away
> his eyelid and the eyeball was left bare.

We can assume that pankration was already structured, at least in its early stages, and was the object of systematic training.

Pankration does not appear in Homer or any other bibliography before the fifth century BCE. It was a sport in the Greek and Roman worlds, and there was nothing like it in the ancient Middle East.[105]

The technique

Pankration began as a form of self-defense; it is possible that it is the evolution of the most primitive form of conflict used by humans against other humans or animals.[106] Almost anything was permitted - strikes, holds and full contact, which is why it is also referred to as *pammachia*[107] or *pammachon*, meaning "contest of all kinds." Philostratus noted that it was the product of combining boxing and wrestling.[108] Plato described it as a combination of imperfect wrestling and imperfect boxing.[109] But the former description is probably more literary. Plato was himself a pankratiast and wrestler, and a skilled one at that, with two victories at the Isthmian and one at the Nemean games, winning once in pankration and twice in wrestling. It is interesting that although he was named Aristocles by his parents, he may have been given the name of Platon, meaning "broad," by his trainer, Ariston of Argos, because of his wide shoulders and generally good build. He was well-aware, therefore, that pankration was more than what he described.

Before we continue, it should be noted that it is not precisely known how exactly the techniques of pankration were performed because the transfer of knowledge from person to person was interrupted over time. Information regarding the techniques of pankration is drawn from texts, but mostly from images painted on ceramic vessels. Nevertheless, these are artistic depictions of the movements and reflect how the artist painting each vessel interpreted

---

105 Michael B. Poliakoff, *Combat sports in the Ancient World: Competition, Violence and Culture* (Sports and History Series, Yale University Press, New Heaven, 1987), p. 54.
106 Albanidis, *Istoria tēs athlēsēs*, p. 161.
107 Michael B. Poliakoff, *Studies in the Terminology of Greek Combat Sports* (Hain, Frankfurt, 1986), p. 64.
108 Philostratus, *Gymnasticus* 11.
109 Plato, *The Republic* 1338.

what he saw. It should also be noted that the human body was the same then as it is nowadays; the joints functioned as levers in the same way and the competitors would have always wanted to emerge the winner; so, they would have developed powerful and effective techniques. One might conclude that the techniques must have resembled those of modern combat sports, but there were probably some differences in the details.

Despite the technical similarities among the three heavy sports, and the references to the first historical record of boxing,[110] wrestling,[111] and pankration,[112] it is not possible to know which came first. However, since pankration was the first form of self-defense, the one in the defensive position would not be thinking about any limitations when under threat. In other words, he would not decide against using his feet to kick, or punching with his fists, or to avoid engaging in hand-to-hand combat if circumstances required it. For these reasons, pankration probably appeared before other combat sports in its initial form, or at least at the same time as the others.

Since the main components of pankration were wrestling and boxing, we will briefly describe these two sports and add whatever elements were included in pankration.

Palē, or wrestling, was particularly popular in the ancient world because it symbolized the struggle of humans as they endeavored to hold their own against nature and their destiny.[113, 114] There were two types of wrestling: upright wrestling, or *orthopalē* or *orthostandēn*, and ground wrestling or *alindēsis* or *kylisis* (rolling in dust). In upright wrestling, the winner was whoever threw his opponent to the ground[115, 116] while in ground wrestling, the match continued on the ground and ended when one of the opponents admitted defeat. The match took place in a sandpit, and there was no time limit, nor points or weight divisions in the contest.

Pygmē, or boxing, was a Laconian invention, according to Philostratus[117]. In order to avoid being struck in the face during combat but also to withstand it if they could not fend off the blow, they trained in how to protect their faces. At a more primitive time, people boxed with bare hands, without leather thongs (*himantes*), or with an open palm. Minoan boxing is depicted

---

110 Albanidis, *Istoria tēs athlēsēs*, p. 152; Mouratidis, *Istoria physikēs agōgēs*, p. 225.
111 Albanidis, *Istoria tēs athlēsēs*, p. 143; Mouratidis, *Istoria physikēs agōgēs*, p. 220.
112 Albanidis, *Istoria tēs athlēsēs*, p. 161; Mouratidis, *Istoria physikēs agōgēs*, p. 233.
113 Thomas Yiannakis, *Archaiognōsia – Philosophia tēs Agōnistikēs* [Philosophy of Competition], Athens, 1979, p. 108.
114 Albanidis, *Istoria tēs athlēsēs*, p. 143.
115 Yiannakis, *Archaiognōsia*, p. 111.
116 Philostratus, *Gymnasticus* 11.
117 Philostratus, *Gymnasticus* 9.

as a match of specialized boxers wearing special gloves and having their palms clenched tighter.[118] There was no specific place for holding the event, like the modern-day ring, nor was there a time limit for competition. No points were given nor weight divisions defined. The athletes boxed continually until one or the other gave up or was knocked out.[119] It was clearly a grueling sport. The boxers used leather *himantes* to protect their knuckles, to prevent sprains and to limit injuries to their opponent.[120] The main components of training included a leather sack (*kōrykos*), like the modern punching bag, and shadowboxing.[121]

Pankration included techniques from boxing, wrestling throws, as well as kicks, strangleholds and pressure locks.[122] Twisting of limbs, bones and fingers was permitted, as well as dislocation, breaking of bones, kneeing, kicking and elbowing, while counterstrikes and other counters were also taught.[123] The mixed use of hands and feet made it look, in modern terms, like a combination of the French Savate, the Japanese ju-jitsu and judo, and freestyle wrestling.[124] The essential difference between wrestling and pankration was that in the former, the goal was for the athlete to throw down his opponent, while in pankration, the contest continued until one of the two pankratiasts admitted defeat.[125] Its two styles - upright (*orthostandēn*) and ground pankration (*alindisēs* or *kylisis*) were also distinguished by technique. In the upright stance, there were strikes with the hands and feet and throwing techniques. On the ground, the pankratiast would use strangleholds, choke holds, limb-twisting or full immobilization[126] to cause his opponent to surrender.[127] It is interesting that the use of violent strikes was possibly permitted, even if the opponent was on the ground.[128]

As in wrestling and boxing, there were no weight divisions, point systems or time limits on pankration matches, nor were there any laws protecting the life and limbs of the opponents. In modern-day terms, one might say the competitor had to grab the win, rather than the rules giving it to him. The

---

118 Achilleas Drivas, *Oi sōmatikes askēseis stēn proistorikē Ellada* [Physical exercise in prehistoric Greece], Athens, 1965, p. 24.
119 Poliakoff, *Combat Sports*, p. 80.
120 Yiannakis, *Archaiognōsia*, p. 129.
121 Mouratidis, *Istoria physikēs agōgēs*, p. 232.
122 Poliakoff, *Combat Sports*, p. 54.
123 Yiannakis, *Archaiognōsia*, p. 142.
124 Roberto Patrucco, *Lo sport nella Grecia Antica*, L. S. Olschki, Firenze, 1972, p. 312.
125 E. Norman Gardiner, "The Pankration and Wrestling. III," The Journal of Hellenic Studies 26, (1906): p. 4.
126 Patrucco, *Lo sport*, p. 312.
127 Patrucco, *Lo sport*, p. 322.
128 Patrucco, *Lo sport*, p. 317.

rules mostly referred to things that were not permitted. Victory could only be achieved if one of the opponents did not wish or was unable to continue.[129] This resignation, or surrender, was expressed by raising one or two fingers, as in boxing.[130]

Pankration was also an exhausting sport, which nowadays might even be called a battle of subjugation. All pankratiasts, like boxers, were knock-outers, and though in modern contact sports, knock-outs were the exception, in antiquity they were the rule.

There were differences, however, both in the defensive stances of the three forms of combat which marked the beginning and end of any conflict. Depending on what was permitted, we note the following:

Greek boxers fought upright and preferred hits to the head, and so kept their hands raised. As shown in the two images that follow,[131] the left hand usually used for defense was extended forward, while the right was flexed and kept close to the body.[132]

ROMAN TERRA-COTTA DISCUS OIL LAMP, 1ST CENTURY AD,
Milavic, "Pankration and Greek Coins", p.187

---

129 Stephen G. Miller, Arete: Greek Sports from Ancient Sources, University of California Press, 2012, p. 225.
130 Philostratus, *Gymnasticus* 9.
131 Anthony Milavic, "Pankration and Greek Coins," *The International Journal of the History of Sport* 18, no. 2 (2001): p. 187.
132 Milavic, "Pankration and Greek Coins," p. 180.

PHILIPPOPOLIS, THRACE, AE-30 (1.5X), AD.198–217
Source: Caracalla/Boxer, Milavic, "Pankration and Greek Coins", p.187

The wrestler's stance aimed at avoiding losing his balance backwards while also being able to attack quickly while moving forward. For this reason, they stood on the balls of their feet, rather than the heels, with one or both knees flexed.[133] This is shown in the two images that follow.[134]

BRONZE FIGURINE, FIRST-SECOND CENTURY, AD
Milavic, "Pankration and Greek Coins", p.188

---

133 Milavic, "Pankration and Greek Coins," p. 181.
134 Milavic, "Pankration and Greek Coins," p. 188.

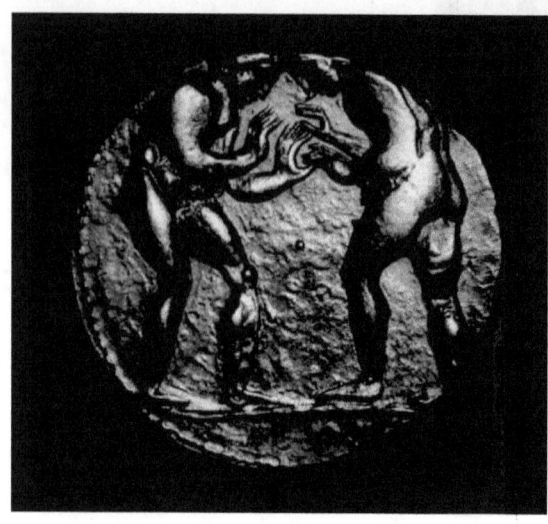

ASPENDUS, PAMPHYLIA, AR STATER (2X), 385–70 BC
Milavic, "Pankration and Greek Coins", p.188

Pankratiasts used techniques of both boxers and wrestlers. Thus, the defensive stance was a combination of these two combative stances. This is how the defensive stance of a pankratiast was described by two ancient writers: Aulus Gellius wrote that when a pankratiast was ready to fight, he would raise his arms and spread his fingers to protect his head and face, and that all his limbs were ready to deflect and deliver blows before the battle began. The second century Greek physician Galen added that the pankratiast kept his fingers flexed to be ready to form a fist to deliver a strike, or to grab his opponent, depending on the opportunity that presented itself.[135] This tactic is used in modern martial sports, with most of the weight on the back foot, leaving the front foot free to function as a punching tool and allowing it to move freely should the opponent attack with kicks, thus avoiding injury.[136]

The differences in defensive positions among the three methods of fighting are apparent in the representations on the amphora.[137]

---

135 Milavic, "Pankration and Greek Coins," p. 181.
136 Milavic, "Pankration and Greek Coins," p. 181.
137 Milavic, "Pankration and Greek Coins," pp. 189, 190.

RED-FIGURE KYLIX. C. 420 BC
Source: British Museum, Milavic, "Pankration and Greek Coins", p.189

ATTIC OENOCHOE, C. 430 BC
Source: Krakow, Poland, Milavic, "Pankration and Greek Coins", p.190

The athletes in the images have placed their weight on the back foot and their hands are bare and flexed at eye-level.[138]

Clearly, pankratiasts were well-rounded athletes. They could wrestle, box, strike with an entire "arsenal" of weapons, engage in fighting from a greater distance that allowed for kicking, at a middle distance with his hands, and at the smallest distance when grappling in close contact. In addition, the large repertory of techniques permitted strikes to be combined with tactics from varying distances, changing angles of attack and the level of engagement, to go from upright combat to ground combat while simultaneously striking

---

138 Milavic, "Pankration and Greek Coins," p. 181.

and grappling, to wear out the opponent with strikes or tire him with different choke holds, and then to finish the match by taking advantage of an opportunity to attack. In order to emerge a victor in pankration, the athletes had to be able to withstand strikes, holds, hard work and pain.[139] Both boxing and pankration were truly brutal and bloody sports.[140] Because of the degree of difficulty and the spectacle it provided, Philostratus considered it the best and most worthy of sports for the men of Olympia.[141]

Ultimately, pankration was a type of scientific unarmed combat[142] that incorporated different styles of engagement, depending on the build and the technical skills of the athlete, which allowed it to be synthesized into a particular technique.[143] It grew into a science of close combat through the ongoing study of competitions, and was supported by knowledge of anatomy, medicine and philosophy.[144]

The rules

The main restrictions were outlined in the *enagonioi nomoi*, or rules of competition. Biting and gouging with fingers anywhere on the body were prohibited. Another rule forbade athletes from grabbing their opponent by the genitals. These regulations were strictly observed and violators were punished by thrashing to make an example of them.[145] In Sparta, pankration was practiced without any of these restrictions; it was practiced as if competitors were on the battlefield and the game was truly deadly. So while choosing to do battle with an Athenian pankratiast may have been misguided, fighting a Spartan could prove fatal. The freedom provided by the Spartan rules led the sport to develop in a very different form. The defense had to be particularly compact, since even a small opening would allow a hand with extended fingers to pass, creating a crack through which subsequent attacks could follow. Sensitive targets such as eyes, neck or ribs were much more vulnerable. Moreover, when a particular hold was used, the arms or legs employing it could not linger un-

---

139 Xenophon, *Symposium* 8, 37-38.
140 H. W. Pleket, "The Olympic Games in antiquity," *European Review* 12, no. 3 (2004): p. 404.
141 Philostratus, *Imagines* 2.6.
142 D. W. Masterson, "The ancient Greek origins of sports medicine", *British Journal of Sports Medicine* 10, no. 4 (1976): p. 197.
143 Lucas Christopoulos, "Greek Combat Sports and their Transmission to Central and East Asia," *Classical World: A Quarterly Journal on Antiquity* 106, no. 3 (2013): p. 456.
144 Christopoulos, «Greek Combat Sports,» p. 456.
145 Mouratidis, *Istoria physikēs agōgēs,* p. 236.

protected near the face of the opponent, as he would be able to use his teeth. Under these circumstances, a match could be over very quickly, with disastrous results, since even a small opening was enough.

Ephedros and anephedros

An *ephedros* was a competitor who was left out of the competition when there were an odd number of competitors and he drew a bye. He would be the third, fifth, seventh and so on. He was fortunate because as he had sat out all the preliminary fights, he would enter the fray at the end against the final winner in better condition, while his opponent would be worn out from the previous rounds.[146] However, an athlete who emerged victorious as an *ephedros* was not valued as highly since his victory was a matter of luck. In contrast, the *anephedros* was the athlete who did not win the victor's crown through chance, but because he participated in all the rounds of competition and won through his efforts. The title "*anephedros*" was related to the value of the victory, since he would be considered worthier.

'Dustless' victory - *akoniti*

Niki akoniti meant winning without effort, since no match took place and the athlete was not covered in dust from the arena.[147] Here is a look at how this facet of competition came about: in the month leading up to the games at Olympia, during which the combatants were trained by the Eleans, the training of wrestlers was more arduous because they exerted equal effort both during training and in competition. As such, the Eleans, rightly decided to award a "dustless win" (*nikē akoniti*) to wrestlers when the occasion presented itself. By comparison, training for boxers and pankratiasts was more restrained to prevent injuries. However, if pankratiasts and boxers were forced to demonstrate their true skills during a preliminary match in order to convince the *Hellanodikēs*, or judges, they were better so they would be selected to take part in the games, then they would give it their all.[148] Aside from the chief reason of preventing injury, there may have been another. Since all techniques were permitted in

---

146 Sakellarakis et al., *Oi Olympiakoi*, p. 123.
147 Albanidis, *Istoria tēs athlēsēs*, p. 128.
148 Philostratus, *Gymnasticus*, 11.

pankration, there was a greater possibility of surprising the opponent in the contest than there was for wrestlers and boxers, since their options were more predictable. Thus, by holding back during training, they reserved their best techniques for the official games to maintain their advantage. Nevertheless, there were cases in Olympia where winners were crowned without fighting both in boxing and in pankration.[149] This occurred when the number of participants was relatively small and thus the chance of a *nikē akoniti* was greater.

In pankration, *nikē akoniti* was the most honorable way of winning because it meant the opponent had not dared show up to compete, thereby acknowledging the superiority of the winner.[150]

Sacred draw

In the event of a tie, where the contest ended without a clear winner after a long duration, the wreath of victory was not given to either of the two competitors, but instead was offered to Olympian Zeus, or to other gods in whose honor the games had been held. This was called an *iera isopalia*, or sacred draw, because the prize was given to the gods. If there was money to be won, the drawn athletes could share the monetary prize. A second century CE podium was found at Olympia which belonged to Tiberius Claudius Rufus. It bears an inscription referring to the sacred *isopalia* and the fact that pankratiast Rufus did not win, but was honored for his physical and mental strength and perseverance.[151]

Training

In a contest that was so varied and complex, the athletes had to be in very good physical condition so they could endure the many hours of daily training. Having achieved the required level of fitness, they then had to learn the entire repertory of boxing and wrestling moves and the additional techniques that combined the two.

Free exercises for the hands constituted a separate cycle called *heironomia*, or hand gesticulation. *Heironomia* looked very much like the shadow-

---

149 Sakellarakis et al., *Oi Olympiakoi*, p. 123.
150 Nigel B. Crowther, *Sport in Ancient Times* (Praeger, Westport, 2007), p. 53.
151 Albanidis, *Istoria tēs athlēsēs*, p. 129.

boxing practiced by boxers. Nowadays, athletes in all contact sports engage in rounds of shadowboxing. The feet also got a workout in shadowboxing since the entire body participated in the move.[152]

In order to increase their stamina, boxers would hold their arms up for a long time. They would also keep their fists raised for long periods while holding *haltēres*, a type of dumbbell, or other weights. To make it even more difficult, they would have another athlete exert downward pressure on their arms to increase resistance.[153] Nowadays, this is known as isometrics. Both pankratiasts and boxers used *haltēres* to exercise.[154] In modern-day terms, this would be eccentric strength-building.

The jumping rope was also used in training. It helped to strengthen the legs, but mostly enhanced arm-leg synchronization and sense of rhythm. It is no surprise that they had developed a number of variations of this exercise.

To increase their striking power, they used a punching bag, or *kōrykos*, as part of their training. The *kōrykos* was a bag filled with fig seeds or flour for the weaker athletes, and sand for the stronger ones. The size of the bag varied according to the athlete's age. According to Philostratus, it had to be lighter for boxers and heavier for pankratiasts. The latter would strike the *kōrykos* with his fists, feet, head, chest or back,[155] as well as knees and elbows. It was common practice to stop the swaying of the bag with the chest or other parts of the body in order to strengthen the internal organs.[156]

Training also included wrestling on the ground (*alindēsē* or *kylisē*, as explained above) as a preparatory exercise for pankration.[157] Another exercise which was used to prepare for wrestling was *akrocheiria*, involving only the hands. The two opponents would grab each other's hands and grapple without using any other holds.

For pankratiasts, this was considered homework.[158] They would study the individual components of combat to improve each one and then observe the match as a whole, paying attention to the combinations and overall competition tactics.

In *Laws*,[159] Plato refers to *pyrrichios*, or *pyrrichē*, as a type of war dance used by boxers and pankratiasts to reenact the offensive and defensive moves

---

152 Evangelos Pavlinis, *Istoria tēs Gymnastikēs [History of Athletics]* (G. Ē. Kallergi, Athens, 1927), p. 217.
153 Pavlinis, *Istoria tēs Gymnastikēs*, p. 220.
154 Pavlinis, *Istoria tēs Gymnastikēs*, p. 218.
155 Pavlinis, *Istoria tēs Gymnastikēs*, pp. 220, 221.
156 Christopoulos, "Greek Combat Sports," p. 447.
157 Pavlinis, *Istoria tēs Gymnastikēs*, p. 221.
158 Pavlinis, *Istoria tēs Gymnastikēs*, p. 220.
159 Plato, *Laws*, Z. 815-816a.

of battle. It included dodging, back-stepping, leaping and crouching.¹⁶⁰ These days, comparable exercises in Asian martial arts are known as *Kata* in Japanese Karate, *Poomsae* in Korean Taekwondo, and "forms" in Chinese Kung fu. The pyrrhic dance was devised by Pyrrhicus of Cydonia, a city-state in Crete.¹⁶¹ As we will see later, the Spartans used the *pyrrichios* to develop the military attributes of their troops.¹⁶² Regardless, these exercises were used throughout each period to improve coordination, rhythm of movement and cohesion.

The older method of physical exercise of that period did not consist of movements with any particular beginning or end, nor was their anticipated outcome specified in detail.¹⁶³ The advantage of that method was that it was natural and thus unhurried and graceful, as each individual¹⁶⁴ executed each technique in his own way to create his own version. Such a regimen was thorough and varied. This explains why older athletes could complete successfully in more than one event. Those competing in the heavy sports sometimes won in two or even in three events, such as the formidable Cleitomachus of Thebes, who won in wrestling, boxing and pankration at almost every competition, and the great Theogenes of Thasos, a pankratiast and boxer who also won the *dolichos* long foot race at Phthia. Another indication of how well-founded their methods of training were was the length of time these athletes remained in peak form. Pankratiast Dorieus, the son of Diagoras of Rhodes, won over a period of sixteen years; Theogenes of Thasos kept winning over twenty years.¹⁶⁵ They were healthy, they were never taken ill while training, aging did not slow them down until they were of advanced age, and they were able to complete at Olympia several times – some eight or nine times.¹⁶⁶

In about the second century BCE, Philostratus wrote that a new system for organizing training had become popular: the tetrad. This was a cycle of four-day training (nowadays it is a seven-day cycle), whereby the first was to prepare the athlete, the second for an intense workout, the third allowed him to rest and on the fourth day, he would train moderately.¹⁶⁷

---

160 Albanidis, *Istoria tēs athlēsēs*, p. 116.
161 Ioannis Chrysafis E., *Ē Gymnastikē ton archaiōn [The fitness training of the ancients]* (National Academy of Physical Education, Athens 1965), p. 172.
162 Thomas Yiannakis, *Istoria physikēs agōgēs: apo tous prōtogonous laous mechri sēmera* [History of physical education: from primitive peoples to the present] (University of Athens Faculty of Physical Education and Sport Science, Athens 1989), p. 36.
163 Pavlinis, *Istoria tēs Gymnastikēs*, p. 254.
164 Pavlinis, *Istoria tēs Gymnastikēs*, p. 254.
165 Pavlinis, *Istoria tēs Gymnastikēs*, pp. 256, 257.
166 Philostratus, *Gymnasticus*, 43.
167 Philostratus, *Gymnasticus*, 47.

From a technical standpoint, pankration was the first and perhaps last method of fighting because it included all of the strikes and holds that could be executed by the human body. Overall, pankration was the absolute form of combat for the following reasons:

1) It essentially included all of the weapons provided by the human body
2) The entire body was a target
3) There were no prohibitions
4) There was no protective apparatus
5) There was no time limit on the rounds of competition
6) The rules were always the same
7) The games took place in a natural environment
8) The games had taken place on the same type of terrain for more than a thousand years, so the outcome was not affected by changes in regulations or arena
9) Victory was achieved through the complete submission of the opponent, since all fighters aimed for a knockout
10) The contest was never interrupted in the event of injury
11) The judges played the same role for more than one thousand years
12) Throughout the sport's presence in the arenas, the spectators continued to hold its athletes in high esteem

Without doubt, pankration would have developed technically a great deal. That is because it survived for more than one thousand years, while the parameters, such as the regulations, the terrain and the role of the judges remained the same. Thus, what would have driven its development would have been improved physical conditioning, techniques and strategy.

Paidotribēs, gymnastēs and aleiptēs

The *paidotribēs*, or physical trainer, was usually a former athlete who undertook to teach the techniques of the sport to youths. Nowadays, mainly in Asian martial arts, this person is addressed as "instructor." The *palaestra* (first a wrestling school, later a training center) usually belonged to him. His duties also included teaching proper manners, discipline and good behavior. Although the *paidotribēs* was usually empirical and lacked theoretical knowledge, in the classical period he was both theoretically trained and possessed a general education. There are numerous references to such *paidotribēs* who were also respected sophists and physicians.[168] As the institution of the *paidotribēs* evolved, they became increasingly more respected, and starting in the second century CE, they were hired for life and usually had an assistant (*ypopaidotribēs*).[169]

Were there particular styles in the way athletes fought one another? Did athletes from each *palaestra* have similar approaches in their fighting? It is quite possible, since each *paidotribēs* trained many young athletes in pankration and therefore would pass on his personal approach to fighting. It was inevitable that these students would have similar technical skills.

The *gymnastēs* was another type of trainer would took on professional athletes or those who were very ambitious.[170] He was able to tell a lot about a person's character based mainly on his external characteristics, and also had extensive theoretical knowledge in pedagogy, kinesiology, anatomy, physiology and psychology. According to Galen and Philostratus, the *gymnastēs* also had to be well-versed in refereeing.[171] The Athenian trainer Menander, who trained Aegina's pankratiasts, was particularly famous.[172] But the best known of all was Melesias, himself a pankratiast, who chalked up 30 victories as a trainer of various winners at sacred games. His achievements were extolled by Pindar.[173]

Trainers of boxing and pankration were most often referred to in classical texts, or depicted on red-figure pottery giving lessons in contact sports. This is not surprising, since many of the trainers were former athletes in these heavy sports and some of them had also been champions in their youth. One can conclude that athletics comprised two closely linked activities: athletic events based on competitive games and lessons in traditional training.[174]

The care of athletes both before and after training included massage and rubdowns with oils which helped to reduce muscle fatigue, to disperse built-up lactic acid after training and to prevent potential injuries. The therapeutic use of oil in the ancient world was widely known, and was first used by the Spartans.[175] Oil was supplied by sponsors at all athletic facilities where athletes could use it freely.[176]

---

168 Mouratidis, *Istoria physikēs agōgēs*, p. 142.
169 Albanidis, *Istoria tēs athlēsēs*, p. 223.
170 Mouratidis, *Istoria physikēs agōgēs*, p. 142.
171 Albanidis, *Istoria tēs athlēsēs*, p. 231.
172 Albanidis, *Istoria tēs athlēsēs*, p. 231.
173 Albanidis, *Istoria tēs athlēsēs*, p. 231.
174 David M. Pritchard, "Sport, War and Democracy in Classical Athens," *The International Journal of the History of Sport* 26, no. 2 (February 2009): pp. 216, 217.
175 Marrou, *Istoria tēs ekpaideusēs*, p. 57.
176 Nikitas N. Nomikos, George N. Nomikos and Demetrios S. Kores, "The use of deep friction mas-

The *aleiptēs* (anointer) was essentially a physiotherapist charged with using appropriate massage techniques with oil, and who was familiar with just how much pressure to exert depending in the age of the athlete in training. The use of deep massage with oil was important both as a warm-up but also to help the athletes achieve their performance goals. There were nine different types of massage. More oil was used in winter than in summer, when the oil would protect the body from the sun and the skin pores from dust and sand. After the massage, the athletes were dusted with a fine sand so their bodies would not be so slippery in combat. There were four different types of dusting powder.[177] Philostratus refers to a type of dust that was *pēlodēs*, or muddy, which helped clean the skin; *ostrakōdēs* (reddish earth) to make dry skin perspire; and *asphaltodēs*, or tar-like, which was meant to warm up the body. Some of these were made in Greece, but at least one of them was imported from Egypt.[178]

The training session was followed by massage to aid recovery, breathing exercises[179] and cleaning of the body with a strigil. This was a curved, sharp scraping tool used to remove the layer of sweat, oil and dirt from the surface of the skin. This sticky glutinous substance was called the *gloios* and it was collected in pots and sold for its supposed medical properties. The scraping was followed by a bath, during which the athletes used a sponge to clean off the residue.[180]

As to the breathing exercises mentioned above: these were much more than a method of post-training recovery. The painting of Eucharides[181] depicts the abdomen of athletes as being unusually distended, as if filled with air. This breathing exercise was called the "exercise of the *pneuma*," meaning breath as well as spirit. The use of the principles of the *pneuma*, along with other concepts of Greek medicine, led to the development of various breathing techniques which were later lost in the West as a result of the mind/body separation introduced by Catholicism. Thus, there is no trace of this practice in the Western world. Oribasius[182] called this type of exercise *apotherapeia*, or restorative treatment. This technique enhanced the stamina of athletes through

---

    sage with olive oil as a means of prevention and treatment of sports injuries in ancient times," Archives of Medical Science 6, no. 5 (2010): p. 642.
177 Albanidis, *Istoria tēs athlēsēs*, p. 257.
178 Mouratidis, *Istoria physikēs agōgēs*, p. 154.
179 Albanidis, *Istoria tēs athlēsēs*, p. 260.
180 Nomikos et al., "The use," p. 643.
181 Eucharides was a Greek painter mainly of pottery and lived from approximately 500 to 470 BCE.
182 Oribasius was an ancient Greek physician and medical writer. He lived from about 320 to 400 CE. He was the personal physician of Roman Emperor Julian, also known as the "Apostate." He studied in Alexandria under physician Zeno of Cyprus.

deep breathing exercises that activated the *pneuma* inside their bodies. He advised athletes competing in combat sports to breathe with the lower part of their abdomen to help push the *pneuma* downward, while also using other types of breathing exercises. He also recommended they speak in a deep voice to open and fill the "empty spaces in the body."[183]

Wages of the paidotribēs

According to testimony, the wages of the instructors at the *palaestrae* were low. Athenaeus reported that the wages paid to a *paidotribēs* in the late four century BCE for one year were about one *mina*, or *mna* (100 drachmas)[184], paid in advance. Since the *paidotribēs* was a leading figure at the palaestra, it would be safe to say that the other instructors were of lower status and would therefore receive lesser amounts. At the same time, the *sōphronistēs*, or gymnasium superintendents who were responsible for discipline and good behavior of the youths, received one drachma a day. From an inscription found in Miletus, we learn that in the second century BCE, the wages for staff at the *palaestra* were paid every month. The four *paidotribēs* received 30 drachmas each per month. The wages of a *paidotribēs* in the second century were the same as those of the Athenian soldiers of the fifth century BCE, which were very low. From another second century BCE inscription, we learn that two *paidotribēs* were paid 500 drachmas each per year, while there is also a reference to hiring an armed combat instructor for not less than two months a year with a salary of 300 drachmas. This amount seems quite generous for someone who worked only two to three months a year.[185]

Diet

According to Philostratus, ancient athletes mostly subsisted on barley unleavened bread, whole wheat barley bread made without sourdough starter

---

183 Christopoulos, "Greek Combat Sports," pp. 442, 443.
184 As a point of reference, 1 drachma was equivalent to 6 *obols*, 100 drachmas were equal to 1 *mina*, and 60 *minas* were equal to 1 Athenian *talent*. Historians have estimated that 1 drachma in the fifth century BCE would have been equivalent to $46.50 in 2015.
185 Mouratidis, *Istoria physikēs agōgēs*, pp. 155, 156.

and any meat of their liking, mostly beef, bull meat, male goat meat and roebuck meat.[186]

Injuries

By modern standards, pankration would be classified as a contact blood sport. According to sources, it featured kicks to the abdomen, bloody blows, a mouth full of blood, eye-gouging and faces rendered formless or deformed by blows.[187] Injuries ranged from light to severe, and there was one recorded death - that of Arrachion, a two-time Olympic champion, who died in 564 BCE.[188]

It should be noted, however, that because the athletes wore no leather thongs on their hands, while blows with hands and feet targeted the whole body and holds engaged all of the joints, the force of the sport was dissipated through several areas, which made it somewhat more moderate. On the other hand, athletes who boxed wore thongs on their hands, making their blows much more painful and destructive, while all of the force was essentially aimed at the head, causing far greater damage. For these reasons, combat sports were described as grievous and terrible.[189]

Medicinal treatment

Even at that time, ancient sports medicine was an interdisciplinary pursuit combining treatment of injuries with providing instructions and preparing the athletes, so that both treatment and prevention played a role.[190]

Nevertheless, the pain experienced by ancient athletes taking part in wrestling, boxing and pankration probably would have been caused by a strike to the face, which would ultimately cause discoloration and bruising. Under these circumstances only, Celsus recommended applying the following remedy twice a day: 8 g aristolochia and thapsia, adding 16 g myrrh, styrax balsam,

---

186 Gogaki, *Oi antilēpseis*, pp. 342, 343.
187 Gogaki, *Oi antilēpseis*, pp. 347, 348.
188 Eleni Konsolaki, "Trauma kefalēs kai trachēlou stēn Archaia Ellada [Head and neck trauma in Ancient Greece]" (doctoral dissertation, University of Crete, Herakleio 2011), p. 60.
189 Gogaki, *Oi antilēpseis*, p. 348.
190 Alan J. Thurston, "Art of preserving health: Studies on the medical supervision of physical exercise," ANZ Journal of Surgery 79, no. 12 (2009): p. 942.

gum ammoniac for fumigation, galbanum gum resin, dried resin, mastic resin, arsenic incense and Illyrian iris wax (Celsus, *Book V*: 18, 24).[191]

From the aspect of modern medicine and pain management, three ancient compounds mentioned by Celsus are particularly interesting: frankincense, saffron and tears of poppy (opium)[192].

Offenses

There were varying penalties depending on the gravity of the offense. Flogging was for minor offenses, and monetary fines were reserved for more serious violations. The fines paid by offending athletes were used to erect statues of Zeus called *Zanes* and were the last ones athletes saw before entering the stadium. They were meant to discourage them from cheating in the games. The reason for the fine was inscribed on the base of the statues as a reminder for future athletes and to expose the violations to ridicule while serving as a deterrent. They were a practical form of atonement, before the god whose sacred agreement they had breached, for violating the oath they had taken. They also exemplified punishment and condemned unethical behavior, and constituted the first rules of honorable sportsmanship, or *eu agōnizesthai* (fair play), in history.[193] If an athlete was unable to pay, his *polis* would assume the obligation to pay the fine. If the *polis* did not pay either, all athletes from there were banned from competing.

Zanes were only found at Olympia.[194] In 1,200 years of Olympic games, only eighteen Zanes were erected.[195] There was a Zan in the *palaestra* made with the fine paid by Sosander of Smyrna and Polyctor of Elis.[196]

Generally, the penalties imposed on an athlete for an improper hold or fatal blow against his opponent were few.[197] It is a fact that the current-day inclination to condemn violence does not appear to have been particularly well developed at that time.[198]

---

191 Else M. Bartels, Judith Swaddling and Adrian P. Harrison, "An Ancient Greek Pain Remedy for Athletes," Pain Practice 6, no. 3 (2006): p. 213.
192 Bartels et al, "An ancient Greek pain," p. 213.
193 Gogaki, *Oi antilēpseis*, pp. 198, 199.
194 Mouratidis, *Istoria physikēs agōgēs*, p. 193.
195 Albanidis, *Istoria tēs athlēsēs*, p. 57.
196 Yiannakis, *Istoria physikēs agōgēs: apo tous prōtogonous*, p. 45.
197 Gogaki, *Oi antilēpseis*, p. 346.
198 Gogaki, *Oi antilēpseis*, p. 348.

Instances of athletes who attempted to ignore the strict regulations enforced at the games were rare, and even on those occasions, the athletes never dared not to comply or not to accept the penalties imposed upon them.[199] One of these regulations was a famous provision declaring that no Olympic champion should receive money,[200] thus establishing the principle of amateur athletics as part of the worldwide cultural heritage of Olympia.[201]

Sarapion

His was the only documented case of a pankratiast exhibiting cowardice. He was from Alexandria and left Olympia one day before the pankration event was to begin, acknowledging the superiority of his opponents although he had entered the competition. Epictetus tells us that athletes who left the games early were punished with a flogging.[202]

The *palaestrae*

For any city to be considered civilized, it was required to have the necessary athletic facilities modeled on those at Olympia.[203] The first and foremost element of any stadium was the foot race.[204] Sports training was held in the *gymnasion*. It was a public institution where athletes trained in the nude; the name *gymnasion* is from the word *gymnos*, meaning "nude." There were three major *gymnasia* in Athens: the Academy, the Lyceum and the Cynosarges (for non-Athenian citizens). A Greek *gymnasion* was usually located in a shady spot, next to a stream. The institution began as a place to train middle-class Greeks for war.[205] The *gymnasia* were decorated with statues of gods, semi-gods, mortals and patrons of athletic events, such as Hermes, Heracles, Theseus and others, to cultivate a religious consciousness and competitive frame of mind. The geometric shapes of the sports facilities, such as the triangle (foot

---

199 Sakellarakis et al., *Oi Olympiakoi*, p. 78.
200 "No money shall be given to anyone for an Olympic victory," Pausanias *V* 21.4
201 Gogaki, *Oi antilēpseis*, pp. 198, 199.
202 Mouratidis, *Istoria physikēs agōgēs*, p. 191.
203 Pausanias, *I* 4.1
204 Dimitris Komitoudis, "Ē proponētikē tōn Archaiōn Ellēnōn [Athletic training of the ancient Greeks] (doctoral dissertation, University of Crete,1997), p. 85.
205 Crowther, *Sport*, p. 75.

race start at the Isthmian games), the square (all *palaestrae*), the rectangle and the circle, were sacred elements interwoven with their religious consciousness.[206]

The layout of every *gymnasion* included: a *xystos* - a covered portico about the length of a stadium (about 200 meters) used for training in bad weather; *paradromis* - an open-air practice track parallel to the *xystos* with a jumping pit and throwing platform; service areas such as a changing room; the *elaiothesion*, the room where athletes had oil applied before training or before the games; the *aleiptērion*, where the anointer (*aleiptēs*) massaged and covered them with oil; the *konistērion*, where the athletes were dusted so they would not slip through holds; the *coryceum*, a room with punching bags;[207] the baths; the *sphairistērion*, where they practiced with balls; and the *palaestra*. This was a small, square building with colonnades and rooms with various functions built around a central sandy courtyard where athletes could train in combat sports. Slaves, tradesmen, other undesirables and women were not permitted to enter the *palaestra* or the *gymnasion* in general. As such, it became one of the social gathering places for men in every Greek community.[208] In the Hellenistic period, other elements were added to the *gymnasion*, including the *akroatērion* (for spectators), the *exedra* (arcade where the sophists would exchange views) and the *ephebeion* (where the younger boys were taught).[209] Aside from the athletic facilities, the gymnasium also included libraries and classrooms for the teaching of rhetoric and philosophy. In Athens, Plato himself was affiliated with the Academy, while Aristotle was associated with the Lyceum.[210]

The *palaestra* was the place for wrestling, boxing and pankration. Hermes' daughter was called Palaestra,[211] and perhaps that is the reason the Greeks and Romans believed Hermes was the protector of the *palaestra*.[212] In fact, it was the first agonistic institute - the first school for fighters. All *palaestrae* on Greek territory were square-shaped. Starting in the fifth century BCE in Athens, there were also private *palaestrae* operated by an owner and managed by

---

206 Thomas Yiannakis, *Ieroi-Panellēnioi agōnes* [Sacred-Panhellenic games] (Athens 1998), pp. 108, 109.
207 Komitoudis, "Ē proponētikē," pp. 86, 87.
208 Crowther, *Sport*, p. 75.
209 Albanidis, *Istoria tēs athlēsēs*, p. 214.
210 Crowther, *Sport*, p. 75.
211 Albanidis, *Istoria tēs athlēsēs*, p. 143.
212 Thomas Yiannakis, *Istoria tēs physikēs agōgēs kai tou athlētismou kata tēn Rōmaikē kai Vyzantinē Epochē* [History of physical education and athletics in the Roman and Byzantine Period] (Athens, 1978), p. 30.

a *paidotribēs* (trainer).²¹³ Many of these *palaestrae* were known by the name of the owner or manager: the *palaestra* of Timaeus, of Antigenes in Athens, the *palaestrae* of Stasius, of Nicias, or Niceratus, a father and son in Delos.²¹⁴

Aeschines called the gymnasium and *palaestra* the *didaktērion*, or school.²¹⁵ The impact of the *palaestra* and gymnasium on the intellect was great if one considers that the greatest intellectuals taught and were taught at the *gymnasia* (Xenophon and Plato came out of Socrates' *palaestra*).²¹⁶

It is worth taking a closer look at the *palaestrae* of the major sacred games, which were the prototypes for all other *palaestrae* in the other major cities:

The palaestra at Olympia

It was located to the left, near the entrance to the gymnasium and enclosed on all sides. It was a beautiful building on the west side of the Olympian sanctuary, built with a donation from Ptolemy II Philadelphus (285-247 BCE) in about 270 BCE.²¹⁷ It was a square space with each side measuring 66 meters. There was an open-air courtyard in the center where training took place. On the north side, towards the corner of the *palaestra*, the remnants of a paved area measuring 24.20 by 5.44 meters with striated ceramic floor tiles are visible today. The area was used for competitive wrestling, and for ground wrestling in particular. The uncovered area of the *palaestra* had to have two pits: one with clay and one with sand. This area was encircled by Doric columns. A covered area (stoa) was formed by the colonnade where athletes could train in inclement weather. For this reason, the interior surface of the Doric columns facing inwards towards the stoa were smoothed to eliminate the fluting of the particular style so that if an athlete stumbled, he would not injure himself falling onto the column. A series of rooms were arranged around the covered area, including: the *elaiothesion*, the *aleiptērion*, the *sphairistērion*, the *kōrykion*, the *ephebeion* and the baths with cold water for washing. A Roman-era pool was discovered toward the north-west corner of the *palaestra* which used warm water. The grandiose entrance to the *palaestra* was on the north-west

---

213 Albanidis, *Istoria tēs athlēsēs*, p. 212.
214 Marrou, *Istoria tēs ekpaideusēs*, p. 250.
215 Yiannakis, *Istoria physikēs agōgēs: apo tous prōtogonous*, p. 53.
216 Yiannakis, *Ieroi-Panellēnioi agōnes*, p. 109.
217 Penelope Kissoudi, "Closing the Circle: Sponsorship and the Greek Olympic Games from Ancient Times to the Present Day," The International Journal of the History of Sport 22, no. 4 (July 2005): p. 621.

side.[218] As for the day of the games, it is possible that the wrestling, boxing and pankration events were held in a movable *palaestra* or in the softened dirt in the pit.[219]

The palaestra at Nemea

The *palaestra*, a square space with sides measuring 20.20 meters, was discovered inside the sacred area of Nemean Zeus. On the west side, there were baths and a pool for the wrestlers, boxers and pankratiasts. Naturally, there were other typical areas, such as the changing rooms, the *sphairistērion*, *konestērion*, *aleiptērion*, equipment room, library, lecture hall, the *prytaneion* and others.[220]

The palaestra at Delphi

This outdoor sixth century BCE institution served the needs of Pythians. In fact, a sixth century BCE grave found nearby contained a strigil, the metal tool which, as mentioned earlier, was used to scrape the layer of oil, dust and perspiration off the athletes' bodies after training. The *palaestra* was square, its sides measuring 13.85 meters, and it was enclosed by columns that formed a peristyle about 4 meters wide. There were various service areas around the peristyle, or colonnade. It must have also had an aleiptērion, and a classroom for foreigners, sophists or rhetoricians to use in case of bad weather. It had two entrances: one from Castalia and the other from Pronaia. There is a reference to a nearby library in the Roman period.[221]

---

218 Yiannakis, *Ieroi-Panellēnioi agōnes*, pp. 107, 108.
219 Yiannakis, *Ieroi-Panellēnioi agōnes*, p. 146.
220 Yiannakis, *Ieroi-Panellēnioi agōnes*, p. 38.
221 Yiannakis, *Ieroi-Panellēnioi agōnes*, p. 63.

Chapter 3

THE GAMES

From the eighth century BCE onward, a number of competitive events gradually appeared throughout the Greek world. At the peak of the Roman Empire, there was a circuit of about five hundred athletic games.[222] Nevertheless, the four sacred panhellenic games were the most important: the Olympian, Pythian, Nemean and Isthmian games.[223] There were also many games of a local nature which were called *topikoi*, *perichōroi* or *perioikoi* (local, regional or neighboring).[224] The sacred games were *stephanites*, which meant the prize was a wreath of minimal value, compared to other games where the prizes had material or monetary value. These games were called *thematikoi* or *chrimatites*.[225] The purpose of popularizing *chrimatites* games and agonistic festivals in individual city-states was to promote civic unity and pride.[226]

After 146 BCE, when Greece came under Roman rule, Elis became part of the Roman province of Achaea and lost its independence. The games withstood the test of time, and the Sanctuary of Olympia was occasionally honored by Roman emperors, but otherwise, only a distant echo remained of its former glory. The games held during Hellenistic and Roman times, in contrast to the austere games of antiquity, now became more luxurious and increasingly less tied to religion, acquiring the character of an enjoyable spectacle.[227]

As we saw previously, for the ancient Greeks, the history of the games dated back to mythical times; from their earliest beginnings, they sprang from

---

222 Pleket, "The Olympic Games," p. 402.
223 Pleket, "The Olympic Games," p. 402.
224 Iakovos Karyotakis, Istoria ton vareon agonismaton [History of heavy sports] (Self-published, Athens, 1974), p. 185.
225 Albanidis, *Istoria tēs athlēsēs*, p. 40.
226 Kyle, "Pan-Hellenism," pp. 188, 189.
227 Gogaki, *Oi antilēpseis*, p. 349.

the gods themselves, and the most important heroes were their descendants. So it was natural to associate the origin of the games with the ancient myths and to attribute their start to the gods and heroes, all the way back to Cronus, the ancestor of the Olympian gods. This would indicate that for the Greeks, the games had a sacred character, as they brought humans closer to god. That was the reason the games were always held in the most sacred places, under the particular god's protection. The agonistic spirit that proved to be decisive in the course of Greek history also achieved a spiritual and religious depth that raised it to a realm much higher than that of a simple game that it may have been at the start. The natural inclination of human beings to test their powers and to outdo their peers was always the primary motivation for the fighting spirit of the Greeks.[228] It should also be noted that the Greek games were far from playful. The objective was nothing short of winning at all costs.[229]

Sacred - panhellenic games

There were about forty official games staged in ancient Greece, more than half of which were dedicated to a god.[230] These were religious gatherings which attracted crowds of merchants and merry-makers, while the games themselves were aristocratic affairs. They only matured and flourished once they acquired their panhellenic status.[231]

But of all of these, the ones to exceed their local character and acquire panhellenic status were the four sacred games held at Olympia, Delphi (Pythian), Nemea and the Isthmus. The Olympic games were the oldest and thus the most prestigious.[232] These were held every four years and the other sacred games took place within the intervening four-year period known as the Olympiad.[233]

These four games defined the *periodos*, or circuit, and the one to win at all four sacred games in the same circuit was called the *periodonikēs*. This title was first used in 190 BCE.[234]

---

228 Sakellarakis et al., *Oi Olympiakoi*, p. 8.
229 Boutet-Lanouette, «La vie agonistique,» pp. 18-22.
230 Evangelos Papakyriakou, "Ē koinonikē sēmasia tēs fysikēs agōgēs kai tou athlētismou stēn Athēna tou 5ou aiōna [The social significance of physical education and athletics in 5th century Athens]" (doctoral dissertation, University of Thessaloniki, 1988), p. 69.
231 Drivas, *Oi sōmatikes askēseis*, p. 158.
232 Pleket, "The Olympic Games," p. 402.
233 Mouratidis, *Istoria physikēs agōgēs*, p. 255.
234 Rudolf Knab, *Die Periodoniken* (Ares Publishers, Chicago, 1934), p. 4.

For the first time in history, the panhellenic games provided the Greeks with a national identity, since there was no central government in the *polis* system. Throughout this period, the panhellenic games became the only link uniting Greeks, while also serving to draw a line between Greeks and non-Greeks.[235]

In most cases, the sites of the panhellenic athletic competitions were already sacred places - well before they came to host the games - and they continued to function as places of worship independently of the sporting events. The fact that these sites became sacred had nothing to do with athletics.[236] However, these powerful religious centers were located in states in their political prime and with considerable military strength. At the same time, the natural setting in which the competition venue was located had a metaphysical effect.[237]

The requirements for those taking part in panhellenic games were much stricter than for other games. Participants were distinguished by their moral grounding and their competitiveness and had to be worthy to take part in the games, which were the most important in the Hellenic world.[238]

At these panhellenic gatherings, where athletics and music brought pleasure to the lives of Greeks and reminded them of their ancient roots, where their sages came for glory and praise and to talk to them about the past and the future, the Greeks would forget their own homeland and everything that divided them and at least temporarily share a life full of excitement. They had cause to speak of an expanded homeland found only in people's hearts.[239] At Olympia, Delphi, the Isthmus and Nemea, these small home states became united into one larger entity: one which they called by their common name - Greece - even though they did not know where its borders lay.[240]

The sacred truce

There is no single Greek tradition to explain the origins of the sacred truce. According to one school of thought, the truce appears to have been an attempt to revive the Mycenaean kingdom. But to start at the beginning. After years of

---

235 Wang Daqing, "On the Ancient Greek αγών [agon]," *Procedia Social and Behavioral Sciences* 2, no. 5 (2010): p. 6807.
236 Hubbard, "Contemporary," p. 380.
237 Yiannakis, *Ieroi-Panellēnioi agōnes*, p. 9.
238 Yiannakis, *Ieroi-Panellēnioi agōnes*, p. 11.
239 Sakellarakis et al., *Oi Olympiakoi*, p. 73.
240 Sakellarakis et al., *Oi Olympiakoi*, p. 73.

hostilities resulting in the fragmentation of the Mycenaean empire, both old and new tribes, winners and losers realized they had no choice but to seek a peaceful coexistence. It resembled a nostalgia for the days of glory of Mycenae, given that they had lived through the misery of incessant fighting and all of its negative impacts: the economic recession in their country, the loss of foreign trade for the Phoenician fleet, the shrinking population due to mass migration, a drop in the cultural level and the temporary loss of the art of the writing and - most importantly - the hatred and enmity fed by the rivalry between old and new religious feeling. A solution had to be found. It was proven in practice that even after centuries of hostility, it was possible for diverse peoples to enjoy the fruits of peaceful coexistence. It was an opportunity for traditional enemies to try the road of reconciliation. The time had come for a new beginning.[241]

Iphitus is mentioned as the restorer of the Olympic games. He was a descendant of Oxylus and was king of Elis. According to tradition, he took on the mission to rid Greece of civil wars and disease. He decided to seek counsel from the Oracle of Delphi, who told him that in order to achieve his goal, he had to revive the Olympic games. However, Olympia initially belonged to Pisa. Peace was thus achieved through a treaty between the kings of the two states: Iphitos of Elis and Cleisthenes of Pisa. The will of the people was not enough, however; the gods also had to agree. Peace needed divine approval in order to endure. So Apollo was asked to lend a hand. After receiving the blessing of the gods, peace came to be associated with the start of the Olympic games and was called "*ekecheiria*" (truce).[242] According to Plutarch, there was another guarantor to the peace agreement: Lycurgus, the lawgiver of Sparta. It would have been unacceptable for Sparta, which embodied the military grandeur of the Dorian tribe, to be absent from such an initiative. Thus, the truce was the work of three major centers, each of which represented the ancestry of its ethnic group. These were the former inhabitants of Pisa, as descendants of the Mycenaeans, the Aetolians of Elis, and the Dorians of Sparta.[243]

It was no surprise that the truce would draw the reaction of other *poleis* in Peloponnesus, which had reservations about the revival of the games and about the prestige and wealth they would bring to Olympia. So they sent their own representatives to the Oracle of Delphi. The Oracle issued a new order to all of the Peloponnesian people to offer their wishes for the success of the

---

241 Papantoniou, «Religiosity,» p. 38.
242 Papantoniou, «Oi epidraseis,» p. 97.
243 Papantoniou, «Oi epidraseis,» pp. 97, 98.

games. It was thus through the persistence of the Oracle that the Olympic games came to be widely accepted.[244]

The terms of the peace treaty among the three cities were written on a bronze disk, the so-called Disk of Iphitus, which was kept inside the Temple of Hera. This provided divine ratification and force to the agreement. As a result, any violation of the truce would be considered an affront and blasphemous towards the god, and by extension, violators would be guilty of sacrilege.[245] These events took place in 884 BCE. Apparently, Aristotle and Pausanias both claimed to have seen the Disk of Iphitus with their own eyes.[246] In fact, Iphitus himself is depicted in art forms at the instant he is being crowned by a woman, the personification of *ekecheiria*.[247]

It should be noted that this was a truce, not peace, and that it applied to fighting taking place in the area around the sites of the panhellenic games to ensure they would be conducted without disturbance.[248] Visitors were permitted to travel towards Olympia as pilgrims. It was mandated by the divine element and not by some powerful central authority. The truce implied silent prohibition of any war involving Elis. So, while the truce may have been a local deterrent, wars between the *poleis* did not stop.[249]

Thanks to the truce, the Sanctuary of Olympia acquired great prestige and reputation. At the same time, the Eleans, who were thus able to keep their homeland out of any conflict for long periods of time, prospered, at least until the fifth century BCE.

The main conditions of the truce were as follows:
- Any prevailing hostilities ceased and passage to Elis, which was declared neutral and inviolable, was unimpeded. In addition, those who wished to attend or to take part in the games were free to pass even through countries with which their homeland was at war.
- Entry into Elis was forbidden to anyone who was armed, or to any military unit.
- Executions were also forbidden.[250]

Initially, the truce was observed for one month, and was called the *ieromēnia*, or "sacred month."[251] Later, it was extended to three months, which was actually a month and a half before the games and a month and a half af-

---

244 Papantoniou, «Religiosity,» p. 37.
245 Papantoniou, «Oi epidraseis,» pp. 97, 98.
246 Yiannakis, Istoria physikēs agōgēs: apo tous prōtogonous, p. 34.
247 Gogaki, Oi antilēpseis, p. 147.
248 Daqing, "On the Ancient Greek αγών [agon]," p. 6807.
249 Kyle, "Pan-Hellenism," p.189.
250 Sakellarakis et al., Oi Olympiakoi, p. 106.
251 Yiannakis, Istoria physikēs agōgēs: apo tous prōtogonous, p. 85.

ter.[252] Some researchers believe it lasted three months before and three months after the games.[253] In the time of Lucian, the truce lasted at least four months. After the fifth century BCE, the truce lasted up to ten or eleven months.[254]

The sacred truce was heralded by the *spondophoroi* (bearers of a proposal for a truce), three[255] young noblemen wearing olive wreaths[256] who set off from Elis and toured all of the Greek cities with expenses paid by their home state.[257]

As a result, the *spondophoroi* traveled against the flow of visitors and athletes along their route.[258] They spread the message of truce in Peloponnesus, Attica, Boeotia, Thessaly, Epirus, Aetolia, Macedonia, Crete, Cyrenaica, Cyprus, the Syrian coast, Southern Italy and Sicily.[259]

The longevity of the ancient games was the direct result of two unchanging rules: firstly, all athletes, trainers and spectators were guaranteed safe travel to and from Olympia; and secondly, while the games were being held, no state could invade Elis, nor were the Eleans allowed to attack anyone else.[260] Throughout the 1,200-year duration of the Olympic games, there were very few violations.[261]

As a competition venue, Olympia had a rather local character until the tenth century BCE, with only the Pisaeans taking part. After 884 BCE, with the establishment of the truce signed by the three main leaders - Lycurgus, Cleisthenes and Iphitus - it acquired a broader Peloponnesian dimension. It took on a more panhellenic character after 728 BCE with all Greeks taking part, and with the entry of the Romans into Greek territory in the second century BCE, the Olympic games became worldwide, since even "barbarians" took part.[262]

Preparations for the festival began once the truce was declared. The law entered into force with the arrival of the special envoys, who traveled all over the Greek world, as mentioned earlier, to announce the religious festival. Oc-

---

252 Nigel Crowther, "Visiting the Olympic Games in Ancient Greece: Travel and Conditions for Athletes and Spectators," The International Journal of the History of Sport 18, no. 4 (December 2001): p. 42.
253 Cindy Burleson, "The ancient Olympic Truce in modern-day peacekeeping: revisiting Ekecheiria," Sport in Society 15, no. 6 (August 2012): p. 798.
254 Yiannakis, Istoria physikēs agōgēs: apo tous prōtogonous, p. 85.
255 Mouratidis, Istoria physikēs agōgēs, p. 187.
256 Gogaki, Oi antilēpseis, p. 147.
257 Albanidis, Istoria tēs athlēsēs, p. 64.
258 Crowther, "Visiting the Olympic Games," p. 42.
259 Albanidis, Istoria tēs athlēsēs, p. 64.
260 Kidd, "The myth," p. 418.
261 Albanidis, Istoria tēs athlēsēs, p. 66.
262 Yiannakis, Istoria physikēs agōgēs: apo tous prōtogonous, p. 50.

casionally, the truce would take effect earlier in certain cities and later in others; it was not put into place everywhere at the same time. In other words, its duration was variable, depending on the distance of the city.[263]

There are references to truces at the Eleusinian Mysteries, and at the Pythian, Isthmian, Nemean and Panathenaic games. It is possible the truce of the Pythian games was in effect for up to a year.[264]

The Hellanodikēs

The *Hellanodikēs* were responsible for staging the games and also werved as judges. The office of the *Hellanodikēs* was first mentioned in Pindar and an inscription at Olympia dated at 475-450 BCE. They wore Tyrian or royal purple, indicating that the *Hellanodikēs* were initially the kings of various tribes.[265] At first, there was just one *Hellanodikēs*, but with the passing of time and the increasing number of events and athletes, their number rose to twelve, equivalent to the number of tribes in Elis.[266] Their president was elected by the body, though some claim it was usually the elder one. After the Persian Wars, there were nine, as many as there were tribes at that time. Three of them supervised the pentathlon, three oversaw the chariot and equestrian events and the other three were responsible for the remaining events, including pankration.[267]

In the beginning, the position of the *Hellanodikēs* was inherited and lifelong; when they increased in number, possibly after 584 BCE, they were chosen by lottery from among all Elean citizens.[268] They were selected for one Olympiad, which was four years, and resided at the *Hellanodikeio* for ten months where they were taught the regulations of the games by the *nomophylakes*, or guardians of the law.[269] The *Hellanodikeio* was associated with the Elis agora and with one of the three *gymnasia* located there.[270]

Their duties included: general oversight of the games and all competitive events, and assigning athletes to age levels and verifying their origins. They also supervised the training of athletes at the *gymnasia* in Elis one month before the games commenced and selected the most suitable to compete at the

---

263 Boutet-Lanouette, «La vie agonistique,» pp. 12-14.
264 Albanidis, Istoria tēs athlēsēs, p. 68.
265 Mouratidis, Istoria physikēs agōgēs, p. 188.
266 Mouratidis, Istoria physikēs agōgēs, p. 189.
267 Mouratidis, Istoria physikēs agōgēs, p. 189.
268 Sakellarakis et al., Oi Olympiakoi, p. 111.
269 Albanidis, Istoria tēs athlēsēs, p. 55.
270 Mouratidis, Istoria physikēs agōgēs, p. 190.

Olympia stadium, while excluding those they considered ill-prepared. They imposed penalties on athletes who violated the rules. The penalties imposed against offending athletes depended on the severity of the misconduct, and ranged from monetary fines and exclusion from the games to flogging by the *mastigophorous* (flagellator) or *rabdouchous* (rod-bearer). The decisions of the *Hellanodikēs* were respected and irrevocable. The Council of Eleans had the power to punish a *Hellanodikēs* with a monetary fine, but it could not overturn his ruling. The *Hellanodikēs* also presented the awards.[271] They were assisted in their work by the *alytarchēs* and the *alytai,* responsible for the smooth running of the games.[272]

Apparently, the role of the *Hellanodikēs* at the ancient games was similar to the role of the referee in modern times: enforcing a predefined set of rules. However, the social status of the *Hellanodikēs* and range of responsibilities exceeded those of a modern sports referee.[273]

The Olympic *prorrhesis*

There was a gymnasium at Elis where the athletes gathered to train in the thirty days leading up to the Olympian games. This period of time was called the Olympic *prorrhesis*, or proclamation.[274] Thus, every four years and for a month prior to the Olympic games, Elis was transformed into a cosmopolitan gathering place where athletes, trainers and parents of young athletes arrived from all over Greece.[275] Elis became the first Olympic village in the world.[276] Competitors who arrived later in the month preceding the games or refused to take part in training were excluded from the games.[277]

One section of the Elis gymnasium was called the *plethrion* (wrestling ground) and the *Hellanodikēs* evaluated the athletes there, classifying them as either boys or men or according to their skills in the wrestling sports.[278] For the most part, they based their ruling on the athletes' body type. As to ages they used to establish the boys' competitive category at Olympia, the most

---

271 Albanidis, Istoria tēs athlēsēs, p. 56.
272 Sakellarakis et al., Oi Olympiakoi, p. 112.
273 Cedric Duvinage, "The Ancient History of Sports Referees," in Referees in Sports Contests (Gabler Verlag, Wiesbaden, 2012), p. 21.
274 Albanidis, Istoria tēs athlēsēs, p. 59.
275 Yiannakis, Ieroi-Panellinioi agōnes, p. 87.
276 Yiannakis, Istoria physikēs agōgēs: apo tous prōtogonous, p. 44.
277 Albanidis, Istoria tēs athlēsēs, p. 59.
278 Yiannakis, Ieroi-Panellinioi agōnes, p. 87.

likely would have been twelve to seventeen, through some say it was seventeen to nineteen. What is certain is that the same age classifications were used in both the Hellenistic period and the Roman imperial era.[279]

It was still no easy matter, since puberty begins at differing ages. One criterion for an athlete to remain in the boys' category was height. Another was the appearance of hair in the genital area (pubic hair), taken as a sign marking the end of childhood. Another factor that was taken into account was whether all of the permanent teeth and second molars had come in.[280] One might say that biological age and physical development were taken into account, which was more appropriate than chronological age.

During the training period and the games themselves, the Greeks went to great lengths to protect the younger athletes from injuries. They discouraged premature intensive involvement with athletics. But there was another reason as well. Plato and Aristotle believed that physical exercise was essential in childhood and that it had to start early on, when the body was developing very quickly. In Aristotle's view, however, specialized athletic activity was tantamount to physical work and was thus unworthy of free citizens. If they were to occupy themselves exclusively with athletics, they would be indifferent to public affairs and would be rendered useless to the state, he postulated.[281]

It should be added that, in contrast to modern times, the contestants themselves volunteered to compete in the Olympic games. The Greek city-sates did not preselect athletes and they showed relatively little interest in the participants until they emerged as winners.[282]

The ritual procession of athletes, trainers, visitors and other officials from Elis to the sanctuary at Olympia - the Sacred Way - was a journey of about 60 kilometers (about 40 miles) and lasted two days.[283] At least the ground there was flat, in contrast to so many other routes in Greece.[284] Nowadays, the distance is closer to 43 kilometers (27 miles) and can be covered in less than an hour by car.

---

279 Aikaterini Samara and Evangelos Albanidis, "Ē agōnistikē parousia kai ē athlētikē proetoimasia tōn paidōn stēn Ellinikē and Romaikē archaiotēta [The competitive presence and athletic preparation of youths in Greek and Roman antiquity" (paper presented at the 19th International Congress on Physical Education & Sport, Komotini, Greece, May 20-22, 2011), p. 6.
280 Samara and Albanidis, "Ē agōnistikē parousia," p. 7.
281 Samara and Albanidis, "Ē agōnistikē parousia," p. 8.
282 Crowther, Sport, p. 47.
283 Crowther, Sport, p. 48.
284 Crowther, "Visiting the Olympic Games," p. 39.

Number of participants

There is no information in the historical sources on the number of adult athletes taking part in the sacred games. One can only approximate the numbers from references in Lucian.[285] Most of the athletes about whom some information is available were from Athens and Sparta. At best, we know about 25 percent of the Olympic victors. We also know that perhaps only two hundred to two hundred and fifty athletes took part in all events at each Olympiad.[286]

The number of athletes competing in contact sports (wrestling, boxing, pankration) at Olympia was very small. The ancient inscriptions make no mention of number of total participants, but only refer to the wins and rounds that it took for the athlete to reach final victory. Thus, it would take three to four wins for boys in heavy sports, meaning that five to sixteen athletes took part. Similarly, in the men's category, there would have been four to twelve contestants, but usually eight.[287] The numbers at Olympia seem to have changed slightly after the fifth century and up to Lucian's era in the second century CE.[288]

As to number of participants, the opposite was true at local games. The number of athletes taking part in local games was much greater compared to the sacred games. For example, we know that in the games in Pisidian Antioch in the Late Empire, a competitor in the men's pankration would have to win seven consecutive bouts to be declared the victor. That means that anywhere from 65 to 128 adult athletes would have taken part. In boys' pankration, the comparable figure was two winning bouts, meaning 3 to 4 athletes taking part.[289]

It is also notable that in Pisidia, an athlete who had won one event could not compete in another. This was probably intended to keep the number of participants low.[290]

At the Roman Capitoline games, the term "*stēsas tous antagōnistas*" was used, which meant "stopping the opponent,"[291] specifically in reference to

---

[285] Nigel B. Crowther, "Numbers of Contestants in Greek Athletic Contests," Nikephoros 6 (1993): p. 43.
[286] Donald G. Kyle, "Greek Athletic Competitions: The Ancient Olympics and More," in A Companion to Sport and Spectacle in Greek and Roman Antiquity, ed. Paul Christensen and Donald G. Kyle (Wiley-Blackwell, Hoboken, 2013), p. 33.
[287] Crowther, "Numbers," p. 48.
[288] Crowther, "Numbers," p. 44.
[289] Crowther, "Numbers," p. 50.
[290] Crowther, "Numbers," p. 52.
[291] Crowther, "Numbers," p. 51.

pankratiast Marcus Aurelius Asclepiades[292] in CE 200. This method of determining the winner was a combination of rounds of competition and drawing lots. Sometimes, a competitor was too intimidated by his opponent to compete so he would forfeit.

On the previous pages, we saw that during the Roman period, about five hundred contests were held each year. Based on this information, we can calculate that the number of pankratiasts taking part in local games could range between 80 and 100. This meant that in any given year, there could more than 40,000-50,000 pankratiasts taking part. Those kinds of numbers would certainly make modern-day sports federation presidents very happy. This number becomes even more significant if we consider the difficulties athletes faced in traveling from one region to another to compete.

The number of athletes and rules of competition also had an impact on how frequently athletes were declared winners without actually having to fight – earning a *nikē akoniti* (literally "winning without getting dusty"). The reason for the relatively large number of dustless victories at Olympia was, firstly, that inferior athletes were eliminated by the *Hellanodikēs*, and secondly, other athletes who did not wish to spend a month of the year with little or no reward were able to withdraw their participation during the training period before the games in Elis.[293]

For example, a spectator who was particularly interested in pankration could travel to Olympia and be satisfied merely with the opportunity to see some of the best athletes around, even though the competition was sparse.[294] The ancient spectators would not feel cheated if an athlete won a contest without much effort, since they were in the fortunate position of proclaiming the winner.[295]

It was normal for the audience not to complain for having been denied their entertainment, nor were there any incidents or disturbances. Apparently everyone's main concern was to see the best athlete crowned, and it seems the Eleans managed things quite well. This represents a distinct difference between the ancient and modern games.[296]

By contrast, it was rare for local games to have a low number of participants, which meant a smaller chance of witnessing a *nikē akoniti* than at the sacred games.[297]

---

292 The entire inscription will be provided later in the Olympic victors section.
293 Crowther, "Numbers," p. 42.
294 Crowther, "Numbers," pp. 42, 43.
295 Crowther, Sport, p. 53.
296 Crowther, "Numbers," p.43.
297 Crowther, "Numbers," p. 52.

The Olympian Games

The location

The Greeks held the ancient Olympic games in a fertile valley in Olympia, in the south-west corner of mainland Greece. It was not an easily accessible venue with outstanding athletic facilities. Olympia was in a rather isolated part of the Greek world and had poor infrastructure. There were no permanent residents, since it was not a community or *polis*. It had barely more than a temple and the basics for certain types of sports, which would have been called primitive even by Greek standards. By modern standards, they could not have found a less appropriate location to hold the most important games in the world. Nevertheless, of all of the ancient Greek influences on the modern era, the Olympic games are probably the best known.[298]

In 776 BCE, Olympia was already a sacred place; it never was and never became a city or a village. Elis was a relatively underdeveloped, non-urbanized agricultural area. It was not until 472 BCE that a voluntary conglomeration of many villages came together in the *polis* of Elis. It could be the significance of Elis itself as a political entity that explains why the Olympic festival, contrary to the modern Olympic Games which change location every four years, never left Olympia.[299]

Ultimately, however, even researchers are not certain about why exactly such an unassuming place like Olympia became so important to athletics. The oracle of Zeus at Olympia had a significant reputation in the ancient world, though it was less famous than the Oracle of Delphi. Moreover, archaeologists discovered about seventy altars to other gods in the area, including Artemis, Aphrodite, Demeter and Gaia. This meant the sanctuary was important for worshipers to visit. Soothsayers from the sanctuary also accompanied Greek settlers who migrated to new homes in what is now southern Italy. These migrants traveling west, like other Greeks, often used Olympia as a meeting point for commerce and diplomatic relations. Some researchers believe it was precisely this relative insignificance of the place, its isolation and conservativism that contributed to its success. Whatever the reason, quite a few of the smaller games in Greece paid the equivalent of a fee for the right to use the name

---

298 Crowther, Sport, p. 45.
299 Pleket, "The Olympic Games," p. 401.

"Olympian" in order to enhance the status of their own games.[300] As we saw earlier, there were about five hundred sporting events during the period of the Roman Empire, but the Olympic games were older and hence better known.[301]

The area around Olympia is a serene, riverside, fertile valley, with thick growths of wild olive, plane and poplar trees that make a perfect setting for peace and quiet and for stimulating religious feelings. The priesthood artfully cultivated it into a multifaceted sacred center. The site has a mysterious, seductive force that is surrounded and cooled by two sacred, therapeutic rivers - the Kladeos and the Alpheios, companions of Cronus.[302] Transcendent values revolving around religion, the state and human condition developed here.[303]

Living in one of the most fertile regions of Greece, the Eleans were naturally occupied with farming and animal breeding. The bounty of the land allowed the population to remain throughout antiquity, dispersed around the towns, villages and farmhouses in the region. Thus, since Elis was independent in its food production, it did not need to engage in extensive commerce and industry.[304]

In this beautiful land, humans came closer to god. The Olympian games were never established or founded; they evolved from religious occasions.[305]

Mythology

According to the myth, the Olympian games began many centuries ago, when there were no mortals, but only gods and demigods who competed against one another in foot races or in wrestling. Pausanias (second century CE) said that Eleans who were familiar with those ancient times affirmed the heavenly sovereignty of Cronus from an even earlier Age of Man, known as the *chryseon genos,* or Golden Age. Zeus overcame Cronus at wrestling, while Apollo outran Hermes in a race and beat Ares at boxing.[306] That is how the legend unfolds: how the early gods prevailed as victors in contests among themselves, and how these contests became the Olympian games.

---

300 Crowther, Sport, p. 45.
301 Pleket, "The Olympic Games," p. 402.
302 Yiannakis, Ieroi-Panellinioi agōnes, p. 95.
303 Yiannakis, Ieroi-Panellēnioi agōnes, pp. 95, 96.
304 Sakellarakis et al., Oi Olympiakoi, p. 85.
305 Yiannakis, Istoria physikēs agōgēs: apo tous prōtogonous, p. 49.
306 Sakellarakis et al., Oi Olympiakoi, p. 82.

History

The earliest human activity at Olympia is dated at seven to ten thousand years ago, while it seems it functioned loosely as a religious center in 3500 BCE. Vaulted buildings were discovered and dated to 1900-1600 BCE.[307]

There are also indications of physical activity in the pre-Hellenic age which was transmitted to the Dorian tribes along with the influence of the Mycenaean civilization in the Peloponnese from the twelfth century BCE onward.[308]

Archaeological findings at the Olympian sanctuary lead to the conclusion that there was systematic religious use of the space starting in 1000 BCE, but it is doubtful that athletic games were held on a large scale there before the end of the eighth century BCE.[309]

In primitive societies, human beings were enraptured by the cycle of plant growth and decline and endeavored to explain it as the work of a supreme divine authority. The power of nature thus took the shape of a fertile female deity, with an accessory young god at her side. Humans worshiped these fertile divine forces and endeavored to appease them and bring about their unity, believing that the result would be abundance, wealth and prosperity. The divine couple was the basis of religions involving fertility, as they passed from the Cretan and Mycenaean civilizations and prevailed from time to time in Olympia. The faithful accepted these religions and worshipped the gods with ritualistic activities. Physical activities, which were believed to be integral to devotional acts, played a leading role in these rituals.[310]

According to the oldest traditions regarding the origins of the Olympic games, when Zeus, the father of the gods, was born, his mother, Rhea, placed him in the care of the Idaean Dactyls - five brothers from Mount Ida in Crete: Heracles, Paionios, Epimedes, Iasios and Idas.[311] Heracles, the eldest of the brothers, entertained his brothers by having them run races, and crowned the winner with a wreath of wild olives. Heracles himself brought the wild olive tree to Greece from the Hyperboreans, the people who lived beyond the north wind, to provide shade for the crowds of visitors descending on the sacred woods of Zeus, but also for use as a crown of virtues.[312]

---

307 Yiannakis, Istoria physikēs agōgēs: apo tous prōtogonous, p. 48.
308 Papantoniou, «Oi epidraseis,» p. 86.
309 Zinon Papakonstantinou, "Prologue: Sport in the Cultures of the Ancient World," The International Journal of the History of Sport 26, no. 2 (February 2009): 141–148, p. 142.
310 Papantoniou, "Oi epidraseis," pp. 87-88.
311 Albanidis, Istoria tēs athlēsēs, p. 44.
312 Gogaki, Oi antilēpseis, p. 144.

First of all, the myth contains the fact that the idea of competition arose from the brothers' game, and is related to the element of rivalry. In other words, the myth contains the competitive factor, and the aspect of each competitor wanting to overcome the rest. Secondly, the winner in the myth is crowned by Heracles himself, the organizer of the games, with a branch of wild olive (the well-known *kotinos*), which became the standard prize for winners at all subsequent Olympic games. And lastly, the myth ordained that the games should be held with some regularity, and thus the spontaneous game became an established institution.[313]

As the god of the olive, Idaean Heracles became an agricultural god at Olympia. The crowning of the winner with the wild olive symbolized the divine presence. Heracles functions as the mate of a female deity - the goddess Demeter, the pre-eminent goddess of fertility who taught mortals the secrets of farming.[314]

Zeus came from the north and was a deity of Indo-European descent. He attempted to impose himself as a dominant male religious figure over the female deities of the eastern civilizations of the Aegean. However, influenced by the local population which was culturally superior, he modified his character and took the place of a fertility deity next to Hera as part of the Olympian Pantheon. Thus, at first, Zeus and Hera were worshiped as a divine couple and appeared at Olympia in this form starting in 2000 BCE.

Pelops, whose roots were in the East, was the most important mythological figure in Peloponnesus. His invasion of Argolis linked him to the local goddess, Hera, at whose side he functioned as a husband with the name Zeus-Pelops, as part of a divine couple of fertility. Pelops becomes associated with the sanctuary of Olympia through a myth, according to which he arrived in Pisa (Elis), dueled with Oenomaus, the local nobleman, overcame him, took over leadership and took his daughter, Hippodamia, for his wife.

When his strength started to wane, he was not permitted to remain in office. The regular staging of a contest was considered essential in evaluating his abilities. The power of the central authoritative figure was not lifelong, but was renewed periodically through competitive games, and this led to the games being held regularly for the purpose of determining the worthy ruler. Victory was considered proof of divine endorsement which transmitted the god's power to the winner. In mythology, people were convinced that the winner of a contest owed the victory to a decision made by god who anointed the victor as the authority. In this way, a contest between two individuals vying

---

313 Papantoniou, «Religiosity,» p. 33.
314 Papantoniou, «Oi epidraseis,» p. 89.

for power functioned as an election of the best candidate and replaced every other type of selection process; this was considered the most valid, as it bore the divine seal of approval.[315]

The descent of the Dorians upon Olympia changed the entire religious framework. Still, the former gods of the defeated people were not driven away, but instead were demoted to the status of heroes, allowing their followers to continue the same type of worship in their honor. These rituals included competitive games which over time had been incorporated into the worship of Olympian Zeus, the god of the victorious invaders.[316]

The cultural value of the ancient Olympic games

The journey to Olympia was a pilgrimage and as such, it implied the existence of a center and every such center had religious value. Therefore, the games were held in places which were also important religious centers. The worshipers flowed into such places to pay their religious respects to the local gods, placating them and renewing sacred bonds with them, while asking for their continued favor. As a result, the games constituted the climax of the events, centrally important to a festival of worshipers, spectators and travelers in a place where civilizations came together and represented the essence of religion through a number of other rituals.[317] Among those meeting in Olympia were Phidias, Pythagoras, Polykleitos, Praxiteles, Myron and Lysippos. Greek historians read their work publicly for the first time: Anaxagoras, Herodotus, Pindar, Plato, Aristotle, Gorgias, Isocrates, Lysias, Dio Chrystostom, Euripides and others.[318] The importance of the institution is also indicated by the fact that despite the ongoing wars of the time, the Olympic games were conducted normally without being canceled even once in the more than one thousand years they endured. Even in 480 BCE, when the Persians were just outside Thermopylae, the 75th Olympiad was held normally.[319] When Xerxes found out, he got angry with Mardonius and wondered, "what kind of men are these

---

315 Papantoniou, «Oi epidraseis,» pp. 89-91.
316 Papantoniou, «Religiosity,» p. 36.
317 Gogaki, Oi antilēpseis, pp.191-194.
318 Gogaki, Oi antilēpseis, pp. 202, 203.
319 Panos Valavanis, Athla, Athlētes kai Epathla [Contests, Athletes and Prizes] (Erevnites, Athens 1996), p. 48.

that you have pitted against us? It is not for riches that they contend but for honor!"[320]

In actuality, the ancient Olympic games did not have medals or second-place prizes; there were no teams, or female athletes; nor were there winter or water sports; and there was no prevailing ideology about global brotherhood and peace.[321] Olympia itself did not promote a spirit of pan-Hellenism, even though some philosophers who gathered there may have espoused its logic. Olympia remained the only major festival in Greece that did not include artistic contests in the program.[322]

But there was another aspect.

Given the origins of the games, which was essentially warfare, it could be assumed that athletics and the competitive spirit were linked to the formation of the Greek nation. In general, early human societies were equal and shared. Though there was a division of labor among men, women and families, the results achieved by the total workforce of the community were also equitably distributed. However, at some point in history - though it is not known exactly when - certain members created a system with which they could enjoy an unequal share of the fruits of the community's labor. This was achieved by subjugating the other members of society with the force of weapons; they made use of the surplus of their work which was over and above what was needed for a simple subsistence. This development contributed to the creation of the better known social divisions of class and gender. In this way, society was divided into groups of men and women who shared a common relationship through the means of production and distribution. The oldest form of a class society included slavery. Society was structured according to gender. This meant that men enjoyed the privilege of male domination almost everywhere in the form of patriarchy. At the same time, a form of authority began to emerge. Its purpose was to promote the interests of the ruling class and gender and to mediate any negative consequences of the struggle among classes and the two sexes, either by instituting reforms or by suppressing dissenters.

Among the Greeks, the state societies based on slavery and patriarchy existed in prehistoric times. Up until *The Iliad*, Greek societies were dominated by small elite groups of male aristocrats. They enjoyed a higher standard of living resulting from the work of slaves who had been seized, exchanged or multiplied, as well as from the taxes paid by subjugated states and the spoils of recent military campaigns.

---

320 Kyle, "Pan-Hellenism," p.196.
321 Kyle, "Greek Athletic Competitions," p. 21.
322 Crowther, Sport, p. 55.

Throughout the existence of the early Olympics, although economic development, urbanization and further conquests led to a more complex social structure, Greek (and Roman) states were very much dependent on forced labor. Even in democratic Athens, 40 to 50 percent of the population were slaves. The Olympic games reinforced this system of power. The connection was even clearer in Sparta, since the ruling class acquired its goods from the subjugated classes, particularly the helot serfs who constituted the overwhelming majority of the population. The Spartans controlled the helots through a campaign of ongoing terror and random murder waged against them. Youths and adult men were trained for this task under conditions of strict discipline, battles and athletics.

Almost every aspect of the games symbolically endorsed this system of authority. Despite the fact the games were open to all Greek citizens, this did not include slaves or women.

The words of Homer, "The ambition of athletes is always to be first and to overcome the rest," seemed to explain the exploitive stance in other areas of life. The ancients were quite honest about the classist role of athletics. The rulers of the city-states liberally subsidized local athletes because their reflected glory enhanced their own prestige. Aristocratic poets like Pindar were well aware that the lyrics of their odes to athletes did not glorify just the individual but an entire class.[323]

As we have seen, the Olympic games were neither above nor outside the structures of authority in classical Greek society. Despite the fact that the high priests who directed the games adopted a neutral stance towards them, the games they staged were an integral part of the prevailing system of authority. Popular rituals assumed they provided powerful ideological support to the upper classes which governed the particular states. Few of the ancients could deny that the Olympic games served a system of power.[324]

The journey to Olympia

The difficulties involved in traveling to Olympia were significant for many athletes and visitors. There are references by people who went there and said it took them five or six days to walk from Athens to Olympia (Xenophon, *Memorabilia* 3.13.5). Therefore, it would take ten to twelve days to travel there and

---

323 Kidd, "The myth," p. 420, 421.
324 Kidd, "The myth," p. 422.

back, with another five to six days for the actual games, making the entire trip two to three weeks long.[325]

Many of the visitors would walk the entire route to Olympia. Others could travel on donkeys or mules (horses were unable to traverse the bumpy terrain). The more well-to-do could travel in a primitive carriage or basket, without springs or suspension of any kind. The roads were very rough or non-existent, particularly in isolated areas like Olympia. Meanwhile, bandits were a constant threat. The best way to travel was probably by boat, though there were no regularly scheduled passenger ships, and there was also the risk of a pirate attack or a shipwreck. Even after arriving in Olympia, spectators were met with amenities far less than luxurious. The ancient Greeks had to endure the stifling heat of summer, the swarms of flies, the noise, the stench, the whips of those charged with keeping order and controlling the crowds, the congestion, the lack of space for spectators in the stadium, and the constant risk associated with open cooking fires. They stayed in small tents or wooden shacks within the sanctuary, or in crowded refuges outside the area. During the games, Olympia became a vast campground. With the passing of time, however, conditions improved; the organizers introduced stalls with food and other amenities. But it took hundreds of years before a complex water system could be built to provide adequate drinking water, elaborate baths and even water to wash down the toilets.[326] One thing was certain: the ancient Olympic games and similar contemporary events in general were not an event for the poor, even though there is no indication there was any type of entrance fee, like a ticket or toll.[327]

So why would anyone go? Just as so many spectators nowadays are willing to endure the discomforts of many modern athletic events, so too visitors in antiquity had various reasons for traveling to Olympia. Many put up with the harsh conditions out of love for the sports; to see the best athletes of the time fight for a victory. They would enjoy the physical beauty, the strength and the level excellence of the athletes. Others went for reasons unrelated to sports; they went for commercial reasons or to listen to the great writers and philosophers. For some Greeks, a visit to Olympia was an aesthetic ideal.[328] But the works of art were also a pole of attraction for visitors. The Greeks and Romans traveled to Olympia often to see the work of Phidias and considered it bad luck to die before having seen it.[329] The statue of Zeus at the Olympia

---

325 Crowther, "Visiting the Olympic Games," p. 38.
326 Crowther, Sport, p. 48.
327 Crowther, "Visiting the Olympic Games," p. 37.
328 Crowther, "Visiting the Olympic Games," p. 46.
329 Crowther, "Visiting the Olympic Games," p. 49.

Bouleuterion (council house) was primarily constructed to intimidate cheats; it was called Zeus Horkios and held a thunderbolt in its hands, Pausanias noted. A custom had been established whereby athletes, fathers, brothers, trainers and even judges would take an oath on the statue that they would commit no violation at the expense of the games.[330]

For still others, it was a type of pilgrimage.

For the Romans, and perhaps for other foreigners, a visit to Olympia was considered an educational experience that formed part of the Roman civilizing process. It is possible that the Romans were less interested in the athletic ideal than the Greeks, but they were intrigued by the spectacle as a whole.[331] Olympia was consistently on the tourism map of elite Romans[332] as the site of an event that offered more than just sport.[333]

The importance and radiance of the games

Of course, Olympia did not lead to some nationwide political unification, but it did achieve something even greater: the prevalance and clearer definition of the common characteristics of the Greek spirit, despite the conflicts, the rivalries and the fragmentation of the Greeks in hostile and isolated Greek cities.[334]

It was customary for Olympian victors to dedicate statues at the sanctuaries. This occurred before the sixth century BCE. Almost all of the statues of Olympic champions were intact in the Altis, the sacred precinct of Zeus at Olympia.[335] The offering and placement of statuary demonstrated the athlete's gratitude, faith and respect toward the god of Olympia, but also promoted the athlete and his *polis* on a national level. The name of the athlete, his father, his state (and in some cases of the trainer) and the event he had won were inscribed on the base of the statue. The cost of the work was covered by the athlete's father or his district. Oftentimes, the sacred oracles encouraged the placement of statues of athletes. In the *Elis* section of *Description of Greece* , Pausanias mentions about 230 statues of athletes, although in his opinion not all of the athletes, nor even the famed ones, were represented.[336]

---

330 Gogaki, Oi antilēpseis, p. 297.
331 Crowther, "Visiting the Olympic Games," p. 48.
332 H. A. Harris, Sport in Greece and Rome (Thames and Hudson, London 1972), pp. 53–54.
333 Crowther, Sport, p. 49.
334 Sakellarakis et al., Oi Olympiakoi, p. 80.
335 Sacred Altis was the wooded area at Olympia. Life began with the dawning of the prehistoric age (2300-2100 BCE).
336 Yiannakis, Istoria physikēs agōgēs: apo tous prōtogonous, p. 67.

Few glories were as great and as long-lasting as for someone to win the Olympic crown.[337] That was because, as Pindar aptly explains in the first Olympic ode, "Water is best, and gold, like a blazing fire in the night, stands out supreme of all lordly wealth. But if, my heart, you wish to sing of contests, look no further for any star warmer than the sun, shining by day through the lonely sky, and let us not proclaim any contest greater than Olympia."[338]

When they were held

The Suda encyclopedia[339] places the first Olympiad in the era of King Solomon, ninth century BCE. The games took place on the sixth day of the season of the year during which the Sun passed through the same point every four years, meaning every leap year[340], during the second full moon after the summer solstice in late summer. They were held in the middle of July.[341] This period of time coincided with a lull in agricultural work and the event was associated with an astronomical phenomenon understood by all.[342] Initially, the event lasted just one day and included only foot races, though it should be noted that historians strongly dispute this.[343]

Let us examine some views on this issue. According to Pindar, they were held during the *Hekatombaion* month, which corresponded to the period July 15 to August 15. Another theory is that they were held during the first full moon of every leap year. A third view was that the games took place every 49 months of the Elean month of Apollonios-July, and the Heraean games were held on the 50th month, the month of Parthenios-August. During the next Olympiad, the Heraean games would take place on the 49th month and the Olympian games on the 50th, but always at the first full moon after the summer solstice of Apollonios and Parthenios.[344] The prevailing opinion is that they took place between July 24 and August 27 by the modern calendar. The

---

337 Kidd, "The myth," p. 418.
338 Sakellarakis et al., Oi Olympiakoi, p. 77.
339 The Suda or Suidas is one of the most important Greek lexicons and was written in the 10th century. It is possible that Soudas or Suidas may have been the name of the author. It contains 30,000 entries, many of which include information based on sources that would have been lost otherwise. This lexicon is one of the most valuable documents on Greek literature, grammar and literary history.
340 Yiannakis, Istoria physikēs agōgēs: apo tous prōtogonous, p. 50.
341 Pavlinis, Istoria tēs gymnastikēs, p. 149; Valavanis, Athla, p. 23.
342 Kyle, "Greek Athletic Competitions," p. 23.
343 Albanidis, Istoria tēs athlēsēs, p. 50; Mouratidis, Istoria physikēs agōgēs, pp. 278-281.
344 Yiannakis, Istoria physikēs agōgēs: apo tous prōtogonous, pp. 77, 78.

first full moon after the summer solstice was the day that the athletes arrived in Elis and had to remain there for thirty days. The first full moon was also the day that the truce was declared.[345]

The period of time between the end of the games and the start of the fifth year, when the next games would begin, was called the Olympiad.[346] The Olympiads were used as the basis of a dating system and replaced the local calendars. This system was superior to local dating systems because it was used throughout the country and was familiar and understood in all the known world.[347] One could say it functioned as the first global calendar.

During Roman rule, there were more than twenty Olympic games outside of Olympia.[348]

The events

There were 23[349] events included in the Olympic games but they never all appeared at once; over time, new ones were introduced while others were eliminated.[350]

The program

The boys' games were held on the second day in this order: the *stadion* footrace, then wrestling, boxing and pankration. On the third day, the most formal day of the games, the men's competitions were held in the same order: *stadion*, wrestling, boxing and pankration.[351]

After 200 BCE, boys competed on the third day and the men on the fourth.[352]

---

345 Albanidis, Istoria tēs athlēsēs, p. 49.
346 Yiannakis, Istoria physikēs agōgēs: apo tous prōtogonous, p. 47.
347 Sakellarakis et al., Oi Olympiakoi, p. 104.
348 Daqing, "On the Ancient Greek αγών [agon]," p. 6808.
349 Pavlinis, Istoria tēs gymnastikēs, p. 149.
350 Pavlinis, Istoria tēs gymnastikēs, p. 151.
351 Pavlinis, Istoria tēs gymnastikēs, p. 172.
352 Albanidis, Istoria tēs athlēsēs, pp. 52, 53.

Pankration

Men's pankration was introduced in 648 BCE in the 33rd Olympiad, and the boys' event was added in 200 BCE in the 145th Olympiad.[353] Once pankration was incorporated into the games, it was never removed from the Olympic lineup until the games were abolished.

Stadium capacity

It is estimated that starting in the mid-fourth century BCE, the stadium could accommodate about 40,000 spectators.[354] Others said that the surrounding mounds were enough for 45,000 spectators.[355, 356]

The prize

The trophy was a branch of wild olive known as *kotinos*. At the Pantheon, a sacred olive tree had been planted at the rear of the temple of Zeus. A child with two living parents would cut 17 branches with a golden sickle for as many events and would take them inside the temple of Hera. He would lay them on a gold and ivory inlaid altar (chryselephantine) decorated with carvings of the sports, a work by sculptor Kolotes, and the *Hellanodikai* would take them from there to crown the victors on the fifth day. The moral significance of winning a prize at Olympia was incalculable.[357]

---

[353] Albanidis, Istoria tēs athlēsēs, p. 161.
[354] Crowther, "Visiting the Olympic Games," p. 38.
[355] Yiannakis, Ieroi-Panellēnioi agōnes, pp. 139, 140.
[356] Sakellarakis et al., Oi Olympiakoi, p. 92.
[357] Yiannakis, Ieroi-Panellēnioi agōnes, p. 153.

The Isthmian Games

Mythology

According to mythology, the Isthmian games, or Isthmia, began as funerary events introduced by Sisyphus, the king of Corinth, in honor of his nephew, Melicertes, who was found drowned on the shore. According to another view associated with the tradition of the city of Athens, the Isthmia were established by Theseus to atone for his killing of two robbers, Sines and Sciron, whom he had killed while traveling to Athens. There is also the version in which Theseus founded the Isthmia to honor Poseidon, as Heracles had dedicated the Olympian games to Zeus.[358]

History

The Isthmia acquired a wide reputation due to their geographical location near the major commercial center in Corinth and the numerous festivals associated with the sporting events.[359] They were considered to be a national festival second in importance only to the Olympian games, which naturally led to rivalry between the two events.

According to historical records, the Isthmia began between 583 and 581 BCE and were held in honor of Poseidon and of the mortal Melicertes or Palaemon. According to the Parian Chronicle,[360] the Isthmia began in 1251 BCE.[361] After the Greeks were subjugated by the Romans in 146 BCE, all Greek games took on a global character. There was a stadium, a *palaestra* and a hippodrome. It is presumed they were abolished around 394 BCE.[362]

---

[358] Papantoniou, «Oi epidraseis,» pp. 99-103.
[359] Sakellarakis et al., Oi Olympiakoi, p. 68.
[360] The Parian Chronicle was a very significant ancient Greek inscribed text, written in the Attic dialect by an unknown author during the time of the archon Diognetus in Athens in 264 or 263 BCE, and was found on a tombstone. It is a chronological list of the most important historical events from the time of Cecrops, the first mythical king of Athens, to the period of Diognetus. Among other things, it contains information about the development of literature, drama, music, the establishment of national games, and the winners from 1581 BCE to 264 BCE. It was so named because it was found on the island of Paros.
[361] Yiannakis, Ieroi-Panellēnioi agōnes, p. 23.
[362] Yiannakis, Istoria physikēs agōgēs: apo tous prōtogonous, pp. 36, 38.

When they were held

Games would be held at Megara in early spring, with the Isthmia following nine days later, followed by the Asklepieia in Epidaurus.[363] These games were held every first and third year of the Olympiad[364] and took place in late April.[365] Other sources say they were held in the middle of the Attic month of Thargelion (late May).[366]

Pankration

There were more events here than at the Olympian games.[367] It is not known when pankration was introduced at Isthmia, however. At both the Isthmian and Nemean games, there was a category for boys in addition to the categories for men and *ageneioi* ("beardless youths").[368] Nowadays, it would be a category for adolescents.

The categories were based on the following age groupings: boys aged 12-16; youths aged 16-20; and men of 20 and over. Other sources say that the boys' category included athletes aged 12-14, the youth class was 15-17 and the men's category was for those 17 and over. Yet another classification had boys of 14-17, youths of 17-20 and men were 20 and over.

From about the 3rd century BCE onward, the boys' category changed considerably with a number of smaller categories, such as first, second and third level boys, older and younger boys, and boys of all ages.

In all events, the criterion for classifying boy athletes was not so much their age as their physical development. Boy athletes were reportedly also present at local games such as the Panathenaic and Theseian games (first, second, and third age level).[369]

---

363 Yiannakis, Ieroi-Panellēnioi agōnes, p. 24.
364 Yiannakis, Ieroi-Panellēnioi agōnes, p. 25.
365 Valavanis, Athla, p. 23.
366 Albanidis, Istoria tēs athlēsēs, p. 98.
367 Yiannakis, Ieroi-Panellēnioi agōnes, p. 30.
368 Pavlinis, Istoria tēs Gymnastikēs, p. 195.
369 Samara and Albanidis, "Ē agōnistikē parousia," p. 8.

Stadium capacity

It is believed that in the late Hellenistic period, the Isthmian stadium could hold 21,000 spectators.[370]

The prize

Initially, the prize for the winners was a crown of celery, which was a plant associated with funerary worship. It was later replaced by a branch of pine.[371] The crowning with celery was also seen in Pindar's time, when it was a plant related to the dead and the chthonic gods. When a prize of celery was presented, it was an offering with significance for Melicertes-Palaemon; on the other hand, when there was greater religious feeling for Poseidon, the prize to the winner would be pine. According to commentators on Pindar, dry celery was given at the Isthmia and fresh celery was given at the Nemean games.[372]

---

370 Crowther, "Visiting the Olympic Games," p. 38.
371 Papantoniou, "Oi epidraseis," pp. 99-103.
372 Yiannakis, Ieroi-Panellēnioi agōnes, p. 31.

The Nemean Games

The location

Nemea lay along the foot of the Arcadian mountains at an altitude of 333 meters (1,100 feet), at the border between the ancient territory of Arcadia, Corinth and Argolis.

Mythology

According to legend, the Nemean games were funerary games held in memory of the death of Opheltes, son of King Lycurgus of Nemea. But here is what history has to say. When the seven Argive generals set off to attack Thebes and seize power from Eteocles and give it to Polynices (both were sons of Oedipus), they looked for a spring to take a drink of water along the way. Then Hypsipyle, young Opheltes' nursemaid, wanting to help them, left the little boy in a bed of celery and hurried to show them to a fountain. But the snake guarding the fountain bit the child and killed him. The seven generals took the death of the boy as a bad omen and decided to dedicate the games to him, posthumously naming him Archemorus (the forerunner of death). According to another version, the games were founded by Heracles when he killed the Nemean lion and they were revived by Adrastus, the King of Sicyon, when he took power.[373]

History

The games appear in history in 573 BCE and were held after that as a panhellenic religious festival, much like the Olympic games. Initially, they were organized by the people of Cleonae and later passed to the Argives, who made the festival even more famous.[374]

When they were held

The games were held in the second and fourth year of every Olympiad. Pausanias refers to winter Nemean games. Perhaps the Nemea that took place in

---

[373] Papantoniou, «Oi epidraseis,» pp. 99-103.
[374] Papantoniou, «Oi epidraseis,» pp. 99-103.

the fourth year of the Olympiad were held in winter so as not to conflict with the Olympic games.[375] Initially, the games were staged inside the sanctuary of Nemean Zeus, which included a stadium, a *palaestra* and a hippodrome.[376] There are references to the Nemea up until 200 CE by Philostratus, and they may have stopped at the same time as the Olympian games.[377] It is presumed they were abolished around 394 CE.[378]

Pankration

Starting in the fifth century BCE, the Nemean games included pankration for boys, which was introduced at the Olympian games in 200 BCE.[379] In addition to the boys' category (ages 12-16) and men's (over 20), there was also a youth category (16-20).[380] According to other sources, the boys' category at the Nemea included athletes aged 12 to 14, the youth class was 15 to17 and the men's category was for men of 17 and over. But here, too, the criterion for classifying boy athletes was not so much their age as their physical development.[381]

Before the Hellenistic period, the Nemea did not include musical events, and the athletic events were limited to just a few sports. That is why in the Hellenic world, these games were the least important of the panhellenic sacred games, though they did not lack the broad-based and significant participation of notable athletes.[382]

The prize

According to Pindar's commentator, before celery was introduced as the prize, athletes received an olive branch, the beloved tree of Zeus-Hellos; it became celery after the Persian Wars. When the organizers of the Nemean games presented the victors with a crown of olive branches, the athletes and spectators were mostly honoring the presence of Zeus and Heracles. However, when they gave them a crown of celery, it indicated the games were dedicated to the worship of Opheltes-Archemorus and were the origin of the funeral nude games. The Delphi oracle called the Nemean prize the "Nemean flower."[383]

---

375 Papantoniou, «Oi epidraseis,» pp. 99-103.
376 Yiannakis, Ieroi-Panellēnioi agōnes, p. 36.
377 Yiannakis, Ieroi-Panellēnioi agōnes, p. 37.
378 Yiannakis, Istoria physikēs agōgēs: apo tous prōtogonous, pp. 38, 40.
379 Yiannakis, Ieroi-Panellēnioi agōnes, p. 42.
380 Pavlinis, Istoria tēs Gymnastikēs, p. 190.
381 Samara and Albanidis, «Ē agōnistikē parousia,» p. 8.
382 Sakellarakis et al., Oi Olympiakoi, pp. 70, 71.
383 Yiannakis, Ieroi-Panellēnioi agōnes, p. 49.

The Pythian Games

The location

From a structural and locational point of view, the stadium at Delphi was superior to the others. It was located at an altitude of 650 meters (2,130 feet) above sea level and was 178 meters (585 feet) in length.[384]

Mythology

The Pythian games appeared about two centuries after the start of the Olympian games, and arose from the prehistoric tradition and history of both places. According to the mythology, the games originated when Apollo killed Python, the dragon of the Underworld, and founded the Pythia to memorialize his victory. It represented the subjugation of the chthonic deity (Python was the monster that symbolized the prehistoric chthonic forces) and the preeminence of the spirit of the Olympian gods and the light of the sky (Apollo was the god of the sun).[385]

History

The first reorganization of the games is attributed to Cleisthenes, tyrant of Sicyon. It took place after the First Sacred War, waged for economic and political reasons. The historical record of the Pythiads begins in 582 BCE, by which time the war had ended.[386] The Delphic Amphictyony clashed with the Phocian city of Kirrha, which controlled the only harbor that served Delphi. The rulers of Kirrha wanted to impose a toll on pilgrims arriving at the harbor before allowing them to proceed to the Delphic oracle. This led the members of the Amphictyony to intervene and put an end to it. Following its victory, the Amphictyony reorganized the Pythian games and declared they would include nude contests and equestrian events in addition to musical competi-

---

384 Mouratidis, Istoria physikēs agōgēs, p. 256.
385 Yiannakis, Ieroi-Panellēnioi agōnes, p. 68.
386 Papantoniou, «Oi epidraseis,» pp. 99-103.

tion.[387] But the musical component always dominated these games. They were first on the program and their glamour overshadowed all the other events.[388]

At the time of the Roman Empire, Pythian games were also held in other cities which had bought the right from the former athletic center.[389]

The Delphic Oracle faded after the decree of Theodosius regarding games and ancient worship rites in 394 CE. However, it seems that the Pythian games had been in decline even earlier.[390] In the fifth century CE, the temple of Apollo was converted into a Christian church. Delphi was pillaged. Meanwhile, earthquakes, storms, rain and rock slides destroyed and covered the sacred site.[391]

The sanctuary at Olympia continued its main mission of cultivating the agonistic spirit and the desire to excel, while Delphi and the Mysteries opened the way for people to achieve a better life.[392]

When they were held

Initially, the Pythian games were held every eight years, which was how long it took for Apollo to atone for killing the dragon Python that guarded the oracle.[393]

The games took place every four years, on the third year of the Olympiad, in the month of Bucatios (August-September),[394] just a few days after the Great Panathenaic games.[395]

The games at Delphi lasted seven days. They began on the evening of the sixth of Bucatios.[396] On the fifth day of the games and the tenth of Bucatios, the nude games and pankration were held. The Pythian games include men and boy athletes.[397]

---

387 Papantoniou, «Oi epidraseis,» pp. 99-103.
388 Albanidis, Istoria tēs athlēsēs, p. 91.
389 Albanidis, Istoria tēs athlēsēs, p. 297.
390 Yiannakis, Istoria physikēs agōgēs: apo tous prōtogonous, p. 40.
391 Yiannakis, Ieroi-Panellēnioi agōnes, p. 69.
392 Sakellarakis et al., Oi Olympiakoi, p. 77.
393 Yiannakis, Ieroi-Panellēnioi agōnes, p. 68.
394 Sakellarakis et al., Oi Olympiakoi, pp. 66, 67.
395 Yiannakis, Ieroi-Panellēnioi agōnes, p. 68.
396 Albanidis, Istoria tēs athlēsēs, p. 91.
397 Samara and Albanidis, "Ē agōnistikē parousia," p. 8.

Pankration

Men's pankration was introduced in 586 BCE.[398] The boys' pankration was introduced at the 61st Pythian games in 346 BCE, and the winner was Iolaus of Thebes.[399] Clearly, the boys' pankration had been introduced at the Pythian games before the Olympian games.[400]

Stadium capacity

At the time of Herodes Atticus, the Delphic stadium could accommodate 7,000 spectators (second century CE),[401] while according to another source it was 8,000.[402]

The prize

Pausanias refers to 586 BCE as the year they began, when the prizes for the winners were the spoils from the Sacred War. This would mean that initially the prizes were monetary, but after 586 BCE, they were bay laurel wreaths. From that point on, the games became *stephanitai*.[403]

---

398 Miller, Arete, p. 202.
399 Yiannakis, Ieroi-Panellēnioi agōnes, p. 71.
400 Yiannakis, Ieroi-Panellinioi agones, p. 71.
401 Crowther, "Visiting the Olympic Games," p. 38.
402 Mouratidis, Istoria physikēs agōgēs, p. 256.
403 Papantoniou, «Oi epidraseis,» pp. 99-103.

Chapter 4

THE ATHLETES

We have seen that victory was a moral ideal. The winners essentially performed feats.[404] The contest was associated with a god and the victory had a divine aspect.[405] The athlete's victory was proof that he possessed special ability and that he enjoyed a divine blessing and seal of approval.[406]

At these supreme moments, all of Greece would be in the stands celebrating the athletes' victory.[407] The cheering, the praises and the rituals glorifying the athletes all reaffirmed that a new god had just been born. In addition, the jubilation that followed the victory, the hymns that were sung, the enthusiastic procession and the delirium of the crowds manifested the deeply rooted need of the people and of society to feel spiritually engaged; a need to identify with the winner and by extension to communicate with their deity. This also expressed the deep admiration of human beings of their ability to overcome physical limitations and reach extremes on their own merit, which was something that approached the limits of art and even the limits of god.[408]

By winning, the athletes also demonstrated the value of their native city and did justice to their heritage.[409] It was not the individual who won; through the athlete, before the whole of Greece and in competition against all of Greece, his ancestry and his homeland were also glorified. That is the reason they competed so zealously. The concept of bravery embodied the moral,

---

404 Gogaki, Oi antilēpseis, p. 172.
405 Gogaki, Oi antilēpseis, p. 173.
406 Gogaki, Oi antilēpseis, pp. 174, 175.
407 Gogaki, Oi antilēpseis, p. 176.
408 Gogaki, Oi antilēpseis, p. 188.
409 Gogaki, Oi antilēpseis, p. 187.

political and spiritual ideals that the athletes believed were worth risking their lives for.[410]

The panhellenic games also had a national value, as they shaped the raw material that would later be called a "national conscience." The concept of national conscience was a revolutionary social intervention at a time when the institutions and the state were faceless forms. The individual aspect of the Olympic victor was transformed into a collective one and the games became a structural element of the community.[411]

Hence, three parameters are evident in the sacred games, and even more so in the Olympics: the religious, the athletic and the socio-political. We also looked at the evolution of the Olympian pantheon through the centuries. All of the symbolism of the old religion, the new deities that appeared with the invaders, and the local beliefs filtered and modified through interactions over time had taken shape through the rituals observed at the most significant religious festival.

The evolution of athletics is the second parameter: a movement that went from an unstructured activity to a game and then to a sport.

And finally, the involvement of the authorities, at first merely tolerating but later encouraging an institution that never challenged the powers that be; instead, it serve to enhance their image and solidify their authority.

We can thus discern a complete structure built on a foundation of athletic activity, with an ideological overlay of religion bolstered by power.

The major protagonists were the athletes taking part in the games. They stood between humans and gods. They mobilized this vast mechanism of primordial rituals, symbolism, ideas, festivals, ceremonies, dedications, votive offerings, expressions of art, philosophical discussions, the attendance of sophists, poets, historians, singers, musicians, sculptors and representatives of the authorities, the military, politicians, merchants, business people of the times and others. With their endeavors, they managed to attract to the places where they competed figures such as Phidias, Pythagoras, Praxiteles, Myron, Lysippos, Anaxagoras, Herodotus, Pindar, Plato, Aristotle, Gorgias, Isocrates, Lysias, Euripides and many others.

The men's pankration became part of the Olympic lineup in 648 BCE, as we saw earlier - 128 years after the Olympic games first began. Boys' pankration followed in 200 BCE, 576 years after the start of the games. These two beginnings were separated by 448 years. They both remained part of the Olym-

---

410 Gogaki, Oi antilēpseis, pp. 238, 239.
411 Gogaki, Oi antilēpseis, pp. 194, 195.

pics until the games were abolished in 393 CE. Therefore, men's pankration was present for 1,041 years and the boys' for 593 years.

By the time the pankratiasts appeared at Olympia, the games had already matured with a centuries-long history behind them. They had had ample time to see and assimilate everything that went on in Olympia. There could not help but be fully aware of the role of the games and know what they were taking part in. Besides, a top-level athlete could avoid suffering the hardship of traveling to Elis, or taking part in the Olympics, or committing to staying in Elis for a month, or risking elimination, or becoming involved in the most demanding competitions, and instead take part in *chrimatites* games and collect monetary prizes. But participating in the sacred games was something different; it was a religious act. They were taking part in a significant religious event that led to purification. Athletes competed to honor the gods, as well as to win for their *poleis* and for themselves.

The process of taking part began when the athletes set off on their journey to Olympia. One could say that the entire time - from the moment they left their homes, traveled under the protection of the truce, arrived in Elis, trained for thirty days under the guidance of the Elean *Hellanodikēs*, marched in the procession over the final 60 kilometers to Olympia where 40,000 Greeks from all over the world awaited them, and until the first three days of waiting before it was their turn to compete and the oaths they took to compete honorably - served to psychologically and mentally prepare the athletes to follow in the footsteps of the gods who had once competed there. They would be ready to experience the ultimate glory, to have their name recorded on the list of victors, to acquire the right to erect their statue in the sacred place and in their homeland, to be memorialized by poets and to be spoken of with admiration by all who had seen and heard of them. They had the opportunity to experience immortality.

However, preparations began much earlier, even years before, because the ten months of compulsory training before the games could hardly assure them of much success. They had to be impeccably prepared as well as experienced; along the way to the Olympian games, they had to win at a number of smaller competitions and learn to protect themselves from injury so that when they reached the ultimate goal of their career, they would be able to compete in perfect condition. The games were the last - and highest - step in their careers and only those who were best-equipped could be chosen.

The sacred games were also a great expense for the organizers, but also brought many economic and political benefits to Elis. It was no accident that the games did not change location throughout their duration. The Eleans and the organizers of the other sacred games sent heralds (*spondophoroi*) throughout the Greek world at their own expense to announce the beginning of the truce. *Hellanodikēs* had to be trained and repairs had to be made to the stadiums in preparation. Huge amounts were invested in the entire event and naturally, they expected to reap certain rewards, whether economic, political or athletic. The "payback" came from the athletes. As we saw earlier, pankration was the most popular of the sports at Olympia, and was therefore the event from which the most was expected in terms of "payback."

The Olympic Victors

But just who were these great athletes? The Olympic games were held from 776 BCE to 393 CE - a period of about twelve centuries. Of the 4,237 athletes who would have emerged as victors in all of the events during the 293 Olympian games, the names, origins and event of only 921 are known today.[412] At best, we know about 25 percent of the Olympic champions.[413] Pankration is mentioned in 83 Olympian games and there is information on 72 champion pankratiasts. By following the trail of information on these athletes, it is possible to form an impression of what was happening at that time.

Three periods can be distinguished during this period of time: the first period: 776 - 480 BCE; the second period: 480 - 146 BCE; and the third period: 146 BCE - 393 CE.

First period: 776 - 480 BCE

This period marked the beginning of the games, their development and their peak. During this time, the games were transformed from local to major national events.[414] Information is available on eleven Olympian games that included pankration, and on eight winners.

The first champion pankratiast was **Lygdamis** of Syracuse, who took part in the 33rd Olympian games in 648 BCE.[415] Lygdamis was better known

---

412 Valavanis, Athla, p. 52.
413 Kyle, "Greek Athletic Competitions," p. 33.
414 Mouratidis, Istoria physikēs agōgēs, p. 559.
415 Luigi Moretti, Olympionikai, I vincitori negli antichi Agoni Olimpici (Academia Nazionale dei Lincei, Rome, 1957), No 51.

for his build; he was a giant.[416] He must have been so large that the length of his foot was equal to a pēchēs (or cubit, based on the length of the forearm); when he measured the length of the Olympic stadium, he found it to be as many feet as the length of his foot in pēchēs.[417] According to Pausanias, Lygdamis was as well developed physically as Heracles of Thebes was, according to his countrymen. Lygdamis' tomb was located near the Syracuse quarries.[418] Naturally, Lygdamis could not imagine that the best pankratiasts would fight in the same *palaestra* over the next thousand years.

The second pankration winner about whom something is known was **Phrynon** of Athens. He was a victor in 636 BCE at the 36th Olympics. He was a general in the war between the Athenians and the Mytilenaeans for control of Sigeion. According to a reference by Diogenes Laertius (1.4.74), he was killed by Mytilenaean general Pittacus. [419, 420]

Arrichion or **Arrachion** won three times - at the 52nd, 53rd and 54th Olympian Games, in 572, 568 and 564 BCE respectively. He was an outstanding pankratiast and the first athlete to develop a regular training method.[421] He was from Phigaleia, a town in Arcadia near modern-day Andritsaina[422]; in fact, the area now belongs to the Province of Trifylia in the Prefecture of Messenia.[423] Arrhachion died while fighting to attain his third Olympic victory, which was earned after death. His is the only verified case of a pankratiast dying in competition; his death resulted from a choke hold. Philostratus and Pausanias provide a detailed description:[424] "The antagonist of Arrhachion, having already clinched him around the middle, thought to kill him; already he had wound his forearm about the other's throat to shut off the breathing, while pressing his legs on Arrhachion's groins and winding his feet one inside each knee of his adversary. But, although the choke was successful and the sleep of death thus induced began to creep over his limbs and senses, as he relaxed the tension of his legs he failed to forestall the scheme of Arrhachion in his swift reaction. Arrhachion kicked back with the sole of his right foot (as the result of which his right side was imperiled since now his knee was hanging unsupported). Then with his groin he holds his adversary tight till he

---

416 Sakellarakis et al., Oi Olympiakoi, p. 230.
417 Philostratus, Gymnasticus, 12.22.
418 Pausanias, V 8.8.
419 Moretti, Olympionikai, No 58.
420 Papantoniou, "Oi epidraseis," p. 131.
421 Moretti, Olympionikai, No 95, 99, 102.
422 Yiannakis, Archaiognōsia, p. 147.
423 K. S. Kitriniaris, Gymnasticus by Philostratus (Patsilinakos, Athens 1961), p. 65.
424 Philostratus, Imagines II.6.4, trans. Arthur Fairbanks, http://www.theoi.com/Text/PhilostratusElder2A.html#6, retrieved Sept. 21, 2016); Pausanias, VIII, 40.1-2.

can no longer resist, and, throwing his weight down toward the left while he locks the latter's foot tightly inside his own right knee, by this violent outward thrust he wrenched the ankle from its socket."[425] At that moment, Arrhachion's trainer, Eryxias, realizing that the contest was up and that a winner would soon be declared, shouted in support, "What a noble epitaph, 'He was never defeated at Olympia.'"[426] Arrhachion took courage and continued past the point of no return. He died from his opponent's choke hold. At the same time, his adversary surrendered, screaming in pain. Thus, Arrhachion was crowned an Olympic champion after death, since his opponent had surrendered.

According to Pausanias, there was an ancient stone statue of Arrhachion in Phigalia[427], but the inscription at the base was not clear. Excavations carried out in the early 20th century found a statue that represented a young, nude athlete which is dated to about the same time as the athlete; it is, therefore, surmised that it belonged to him.[428]

Rexibius of Opuntia in Antioch was a winner at the 61st Olympic games in 536 BCE.[429] His statue was the second-oldest at Olympia, after that of Praxidamas, a boxing champion from Aegina.[430] It was made of the wood of a fig tree.[431]

At the 62nd Olympian games in 532 BCE, the victor was **Eurymenes** of Samos. He was an athlete in wrestling, boxing and pankration.[432] Pythagoras the philosopher and mathematician makes a reference to him, as they must have been of the same age. In contrast to other athletes of the time whose diet consisted mostly of dried figs and cheese, Eurymenes mainly ate meat (animal protein).

Timasitheus of Delphi won twice: in 516 and 512 BCE at the 66th and 67th Olympics respectively. His statue at Olympia was made by sculptor Ageladas the Argive.[433] But his was not a happy ending. He became involved in politics and in his final effort to seize the Acropolis of Athens with Isagoras and install the latter as the tyrant of the city, he was arrested along with others and condemned by the Athenians to death for his crime in 507 BCE.[434]

Hagias, son of Acnonius of Pharsalus, was also a great athlete. He won at the 74th Olympics in 484 BCE and was the first Olympic pankratiast champion from his region.

---

425 Yiannakis, Archaiognosia, p. 149.
426 Philostratus, Gymnasticus, 21.
427 Pausanias, VIII 40.1
428 Mouratidis, Istoria physikēs agōgēs, p. 335.
429 Moretti, Olympionikai, No 119.
430 Pausanias, VI, 18.7.
431 Pavlinis, Istoria tēs Gymnastikēs, p. 132.
432 Moretti, Olympionikai, No 123.
433 Moretti, Olympionikai, No 140, 146.
434 Gogaki, Oi antilēpseis, p. 300. (Pausanias 6.8.6.)

The inscriptions referring to him are as follows:

Inscription **FD III 4:460** was found at Delphi and is dated to between 337/6 and 333/2 BCE. Here it is in its entirety:

1.1 Ἀκνόνιος Ἀπάρου τέτραρχος Θεσσαλῶν.

2.1 πρῶτος Ὀλύμπια παγκράτιον, Φαρσάλιε, νικᾶις,
Ἁγία Ἀκνονίου, γῆς ἀπὸ Θεσσαλίας,
πεντάκις ἐν Νεμέαι, τρὶς Πύθια, πεντάκις Ἰσθμοῖ·
καὶ σῶν οὐδείς πω στῆσε τροπαῖα χερῶν.
5

3.1 κἀγὼ τοῦ{ο}δε {²⁶τοῦδε}²⁶ ὁμάδελ[φος ἔ]φυν, ἀριθμὸν δὲ τὸν αὐτὸν
ἤμασι τοῖς αὐτοῖς [ἐχφέρ]ομαι στεφάνων,
νικῶν μουνοπά[λης], Τ[..]σηνῶν δὲ ἄνδρα κράτιστον
κτεῖνα, ἔθελον τό[γε δ' οὔ]· Τηλέμαχος δ' ὄνομα.
5

4.1 οἵδε μὲν ἀθλοφόρου ῥώμης ἴσον ἔσχον, ἐγὼ δὲ
σύγγονος ἀμφοτέρων τῶνδε Ἀγέλαος ἔφυν·
νικῶ δὲ στάδιον τούτοις ἅμα Πύθια παῖδας·
μοῦνοι δὲ θνητῶν τοῦσδ' ἔχομεν στεφάνους.
5

5.1 Δάοχος Ἁγία εἰμί, πατρὶς Φάρσαλος, ἁπάσης
Θεσσαλίας ἄρξας vac. οὐ βίαι ἀλλὰ νόμωι,
ἑπτὰ καὶ εἴκοσι ἔτη, πολλῆι δὲ καὶ ἀγλαοκάρπωι
εἰρήνηι πλούτωι τε ἔβρυε Θεσσαλία.
5

6.1 οὐκ ἔψευσέ σε Παλλὰς ἐν ὕπνωι, Δαόχου υἱὲ
Σίσυφε, ἃ δ' εἶπε σαφῆ θῆκεν ὑποσχεσίαν·
ἐξ οὗ γὰρ τὸ πρῶτον ἔδυς περὶ τεύχεα χρωτί,
οὔτ' ἔφυγες δήϊους οὔτε τι τραῦμ' ἔλαβες.
5

7.1 αὔξων οἰκείων προγόνων ἀρετὰς τάδε δῶρα
στῆσεμ Φοίβωι ἄνακτι, γένος καὶ πατρίδα τιμῶν,
Δάοχος εὐδόξωι χρώμενος εὐλογίαι,
τέτραρχος Θεσσαλῶν
5 ἱερομνήμων Ἀμφικτυόνων.

8.1 Σίσυφος Δαόχου.

Here is a translation of the text:

1.1 Acnonius, son of Aparus, Tetrarch of the Thessalians

2.1 First victory at the Olympian pankration you scored,
Pharsalian **Agias, son of Acnonius**, from the Thessalian land,
five victories at the Nemea, three at the Pythia, five at the Isthmus;
and no one has yet taken this record from your hands.

3.1 And I was born his full-brother; and on the selfsame day
I carried off the same number of crowns
having scored victory in wrestling. I killed a mighty man from T[- -],
but not on purpose. My name is Telemachus.

4.1 And these have shared an equal strength for victory, while I,
Agelaus, was born a kinsman of both;
I won the stadion for youths at Pythia, just like they did;
we alone of all mortals have carried off these crowns.[435]

5.1 I am Daochos, son of Hagias, Pharsalus is my native city, (and I) ruled over all of Thessaly, not by force but by law, for twenty-seven years, and Thessaly prospered with great and splendid fruit-bearing peace and wealth.[436]

6.1 Pallas did not deceive you in a dream, Sisyphus son of Daochos, and the clear things which she told you she set down as a promise. For from the moment you first clothed your skin with armour, you never fled your foes nor received a single wound.

7.1 Increasing the virtues of my family's ancestors, I set up these gifts to lord Phoibos, honouring my people and my homeland – I, Daochos, possessed of glorious praise, tetrarch of the Thessalians, hieromnemon of the Amphictyons[437].

8.1 Sisyphus son of Daochos.[438]

---

435 Elizabeth Kosmetatou, "Constructing Legitimacy: The Ptolemaic *Familiengruppe* as a Means of Self-Definition in Posidippus' *Hippika*," in *Labored in Papyrus Leaves: Perspectives on an Epigram Collection Attributed to Posidippus (P.Mil.Vogl. VIII 309)*, ed. Benjamin Acosta-Hughes, Elizabeth Kosmetatou and Manuel Baumach (Center for Hellenic Studies, Washington, D.C., 2004) http://nrs.harvard.edu/urn-3:hul.ebook:CHS_AcostaHughesB_etal_eds.Labored_in_Papyrus_Leaves.2004, retrieved Sept. 20, 2016.

436 Translation retrieved from http://www.perseus.tufts.edu/hopper/artifact?name=Delphi,+Daochos+Monument,+Daochos+I&object=sculpture, Sept. 20, 2016.

437 The *amphictyonai* were to the Pythian games what the *Hellanodikai* were to the Olympian games. They oversaw the games, and along with the *hieromnēmonai* (sacred secretaries), they were resposible for judging the games, the preparations, the expenses, the delegations of envoys and proclaiming the games. It was a particularly prestigious office.

438 Translation by Emma M. Aston, "Thessaly and Macedon at Delphi," *Electrum* 19, (2012): pp 41-60, doi: 10.4467/20843909EL.12.002.0743, retrieved Sept. 20, 2016.

Inscription **IG IX,2 249** below also refers to Hagias and was found in Pharsalus. It is dated later than 338 BCE. The inscription records his achievements in the sacred games:

```
1  ....κ[– – – – – – – – – – – – –]
   .....γεσ.......ουσι ΣΟ[–τιμῶν(?)]
   [πατ]<ρ>[ί]δα Φάρσ[αλον] καὶ πατέ[ρων? ἀρετάς(?)]
   [πρῶ]τος Ὀλύμπ[ια πα]γκράτιο[ν, Φαρσάλιε, νικᾶις],
5  [Ἀγ]ία Ἀκνονίο[υ, γῆς ἀ]πὸ Θεσσ[αλίας],
   [πε]ντάκις ἐν Νε[μέοις], τόσα Π[ύθια, πεντάκις Ἰσθμοῖ].
   [κα]ὶ σῶν οὐδείς [πω στῆσ]ε τρ[όπαια χερῶν].
      vacat
8  Λύσιππ[ος Σικυώνιος ἐποίησε(?)].
```

Translated:

[---] Honors (?)
for the homeland Pharsalus and the virtues of the fathers (?)
you are the first from the Thessalian land, **Hagias, son of Acnonius** of Pharsalus,
to be victorious in pankration at the Olympic games, (having been victorious) five times at Nemea, three times at the Pythia, (and) five times at the Isthmia; and no one yet has grasped the trophies from your hands.

Erected by Lysippos of Sicyon.

Hagias was also a *periodonikēs*[439], which meant he had won in all four sacred games: Olympian, Nemean, Pythian and Isthmian. Aside from the Olympian games, he had achieved a total of five wins at Nemea, three in Delphi and five at the Isthmian games. His homeland paid him particular tribute.[440] The offering of Daochos, the monument erected in his honor at the Temple of Apollo at Delphi, consisted of nine statues standing on a rectangular base. A statue of Apollo stood at the right end, and to its left were six statues of the ancestors of Daochos: The family patriarch Acnonius, Agias, Telemachus, Agelaus, Daochos I, Sisyphus I, Daochos II (the dedicator) and his son, Sisyphos II; in other words, the father, his sons and his four descendants. It was erected at Delphi in 337/6-333/2 BCE. The inscription on the statue refers to a victory at Olympia, five at Nemea, three at the Pythian games, and five at the Isthmian games. The three brothers all won at the Pythian games: Hagias at pankration, Telemachus at wrestling and Agelaus in the boys' *stadion* competition. The vo-

---

439 Knab, Die Periodoniken, No 11, 12.
440 Moretti, *Olympionikai*, No 192.

tive monument was the work of outstanding sculptor Lysippos, as noted in the above inscription.[441] The 1.97 meter (6½ feet) statue of the great pankratiast[442] is now at the Delphi Museum.

Dromeas was originally from Mantinea and was a pankration winner at the 75th Olympics in 480 BCE.[443] He was to compete in the final against Theagenes, son of Timosthenes of Thasos, a boxer and pankratiast who was perhaps the greatest athlete of the ancient world. In 480 BCE, Theagenes was still quite young.[444] Carried away with the enthusiasm of youth, he sought to achieve a double win in two different events: boxing and pankration. This overestimation of his abilities was considered arrogant and disrespectful of the gods. He was punished for his inappropriate behavior with a fine of one talent for insulting the gods. Theagenes was similarly punished for his stance against his fellow athlete in boxing, Euthymus of Locri-Southern Italy, because it was determined that he acted out of personal animosity against him and he was stripped of his victory. Pausanias refers to a hostile attitude, which was contrary to the established principles of the games: the contest between the rivals had to be within the scope of fair play and good sportsmanship.[445] Theagenes had beaten Euthymus in the boxing competition. But he was very tired from his efforts and could not compete in the pankration. Thus, Dromeas earned a *nikē akoniti*, which meant he did not have to compete; it would have been unfair for Dromeas to lose through the fault of Theagenes.[446] In fact, he was the first pankratiast to be declared an *akoniti* victor.[447] For his absence, which was considered scandalous, Theagenes was fined one talent. If an athlete did not pay the imposed fine, it was paid by his *polis*; otherwise, the Eleans would have barred all of the athletes from Thasos from the games.[448] But that was not all. His victory in boxing was annulled and the match was repeated. He won once again, but because Euthymus was forced to compete twice because of Theagenes, the latter was required to pay compensation of one talent. He paid the one talent to Olympian Zeus[449] for his absence, but instead of paying the

---

441 Giorgos P. Kostouros, *Nemeōn Athlōn Diēgēsis* [Record of Nemean feats], Vol. 2 (Athens, Nisos 2008), p. 33.
442 Yiannakis, *Ieroi-Panellēnioi agōnes*, p. 82.
443 Moretti, *Olympionikai*, No 202.
444 Papantoniou, "Oi epidraseis," p. 169.
445 Papantoniou, «Oi epidraseis,» pp. 164-169.
446 Pavlinis, *Istoria tēs Gymnastikēs*, p. 158.
447 Pausanias, *VI* 11.4.
448 Pavlinis, *Istoria tēs Gymnastikēs*, p. 161.
449 Mouratidis, *Istoria physikēs agōgēs*, p. 191.

other, he agreed with his opponent that he would not compete in the next two Olympics (476 and 472 BCE), giving Euthymus a chance to win.[450]

TABLE 1: Olympic pankratiast victors 776 - 480 BCE

	Year	Olympics	Name
1	648 BCE	33rd	Lygdamis
2	636 BCE	36th	Phrynon
3	572 BCE	52nd	Arrachion
4	568 BCE	53rd	Arrachion
5	564 BCE	54th	Arrachion
6	536 BCE	61st	Rexibius
7	532 BCE	62nd	Eurymenes
8	516 BCE	66th	Timasitheus
9	512 BCE	67th	Timasitheus
10	484 BCE	74th	Hagias
11	480 BCE	75th	Dromeas

Second period: 480 - 146 BCE

In moving into the classical period and the prevalence of philosophical theories, the religious convictions of the people began to disintegrate and the existence of the gods to come into doubt. At the same time, the sophist teachings of utilitarianism were gaining popularity, as a result of which human beings deviated from their religious beliefs and turned to the pursuit of personal interests. Thus, the Olympic games evolved from a purely ritualistic act into an athletic event with an institutional underpinnings.[451] The athletes gradually acquired the attitude of professionals and would take part in the games not in worship of Olympian Zeus, but to seek a victory with lucrative potential. In this way, athletics became a type of work. Through this new moral reality, from the late fifth century and more so during the fourth century BCE, it was no coincidence that the first violations began to arise. There were violations of the truce; athletes were traded to wealthy cities in exchange for monetary gain; and opponents were bribed to ensure victory. This crisis continued throughout the remaining course of the games until they were abolished.[452] It was

---

450 Pausanias, *VI* 6.5.
451 Papantoniou, «Oi epidraseis,» p. 15.
452 Papantoniou, «Oi epidraseis,» pp. 9, 10.

a golden period for professional athletes who earned enormous amounts of money, but the physical beauty of athletes was lost.[453]

Yet another threat was emerging outside the *palaestrae* at the beginning of the fifth century BCE. The first two decades of this century were overshadowed by impending war. From the East, the Persian expansion was coming to strike at the heart of Greece after suppressing the Ionian Revolt of 500 BCE. From the West, the Carthaginians, a powerful enemy, were threatening the prosperous Greek cities in Sicily. The Greeks were coming to realize more than ever before that they had to act together as a nation to fend off this great enemy. The profound religiosity of the people proved most effective in uniting them on a national level. The Greeks turned to their common gods - the great deities of the Olympic pantheon. The double victory at the Battle of Himera of the Greek cities of Syracuse and Akragas against the Carthaginians, and the united Greek fleet against the Persian imperial fleet in the Battle of Salamis on September 22 of the same year (480 BCE) were landmark events. If the Greeks had been beaten, the evolution of Greece would have come to a halt and Western civilization would not be what it is today.

Meanwhile, the Olympian games were to take place in the summer of 480 BCE. Thus, in the days preceding this major and decisive confrontation, the truce went into effect once more and the Greek *poleis* gathered at Olympia to celebrate the 75th Olympics as usual, in a climate of national unity and religious fervor. The Eleans welcomed the athletes and visitors even from cities whose position had been neutral or even sympathetic to the enemy. They set aside their differences and demonstrated the accustomed neutrality of the organizing authority.

But at the same time, the Olympiad of 480 BCE posed a challenging dilemma for the first time. They had to decide in the face of advancing threat whether to respond directly and become involved in the war, or to celebrate the Olympian games and then resume their military operations afterwards. The Greeks chose to follow their religious conscience and adopted a relaxed response to the hostilities until they could complete their agonistic obligations to the god of Olympia.[454] This unwavering devotion of the Greeks to the ritual of the games cannot be overlooked; it was something that led Xerxes to wonder, after the Battle of Thermopylae and seeing no serious response on their part, "what on earth is occupying those Greeks." He could not imagine that, as he was invading, the Greek *poleis* were celebrating the Olympian games, the Greek visitors were enjoying the spectacle of the games and the athletes were

---

453 Mouratidis, *Istoria physikēs agōgēs*, p. 559.
454 Papantoniou, "Oi epidraseis," p. 167.

competing in the name of virtue.[455] In such an atmosphere of intense religious feeling, it was natural that a victory at the games would be associated with the moral reward of the athletes.[456]

Information related to this period refers to 38 Olympian games that included pankration and to 30 victors.

The 76th Olympiad in 476 BCE, which followed the Persian Wars, was the most brilliant in the history of the games.[457] The spectators included Themistocles, who had led the Greeks to victory in the naval Battle of Salamis. The audience cheered for him as if he were an Olympic champion himself and all eyes were turned to him instead of the competitors that day, as Plutarch tells us.[458] At these games, **Theagenes** took part only in the pankration and won.[459] He was the greatest athlete in antiquity and was active in the first half of the fifth century, as we saw earlier. His father's name was Timosthenes, but because there was also a priest of Heracles of Thasos with the same name, the Thasians believed that Theagenes was the fruit of the union between his mother and Heracles' ghost, which had taken the form of Timosthenes. Aside from the Olympian games, he also won three times at the Pythia, nine at the Nemea and ten at the Isthmia, sometimes in pankration and at other times in boxing. He decided to compete and won in the *dolichos* long race at Phthia, Thessaly, Achilles' home. He also won the *dolichos* at the Hecatomb festival in Argos. Theagenes began his athletic career at the Pythian games in 482 BCE. He was considered a big eater, and it was said that he ate a bull entirely by himself.[460]

A name is a word with which an individual addresses society and by which he is known. When early organized societies were taking form in antiquity, their members used names to distinguish themselves from one another. They came to believe that the name of an individual was an integral part of his person and that it played a significant role in his life and personality. Thus, careful attention was paid to choosing the best possible name. In addition, the name of an individual was not the only factor that set him apart in society; it was always associated with the customs and convictions that were based on people's belief in the magical powers of names. It was also commonly understood that the name and its bearer were one and the same.[461] Thus, Theagenes

---

455 Kyle, "Pan-Hellenism," p. 196.
456 Papantoniou, «Oi epidraseis,» p. 168.
457 Mouratidis, *Istoria physikēs agōgēs*, p. 559.
458 Sakellarakis et al., *Oi Olympiakoi*, p. 81.
459 Pavlinis, *Istoria tēs Gymnastikēs*, p. 77.
460 Athenaeus, *Deipnosophistae* [*Dinner-table philosophers*], 10.412.d
461 Thomas B. Yiannakis and Sylvia T. Yiannaki, "The Meaning of Names in Greek Antiquity, with Special Reference to Olympic Athletes," *The International Journal of the History of Sport* 15, no. 3 (December 1998): p. 103.

was the son of the demigod Heracles (Theagenes meant "theos" [god] + genus = god + birth = he of divine or sacred origins).[462]

Inscription **Syll.³ 36A** was found in Phocis, near Delphi, and is dated at between 370 and 365 BCE. It refers to Theagenes as Theugenes, and to his father Timosthenes as Timoxenes. It includes a partial list of his victories and is included here:

a.1 ὀλ[βίστη θρέπτειρα Θ]άσος, Τιμοξένου υἱέ, | καὶ [γὰρ ἀφ' Ἑλλή]νων
[π]λ[εῖστ]ον [ἔπαινο]ν ἔχει[ς] | καρτερίας. οὐ γάρ τις Ὀλυμπίαι ἐστεφ-
ανώθη | ὠὑ[τὸ]ς [ἀνὴ]ρ πυγμῆι παγκρατίωι τε κρατῶν. | σοὶ δὲ καὶ ἐμ Π-
υθῶνι τριῶν στεφάνω[ν ἀκ]ονιτί | ες ——τόδε θνητὸς ἀνὴρ οὔτις ἔρε-
5 ξε ἕτερος—— · | ἐνέα δ' Ἰσθ[μι]άδων νῖκαι δέκα, δὶς γὰρ ἄϋσεν | κῆρυξ
ἐγ κύκλωι μοῦνον ἐπιχθονίων | πυγμῆς παγκρατίου τ' ἐπινίκι-
ον ἤματι τωὐτῶι | ἐνάκι δ' ἐν Νεμέαι, Θεόγενες· αἱ δὲ ἴδιαι | νῖκαι
τρίς τε ἑκατὸν καὶ χίλιαι, οὐδέ σέ φημι | πυγμῆι νικηθῆναι ἔκοσι καὶ δύ' ἐτῶν. |

b.9 **Θευγένης Τιμοξένου Θάσιος** ἐνίκησεν τάδε·
I.10 Ὀλύμπια πύξ
Ὀλύμπια παγκράτιον.
Πυθοῖ πύξ
Πυθοῖ πύξ
Πυθοῖ πὺξ ἀκονιτί.
15 Ἰσθμοῖ πύξ
Ἰσθμοῖ πύξ
Ἰσθμοῖ πύξ
Ἰσθμοῖ πύξ
Ἰσθμοῖ πύξ
II.20 Ἰσθμοῖ πύξ
Ἰσθμοῖ πύξ
Ἰσθμοῖ πύξ
Ἰσθμοῖ πύξ
καὶ παγκράτιον
25 τῆι αὐτῆι
Ἰσθμιάδι.
III.27 Νέμεα πύξ
Νέμεα πύξ
Νέμεα πύξ
30 Νέμεα πύξ
Νέμεα πύξ

---

462 Yiannakis and Yiannaki, "The Meaning of Names," p. 108.

         Νέμεα πύξ
         Νέμεα πύξ
         Νέμεα πύξ
IV.35   Νέμεα πύξ.
         Ἑκατόμβοια
         δόλιχον
         ἐν Ἄργει.

In translation:

a1.   Your fortunate nurturer Thasos, o son of Timoxenes, and (hence) the Greeks praise you greatly for your endurance. Because no one took the victor's crown at Olympia as you prevailed over all in boxing and pankration. You have also won three crowns at Pythia without facing an opponent – something that no other mortal man has achieved. You had ten victories at Isthmia, and twice the herald called you into the ring, the only mortal, winning on the same day both in boxing and the pankration; nine times at Nemea, o Theogenes; and your total personal victories are 1,300, I declare that you have never been defeated in boxing for 22 consecutive years.

      Theogenes, son of Timoxenes of Thasos, won the following:
      At Olympia in boxing
      At Olympia in pankration.
      At Pythia in boxing
      At Pythia in boxing
      At Pythia in boxing after opponent's refusal to compete (*akoniti*).
      At Isthmia in boxing
      At Isthmia in boxing
      At Isthmia in boxing
      At Isthmia in boxing
      At Isthmia in boxing
      At Isthmia in boxing
      At Isthmia in boxing
      At Isthmia in boxing
      At Isthmia in boxing
      and in pankration
      on the same day of the Isthmia.
      At Nemea in boxing
      At Nemea in boxing
      At Nemea in boxing
      At Nemea in boxing
      At Nemea in boxing

> At Nemea in boxing
> At Nemea in boxing
> At Nemea in boxing
> At Nemea in boxing.
> At the Hecatomb
> in dolichos
> at Argos.

A bronze statue of him had been erected in the central marketplace of Thasos. But a man who hated him passionately would go every night and strike it. One night, the statue fell on him and killed him. At the request of the dead man's family, the Thasians threw the statue into the sea. It was a reckless act and punishment from the gods came swiftly: the island was afflicted with famine and misery. They asked the Oracle of Delphi why this was happening and the Oracle advised them to bring back their exiles. They followed the advice, but nothing changed. They returned to the Oracle and learned that the prophecy meant they had to restore the statue of Theagenes to its rightful place. Once they had done so, the curse was lifted. From that point on, the Thasians adopted the custom of offering sacrifices and paying divine honors to the statue of their athlete.[463]

Pausanias[464] refers to 1,400 victories for Theagenes, while Plutarch refers to 1,200. Because of his athletic performance, he was called a *disolympios*, meaning "twice at Olympia", and a *myriaethlos*, meaning "with victories in a thousand feats."[465]

Traveling from event to event was not as simple as it is nowadays. Those 1,400 victories meant 1,400 journeys in harsh conditions. At that time, athletes traveled either by road or by sea. One academic noted that Theagenes would have had difficulty sailing from Thasos to so many games throughout the Greek world because the safe sailing season (May to October) was so short. For athletes at his level, there would have been up to 500 competitions around the Mediterranean when the sporting circuit was at its peak. Obviously, the athletes would have had to pick and choose the games they would attend, since it would have been impossible to compete in all of them.[466]

Winning so many events even in the modern world would be highly unlikely, though in ancient Greece, we can assume that Theagenes probably

---

463 Wayne Andersen, "Chasing shadows: lives of ancient Greek statues as lived by writers," *The European Legacy* 9, no. 4 (2004): pp. 510, 511.
464 Pausanias, *VI* 11.6.
465 Albanidis, *Istoria tēs athlēsēs*, p. 79.
466 Crowther, "Visiting the Olympic Games," pp. 41, 42.

achieved a fair number of victories without actually competing (*akoniti*); his opponents would have withdrawn because of his outstanding reputation. That was the greatest level of success. We can also assume that Theagenes competed up to the age of 40, since sources say he remained undefeated in boxing for 22 years. Theagenes was one of the few athletes in the early fifth century who is known to have had an athletic career. He was one of the first professionals to be occupied full-time in the sports circuit. He had amassed a significant fortune from his victories and numerous tributes from his homeland, which included honorary distinctions, sponsorships and other financial benefits. As we saw earlier, the vast amount of two talents that he was forced to pay for not taking part in the pankration at the Olympian games in 480 BCE would have been the equivalent of more than 250,000 dollars by current standards, according to researchers. Theagenes would have had no trouble paying that amount, considering the vast wealth to be gained by successful athletes; it is also possible that this son of a priest also had considerable family wealth.[467]

Another outstanding athlete - **Callias**[468], son of Didymias of Athens - appeared at the 77th Olympian games in 472 BCE. He was born in about 505 BCE and must have been about thirty-three years old when he won at Olympia. A larger-than-life bronze statue of him[469], created by renowned Athenian sculptor Micon, was erected at Olympia.[470] According to Pausanias, the equestrian events were held on the same day as the human competitions at the 77th Olympics. This meant that there was a delay in the pankration bout. The delay was due both to the equestrian races and to the pentathlon. As a result, Kallias was crowned the victor after a nighttime contest. But that was the last time such a delay occurred. The problem was resolved by the following Olympian games.[471]

Here are the inscriptions that refer to him: inscription **IG I³ 1473** was found at Olympia and is dated at approximately 470 BCE. It simply states the name of the athlete, his father and the sculptor - Micon of Athens - who made the statue.

A.1 **Καλλίας Διδυμίο: Ἀθηναῖος**
παγκράτιον.

B.1 Μίκων : ἐποίησεν : Ἀθηναῖος.

---

467 Crowther, *Sport,* pp. 140, 141, 142.
468 Moretti, *Olympionikai,* No 228.
469 Pavlinis, *Istoria tēs Gymnastikēs,* p. 132.
470 Luigi Moretti, *Inscrizioni Agonistiche Crèche* (Angelo Signorelli, Rome 1953), p. 33.
471 Pausanias, *V* 9.3.

Inscription **IG I³ 893** was found at the Acropolis in Athens and is dated to approximately 430 BCE. It lists his most significant victories:

I.1 **Καλλίας Δ[ιδυμίο]**.
II.2 νῖκαι·
Ὀλυ[μ]πίασι
Πύθια : δίς
5 Ἴσθμια : πεντάκις
Νέμεια : τετράκις
Παναθέναια με<γά>λ[α].

In translation:

Kallias, [son] of Didymias
Won at Olympia
Twice at Pythia
Five times at Isthmia
Four times at Nemea
At the Great Panathenaia

The winner at the 78th Olympics in 468 BCE was **Epitimadas** or Epitimidas, who was from Argos.[472]

The next Olympian at the 79th Olympic games in 464 BCE was **Ephotion** from Maenalus. His name also appears as **Ephoudion** or **Ephodion**. He is believed to have achieved victories at the Pythia, Isthmia and Nemea in 466, 465 and 464 BCE.[473] Nothing is known about the number of wins, however. He had won more than once at Olympia, and had also completed the *periodos*, or circuit, at a younger age. His career ended respectably when, as a veteran athlete with his hair turning gray, he achieved an unexpected win against young Ascondas.[474]

At the 80th Olympian games in 460 BCE, the winner was **Timodemus**, son of Timonoos of Acharnae in Athens.[475] He won at Olympia after his success at Nemea, which he achieved no later than 485 BCE.[476] A descendant of the Timodemides, he had collected seven wins at Nemea, eight at Isthmia and four at Pythia. His first victory was at Nemea. Pindar's ode Nemean 2 is ded-

---

472 Moretti, *Olympionikai*, No 241.
473 Moretti, *Olympionikai*, No 253.
474 Knab, *Die Periodoniken*, No 10.
475 Moretti, *Olympionikai*, No 262.
476 Moretti, *Olympionikai*, No 262.

icated to him.[477] His name, Timodemus, is derived from "*timē*" and "*dēmos*", meaning "honor of the people," or "the glory of the people."[478]

At the 81st Olympian games in 456 BCE, the winner was **Timanthes** of Cleone. A statue of him at Olympia was made by Myron. Timanthes came to an unfortunate end, however, as he committed suicide by falling into fire[479]. Nothing more is known.

Damagetus, eldest son of Diagoras of Rhodes, had two consecutive wins in the 82nd and 83rd Olympian Games in 452 and 448 BCE respectively.[480]

Inscription **IvO 152**, found at Olympia, is dated at 436 BCE and contains a reference to him, but unfortunately does not provide much information: the name of the athlete, his father, Diagoras, and his place of origin, Rhodes.

1 Δαμάγητος Διαγόρα Ῥ[όδιος].

Dorieus, the younger son of Diagoras of Rhodes, was victorious at the next three Olympian games, the 87th in 432, the 88th in 428 and the 89th in 424 BCE.

Here are the inscriptions referring to him:

IvO 153 was found at Olympia and has been dated at 424 BCE. It lists his achievements in the sacred games, along with the event in which he competed:

      [Δωριεὺς Διαγόρα Ῥόδιος]
      1
col. I.2 [Ὀλυμπίαι παγκράτιον]
      [Ὀλυμπίαι παγκράτιον]
      [Ὀλυμπίαι παγκράτ]ιον
    5 [Πυθοῖ πύξ]
      [Πυθοῖ πύ]ξ
      [Πυθοῖ π]ὺξ ἀκονιτεί
      [Ἰσθμο]ῖ πύξ
      [Ἰσθ]μοῖ πύξ
  10 [Ἰσθ]μοῖ πύξ
      [καὶ πα]νκράτιο[ν]
col. II.2 [Ἰσθμοῖ πύξ]
      [Ἰσθμοῖ πύξ]

---

477 Kostouros, *Nemeōn* 2, p. 180.
478 Yiannakis and Yiannaki, "The Meaning of Names," p. 108.
479 Moretti, *Olympionikai*, No 273.
480 Moretti, *Olympionikai*, No 287, 300.

  Ἰσθμ[οῖ]
5 Ἰσθμ[ο]ῖ
  Νεμῆ[ι] πύξ
  Νεμῆι πύξ
  Ν[εμ]ῆι πύξ
  Νε[μ]ῆι πύξ
10 [Νεμ]ῆι πύξ
  [Νεμῆι] π[ύξ]
  [Νεμῆι πύξ]

In translation:
  Dorieus, [son] of Diagoras of Rhodes
  At Olympia in pankration
  At Olympia in pankration
  At Olympia in pankration
  At Pythia in boxing
  At Pythia in boxing
  At Pythia in boxing *akoniti*
  At Isthmia in boxing
  At Isthmia in boxing
  At Isthmia in boxing
  and pankration
  At Isthmia in boxing
  At Isthmia in boxing
  At Isthmia
  At Isthmia
  At Nemea in boxing
  At Nemea in boxing
  At Nemea in boxing
  At Nemea in boxing
  At Nemea in boxing
  At Nemea in boxing
  At Nemea in boxing

  The inscription **Syll.³ 82** was found at Delphi and is dated at 426 to 420 BCE. Here is a brief summary of his victories at the sacred games:

1 [Δωριεὺς Διαγόρα Ῥόδιος]
  [ἐνίκησε παγκράτιον]·
  Ὀλύ[μπια τρίς, Πύ]θια τετράκις,
  Ἴσθ[μ]ι[α ὀκτ]άκις, Νέμεα ἑπτάκις,

Translated, it says:
> **Dorieus, [son] of Diagoras of Rhodes**
> Won in pankration
> At Olympia three times, at Pythia four times
> At Isthmia eight times, at Nemea seven times

In terms of wins at major games, Dorieus was the most successful member of the Diagoras family, the largest athletic family in ancient Greece.[481] He had collected twenty-six wins in pankration at various athletic competitions.[482] He also won eight times at Isthmia and seven at Nemea. Both he and his nephew, wrestling champion Peisidorus, competed not as Rhodians but as Thurians because they had fled to Thurii in Italy after being exiled by their political rivals. Dorieus later returned to Rhodes and openly supported the Spartans. He took part in the Peloponnesian War, fought in a naval battle against the Athenians, who captured and wanted to kill him. But when they gathered at the assembly and saw him, they were overcome by the glory he had achieved as an Olympic champion and changed their minds. They let him go without harming him.[483] These events took place in 407 BCE. His death is described by Androtion. Here is what happened: at that time, the king's fleet was in Kaunus under general Conon. Conon had convinced the Rhodians to abandon the Spartans and form an alliance with the king of Persia and the Athenians. Dorieus was not in Rhodes at the time but in Peloponnesus, where he was taken prisoner by the Spartans who believed his actions had done them harm and they condemned him to death.[484] This is one of the most typical cases regarding the reputation of Olympic champions.

Androsthenes, son of Lochaios from Maenalus, won the next two events, in 420 and 416 BCE at the 90th and 91st Olympian games. His statue at Olympia is one of the first works made by his countryman, Nicodamos, and is from the first quarter of the century.[485]

In 408 BCE at the 93rd Olympics, the winner was the great athlete **Polydamas**, or Pulydamas, son of Nicias, from Scotussa in Thessaly, which was destroyed by Alexander of Pherae in 372 BCE.[486] His statue was larger than all the other statues of athletes, including that of Milon.[487] According to Paus-

---
481 Moretti, *Olympionikai*, No 322, 326, 330.
482 Mouratidis, *Istoria physikēs agōgēs*, p. 333.
483 Gogaki, *Oi antilēpseis*, p. 307; (Pausanias 6.7.5.)
484 Kostouros, *Nemeōn 2*, p. 72
485 Moretti, *Olympionikai*, No 336, 343.
486 Pavlinis, *Istoria tēs Gymnastikēs*, p. 75.
487 Moretti, *Olympionikai*, No 348.

anias[488], he was defeated by Promachus of Pellene, but his countrymen always considered him undefeated. He was the tallest and strongest man of his generation. He was better known for his achievements outside of competition rather than his victories. In Persia, he bent thick pieces of iron and overcame lions.[489] He immobilized a bull by holding on to his rear legs and had stopped a chariot with one hand. Polydamas trained according to the old methods, which focused only on physical strength. He lifted heavy weights, ran against horses and hares for speed, straightened and bent iron bars and lifted bulls onto his shoulders.[490] Darius II learned of Polydamas' feats and sent envoys with gifts to convince him to go to Sousa in Persia. When he arrived, he was asked to fight unarmed against three of Persia's best soldiers, the so-called Immortals. He overcame and killed all three of them. Despite his achievements, he died a rather prosaic death[491] resulting from excessiveness and arrogance.[492] He had gone to a cave with his friends to escape the unbearable summer heat. The cave began to collapse and he attempted to hold up the ceiling. His friends managed to save themselves but he was crushed.[493]

Inscription **IG XII,6 2:640** referring to him was found at Pythagoreion in Samos and is dated at between 450 and 400 BCE. No additional information is provided, other than the name of the athlete and of his father.

1 **Πολυδάμας**
   Νικίωνος.

At the 94th Olympian games in 404 BCE, the winner was **Promachus**, son of Dryon of Pellene. Pellene was a city in Achaea referenced by Homer in the catalog of ships and had been built on the west bank of the Sythas River, along the border with Sicyon, near the village of Zougra in Corinthia.[494] Promachus had beaten Polydamas who had returned from Sousa to once again take part in the games. He had taken part and distinguished himself in a war against Corinth that may have been the Battle of Nemea in 394 BCE, when Pellene was allied with Sparta. To honor Promachus, his countrymen had built two statues - a bronze one in Olympia and a marble one at the gymnasium in Pellene.[495] But love provided incentive for victory. Promachus' trainer realized

---

488 Pausanias, *VII* 27.2.
489 Kitriniaris, *Gymnasticus*, p. 96.
490 Philostratus, *Gymnasticus*, 43.72.
491 Gogaki, *Oi antilēpseis*, p. 331.
492 Gogaki, *Oi antilēpseis*, p. 332.
493 Mouratidis, *Istoria physikēs agōgēs*, p. 362.
494 Kostouros, *Nemeōn* 2, p. 263.
495 Moretti, *Olympionikai*, No 355.

that the young man was in love and as the games approached, he brought him a fake letter supposedly from his beloved. The letter said that "he would not be considered worthy of her love unless he was a victor at the Olympian games." The message of love gave him such strength that he overcame famous Polydamas.[496] One might say this incident demonstrates two things: that love overcomes all obstacles and that coaching is indeed an art.

At the 95th Olympian games in 400 BCE, the winner was **Antiochus** of Lepreon. Lepreon was slightly to the north of the modern village of Strovitzi.[497] Antiochus also had two wins at Isthmia and Nemea. A statue of him at Olympia was made by Nicodamos.[498]

The name of the winner at the 96th Olympics in 396 BCE has not been recovered. The only information available about him is that he was from Acarnania, but even that is not certain.[499]

At the 100th Olympian games in 380 BCE, the winner was **Xenophon**, son of Menephylos from Aegium.[500] The existence of a statue at the *Altis*, the sacred grove where statues were usually erected at Olympia, is confirmed by Pausanias. It is dated at between 400 and 360 BCE, which coincides with the athlete's age.[501]

Local athlete **Stomios** won in 376 BCE at the 101st Olympics.[502] According to Pausanias, the inscription at the base of the statue at Olympia indicates Stomios had also achieved three victories at Nemea between 380 and 370 BCE.[503] He had also earned distinctions at war. He took part as a commander in the Elean cavalry in a war before the Battle of Leuctra (371 BCE), and he killed the opposing general.

Although the name of the winner at the 103rd Olympics in 368 BCE is not known, it is known that he was from Acarnania. The name of the athlete may have been **Philandrides**. Some believe that was the name of his father. Pausanias saw the statue of the athlete at Olympia, which was the work of sculptor Lysippos.[504]

Sostratus, son of Sosistratus of Sicyon, was victorious at three successive Olympics: the 104th, the 105th and the 106th, in 364, 360 and 356 BCE.[505]

---

496 Gogaki, *Oi antilēpseis*, p. 184.
497 Moretti, *Olympionikai*, No 360.
498 Moretti, *Olympionikai*, No 360.
499 Moretti, *Olympionikai*, No 367e.
500 Moretti, *Olympionikai*, No 400.
501 Pausanias, *VI* 3.13.
502 Moretti, *Olympionikai*, No 404.
503 Pausanias, *VI* 3.2.
504 Moretti, *Olympionikai*, No 415.
505 Moretti, *Olympionikai*, No 420.

He was the most successful athlete of the era, and managed to win twice at the Pythia and a total of twelve times at the Isthmia and the Nemea, in addition to his three Olympic wins throughout his career from 367 to 356 BCE.[506] He had an interesting way of competing. He was known as an *akrochersitēs*, which referred to his propensity for breaking his opponents' fingers and causing them to surrender. One wonders if he was unique in his use of this technique, or if it was a widely accepted style of fighting at his particular *palaestra* (wrestling school). No one can say. What is certain is that this style of competing was very clever since he overcame his opponents by attacking their weakest point - their fingers - which were unavoidably exposed. One can easily conclude that he had very strong fingers. He must also have had strong hands to be able to hold the fingers locked. Was he tall? Probably not; if he had been, he would also have had long limbs, and therefore hands. It would have made more sense for him to make use of the length of his arms and to strike from a distance, engaging in combat from further away. But with his smaller build, he would have been able to execute holds near his trunk; he had a lower center of gravity and would have changed position quickly to put all of his weight into his holds for greater force.

Being aware of his approach, his opponents would have avoided attacking with holds that required them to extend their fingers to grab him, thus giving him access. They would opt for fewer attacks using closed fists, which would be faster while protecting the fingers. He would have certainly been good at defense to protect himself from his opponents' hands and to give himself time to grasp them. This rationale is borne out by two additional details: why attack only the fingers and not the toes as well, given that feet moved more slowly and were therefore more exposed? For this reason, his opponents knew that if their hands were at risk, their feet had no hope at all of returning to protective position intact. The fact that he was relatively short lessened his chances of striking his larger opponents. He would not hope to achieve a good outcome against his rivals unless they were of about the same height. The method he chose to fight essentially leveled the playing field.

At the 111st Olympian games in 336 BCE, the winner was **Dioxippus** of Athens. He was part of Alexander the Great's campaign to India.[507] According to historian Diodorus of Sicily[508], Alexander was wounded in battle and later held a huge symposium for his friends to celebrate his recovery in 325 BCE. Among the king's friends was also a Macedonian named Coragus, who

---

506 Mouratidis, *Istoria physikēs agōgēs*, p. 238; Knab, *Die Periodoniken*, No 15.
507 Moretti, *Olympionikai*, No 458.
508 Diodorus of Sicily, *17, 100, 2-6*.

was physically very strong and often stood out in battle. During the celebration, Coragus became belligerently drunk and challenged Dioxippus to a duel, which Dioxippus accepted. Alexander then set the time and place for the confrontation. As the time for the duel approached, thousands of people gathered to watch. As a Macedonian, Coragus had the support of his countrymen and of Alexander. The rest of the Greeks were behind Dioxippus. Coragus arrived at the field of honor wearing the best armor available, while the Athenian was nude, his body oiled and carrying a well-weighted club.

Both men were in excellent physical condition and fervently wished to win. The spectators fully expected to witness a true battle of the gods. The Macedonian, with his stature and gleaming armor resembling the god Ares, inspired fear. Dioxippus resembled Heracles in strength and athletic training, and even more so with the club in his hands. As they approached one another to arrive at the correct distance, the Macedonian threw his spear, but Dioxippus crouched slightly and evaded it. Then Coragus prepared to throw his long spear, but the pankratiast broke it with his club. Coragus then attempted to draw his sword, but Dioxippus managed to grab his armed hand with his own left as he used his other hand to knock him off balance, striking him in the legs and throwing him down. The Olympic champion put his foot on Coragus' throat and raised his club over his head as he looked at the crowd. The spectators were in awe over the incredible abilities and superior strength of the pankratiast. Alexander nodded to Dioxippus, indicating that he should release Coragus, and then he broke up the gathering, clearly irritated by the Macedonian's defeat. The Athenian departed the winner with a triumphant victory. His countrymen showered him with praise and ribbons for his achievement. But he was not able to enjoy his victory for long. The king and his friends were becoming increasingly more competitive against Dioxippus and all of the Macedonians in Alexander's court were envious of the Olympic champion. They convinced one of his servants to hide a golden cup under Dioxippus' pillow. At the next symposium, they pretended to find the cup and accused Dioxippus of theft. The Athenian was very embarrassed, but he realized they were plotting against him and he left the gathering. When he returned to his quarters, he wrote a note to Alexander about the trick played against him. He gave it to his servants to deliver to the king and then he committed suicide.[509]

Alexander was greatly saddened and he often recalled the exceptional skills of the Olympic pankratiast which he had not appreciated while Dioxippus was alive.[510] **Dioxippus** was criticized for his folly of having great strength

---

509 Miller, *Arete*, pp. 117, 118.
510 Kostouros, *Nemeōn* 2, p. 70.

but a small mind.[511] But what conclusion should we draw about Coragus, who challenged this extraordinary athlete in the sport in which he excelled to a man-to-man duel? Coragus opted to wear all of the cumbersome equipment of a military battle, with his own fighting skills clearly inferior to those of Dioxippus, who nevertheless appeared as a nude Olympic fighter whose only extra weight was a light and swift club. The insolent Coragus never realized what a humanitarian the Olympic champion was.

Astyanax of Miletus had won at three Olympics – the 114th, 115th and 116th in 324, 320 and 316 BCE.[512] Athenaeus[513] reported that when Astyanax was once invited to dine with the Persian satrap Ariobarzanes, he promised when he arrived to eat all of the food prepared for the nine guests, which he did. When the Persian asked him to do something to demonstrate his physical strength, he broke off a bronze ornament on the couch, crushed it flat with his hands and threw it away.[514]

At the 117th Olympian games in 312 BCE, the winner was **Aristophon**, son of Lysinus of Athens.[515] Pausanias refers to having seen his statue at Olympia and that it was made by Athenians.[516]

Antenor, son of Xenares of Miletus or Athens[517], won *akoniti* at the 118th Olympic games in 308 BCE.[518] He was not merely an Olympic champion, though that was certainly no small feat; he achieved something quite rare - he was undefeated in three age categories; he competed in the boys', youth (*ageneioi*)[519] and men's class without ever losing.[520]

The inscription **Miletos 104 Ionia** below is a list of well-known crowned victors dated between 313/2 and 260/259 BCE. It is included here in its entirety:

1 vacat οἴδε μολπῶν ἠισύμνησαν·
  Ἱππόμαχος Θήρωνος: ἐπὶ τούτου ἡ πόλις
  ἐλευθέρα καὶ αὐτόνομος ἐγένετο ὑπὸ
  Ἀντιγόνου καὶ ἡ δημοκρατία ἀπεδόθη.
5 Ἀπόλλων Διός

---

511 Gogaki, *Oi antilēpseis*, p. 328.
512 Moretti, *Olympionikai*, No 479.
513 Athenaeus, *Deipnosophistae [Banquet philosophers]*, 10.413.a-c.
514 Kostouros, *Nemeōn* 2, p. 49.
515 Moretti, *Olympionikai*, No 484.
516 Pausanias, *VI* 13.11 & 14.1.
517 Sakellarakis et al., *Oi Olympiakoi*, p. 293.
518 Moretti, *Olympionikai*, No 488.
519 Mouratidis, *Istoria physikēs agōgēs*, pp. 263, 268, 395.
520 Knab, *Die Periodoniken*, No 18.

  Βαῦκος Λυκομήδους
  Μητρόδωρος Ἀντιφάνους
  Ἱπποθῶν Ἱππέως
  Ἀναξίλεως Φιλίσκου
10 Λύκος Δεξικράτεω
  Ἀριστόδημος Παρθενίου
  Ἀντίπατρος Φιλίσκου
  Δάμων Δαμέω
  Νέων Ἀλεξάνδρου
15 Πάμφιλος Παρθενίου
  Κριτόβουλος Ἀγασικράτους
  Ἀθήναιος Δαμέω
  Ἀπόλλων Διός
  Σωσίπ<ολ>ις Ἀρίστωνος
20 Ἀρισταγόρας Στησίλεω
  Σωσίστρατος Φανοδίκου
  Δημήτριος: Ἀντιγόνου
  Πάνταινος: Πανταίνου
  Δημήτριος: Φιλιστίδου
25 Φιλίσκος Δεξικράτους
  Στράττις Νόσσου
  Λέων: Μολπαγόρου
  Τελεσίας Κορινθίου
  Ποσείδιππος: Εὐπόλιδος
30 Θεόδωρος Βάτωνος
  Μητρόδωρος Σωσιστράτου
  Ἀγασικράτης Κριτοβούλου
  Γόργος Ἀντιπάτρου
  Ἀλέξιππος Σίμου
35 Ἀπόλλων Διός
  Εὔπολις Ποσειδίππου
  Ἀντίοχος Σελεύκου
  Ἀντήνωρ Ξενάρους: ἐπὶ τούτου ἐδό-
  θη ἡ χώρα τῶι δήμωι ὑπὸ τοῦ βασιλέως
40 Πτολεμαίου.
  Λεωσθένης Λεωκέστορος
  Ποσείδιππος Ποσειδωνίου
  Ἀπόλλων Διός
  Ἀπόλλων Διός
45 Αἰσχυλῖνος Θεοκρίνους

    Ἀλέξανδρος Δημητρίου τοῦ Φιλιστίδου
    Σῖμος Ποσειδίππου
    Ποσειδώνιος Θεοδέκτους
    Λυκόφρων Εὐδήμου
50 Ἀθηνόδωρος Δρύμωνος
    Ζήνων Δημοστράτου
    Αἰσχύλος Πανταίνου
    Ἀπόλλων Διός
    Ἀπόλλων Διός
55 Ἀπόλλων Διός
    Ἀπόλλων Διός
    Τάχως Γογγύλου
    Πειθένους Θαρσαγόρου
    Ἀπόλλων Διός

Translated:
    They praised with laudatory odes;
    Hippomachus, son of Theron: in the year the city was freed and became autonomous by Antigonus and democracy was restored.
    Apollo, son of Zeus
    Baucus, son of Lycomedes
    Metrodorus, son of Antiphanes
    Hippothon, son of Hippeus
    Anaxileus, son of Philiscus
    Lycus, son of Dexicrates
    Aristodemus, son of Parthenius
    Antipatrus, son of Philiscus
    Damon, son of Dameas
    Neon, son of Alexander
    Pamphilus, son of Parthenius
    Critobulus, son of Agasicratus
    Athenaeus, son of Dameas
    Apollo, son of Zeus
    Sosipolis, son of Ariston
    Aristagorus, son of Stesileus
    Sosistratus, son of Phanodicus
    Demetrius, son of Antigonus
    Pantaenus, son of Pantaenus
    Demetrius, son of Philistides
    Philiscus, son of Dexicrates
    Strattis, son of Nossos

Leon, son of Molpagorus
Telesias, son of Corinthius
Poseidippus, son of Eupolis
Theodorus, son of Baton
Metrodorus, son of Sosistratus
Agasicrates, son of Critobulus
Gorgos, son of Antipatres
Alexippus, son of Simos
Apollo, son of Zeus
Eupolis, son of Poseidippus
Antiochus, son of Seleucus
Antenor, son of Xenares, in his time, the territory was given to the people by king Ptolemy
Leosthenes, son of Leokestor
Poseidippus, son of Posidonius
Apollo, son of Zeus
Apollo, son of Zeus
Aeschylinus, son of Theocrines
Alexander, son of Demetrius, son of Philistides
Simos, son of Poseidippus
Posidonius, son of Theodectes
Lycophron, son of Eudemus
Athenodorus, son of Drymon
Zenon, son of Demostratus
Aeschylus, son of Pantaenus
Apollo, son of Zeus
Apollo, son of Zeus
Apollo, son of Zeus
Apollo, son of Zeus
Tachus, son of Gongylus
Pithenus, son of Tharsagoras
Apollo, son of Zeus

The winner at the 119th Olympics in 304 BCE was **Leontiscus**, a contemporary of Antenor.[521]

Nicon of Anthedon in Boeotia, a great pankratiast, won two consecutive Olympics, the 120th and 121st in 300 and 296 BCE. During his career, he achieved two victories at the Pythian games, two at the Isthmian and four at the Nemean games, in addition to his Olympic wins. As such, Nicon was twice a *periodonikēs*.[522]

---

521 Moretti, *Olympionikai*, No 495.
522 Moretti, *Olympionikai*, No 517; Knab, *Die Periodoniken*, p. 33.

Agesidamus of Messene won at the 140th Olympics in 220 BCE.[523]

Cleitomachus, son of Hermocrates of Thebes, was a unique case. He was famous for winning at wrestling, boxing and pankration. His victory came at the 141st Olympics in 216 BCE.[524] He won at wrestling, boxing and pankration at the Isthmia, and three times in pankration at the Pythian games (possibly in 218, 214 and 210 BCE). Although the order of events was specific, it could be changed if the *Hellanodikai* determined it was appropriate. Cleitomachus asked that pankration be held before boxing at the 142nd Olympiad in 212 BCE so that he would not risk competing in pankration with an injury, since he was competing in both.[525]

At the 142nd Olympian games in 212 BCE, the winner was **Caprus**, son of Pythagoras and an outstanding athlete from Elis. He was one of a small group of athletes who managed what was considered to be the ultimate achievement for the Olympics: he won in wrestling and pankration on the same day and became the first mortal after Heracles to achieve this. He was thereafter described as the "first after Heracles."[526]

Boys' pankration was introduced for the first time at the 145th Olympics in 200 BCE, and the first winner was **Phaedimus** of Alexandria Troas[527, 528]. However, Philostratus claims that Phaedimus was from Naucrates of Egypt.[529]

Diallos, son of Pollis of Smyrna, won the boys' pankration at the 152nd Olympics in 172 BCE.[530]

Inscription **IG XI, 4 1216**, which refers to him, was found in Delos and is dated to the early second century BCE. Here it is in its entirety:

col. I.1 Σαράπιδι, Ἴσιδι, Ἀνούβιδι
οἵδε ἀνέθηκαν·
Δημήτριος Διάλλου
Ἀνδροσθένης Δημητρίου
col. II.1 **Δίαλλος** Ἡρογείτονος
Ἑρμαγόρας Διάλλου
Δίαλλος Πόλλιδος
Σωκράτης Πόλλιδος

---

523 Moretti, *Olympionikai*, No 580.
524 Moretti, *Olympionikai*, No 584.
525 Pavlinis, *Istoria tēs Gymnastikēs*, pp. 169, 170.
526 Moretti, *Olympionikai*, No 587-588.
527 Moretti, *Olympionikai*, No 603.
528 Pausanias, *V*, 8.11.
529 Philostratus, Gymnasticus, 13.24.
530 Moretti, *Olympionikai*, No 616; Pausanias, *VI*, 13.6.

col. III.1 Διονύσιος Νουμηνίου
Συβαροκλῆς Κριτίου
Ἱππίας Ἀντιγόνου
Ζώπυρος Ἐρξίνου
col. IV.1 Ξένων Ξενοκ[ι]λείου {²⁶Ξενοκλείου}²⁶
Γλαυκίας Καλλιφάνου
Ἀφροδίσιος Δημητρίου
Ἡρακλείδης Δημοκράτου
col. V.1 Εὐβούλη[ι] Ἀρχεστράτου
Ἀριστόβουλος Ἱππάκου
Διοτρέφης Αἰαντίδου
Ἀγάθων Ξενοκράτου
col. VI.1 Ξενοκράτης Ἀγάθωνος
Ζήνων Πάτρωνος·
col. VII.1 ἐπιμεληθέντος
Δημητρίου τοῦ Διάλλου.

In translation:
This is dedicated to
Sarapis, Isis, and Anubis.
Demetrius, son of Diallos
Androsthenes, son of Demetrius
Diallos, son of Herogeiton
Hermagoras, son of Diallos
Diallos, son of Pollis
Socrates, son of Pollis
Dionysios, son of Numenius
Sybarocles, son of Critias
Hippias, son of Antigonus
Zopyrus, son of Erginus
Xenon, son of Xenokles
Glycon, son of Calliphanes
Aphrodisius, son of Demetrius
Heraklides, son of Democrates
Euboule, daughter of Archestratus
Aristobulus, son of Hippasus
Diotrephes, son of Aeantides
Agathon, son of Xenocrates
Xenocrates, son of Agathon
Zenon, son of Patronus;
This was done under the supervision of Demetrius, son of Diallos.

At the 156th Olympics in 156 B.C, the winner was **Aristomenes** of Rhodes, who won both the wrestling and pankration events for the ultimate Olympic achievement. He was thus named "second after Heracles."[531]

Amyntas, son of Hellanicus of Eresos in Lesvos or of Ephesus[532], won the boys' pankration at the 156th Olympics in 156 BCE. Pausanias saw his statue, which had been made by sculptor Polycles of Athens, at Olympia.[533]

TABLE 2: Olympic pankration champions 480 - 146 BCE

	Year	Olympics	Name
1	476 BCE	76th	Theagenes
2	472 BCE	77th	Callias
3	468 BCE	78th	Epitimadas
4	464 BCE	79th	Ephotion
5	460 BCE	80th	Timodemus
6	456 BCE	81st	Timanthes
7	452 BCE	82nd	Damagetus
8	448 BCE	83rd	Damagetus
9	432 BCE	87th	Dorieus
10	428 BCE	88th	Dorieus
11	424 BCE	89th	Dorieus
12	420 BCE	90th	Androsthenes
13	416 BCE	91st	Androsthenes
14	408 BCE	93rd	Polydamas
15	404 BCE	94th	Promachus
16	400 BCE	95th	Antiochus
17	396 BCE	96th	
18	380 BCE	100th	Xenophon
19	376 BCE	101th	Stomios
20	368 BCE	103rd	
21	364 BCE	104th	Sostratus
22	360 BCE	105th	Sostratus
23	356 BCE	106th	Sostratus

---

531 Moretti, *Olympionikai*, No 629-630; Pausanias, *V*, 21.10.
532 Sakellarakis et al., *Oi Olympiakoi*, p. 294.
533 Moretti, *Olympionikai*, No 632; Pausanias, *VI*, 4.5.

	Year	Olympics	Name
24	336 BCE	111th	Dioxippus
25	324 BCE	114th	Astyanax
26	320 BCE	115th	Astyanax
27	316 BCE	116th	Astyanax
28	312 BCE	117th	Aristophon
29	308 BCE	118th	Antenor
30	304 BCE	119th	Leontiscus
31	300 BCE	120th	Nicon
32	296 BCE	121st	Nicon
33	220 BCE	140th	Agesidamus
34	216 BCE	141st	Cleitomachus
35	212 BCE	142nd	Caprus
36	200 BCE	145th	Phaedimus (boys)
37	172 BCE	152nd	Diallos (boys)
38	156 BCE	156th	Aristomenes
39	156 BCE	156th	Amyntas (boys)

Third period: 146 BCE - 393 CE

The games during this period became more secular, losing a large part of their sacred character. They were no longer national competitions, but international. People known up to that point as "barbarians" (non-Greeks) now began to take part.[534] The games had now almost run their course and were abolished when Roman emperor Theodosius I issued a decree in 393 CE. It is possible that they survived until the age of Theodosius II (426 CE).[535]

Information on this period refers to thirty-six Olympian games that included pankration and to thirty-two winners.

At the 172nd Olympian games in 92 BCE, **Protophanes**, son of Maeander of Magnesia, won in both wrestling and pankration on the same day. He was named "third after Heracles."[536] Pausanias disagrees as to the origins of the

---

534 Mouratidis, *Istoria physikēs agōgēs*, p. 559.
535 Mouratidis, *Istoria physikēs agōgēs*, p. 559.
536 Moretti, *Olympionikai*, No 666-667.

athlete, claiming that he was descended from the Magnetes of the Lethaeus River.[537]

At the 177th Olympics in 72 BCE, the winner at men's pankration was **Sphodrias** of Sicyon and at boys' pankration, **Calas** of Elis.[538]

Straton, son of Corrhagus of Alexandria, was a great athlete who won at the next two Olympics, the 178th and 179th in 68 and 64 BCE respectively. In 68 BCE, he won both the pankration and wrestling and was named "fourth after Heracles." He was not able to repeat the feat, however. He won four times at the Nemean games, competing in both the boys' and youth classes on the same day, possibly in wrestling and pankration.[539]

The victory at the 182nd Olympics in 52 BCE went to **Marion** of Alexandria in both wrestling and pankration on the same day. He thus became "fifth after Heracles."[540]

At the 189th Olympian Games in 24 BCE, the winner was **Philippus Glycon**, son of Asclepiades of Pergamon.[541] He was an outstanding pankratiast, and no one has matched his singular achievement: he won twice at Olympia in both the boys' and men's categories. He also won twice at Delphi, once at the Isthmian games in men's boxing and two consecutive times at the Nemean games in boxing, as well as in many other competitions in Asia, Italy and Greece. He also managed to come first in youth pankration on the same day that he finished second in boys' wrestling.[542] He was the only one who could win in different styles of fighting at all age levels. From a technical standpoint, he was unsurpassed, as he was able to assimilate different fighting styles from an early age with victories at levels equivalent to the sacred games.

Both of the inscriptions that follow were found at Pergamon and are probably from the 1st century BCE. They list his achievements:

IvP II 534

```
1      [ὁ δῆμος ἐτί]μησεν
       [Φίλιππον Ἀσκλ]ηπιάδου Γλύκωνα,
       [...... τὸ δεύ]τερον νικήσαντα
       [παῖδας πάλην], ἀγενείους παγκρά-
5      [τιον μιᾶι ἡμ]έραι πρῶτον τῶν
       [Περγαμη]νῶν. {²vacat}²
```

---

537 Pausanias, *V* 21.10.
538 Moretti, *Olympionikai*, No 688.
539 Moretti, *Olympionikai*, No 700, 701, 703, Pausanias, *V*, 21.9, Knab, *Die Periodoniken*, No 32.
540 Moretti, *Olympionikai*, No 709-710, Pausanias, *V*, 21.10.
541 Moretti, *Olympionikai*, No 725.
542 Knab, *Die Periodoniken*, No 34.

In translation:
> The people praised **Philippus Glycon, son of Asclepiades**, the second to win in boys' wrestling, (and) the first from Pergamon (who won) in pankration in the youth category within one day.

IvP II 535

```
       [ὁ δῆμος ἐτίμησεν]
1  [Φίλι]ππον Ἀσκληπιάδου Γλύκω[να, νικήσαντα]
   [Ὀλύμ]πια Πύθια Ἄκτια ἄνδρα[ς παγκράτιον],
   [παῖδας] παγκράτιον· Ἴσθμια [ἄνδρας πυγμήν]·
   [Νέμεια ἐ]ν Ἄργει δὶς κατ[ὰ τὸ ἑξῆς πυγμήν],
5  [καὶ τοὺς λοι]ποὺς ἱεροὺς [καὶ στεφανίτας ἀγῶ]-
   [νας ἔν τε Ἀ]σίαι καὶ Ἰ[ταλίαι καὶ Ἑλλάδι].
```

In translation:
> The people praised **Phillipus Glycon, son of Asclepiades**, who won in the Olympian, Pythian and Actian games in pankration in the men's category and in the boy's pankration; at the Isthmia in men's boxing; at the Nemea in Argos, two consecutive times in boxing, and in the other sacred games with the prize of a crown in Asia, Italy and Greece.

At the 198th Olympics in 13 CE, the winner was **Aristeas** of Stratoniceia,[543] or Menander[544] (formerly known as Chrysaoris[545]), in wrestling and in pankration on the same day. He became the sixth member of the group of elite athletes to bear the title "after Heracles."

Hermas, son of Ision, from Antioch on the Orontes River in Syria, won at two Olympian games, the 201st and 202nd in 25 and 29 CE. He also won once at Delphi, once at Isthmus and twice at Nemea, along with wins at the Actian and Heraean games.[546]

Inscription **IvO 231** was found in Olympia and is from the 1st century CE. It lists his achievements:

```
face a.1  Ἑρμᾶς Ἰσίωνος Ἀντιοχε-
          ὺς ἀπὸ Δάφνης, νεικήσας
          Ὀλύμπια δὶς καὶ τὴν
face b.4  λοιπὴν περίοδον ἐν τῇ [πε]-
```

---
543 Moretti, *Olympionikai*, No 747-748.
544 Sakellarakis et al., *Oi Olympiakoi*, p. 295.
545 Pausanias, *V* 21.10.
546 Moretti, *Olympionikai*, No 754, 757.

     5 ριόδῳ σὺν δ[ὶ]ς Νεμείοις [καὶ]
        Ἀκτίοις καὶ Ἡραίοις, Διὶ Ὀ[λ]-
              υμπίῳ
face c.8 ἄνδρας πανκράτιον.

Here is the translation:
> **Hermas, son of Ision of Antioch** from Daphne, (who) won at the Olympia twice as well as at the other games in the same period and an additional two times at the Nemea, the Actia and Heraea, in honor of Olympian Zeus in men's pankration.

Heras, which was an abbreviated form of Herodorus from Laodiceia of Phrygia, won at the 203rd Olympics in 33 CE.[547] Philippus of Thessaloniki recalled victories at Delphi (Pythian Games), Corinth (Isthmia), Elis (Olympia), Argos, and perhaps Heraea, and certainly at Nemea.[548] Heras then became a *periodonikēs*. He also had wins at Actium, Smyrna and Pergamon.

Nicostratus, son of Isidotus from Aegae in Cilicia, won at the 204th Olympics in 37 CE in wrestling and pankration on the same day, and became the "seventh after Heracles."[549] Pausanias tells a story about Nicostratus, who, when he was young, was seized by pirates from Prymessus in Phrygia because he was from a wealthy family. He was taken to Aegae, where he was sold. The buyer had a dream in which he saw a young lion cub lying under the mattress on which Nicostratus was sleeping. The dream was taken as a sign of what was to come. And indeed, when Nicostratus got older, he became a pankratiast and among his other victories he also became an Olympic champion in pankration and wrestling.[550]

The winner of the boys' pankration at the 207th Olympia in 49 CE was **Publius Cornelius Ariston**, son of Irenaeus of Ephesus.[551]

The name of the winner at the 208th Olympian games in 53 CE is not known; only that he was from Stratoniceia of Caria.[552] It is possible he was [-] **us [-] Aristeas Corazeus**, who was a pankration athlete and son of Aristeas Corazeus. The younger was a winner in the youth category at the Nemean and Actian games, at a competition of the Asian League, as well as the Olympian and Pythian games, and possible the Isthmian games.[553]

---

547 Moretti, *Olympionikai*, No 760.
548 Knab, *Die Periodoniken*, No 36.
549 Moretti, *Olympionikai*, No 762-763.
550 Pausanias, *V* 21.10, 11.
551 Moretti, *Olympionikai*, No 777.
552 Moretti, *Olympionikai*, No 780.
553 Kostouros, *Nemeōn* 2, p. 214.

Xenodamus of Anticyra, Phocis, won in the 211th Olympic Games in 67 CE.[554] Pausanias refers to a bronze statue at the ancient school in the athlete's town. It is generally believed that the statue was not erected at Olympia, but in Xenodamus' home town, most likely because it would have been forbidden as these Olympian games were not sanctioned.[555]

The pankration victor at the 212th Olympics in 69 CE was **Tiberius Claudius Artemidorus** of Tralles.[556] Pausanias refers to him simply as Artemidorus[557] and says that the young fighter failed at the boys' pankration events at Olympia because of his age. But when it came time to compete in the Ionian games in Smyrna (Olympia), he was so much stronger that in a pankration match on the same day he overcame the athletes he had fought against at Olympia. After the boys' and youth events, he won against the most select men. It is said he competed against youths on a dare from a trainer and against men because an adult pankratiast challenged him.[558] Artemidorus also competed at Achaea and perhaps at Ionia and Egypt.[559]

Artemidorus followed a diet that combined dishes from all types of cuisines of his era.[560]

Inscription **Ephesos 756**, which the athlete dedicated to Artemis of Ephesus, was found there and dated at 96/98 CE.

It is included here:

1 [Ἀρτέμ]ιδι [Ἐφεσίᾳ]
[κ]αὶ Αὐτοκράτορι Νέρ-
ουᾳ Καίσαρι Σεβαστῷ
καὶ τῷ δήμῳ τῷ Ἐφεσίων
5 **Τιβ(έριος) Κλ(αύδιος) Ἀρτεμίδωρος** Και-
σαρεὺς Τραλλιανὸς ὁ
καὶ Ἀλεξανδρεὺς καὶ
Ἐφέσιος, παγκρατιαστής,
περιοδονείκης καὶ πα-
10 ραδοξονείκης, ἀρχιε-
ρεὺς ξυστοῦ καὶ διὰ βίου

---

554 Moretti, *Olympionikai*, No 789.
555 Pausanias, *X* 36.9.
556 Moretti, *Olympionikai*, No 799.
557 Pausanias, *VI* 14.2.
558 Kostouros, *Nemeōn* 2, p. 175.
559 Robert G. A. Weir, *Roman Delphi and its Pythian Games* (Archeopress, Oxford, 2004) p. 127.
560 Artemis P. Simopoulos, "Nutrition and fitness from the first Olympiad in 776 BC to 393 AD and the concept of positive health," *The American Journal of Clinical Nutrition* 49, no. 5 (1989): p. 923.

ξυστάρχης.

In translation:
> From the temple of Artemis of Ephesus and the Emperor Nerva Caesar Augustus and the deme of Ephesians **Tiberius Claudius Artemidorus** of Tralles of Caesarea (Cappadocia), the Alexandrian[561] and Ephesian[562], the pankratiast, the periodonikēs, paradoxonikēs[563], high priest of the athletic guild (xystos) and lifetime president (xystarchēs)[564] of the guild.

At the 215th Olympian games in 81 CE, the winner was **Tiberius Claudius Rufus** of Smyrna.[565] He was an outstanding athlete and was highly honored by his fellow citizens. He was the head of the athletic family that later included Claudius Rufi, Claudius Rufus Psapharius and Claudius Apollonius.

Titus Flavius Artemidorus, son of Artemidorus of Adana and honorary citizen of Syrian Antioch, won at the 216th and 217th Olympian games in 85 and 89 CE. This was a great athlete whose long career is recorded by an inscription found in Naples, Italy, and refers to two Olympian victories, two at the Pythian games, two at the Nemean games, one at the Isthmian games in the youth category, another at Aegium, the Augustan Games in Naples, at Actium, in Smyrna, in Pergamon, at the Balbilleia in Ephesus, Alexandria, Syria, Sardis, Laodiceia, Argos and one at the first Capitoline festival in Rome.[566] The inscription below is **I.Napoli 50**, which was found in Naples and dated at 90 CE.

```
 1  Τ(ίτος) · Φλάουιος Ἀρτεμιδώρου
    υἱὸς Κυρείνα Ἀρτεμίδωρος
    Ἀδανεὺς ὁ καὶ Ἀντιοχεὺς ἀπὸ
    Δάφνης, νεικήσας τὸν ἀγῶνα τῶν
 5  μεγάλων Καπετολείων τὸν πρώτως ἀχθέντα
    ἀνδρῶν πανκράτιον, Ὀλύμπια β, Πύθια β, Νέμεια β,
    Ἄκτια, Νέαν πόλιν ἀνδρῶν πανκράτιον, Ἴσθμια ἀγε-
    νείων πανκράτιον, κοινὸν Ἀσίας ἐν Ζμύρνῃ ἀγενεί-
    ων πανκράτιον καὶ τῇ ἑξῆς πενταετηρίδι ἀνδρῶν
10  πάλην καὶ πανκράτιον καὶ πάλι ἀνδρῶν πανκράτιον
```

---

561 Note: an honorary citizen of Alexandria
562 Note: an honorary citizen of Ephesus
563 Extensive reference in the next chapter.
564 Extensive reference in the next chapter.
565 Moretti, *Olympionikai*, No 808.
566 Moretti, *Olympionikai*, No 815.820.

```
       πρῶτος ἀνθρώπων, κοινὸν Ἀσ(ίας) ἐν Περγάμῳ
       ἀνδρῶν πανκράτιον, ἐν Ἐφέσῳ Βαλβίλληα παίδω[ν]
       [πανκράτ]ιον κ[α]ὶ πάλι κατὰ τὸ ἐξῆς ἀνδρῶν πανκρά-
       τιον, ἐν Ἀλεξανδρείᾳ τὸν ἱερὸν πενταετη-
   15  [ρικόν], κοινὸν Συρίας Κιλικίας Φοινείκης ἐν Ἀν-
       τιοχείᾳ β ἀνδρῶν πανκράτιον, Ἐφέσηα, Τράλ-
       [λεις] δ, Σάρδεις ε, Λαυδίκειαν ε [— — ἔχει]
       [δὲ τὴ]ν ἐξ Ἄργους ἀσπίδα, καὶ ἄλλους πεν[τα]-
       [ετηρικ]οὺς ἀγῶνας ιζ' ὑ[πὸ ἐπι]σ[τάτην]
   20         Ἀρτεμίδωρον Ἀθηνοδώρου Ἀδ[ανέα — — ἐπι]-
       [μελ]ηθέντος Ἀθηνοδώρ[ου — — — — —]⁵⁶⁷
```

Here is the translation:

Titus Flavius Artemidorus, son of Artemidorus
of Adana and Antioch of Daphne,
won the match of the great Capitoline games, being first in the men's pankration, twice at the Olympian games, twice at the Pythian games, twice at the Nemean games, the men's pankration at Actia and Naples, the youth pankration at the Isthmian Games, the youth pankration at the League of Asia in Smyrna, and at the next quinquennial[568], in men's wrestling and pankration and again in men's pankration, the best of all, at the Asian games in Pergamon (victory) in men's pankration, at the Balbilleia at Ephesus in boys' pankration and again in men's pankration, at Alexandria (won) at the sacred quinquennial games of the Syrian League, Cilicia, Phoenicia at Antioch twice (winner) in men's pankration, at the Ephesian games, four time at Tralles and five times at Sardis.
at Laodiceia five times [...] he has won the shield at Argos and (won) another 17 quinquennial games during the time that Artemidorus of Adana, son of Athenodorus, oversaw the games.
Athenodorus was in charge.

Nicanor, son of Socles of Ephesus, won the boys' pankration at the 217th Olympics in 89 CE. His brother, Diodorus, erected a statue at Olympia which bears the inscription stating that Nicanor had won without a bye meaning he had fought all his rounds.[569]

Titus Flavius Archibius of Alexandria was the winner at the 220th and 221st Olympian games in 101 and 105 CE. He had earned two Olympic victories, four at the Pythian games (one in pankration in the youth category, two in men's pankration and one in men's wrestling), and four at the Nemean

---
567 Boutet-Lanouette, «La vie agonistique,» p.46.-
568 Games held at the beginning of the 5th lunar year, Albanidis, *Istoria tēs athlēsēs*, p. 41.
569 Moretti, *Olympionikai*, No 822.

games (one in boys' pankration and three in men's pankration). He also won at the Capitoline games in Rome, several times at Aegium and at the Augustan Games in Naples.[570] He also had wins in Italy, Achaea, Macedonia, Ionia, Syria and Egypt.[571] He had other wins at the Capitoline games in Rome, at Actium, at the Balbilleia of Ephesus, at an Actian boys' contest in Antioch, in Smyrna, in his homeland of Argos and elsewhere, both in pankration and wrestling, in the boys' and men's category.[572]

The inscription **I.Napoli 51** which follows was found in Naples and is dated at approximately 110 CE:

1   ἀγαθῆι τύχηι.
          ἡ φιλοσέβαστος καὶ φιλορώμα[ιος Ἀλε]-
          ξανδρέων περιπολιστικὴ εὐσεβὴ[ς σύνοδος]
          ἐτίμησεν · **Τ(ίτον) · Φλάουιον · Κυρ(είνα) · Ἀρχίβιον** τὸν [...c.7..]
5   Ἀλεξανδρέα, ἀρχιερέα διὰ βίου τοῦ σύμπ[αντος ξυστοῦ],
          παραδοξονίκην, νικήσαντα τὴν · σκ · ὀλυ[μπιάδα καὶ]
          τὴν · σκα · ὀλυμπιάδα ἀνδρῶν παγκράτ[ιον καὶ ἐν]
          Ῥώμηι τὰ μεγάλα Καπετώλεια τὴν τρίτη[ν πενταετηρίδα]
          ἀγενείων παγκράτιον στεφανωθέντα κα[ὶ τὴν τετάρτην]
10   ἀνδρῶν παγκράτιον νικήσαντα καὶ τὴν πέμπ[την ἀνδρῶν]
          παγκράτιον στεφανωθέντα καὶ τὴν ἕκτην ὁ[μοίως ἀνδρῶν]
          παγκράτιον στεφανωθέντα πρῶτον ἀνθρώπω[ν· τὰ ἐν .c.5.]
          Ἡράκλεια ἐπινίκια Αὐτοκράτορος Νέρουα Τραιανοῦ Κ[αίσαρος Σεβαστοῦ]
          Γερμανικοῦ Δακικοῦ στεφανωθέντα ἀνδρῶν παγκρά[τιον· Πύθια ἀγενείων]
15   παγκράτιον καὶ τῆι ἑξῆς πυθιάδι ἀνδρῶν πάλην καὶ π[αγκράτιον καὶ τῆι]
          ἑξῆς ἀνδρῶν παγκράτιον πρῶτον ἀνθρώπων· Νέμεια π[αίδων παγκράτιον]
          καὶ τρὶς κατὰ τὸ ἑξῆς ἀνδρῶν παγκράτιον πρῶτον ἀν[θρώπων· ...c.9...]
          ἀνδρῶν παγκράτιον· Ἄκτια ἀγενείων πάλη<ν> παγκράτ[ιον καὶ (num.) κατὰ]
          τὸ ἑξῆς ἀνδρῶν παγκράτιον πρῶτον ἀνθρώπων· Νέαν π[όλιν ἀγενείων]
20   παγκράτιον καὶ δὶς κατὰ τὸ ἑξῆς ἀνδρῶν παγκράτιον· [...c.8... ἀγενεί]-
          ων πάλην παγκράτιον καὶ δὶς κατὰ τὸ ἑξῆς ἀνδρῶν πάλην παγκρ[άτιον, καὶ τῇ ἑξῆς]
          ἀνδρῶν παγκράτιον πρῶτον ἀνθρώπων· τὰ ἐν Ἐφέσωι Βαλβίλλεια [ἀνδρῶν πάλην πυγ]-
          μὴν παγκράτιον πρῶτον ἀνθρώπων καὶ τὸν ἐν Ἀντιοχείαι ἱερὸν πεν[ταετηρικὸν ἀγῶνα]
          Ἀκτιακῶν παίδων παγκράτιον καὶ τῆι ἑξῆς πενταετηρίδι ἀγεν[είων πάλην καὶ πυγ]-

---

570 Moretti, *Olympionikai*, No 830-832.
571 Weir, *Roman Delphi*, p. 127.
572 Kostouros, *Nemeōn* 2, p. 184.

25 μὴν καὶ τῆι ἑξῆς ἀνδρῶν παγκράτιον καὶ τῆι ἑξῆς ὁμοίως ἀνδ[ρῶν παγκράτιον]
πρῶτον ἀνθρώπων· Σμύρναν κοινὸν Ἀσίας ἀγενείων πά[λην παγκράτιον]
καὶ τὸν ἐν Ἀλεξανδρείᾳ ἱερὸν πενταετηρικὸν ἀγῶνα Ἀκ[τιακῶν παίδων]
παγκράτιον καὶ μετὰ μίαν πενταετηρίδα ἀνδρῶν πα[γκράτιον]
καὶ τῆι ἑξῆς ὁμοίως ἀνδρῶν παγκράτιον καὶ τῆι ἐ[ξῆς — — —]
30 ἀνδρῶν πάλην παγκράτιον πρῶτον ἀνθρώπων· ἔχε[ι δὲ καὶ τὴν ἐξ]
Ἄργους ἀσπίδα καὶ ἄλλους πλείστους πενταετηρικ[οὺς ἀγῶνας]
παίδων, ἀγενείων, ἀνδρῶν πάλας καὶ παγκράτια. [573]

Here is the translation:
> The venerable and Roman-loving synod of the people of Alexandria honored **Titus Flavius Quirina Archibios** of Alexandria, lifetime high-priest of the entire athletic guild, extraordinary victor, who won at the 220th and 221st Olympic games in men's pankration. At the Capitoline games in Rome, he was crowned in youth pankration in the third quinquennial games, won the men's pankration in the fourth, the men's pankration in the fifth and in the sixth, the first among mortals; he was crowned at the Heraclean games under Nerva Trajan Caesar Augustus, with victories in Germany and Dacia, in men's pankration; at the Pythian games in youth pankration and then (at the next Pythia) in men's wrestling and in pankration; and then at the next Pythia in men's pankration, first among mortals; at the Nemean games in boys' pankration and three consecutive times at men's pankration, first among mortals (succeeded);
>
> [...] in men's pankration; at the Actian games at pankration and youth wrestling and then in men's pankration, first among mortals; in Naples, at youth pankration and two consecutive times at men's pankration; in youth wrestling and pankration, and two consecutive times in men's wrestling and pankration, first among mortals; at the Balbilleia in Ephesus, in wrestling, boxing and pankration, he won first prize in all and won at the sacred quinquennial games in Actium of Antioch, in boys' pankration and in the next quinquennial, the youth wrestling and boxing and in the next, the men's pankration, and in the following likewise in men's pankration, first above all; at Smyrna, at the Asian League games, in youth wrestling and pankration and at the sacred quinquennial games of Actium in Alexandria, in the boys' pankration, and then won in one quinquennial, in the men's pankration, as in the following, and the one after that, in wrestling and pankration, first above all; in addition, he has won the Shield from Argos and (has won) many more quinquennial contests in the boys', youth and men's categories in wrestling and pankration.

Publius Aelius Aristomachus of Magnesia won the boys' pankration at the 224th Olympian Games in 117 CE. His sporting career has been memo-

---

573 Boutet-Lanouette, «La vie agonistique,» p.56.

rialized in two inscriptions from Magnesia. He had also won at the Isthmian games in the boys' category and then in the youth category at the Nemean and Capitoline games, at Aegium, and at the Augustan games in Naples.[574]

One of these inscriptions, **Magnesia 220**, is dated at 138 CE and describes his victorious career:

1 **Πό(πλιος) Αἴλιος Ἀριστόμαχος**
   περιοδονείκης ξυστάρ-
   χης πρῶτος καὶ μόνος τῶν
   ἀπ' αἰῶνος νεικήσας Ὀλύμ-
5 πια παίδων πανκράτιον
   Ὀλυμπιάδι σκδ' καὶ κατὰ
   τὸ ἑξῆς Καπετώλεια ἐν Ῥώμῃ, Σεβαστὰ ἐν Νεαπόλει,
   Ἄκτια, Παναθήναια τὰ πρῶτα
10 δοθέντα εἰσελαστικὰ ὑπὸ
   θεοῦ Ἀδριανοῦ, ἐν Σμύρνῃ κοινὸν Ἀσίας, Ἴσθμια, Νέμεια, Οὐράνια
   ἐν Λακεδαίμονι καὶ τὸ δεύτερον Ἴσθμια ἀγενείων πανκρά-
15 τιον, μήτε ἱεράν ποτε ποιήσας
   μήτε συνεξελθών, τειμηθείς τε
   ἐπὶ τούτοις ὑπὸ θεοῦ Ἀδριανοῦ
   Ῥωμαίων πολειτείαις εἴς τε τὸν
   πατέρα καὶ τὴν μητέρα καὶ τοὺς
20 ἀδελφοὺς καὶ τὴν Κυζικηνῶν ξυσ-
   ταρχίαν, πρεσβεύσας τε πολλάκις πρὸς τοὺς αὐτοκράτορας
   εἴς τε τὴν βασιλίδα Ῥώμην καὶ εἰς
   Παννονίαν τῇ γλυκυτάτῃ πα-
25 τρίδι τοὺς ἑαυτοῦ ἀνδρι-
   άντας.

Here is the translation:
Publius Aelius Aristomachus, periodonikēs, guild president and first and only mortal ever to win at the Olympian games in boy's pankration at the 224th Olympics and then at the Capitoline games in Rome, the Augustan Actian games in Naples, the Panathenaic games , the first eiselastic[575] games by the god Hadrian,

---

574 Moretti, *Olympionikai*, No 838.
575 Eiselastic games were those in which victors were awarded the highest honor of entering their city

at the League of Asia in Smyrna, at the Isthmian and Nemean games and the festival of Urania in Sparta, and again at the Isthmian games in youth pankration, because he was not allowed to make a sacred offering nor to join the celebratory procession with the others, he was honored for these by Hadrian and the states of Rome before his father and mother and brothers, and the guild of Cyzicus, serving many times as the envoy of emperors before the Empress of Rome and Pannonia, by his sweet homeland with statues.

The winner at the 227th Olympics in 129 CE was **Marcus Ulpius Domesticus** of Ephesus. He was a successful athlete who had received a great many honors.[576] The following inscriptions refer to him:

Inscription **IG V, 1 669** was found in Sparta and is dated to the period of the Roman Empire:

> 1 Μ(ᾶρκος) Οὔλπιος Δομεστικὸς
>   Ἐφέσιος · Ἀντινοεὺς καὶ
>   Ἀθηναῖος, πανκρατια-
>   στής · παράδοξος · περιο-
> 5 δονείκης, ξυστάρχης
>   διὰ βίου καὶ ἀρχιερεὺς τοῦ
>   σύνπαντος ξυστοῦ
>   καὶ ἐπὶ βαλανείων Σεβα-
>   στοῦ.
>   Θαυμαστὸς

In translation:

> **Marcus Ulpius Domesticus** of Ephesus; an Antinoite and Athenian, a pankration athlete, extraordinary, *periodonikēs*, lifetime president of the athletic guild and high priest of the entire athletic assembly and the imperial baths.

The inscription **Ephesos 3581** was found at Ephesus and refers to the high priest of the entire athletic assembly, which was the athletic synod, as we will see in the chapter on the honors bestowed upon pankration victors.

> 1 [—]ετει[—].[—]ο[—]
>   [—ο]υ Παύλου
>   [Μᾶρκος] Οὔλπιος

---

by having a section of the city walls torn down, signifying that such heroes did not need walls. Mouratidis, *Istoria physikēs agōgēs*, p. 185.

576 Moretti, *Olympionikai*, No 844.

    [**Δομεστικὸς**] ὁ ἀρχιερεὺς
5 [τοῦ σύμπαντος ξ]υστοῦ
    [—]ν ἅπασι
    [— το]ῦ ξυσ-
    [τοῦ —].υ
9/15 {²lines 9 to 15 lost}²
16 [—].
    [—] Ἐφε-
    [σι—]αρ
    [—].ι

Translated:
    [...] the year [...] of Paul **Marcus Ulpius Domesticus** the high priest of the entire assembly, (in Ephesus) [...]

Inscription **IGUR I 236** was found in Rome and dates to 143 CE:

face a, front.1 [Αὐ]τοκράτορι
    [Κα]ίσαρι · Τίτωι · Αἰλίωι
    Ἁδριανῶι
    Ἀντωνείνωι · Σεβαστῶι
5 Εὐσεβεῖ
    Μ(άρκος) · Οὔλπιος
    Δομεστικὸς
    ὁ ἀρχιερεὺς
    τοῦ · σύνπαντος · ξυστοῦ · καὶ
10 ἐπὶ · βαλανείων · Σεβαστοῦ.

face b, right.1 ἀγαθῆι · τύχηι
    Αὐτοκράτωρ · Καῖσαρ · θεοῦ · Ἁδριανοῦ · υἱός,
    θεοῦ · Τραιανοῦ · Παρθικοῦ · υἱωνός · θεοῦ · Νέρουα
    ἔγγονος · Τίτος · Αἴλιος · Ἁδριανὸς · Ἀντωνεῖνος
5 Σεβαστός · ἀρχιερεὺς · μέγιστος · δημαρχικῆς · ἐξουσίας
    τὸ · ς, αὐτοκράτωρ · τὸ · β, ὕπατος · τὸ · γ, πατὴρ · πατρίδος · συνόδῳ
    ξυστικῇ · τῶν · περὶ · τὸν · Ἡρακλέα · ἀθλητῶν · ἱερονεικῶν · στεφα-
    νειτῶν · χαίρειν·
    ἐκέλευσα · ὑμεῖν · ἀποδειχθῆναι · χωρίον · ἐν · ᾧ · καὶ · τὰ · ἱερὰ · κατα-
10 θήσεσθε · καὶ · τὰ · γράμματα · πρὸς · αὐταῖς · ταῖς · Θερμαῖς · ταῖς · ὑπὸ

τοῦ · θεοῦ · πάππου · μου · γεγενημέναις · ὅπου · καὶ · μάλιστα · τοῖς Καπιτωλείοις · συνέρχεσθε · εὐτυχεῖτε · ἐπρέσβευεν Οὔλπιος · Δομεστικὸς · ὁ ἐπὶ βαλανείων · μου. ἐγράφη · πρὸ · ιζ · καλ(ανδῶν) · Ἰουν(ίων) · ἀπὸ · Ῥώμης · Τορκουάτῳ · καὶ · Ἡρώδῃ · ὑπάτ(οις).

Here is the translation:
    In honor of Caesar Titus Aelius Hadrianus Antoninus Augustus Pius, **Marcus Ulpius Domesticus** the high priest of the entire athletic assembly and Augustan baths.

    With good fortune, Caesar Titus Aelius Hadrianus Antoninus Augustus Pius, son of the god Hadrian, grandson of the god Trajan of the Parthian War, descendant of the divine Nerva
most high priest, president of the tribunate, emperor, supreme father of the country, hails the athletic synod of athletes in the Heracleian games and who won at the sacred stephanite games

    I gave the order to show where you will place your sacred offerings and inscriptions about the Thermae here which have been erected by the god my grandfather, where you often gather for the Capitoline games; Good fortune to you. Ulpius Domesticus was the envoy and the one responsible for my baths. Written seventeen days before the calends[577] of June (~13 May) by the Consuls of Rome Torquatus and Herodes.

    Inscription **IGUR I 235** was found in Rome and dates to between 139 and 143 CE:

face a, front.1   ἀγαθῇ · τύχῃ

    Μ(άρκωι) · Αἰλίωι
    Αὐρηλίωι · Καίσαρι
    Τ(ίτου) · Αἰλίου · Ἁδριανοῦ
5   Ἀντωνείνου
    Σεβαστοῦ · Εὐσεβοῦς · υἱῷ
    Μ(άρκος) · Οὔλπιος
    Δομεστικὸς
    ὁ ἀρχιερεὺς
10 τοῦ · σύνπαντος ξυστοῦ · καὶ
    ἐπὶ βαλανείων Σεβαστῶν.

---

577 Note: The calends is the first day of the month in the ancient Roman calendar, and the origin of the word "calendar."

face b, right.1   ἀγαθῆι · τύχηι

    Αὐτοκράτωρ · Καῖσαρ θεοῦ Τραιανοῦ Παρθικοῦ υἱός,
    θεοῦ · Νέρουα · υἱωνός, Τραιανός · Ἀδριανός · Σεβαστός, ἀρχιερεὺς
    μέγιστος · δημαρχικῆς · ἐξουσίας · τὸ · ιη · ὕπατος · τὸ · γ ·
5 πατὴρ · πατρίδος · συνόδῳ · ξυστικῇ · τῶν · περὶ τὸν
    Ἡρακλέα · ἀθλητῶν · ἱερονεικῶν · στεφανειτῶν · χαίρειν·
    καὶ τόπον ἔνθα · βούλεσθε · κελεύσω δοθῆναι ὑμεῖν · καὶ · οἴκημα
    ὡς τὰ γράμματα ἀποτίθεσθαι τὰ κοινά· καὶ εἰ τῶν διπλῶν τὴν
    μεταποίησιν · ἀνανκαίαν · νομίζετε, τοῦτο ἐφ' ὑμεῖν ἐστιν.
10 ἐπρέσβευεν Οὔλπιος · Δομεστικός · εὐτυχεῖτε.
    πρὸ · γ · νωνῶν · μαίων · ἀπὸ · Ῥώμης.

In translation:

    With good fortune, Marcus Aelius Aurelius Caesar, son of Caesar Titus Aelius Hadrianus Antoninus Augustus Pius.
    Marcus Ulpius Domesticus the high priest of all of the athletic assembly and Augustan baths.
    With good fortune, Emperor Caesar Trajan Hadrianus Augustus, son of the god Trajan of the Parthian War, grandson of the god Nerva, the greatest high priest, president of the tribunate, supreme father of the country, hails the gathering of athletes for the Heracleian games who won at the sacred stephanite games;
    If you desire this place (for sport/games), I will give the order that you be provided a building so that you may place the public inscriptions; and if you decide it is necessary, to be written twice, that will be your responsibility;
    Represented by Ulpius Domesticus; prosper;
    before [...] of Rome.

Inscription **IGUR I 26** was found in Rome and also dates to CE 154:

[Αὐτοκ]ράτορι Καίσαρι Τίτῳ Αἰλίῳ Ἀδριανῷ Ἀντωνείνῳ Σεβαστῷ Ε[ὐσεβ]εῖ καὶ
1 Μάρκῳ Αὐρηλίῳ Καίσαρι καὶ τῷ [— — —]
[Ἐφεσί]ων τῆς πρώτης καὶ μεγίστης μητροπόλεως τῆς [Ἀ]σίας καὶ δὶς νε<ω>κόρου
τῶν Σεβαστῶν ναυκλήροις καὶ ἐ[μπόροις **Μ(άρκος) Οὔλπιος Δομεστικός** — —]
[περιο]δονε<ί>κης παράδοξος καὶ ἐπὶ βαλανείων Σεβαστῶν [..]του ἐκ θεμελίων
σὺν ἅπαντι τῷ περὶ αὐτὸν κόσμῳ καὶ τοῖς ἀγάλμ[ασιν — — —]
ἐπ<ὶ> ὑπάτων Λουκίου Α[ἰ]λίου Αὐρηλίου Κομμόδου καὶ Τίτου Σεξτίου Λατερανοῦ
πρὸ ιε' καλ(ανδῶν) Φεβ(ρουαρίων).

Here is the translation:
> From Emperor Caesar Titus Aelius Hadrianus Antoninus Augustus Pius and Marcus Aurelius Caesar and from [...] and the shipowners and merchants of Ephesus, the first and grandest metropolis of Asia and twice Neokoros[578] of the Augustans, **Marcus Ulpius Domesticus**, extraordinary periodonikēs and superintedent of the Augustan baths [...] from the base along with all the people around him and (along with) the statues [...]
> (erected) under the consulate of Lucius Aelius Aurelius Commodus and Titus Sextius Lateranus fifteen days before the calends of February. (~15 January)

The only information available on the Olympic winner of the 232nd games in 149 CE is his name, **Socrates**, of an unknown family.[579] He later became a citizen of Antioch and Athens. He was a *periodonikēs* in pankration. It is also known that he was on friendly terms with Emperor Hadrian, who apparently urged him to compete at the Olympian games to achieve a victory that would raise his social standing.[580, 581]

Marcus Aurelius Demetrius of Alexandria[582] or Hermopolis[583] was the winner at the 233rd Olympics in CE 153. He was also a successful wrestler. Based on the fact that the son of Marcus Aurelius Asclepiades won in 181 CE, Demetrius can be placed around 150 CE. An inscription found in Rome (IGUR I 239) dated to the late second century CE indicates that Demetrius of Hermopolis and Alexandria had been crowned a *periodonikēs* in pankration, like the son of Marcus Aurelius Asclepiades, also known as Hermodorus.[584] Here is the entire inscription **IGUR I 239**:

face a.1 Δημήτριος
ἀρχιερεύς.

face b.1 **[Δη]μήτριον · Ἑρμοπολείτην**
Ἀλεξανδρέα · πανκρατιαστὴν · περιοδονείκην ?
παλαιστὴν · παράδοξον · ἄλειπτον ?
τὸν ἀρχιερέα · τοῦ · σύνπαντος · ξυστοῦ
5 διὰ βίου · ξυστάρχην · καὶ · ἐπὶ βαλανί-
ων · Σεβ(αστοῦ) · τὸν πατέρα ?

---

578 Note: name of the city.
579 Moretti, *Olympionikai*, No 862.
580 Kostouros, *Nemeōn* 2, p. 129.
581 Sakellarakis et al., *Oi Olympiakoi*, p. 296.
582 Moretti, *Olympionikai*, No 865.
583 Knab, *Die Periodoniken*, No 47.
584 Kostouros, *Nemeōn* 2, p. 64.

    Μ(άρκος) · Αὐρ(ήλιος) · Ἀσκληπιάδης · ὁ καὶ · Ἑρμόδωρος,
    νεωκόρος · τοῦ · μεγάλου · Σαράπιδος,
    Ἀλεξανδρεύς · Ἑρμοπολείτης · πανκρα-
10 τιαστὴς · περιοδονείκης · ἄλειπτος ☐
    ἀσυνέξωστος · ἀνέκκλητος · ξυστάρ-
    ὁ υἱὸς χης · διὰ βίου
    ὁ ἀρχιερεὺς · τοῦ σύμπαντος ξυστοῦ διὰ βίου ☐
    ξυστάρχης · καὶ ἐπὶ βαλανείων τοῦ Σεβαστοῦ. ☐

In translation:
  Demetrius the high priest.

  Demetrius the Hermopolitan of Alexandria, pankratiast, *periodonikēs*, wrestler, extraordinary, who was not absent from any of the trials, the high priest of all the assembly and lifetime president of the athletic guild and superintendent of the Augustan baths, the father [...]
  Marcus Aurelius Asclepiades, also known as **Hermodorus**, the warden of the Serapeum (temple), of Alexandria, Hermopolitan, pankratiast, *periodonikēs*, who was never absent from any of the trails, who has never lost
  lifetime president of the athletic guild, the son [...]
  the high priest of the athletic assembly and lifetime president of the guild and superintendent of the Augustan baths.

    Marcus Aurelius Demostratus Damas of Sardis was more than an outstanding athlete. He was a two-time *periodonikēs* in pankration with a large number of victories. The crowning moment of his career were two wins at the Olympian games - the 238th and 239th, in 173 and 177 CE respectively.[585] His peak is dated during the reign of Marcus Aurelius, while at the end of his career, he also distinguished himself in boxing. No other athletic figure in the imperial period appeared in so many different places outside of his home city of Sardis. He earned victories everywhere: in Italy, Greece, Asia and Alexandria.[586] In determining the exact time line, the reference to the city of Antinoe in Egypt, founded in 130 CE, is also taken into account in addition to the athletic guild honoring Demostratus through the inscription. Aside from the inscription on his statue in Rome, Demostratus is also known by another inscription dedicated to him by his sons and found in his home city of Sardis. He is also mentioned on a papyrus, dated at 194 CE, in which he is referred to

---

585 Moretti, *Olympionikai*, No 878, 881.
586 Jean-Yves Strasser, «La carrière du pancratiaste Markos Aurèlios Dèmostratos Damas,» Bulletin de correspondance hellénique, 127, no. 1 (2003): p. 268.

as the *high priest of the entire athletic guild*. Thus, Demostratus' activity can be dated to the second half of the second century CE. Two inscriptions found at Delphi also refer to Demostratus. It is quite clear that at that time, Demostratus was an excellent boxer and pankratiast who managed to win twenty times in the boys' category and forty-eight times in the men's category at the sacred games. One of the Delphic inscriptions is attributed to Demostratus' son.[587] As an adult, Damas had at least two Olympic wins, three at the Pythian games, five at the Isthmus, at least three at Nemea, three at Argos, two at the Capitoline games in Rome, two in the Eusebeian (Piety) games in honor of Antoninus Pius, at least three at Naples, two at the Actian games, ten in Athens (three in the Panathenaic games, three at the Olympian, one at the Hadrianeia, three at the Panhellenic games), three at Rhodes, four at Sardis, nine at Ephesus, six at Smyrna (two at the League of Asia, two at the Olympia and two at Hadrian's Olympic games), three at Pergamon, four at Alexandria and one at the Epinicean games in Rome.[588]

Here is a look at the inscriptions. The first is from Delphi from the late second century to early third century CE.

BCH 68/69 (1944/5) 125,37

1 **Μ. Αὐρ. Δημόστρατος**
  _ **Δαμᾶς** Σαρδιανὸς
  _ Δαμᾶς Σαρδιανὸς
  παγκρατιαστὴς β'
  περ[ι]οδονείκης.

Translated:
  Marcus Aurelius Demostratus Damas of Sardis
  Pankratiast two-time *periodonikēs*

Inscription **FD III 1:556** which follows was found at Delphi. It is dated at between 212 and 217 CE.

1 **Μ. Αὐρ. Δημόστρατος Δα-**
  μᾶς Σαρδιανὸς πανκρατιαστὴς δὶς περιοδονείκης,
  πύκτης ἄλειπτ%[81]ος π<α>-

---

587 Knab, *Die Periodoniken*, No 52.
588 Strasser, «La carrière due pancratiaste,» p. 293.

5 [ρ]ά%⁸¹δο[ξ]ος

Translated:
> **Marcus Aurelius Demostratus Damas** of Sardis
> Pankratiast two-time *periodonikēs*,
> Boxer who was never absent from any trials, extraordinary

The honorary inscription **Ephesos 1134** was found at Ephesus and is dated at between 161 and 180 CE. It describes Damas as a high priest and is obviously related to the athletes' guild.

1 ἀγαθῇ τ[ύχῃ·]
[Μ(ᾶρκος) Αὐρ(ήλιος)] Δημόστρατος Δαμᾶς
[ἀρχιε]ρεὺς τοῦ σύμπαντος
[ξυστο]ῦ διὰ βίου, ξυστάρχης
5 [καὶ] ἐπὶ βαλανείων τῶν Σεβ(αστῶν), παν-
[κρατιαστὴς] περιοδονείκ[ης δίς,]
[πύκτης] ἄλειπτος [παράδοξος.]

Here is the translation:
> With good fortune;
> **Marcus Aurelius Demostratus Damas**
> high priest of the entire athletic assembly, lifetime head of the guild and superintendent of the Augustan baths, pankratiast, *periodonikēs*, boxer, who was never absent from any trials, extraordinary.

The inscription I. **Ephesos 1612** was found at Ephesus:
[Μ. Αὐρ. Δημόστρατον Δαμ]αν
[περ]ιοδο-
[νίκην ἐπι π]ρυτά-
[νεως -αγ]όρου
[γυμνασιαρχοῦντος]ιου

Translated:
> **Marcus Aurelius Demostratus Damas**, *periodonikēs*
> when he was the head of athletic training and president of the assembly.

Inscription **Sardis 7,1 79** was found at Sardis and is dated at between 212 and 217 CE. It lists many of his achievements and honorary titles. Here it is in its entirety:

A **[Μᾶρκος Αὐρήλιος Δημόστρατος Δαμᾶς**, Σαρδι]-
[ανός, Ἀλεξανδρεύς, Ἀντινοεύς, Νεικομηδεύς],
[Τραλλιανός, Ἐφέσιος, Σμυρναῖος, Μειλήσι]-
1 [ο]ς, Περγαμηνός, Κ[ορίνθιος, Ἀθηναῖ]-
ος, Ἀργεῖος, Λακεδ[αιμόνιος, Δελφός, Ἠ]-
[λ]εῖος, νεικήσας ἀ[γῶνας τοὺς πάντας]
[ρ..], ὧν ἱεροὺς εἰσελαστικο[ὺς ξη΄ Ἰταλίας]
5 Ἑλλάδος Ἀσίας Ἀλεξανδρεί[ας τοὺς ὑ]-
πογεγραμμένους· Ὀλύμπια ἐ[ν Πείση],
Πύθια ἐν Δελφοῖς γ΄, Ἴσθμια ε΄, [Νέμεα],
τὴν ἐξ Ἄργους Ἀσπίδα γ΄, Ῥώμη[ν Καπι]-
τώλια β΄, Ποτιόλους β΄, Νέαν πόλ[ιν],
10 Ἄκτια β΄, Ἀθήνας ι΄, Παναθήναια μ[ὲν],
Πανελλήνια δὲ γ΄, Ὀλύμπεια [Ἀδριά]-
[ν]εια α΄, Ῥόδον Ἄλεια γ΄, Σάρδεις [Χρυσάν]-
θινον δ΄, Ἔφεσον θ΄, Σμύρναν ς΄, [Πέργα]-
μον Αὐγούστεια γ΄, Ἀλεξάνδρει[αν, Ῥώ]-
15 μην ἐπινείκια τῶν κυρίων Αὐτοκρα[τόρων]
Ἀντωνίνου καὶ Κομμόδου, ἐστεφα[νώθη]
χρυσῷ στεφάνῳ καὶ ἔλαβε χρυσοῦν [βραβεῖ]-
ον, αἰτησάμενος καὶ τυχὼν παρὰ τ[ῶν κυ]-
[ρ]ίων ἡμῶν θειοτάτων Αὐτοκρατόρ[ων]
20 Σεουήρου καὶ Ἀντωνίνου τήν τε ἀρ[χιερ]-
[ω]σύνην καὶ τὰς ξυσταρχίας εἰς τὴ[ν τῶν]
παίδων διαδοχήν·
ἀναστησάντων τὸν ἀνδριάντα Αὐ[ρηλίου]
Δαμᾶ ἀρχιερέως τοῦ σύμπαντος ξ[υστοῦ]
25 διὰ βίου, ξυστάρχου καὶ ἐπὶ βαλ[ανείων]
[τ]οῦ Σεβαστοῦ, πλειστονείκου π[αραδόξου]
καὶ Μάρκου Δημοστρατιανοῦ π[λειστο]-
νείκου παραδόξου καὶ Δημο[στράτου]
Ἡγεμονίδου πλειστονείκο[υ παραδό]-
30 ξου καὶ Δαμιανοῦ ξυστάρ[χου]
τῶν πα[ίδω]ν·
καὶ ὅσου[ς] θε[ματικοὺς]
B [ἠγωνίσατο]·
....
1 ....ς γ΄

[κοινὸν Θ]εσ[σα]λίας γʹ
[Θεσπιὰς Ἐρω]τίδεια αʹ
.... αʹ,
5 .... βʹ
[......α]ς αʹ
......α δʹ
........ν αʹ
αʹ, νῦν ἱερός.........
10 αʹ, νῦν ἱερός.........
.....γ..ον αʹ, νῦν ἱερός
αʹ, νῦν ἱερός.....θον
[Ὀλύμπ]εια τῆς Μακεδονίας [.]
βʹ........
15 [κοινὰ Ἀρκ]άδων ἐν Μαντινείᾳ γʹ
[Λακεδαί]μονα ϛʹ
[Εὐρύκλ]εια βʹ, νῦν ἱερός
[Οὐράνη]α γʹ
[Λεωνίδ]εια αʹ
20 [Δημητρι]άδα Μακεδονίας αʹ
[Ἑλλώτ]εια ἐν Ἰσθμῷ δʹ
[Εὐκλεῖ]α ἐν Ἰσθμῷ γʹ
......ονα αʹ

C.1 μόνος καὶ πρῶτος τῶν [ἀπ' αἰ]-
ῶνος ἀνθρώπων νεικήσ[ας]
παίδων μὲν ἱεροὺς κʹ,
ἐκ παιδὸς δὲ τὸν ἄνδρα
5 προσβὰς ἱεροὺς μηʹ,
ἐν οἷς πυγμῆς Πύθια ἐν
Δελφοῖς, Ἴσθμια, Νέμεα,
Ἁδριάνεια Φιλαδέλφειον
ἐν Ἀλεξανδρείᾳ·
10 τειμηθεὶς ὑπὸ θεοῦ Μάρκου
καὶ θεοῦ Κομμόδου πολει-
[τ]είᾳ μὲν Ἀλεξανδρέων ἰθ[α]-
[γ]ενεῖ, ξυσταρχίαις δὲ ταῖς
ὑπογεγραμμέναις·
15 Ῥώμης Καπιτωλίων,
Σάρδεων Χρυσανθίνου,
Σάρδεων κοινοῦ Ἀσίας,
Μειλήτου Διδυμείων,

```
      Ἀλεξανδρείας Ἁδριανείου
20  Φιλαδελφείου,
      Ἀλεξανδρείας Σεβαστείου,
      Ἀλεξανδρείας Σελευκείου,
      Ἀντινόου πόλεως καὶ τῶν
      ἐν Αἰγύπτῳ πάντων,
25  Τράλλεων κοινοῦ Ἀσίας,
      Νεικομηδείας κοινῶν Βειθυν[ίας],
      Λακεδαίμονος Εὐρυκλείων,
      καὶ ὑπὸ θεοῦ Σεουήρου καὶ τοῦ κυ-
      ρίου ἡμῶν θειοτάτου Αὐτοκράτο-
30  ρος Ἀντωνίνου ἄλλαις τε πολ-
      λαῖς καὶ μεγάλαις τειμαῖς κα[ὶ]
      ξυσταρχίαις Εὐσεβείων ἐν Πο-
      τιόλοις καὶ Σεβαστῶν ἐν Νέᾳ
      πόλει.
```

Its translation is particularly interesting:

Marcus Aurelius Demostratus Damas of Sardis, Alexandria, Antinoe, Nicomedia, of Tralles, Ephesus, Smyrna, Miletus, of Pergamon, a Corinthian, an Athenian, an Argive, a Spartan, of Delphi (and) of Elis, (who) won at all of the games [...], of these fifty-eight times at the sacred eiselastic games in Italy, in Greece, in Asia, in Alexandria, as written below; at the Olympian games at Pisa (Elis), the Pythian games at Delphi three times, at the Isthmian games five times, at Nemea, three times winner of the shield at Argos, twice at the Capitoline games in Rome, twice at the Puteolian games, in Naples, twice at the Actian games, ten times at the Panathenaic games in Athens and three times at the Panhellenic games, once at the Hadrian Games in Olympia, three times at the Aleian games in Rhodes, four times in Sardis at the Chrysanthinus, nine times at Ephesus, six times at Smyrna, three times at the Augustan games in Pergamon, at Alexandria, his victory was celebrated in Rome by the ruling emperors Antoninus and Commodus, (where) he was crowned with a golden crown and received a golden trophy, (and after) asking, he was given by our divine ruling emperors Severus and Antoninus the offices of high priest and president of the athletic guild for all future generations. The statues of Aurelius Damas, lifetime high priest of the entire athletic guild, head of the assembly and of the Augustan baths, a *pleistonikēs*,[589] and of Marcus Demostratianus, a multiple and extraordinary victor, and Demostratos Hegemonides, also an extraordinary multiple victor, and Damian, head of the boys' association;

---

[589] Mark Golden, *Sport in the Ancient World from A to Z* (Routledge, London 2004), p. 136, "victor in very many contests."

and those *thematikoi* games (with monetary prizes) in which he competed;

[…] three times
at Thessaly, three times
at the Erotideia at Thespiae, once
[…] once
[…] twice
[…] once
[…] four times
[…] once
[…] once, now sacred […]
[…] once, now sacred […]
[…] once, now sacred […]
[…] once, now sacred […]
At the Olympian games in Macedonia […] two times
At the Guild of Arcadians at Mantineia three times
At Sparta six times
At the Eurycleian games six times, now a sacred contest
At the Ouraneia three times
At the Leonideia once
At the Demetrias games in Macedonia, once
At the Helloteia at Isthmus, four times
At the Eucleia at Isthmus, three times
[…] once
The first and only one in human history to win the boys' category at the sacred games twenty times, and from his youth through his adult career, he won a total of forty-eight sacred games, which included the sport of boxing at the Pythian games at Delphi, the Isthmian and the Nemean games, at the Hadrianeia Philadelpheius Games in Alexandria;
honored by the divine Marcus and Commodus with citizenship as a native Alexandrian and with the presidency of the athletic guild of the contests that follow;
the Capitoline games in Rome
the Chrysanthinus in Sardis
the Guild of Asia in Sardis
the Didymeia in Miletus
the Hadrianus Philadelphus in Alexandria
the Sebasteion in Alexandria
the Seleucion in Alexandria
the city of Antinoe and all cities of Egypt
the Guild of Asia in Tralles
the Guild of Bithynia (games) at Nicomedia
the Eurycleia in Sparta

and by the divine Severus and our most divine leader Emperor Antoninus and many other great honors and presidencies of the athletic guilds at the Eusebeia at Puteoli and the Augustan games in Naples.

Inscription **IGUR I 243**, found in Rome, is dated at between 170 and 180 CE and refers to him as a *periodonikēs*, also listing the cities of which he was an honorary citizen.

1 ἡ · ἱερὰ · ξυστικὴ · σύνοδος · τῶν
[περ]ὶ · τὸν · Ἡρακλέα · ἀπὸ καταλύσεως
ἐν · τῆι · βασιλίδι · Ῥώμηι · κατοικούντων
Μ(άρκον) · Αὐρήλιον · Δημόστρατον · Δαμᾶν
5 Σαρδιανόν · Ἀλεξανδρέα · Ἀντινοέα · Ἀθηναῖον,
Ἐφέσιον · Σμυρναῖον · Περγαμηνόν,
Νεικομηδέα · Μιλήσιον · Λακεδαιμόνιον,
ἀρχιερέα · τοῦ · σύνπαντος · ξυστοῦ · διὰ · βίου,
ξυστάρχην · καὶ · ἐπὶ · βαλανείων · Σεβαστῶν,
10 πανκρατιαστὴν · περιοδονείκην · δίς,
πύκτην · ἄλειπτον · παράδοξον

Here is the translation:
> The holy synod of the athletic guild of Heracleian athletes now living in the royal city of Rome
> honors **Marcus Aurelius Demostratus Damas**, honorary citizen of Sardis, Alexandria, Antinoe, Athens, Ephesus, Smyrna, Pergamon, Nicomedia, Miletus, Sparta, high priest of all of the athletic assembly and lifetime president of the athletic guild and superintendent of the Augustan baths, pankratiast, *periodonikēs*; twice, boxer, never absent from any trials, extraordinary.

Inscription **III 1178** at Hermopolis provides more or less the same information as the previous one:

> ἐπ[ὶ ἀρ]χιε[ρέ]ων του σύμπαντος ξυστοῦ και ξυσταρχῶν δια βίου καΐ
> [ἐπι βαλανεί]ων τοῦ Σεβαστοῦ **Μ. Αὐρ. Δημοστράτου Δαμα**
> [Σαρδιανοῦ, Ἀλεξανδρέως, Ἀν]τινοέως, Ἀθηναίου, ‹Εφεσίου, Σμυρναίου,
> Περ[γαμηνοῦ, Νε]ικομηδέως, Μειλησίου, Λακεδαιμονίου, Τραλλιανοῦ,
> παγκρα[τιασ]τοῦ δις περιοδονείκου, πύκτου ἀλείπτου παραδόξου κτλ.

Translated:
> In honor of the high priests of the entire athletic assembly and lifetime presidents of the athletic guilds and the superintendents of the Augustan baths and **Marcus Aurelius Demostratus Damas**, the Sardian, Alexandrian, Antinoan, Athenian,

Ephesian, Smyrnean, Pergamenian [...etc.], pankratiast and twice *periodonikēs*, boxer who never lagged behind in any trial, incredible athlete, etc.

Inscription **SEG39, 1292** in Sardis provides substantial information about his victories. It is included here:

[**Μ. Αύρ. Δημόστρατος Δαμας**, ό άρχιερεύς]
[του σύμπαντος ξυστού, δια βίου ξυστάρ]-
[χης και επί βαλανείων των Σεβαστών],
4 [πανκρατιαστης δις περιοδονείκης],
[πύκτης αλειπτος παράδοξος, Σαρδια]-
[νός, Άλεξανδρεύς,]
[ ]
8 [ο]ς, Περγαμηνός, Κ[ορίνθιος,]
ος, Άργεῖος, Λακεδ[αιμόνιος, , Ή]-
[λ]εῖος, νεικήσας ά[γώνας τους πάντας]
[ρ./] ων ιερούς είσελαστικο[ύς ξζ', Ιταλίας]
12 Έλλάδος, Ασίας, Άλεξανδρεί[ας, τους ύ]-
πογεγραμμένους· Όλύμπια έ[ν Πείση .],
Πύθια έν Δελφοίς γ›, «Ισθμια ε», [Νέμεα .],
την εξ Άργους ασπίδα γ›, ‹Ρώμη[ν Καπι]-
16 τώλια β', Ποτιόλους β', Νέαν Πόλ[ιν .]
Άκτια β›, Αθήνας ι›, Παναθήναια μ[έν .],
Πανελλήνια δε γ›, Όλύμπεια [., Άδριά]-
[ν]εια α, 'Ρόδον 'Άλεια γ', Σάρδεις [Χρυσάν]-
20 θινον δ', «Εφεσον θ', Σμύρναν ς', [Πέργα]-
μον Αύγούστεια γ›, Άλεξανδρεί[αν . . ‹Ρω]-
μην έπινείκια των κυρίων αύτοκρα[τόρων]
Άντωνίνου και Κομμόδου, έστεφα[νώθη]
24 χρυσω στεφάνφ και έλαβε χρυσούν [βραβεῖ]-
ον vac. αίτησάμενος και τυχών παρά τ[ών κυ]-
[ρ]ίων ημών θειοτάτων αύτοκρατόρ[ων]
Σεουήρου και Άντωνίνου τήν τε άρ[χιερ]-
28 [ω]σύνην και τάς ξυσταρχίας εις τη[ν των]
παίδων διαδοχήν
άναστησάντων τόν ανδριάντα Αύ[ρηλίου]
Δαμα άρχιερέως τού σύμπαντος ξ[υστού],
32 δια βίου ξυστάρχου και έπ! βαλ[ανείων]
[τ]ού Σεβαστού, πλειστονεικου π[αραδόξου],
και Μάρκου Δημοστρατιανού π[λειστο]-
νείκου παραδόξου και Δήμο [στρατού] .
36 ' Ηγεμονίδου πλειστονείκο[υ παραδό]-

ξου και Δαμιανού ξυστάρ[χου vac. ?]
των πα[ίδω]ν
και δσον[ς] θε[ματικούς]
μόνος και πρώτος των [άπ1 αί]-
ώνος ανθρώπων νεικήσ[ας]
παίδων μέν ιερούς κ›,
έκ παιδός δε τόν άνδρα
προσβας Ιερούς μη›,
εν οίς πυγμής Πύθια εν
Δελφοΐς, Ίσθμια, Νέμεα,
8 ʹ Αδριάνεκο>ν Φιλαδέλφειον
έν Αλεξάνδρεια*
τειμηθείς ύπό θεοΰ Μάρκου
και θεοΰ Κομμόδου πολει-
12 [τ]εία μέν Άλεξανδρέων ίθ[α]-
[γ]ενεΐ, ξυσταρχίαις δε ταΐς
ύπογεγραμμέναις·
ʹΡώμης Καπιτωλίων,
16 Σάρδεων Χρυσανθίνου,
Σάρδεων κοινού Ασίας,
Μειλήτου Διδυμείων,
Αλεξανδρείας ‹Αδριάνειου
20 Φιλαδελφείου,
Αλεξανδρείας Σεβαστείου,
Αλεξανδρείας Σελευκείου,
Άντινόου πόλεως καί των
24 έν Αίγυπτο) πάντων,
Τράλλεων κοινοΰ Ασίας,
Νεικομηδείας κοινών Βειθυν[ίας],
Λακεδαίμονος Εύρυκλείων,
28 και ύπό θεοΰ Σεουήρου και τοΰ κυ-
f, ρίου ημών θειοτάτου αύτοκράτο-
ν - ρΟς Αντωνίνου αλλαις τε πολ-
λαις και μεγάλαις τειμαΐς κα[1]
32 ξυσταρχίαις Ευσεβειών έν Ποτιόλοις καί Σεβαστών έν Νέα
πόλει.

Here is the translation:

Marcus Aurelius Demostratos Damas, high priest of the entire athletic assembly, lifetime president of the athletic guild and superintendent the imperial baths, pankratiast and twice *periodonikēs*, an extraordinary boxer who was never defeated, Sardian, Alexandrian, Pergamenian, Corinthian, Argive, Spartan, Elean, (who) was victorious in all of the games, sixty-seven times at the sacred eiselastic games in Italy, Greece, Asia, Alexandria, as listed below;

At the Olympian Games in Pisa (Elis), three times at the Pythian games in Delphi, five times at the Isthmian games, at the Nemean games, three times at the Aspis games at Argos, twice at the Capitoline games in Rome, twice at the Puteolian games, in Naples, at the Actian games two times, in Athens ten times at the Panathenaic games, three times at the Panhellenic games, at the Olympian and once at the Hadrian games, at the Haleian games in Rhodes three times, four times at the Chrysanthinos in Sardis, nine times at Ephesus, six times at Smyrna, three times at the Augustan games in Pergamon, in Alexandria. [...]

He received the honors of victory from the divine emperors Antoninus and Commodus, was crowned with a gold wreath and received a gold trophy and at his request was granted the office of high priest and head of the athletic guild for his sons in succession by the divine emperors Severus and Antoninus.

The statue of Aurelius Damas, lifetime high priest of the entire athletic assembly, head of the guild and superintendent of the imperial baths, an athlete with an incredible record of victories, and of Marcus Demostratianus, also with an incredible series of victories, and of Demostratus Hegemonides, likewise a victor, and of Damian, head of the boys' athletic guild;

and at the thematikoi games [...],

the one and only in human history to win at the sacred games in the boys' category twenty times, forty-eight times in his record of achievements in the sacred games, which included boxing at the Pythian games at Delphi, the Hadrianius Philadelpheios games in Alexandria, he was honored by the divine Marcus and Commodus[590] with citizenship as a native Alexandrian and with the leadership of the following athletic guilds;

at the Capitoline games in Rome
at the Chrysanthinos in Sardis
at the League of Asia in Sardis
at the Didymeia in Miletus
at the Hadrianeia in Alexandria
at Philadelpheios
at the Sebasteion in Alexandria
at the Seleucion in Alexandria
at the city of Antinoe
and all of the cities of Egypt,
at the League of Asia in Tralles
at the Guild of Bithynia in Nicomedia

---

590 The "divine Marcus and Commodus" are the emperors Marcus Aurelius and the son of Commodus of the Antonine dynasty. Emperors were worshiped as gods and sought to take advantage of the glory and cultural supremacy that accompanied Greek athletics to strengthen their image and, by extension, their authority.

at the Eurycleia in Sparta

and by the divine Severus and our most divine leader Emperor Antoninus and many other great honors and presidencies of the athletic guilds at the Eusebeia at Puteoli and the Augustan games in Naples.

He stopped competing between 176 and 180 CE.[591] He had achieved a total of 108 victories, 68 of which were at sacred games and 40 at competitions with monetary prizes (*thematikoi* or *thematitai*).[592]

Marcus Aurelius Asclepiades, also known as **Hermodorus**, son of Marcus Aurelius Demetrius of Alexandria, was the winner at the 240th Olympian games in 181 CE. He was a *periodonikēs* with one win at the Olympic games, two at the Pythia, two at the Isthmia, two at the Nemea, and had won at many other competitions, such as at Aegium, the Capitoline games and the Sebasteion at Naples. There is also information on his competing in Italy, Achaea, Macedonia, Bithynia, Mysia, Lydia, Ionia, Egypt and Rhodes.[593] He also had victories at the Aspis games at Argos in honor of Hera, in Athens, at the Panathenaic Games, at the Olympian games, the Panhellenic and Hadrianeian games, the Augustan Games at Pergamon, at Smyrna, at the Actian games at Nicopolis, at the Asclepeia in Epidaurus, the Aleia in Rhodes, the Chrysanthinos at Sardis, the Eucleia at Sparta, at Mantineia, and others.[594] He was born in 157 or 158 CE. He was only active for six years and in 182 CE, at the age of twenty-five, he withdrew from competition. He returned years later, but only once, on the occasion of the festival of Olympia of Alexandria (196 CE).[595] He was a citizen and councilor of many cities and was involved in pankration, like his father.

Here are three inscriptions referring to him: Inscription **IGUR I 239** was found in Rome and is dated as late second century CE. It is included in the section referring to Marcus Aurelius Demetrius.

Inscription **IGUR I 250** was found in Rome and is dated as late second century CE. It mostly refers to the honors bestowed upon Asclepiades:

1 [Μάρκος Αὐρήλιος Ἀσκληπιάδης ὁ καὶ Ἑρμόδωρος Δημητρίου υἱὸς παγκρατιαστὴς περιοδονεί]κης ἄλειπτος ἀρχιερεὺς · τοῦ σύμπαντος ξυ[στοῦ] [διὰ βίου καὶ πρεσβύτατος νεωκόρος τοῦ μεγάλου Σαράπιδος καὶ τῶν ἐν τῷ Μουσείῳ σει]τουμένων ἀτελῶν φιλοσόφων.

---

591 Strasser, «La carrière due pancratiaste,» p. 298.
592 Kostouros, *Nemeōn* 2, p. 115.
593 Weir, *Roman Delphi*, p. 126.
594 Kostouros, *Nemeōn* 2, p. 112.
595 Moretti, *Olympionikai*, No 884.

[M (arcus) Aur (elius) Asclepiades Demetri] f (ilius) · a balnearibu[s].

Translated:
> **Marcus Aurelius Asclepiades**, also known as **Hermodorus**, son of Demetrius, pankratiast *periodonikēs*, undefeated lifetime high priest of the entire athletic assembly and most senior warden of the Serapeum Temple and the unpaid philosophers served food at the Museum.

The inscription **IGUR I 240** was also found in Rome and dates to 200 CE.

face a, front.1
Μ(άρκου) · Αὐρηλίου · Δημητρίου · ἀρχιερέως · τοῦ σύνπαντος
ξυστοῦ · διὰ βίου, ξυστάρχου · καὶ · ἐπὶ · βαλανείων · τοῦ · Σεβαστ[οῦ],
Ἀλεξανδρέως · Ἑρμοπολείτου · πανκρατιαστοῦ · περιοδον[είκου],
παλαιστοῦ · παραδόξου · υ·ἱὸς · **Μάρκος · Αὐρήλιος**
5 **Ἀσκληπιάδης** · ὁ καὶ · **Ἑρμόδωρος** · ὁ πρεσβύτατος · τῶν νεω-
κόρων · τοῦ μεγάλου · Σαράπιδος · ὁ ἀρχιερεὺς · τοῦ · σύνπαντος
ξυστοῦ · διὰ βίου · ξυστάρχης · καὶ · ἐπὶ βαλανείων · τοῦ Σεβαστοῦ,
Ἀλεξανδρεύς · Ἑρμοπολείτης · Ποτιολανός · Νεαπολείτης καὶ
Ἠλεῖος · καὶ · Ἀθηναῖος · βουλευτὴς · καὶ · ἄλλων πόλεων · πολλῶν
10 πολείτης · καὶ · βουλευτής · πανκρατιαστὴς · περιοδονείκης · ἄλειπτος,
ἀσυνέξωστος · ἀνέκκλητος · ὅσους ποτὲ ἀγῶνας · ἀπεγραψάμην
πάντας · νεικήσας · μήτε · ἐκκαλέσαμενος · μήτε · ἑτέρου · κατ' ἐμοῦ · τολμή-
σαντος · ἐκκαλέσασθαι · μήτε συστεφανωθεὶς · μήτε · ἐπεξελθὼν μήτε
παραι-
τησάμενος · μήτε · ἀγῶνα · παραλιπὼν · μήτε κατὰ χάριν · βασιλικὴν · ἀγῶνα
15 ἔχων · μηδὲ · καινὸν · ἀγῶνα · νεικήσας · ἀλλὰ · πάντας οὕς ποτε · ἀπεγραψάμην ἐν αὐτοῖς · τοῖς · σκάμμασιν · στεφανωθεὶς · καὶ · ταῖς · προπείραις
τούτων · πάσαις · δοκιμασθεὶς · ἀγωνισάμενος · ἐν ἔθνεσιν · τρισίν · Ἰταλία,
Ἑλλάδι · Ἀσία · νεικήσας · ἀγῶνας · τοὺς · ὑπογεγραμμένους · πάντας ·
πανκρα-
τίου · Ὀλύμπια τὰ ἐν Πείσῃ · σμ · ὀλυμπιάδι · Πύθια ἐν Δελφοῖς · Ἴσθμια δίς,
20 Νέμεα · δίς · τὸ δεύτερον · στήσας · τοὺς · ἀνταγωνιστάς · καὶ · τὴν ἀσπίδα
Ἥρας ΕΜ
ΜΙ · Καπετώλια · ἐν Ῥώμῃ · δίς · τὸ · δεύτερον · μετὰ πρῶτον κλῆρον · στήσας
τοὺς ἀνταγωνιστάς · Εὐσέβεια · ἐν Ποτιόλοις · δίς · τὸ δεύτερον · μετὰ
δεύτερον
κλῆρον · στήσας · τοὺς ἀνταγωνιστάς · Σεβαστὰ ἐν Νεαπόλι · <δίς>, τὸ
δεύτερον μετὰ

δεύτερον · κλῆρον στήσας τοὺς · ἀνταγωνιστάς · Ἄκτια · ἐν Νεικοπόλι δίς · τὸ δεύ-
25 τερον στήσας · τοὺς ἀνταγωνιστάς · Ἀθήνας · ε · Παναθήναια · Ὀλύμπεια · Πανελ-
λήνια · Ἀδριάνια · δίς · Ζμύρναν · ε · κοινὰ · Ἀσίας δίς · τὸ δεύτερον · στήσας τοὺς ἀνταγωνιστάς · ὁμοίως · ἐν Ζμύρνῃ · Ὀλύμπια καὶ Ἀδριάνια · Ὀλύμπια· Πέργαμον · Αὐγούστεια · τρίς · τὸ δεύτερον · ἐξ ἀρχῆς στήσας τοὺς ἀνταγωνιστ[άς],

face b, right.29 τὸ τρίτον μετὰ πρῶτον κλῆρον στήσας τοὺς
30 ἀνταγωνιστάς· Ἔφεσον τρίς, Ἀδριάνια, Ὀλύμπια, Βαρβίλληα, μετὰ πρῶτον κλῆρον στήσας
τοὺς ἀνταγωνιστάς· Ἐπίδαυρον Ἀσκλήπεια· Ῥόδον
Ἄλεια· Χρυσάνθινα ἐν Σάρδεσιν, καὶ θεματεί-
τας πλείονας, ἐν οἷς Εὐρύκλεια ἐν Λακεδαίμονι
35 καὶ Μαντίνιαν καὶ ἄλλους. ἀθλήσας τὰ πάντα ἔτη
ἕξ, παυσάμενος τῆς ἀθλήσεως ἐτῶν ὢν κε
διὰ τοὺς συνβάντας μοι κινδύνους καὶ φθό-
νους καὶ μετὰ τὸ παύσασθαι μετὰ πλείονα χρόνον
ἀνανκασθεὶς ἐν τῇ πατρίδι Ἀλεξανδρείᾳ καὶ
40 νεικήσας Ὀλύμπια πανκράτιον
Ὀλυμπιάδι ἕκτῃ.

Here is the translation:

The son of Marcus Aurelius Demetrios, high priest of the entire athletic assembly and lifetime president of the athletic guild and superintendent of the imperial baths, citizen of Alexandria and Hermopolis, pankratiast, *periodonikēs* wrestler, the extraordinary, son **Marcus Aurelius Asclepiades**, also known as **Hermodorus**, the senior-most warden of the Serapeum Temple, the high priest of the entire athletic aseembly, lifetime president of the guild and superintendent of the imperial baths, Alexandrian, Hermopolitan, Puteolian, Neapolitan and Elean, and an Athenian councilor, and a citizen and councilor of many other cities, pankratiast, *periodonikēs*, unconquered, never defeated, tenacious, never absent from a trial, never thrown off the sand and never in the games I recorded I beat them all without being penalized, without my opponent being able to hold me off for very long, causing me to be penalized, without finishing even with another, without ever kneeling or reaching my limit or giving up, without avoiding any contest, without ever winning a contest by royal favor, without winning at any new contest, but I recorded all those games during which I was crowned at some time in these sand pits, and I was successfully tested at all preliminary games before these and competed in three nations, Italy, Greece and Asia and won in all of the pankration competitions listed below;

At the Olympian games in Pisa (Elis) at the 250th Olympiad
at the Pythia in Delphi
At the Isthmia two times
at the Nemea two times and then won the shield of Hera by "*stēsas tous antagonistas*" (stopping the opponent) [...]
at the Capitoline games in Rome twice in the second round after the first draw by *stēsas tous antagonistas*
at the Eusebeia in Puteoli twice in the second round after the second draw by *stēsas tous antagonistas*
at the Augustan games in Naples twice in the second round after the second draw by*stēsas tous antagonistas*
at the Actia in Nicopolis twice in the second round after the second draw by *stēsas tous antagonistas*
in Athens five times
at the Panathenaic games
At the Panhellenic Olympics twice
in Smyrna five times
at the League of Asia Games twice in the second round by *stēsas tous antagonistas*
the same in Smyrna
at the Olympia and Hadrianeia Olympia;
at the Augustan games in Pergamon three times in the second round at the beginning *stēsas tous antagonistas*
in the third round after the first draw by *stēsas tous antagonistas*
in Ephesus, three times
at the Hadrianeia, the Olympia, the Barbilleia, with the first draw *stēsas tous antagonistas*
in Epidaurus at the Asclepeia;
in Rhodes at the Aleia;
at the Chrysanthinos in Sardis, and even more *thematikoi* games, including: the Eurycleia in Sparta and Mantineia and others.
I competed in all of the games (everything) for six years, though I stopped competing at the age of twenty-five because of the risks I would be exposed to and because of the malice that I faced after I had stopped, and then after a long time I was convinced to take part in my home of Alexandria and I won the pankration at the Olympian games in the sixth Olympiad.

At the 242nd Olympian games in 189 CE, the winner was **Claudius Apollonius** of Smyrna. He was most likely a descendant of Tiberius Claudius

Rufus of Smyrna.[596] He was a *periodonikēs* in wrestling and perhaps in boxing or in pankration as well.[597]

At the 247th Olympian games in 209 CE, the winner was **Perelius Aurelius Alexander** from Thyateira of Lydia.[598] He lived during the period of Roman Emperor Caracalla (198-217 CE; nickname of Marcus Aurelius Severus Antoninus Augustus).[599]

At the 248th Olympian Games in 213 CE, the winner was **Lucius Silicius Firmus Mandrogenes** of Magnesia. He also lived during the era of Emperor Caracalla.[600] The role of those close to the athlete in his achievements was apparently quite significant. Mandrogenes of Magnesia earned his first victory at pankration from the respect expressed in a letter that his trainer sent to his mother, who had raised the athlete on her own. According to Philostratus, the letter said: "If you hear that your son has died, believe it. But if you hear that he was defeated in competition, do not believe it." Thus Mandrogenes competed with his heart and soul so as not to disappoint his mother and he won.[601]

At the 249th Olympian games in 217 CE, the winner was **Aurelius Aelix** of Phoenicia. He had won at the Capitoline games in Rome in 218 CE.[602]

At the 250th Olympics in 221 CE, the winner was **Aurelius Phoibammon**, son of Poseidonius[603] of Egypt.[604]

The winner at the 252nd and 253rd Olympian games in 229 and 233 CE[605] was **Claudius Rufus**, who was also called Apollonius and was the son of Claudius Apollonius. The event he competed in is not known with certainty, but it may have been boxing or pankration.[606]

Neither the name nor origin is known of the winner at the 254th Olympics in 237 CE. He may have also won at wrestling or pankration. He also had victories at the Isthmia and at wrestling and pankration competitions at Smyrna. There is no doubt that he was an athlete who had won at least once even at Olympia.[607, 608]

---

596 Moretti, *Olympionikai*, No 890.
597 Knab, *Die Periodoniken*, No 55.
598 Moretti, *Olympionikai*, No 908.
599 Kostouros, *Nemeōn* 2, p. 58.
600 Moretti, *Olympionikai*, No 912.
601 Gogaki, *Oi antilēpseis*, pp. 182, 183.
602 Moretti, *Olympionikai*, No 915.
603 Moretti, *Olympionikai*, No 919.
604 Sakellarakis et al., *Oi Olympiakoi*, p. 296.
605 Sakellarakis et al., *Oi Olympiakoi*, p. 296.
606 Moretti, *Olympionikai*, No 924.
607 Moretti, *Olympionikai*, No 929.
608 Sakellarakis et al., *Oi Olympiakoi*, p. 296.

Philumenus of Lydian Philadelphia won one of the heavy events, either wrestling or boxing or pankration at the 287th Olympic Games in 369 CE.[609]

There are two more winners, though they are in doubt. One is among the hotly disputed Olympic champions, as they are described. His name was **Rufus**, and nothing is known about his family name or his native land. He had won at either wrestling or boxing or pankration. It is possible that this athlete was a member of the well-known family of Claudii Rufi.[610]

Also among the questionable Olympic athletes is **Aurelius Toalius** of Oenoanda[611], in boys' pankration. There are references to two Olympian victories, two at Aegium and one at the Pythian games. However, this could be alluding to a city named Olympia in Asia Minor.[612]

Here is the inscription that refers to him. It is **BCH 10 (1886) 233,13** and was found in Lycia:

ἀγωνοθετοῦντος διὰ βί-
1
ου Ἰουλίου Λουκίου Πει-
λίου Εὐαρέστου πανηγύ-
ρεως δευτέρας Σευηρεί-
5 ων [Ἀλεξανδρείων] Εὐα-
ρεστείων ἧς αὐτὸς συν-
εστήσατο ἐξ ἰδίων χρη-
μάτων εἰς πάντα τὸν
χρόνον,
10 **Αὐρ. Τοάλιος** νεικήσας ἐν-
δόξως παίδων πανκρά-
τιον κοινὰ Λυκίων.
Ὀλύμ-
πια.
15 Πύθι-
α.
Ἄκτι-
α.
Ὀλύμ-
20 πια.
Ἄκτι-
α.

---
609 Moretti, *Olympionikai*, No 943.
610 Moretti, *Olympionikai*, No 977.
611 Sakellarakis et al., *Oi Olympiakoi*, p. 297.
612 Moretti, *Olympionikai*, 1005, 1006.

Here is the translation:
> During the term of the *agonothetēs* [613]Julius Lucius Pilius Euarestus of the second festival of the Severeian Alexandrian Eurasteian games during which he himself founded for all time with his own money, **Aurelius Toalius** honorably won the boys' pankration at the League of Lycia games, at the Olympian games, at the Pythia, at the Actia, at the Olympia, at the Actia.

MARBLE BASE OF THE STATUE OF PANKRATIAST POLYDAMAS,
SECOND HALF OF THE 4th CENTURY BCE.
OLYMPIA ARCHAEOLOGICAL MUSEUM
(photo from the author's collection)

---

613 Translator's note: judge or president of the games

Another disputed Olympic champion is **Leucarus** of Acarnania.[614]

	Year	Olympics	Name
1	92 BCE	172nd	Protophanes
2	72 BCE	177th	Sphodrias
3	72 BCE	177th	Calas (boys)
4	68 BCE	178th	Straton
5	64 BCE	179th	Straton
6	52 BCE	182nd	Marion
7	24 BCE	189th	Philippus Glycon
8	CE 13	198th	Aristeas
9	CE 25	201st	Hermas
10	CE 29	202nd	Hermas
11	CE 33	203rd	Heras
12	CE 37	204th	Nicostratus
13	CE 49	207th	Publius Cornelius Ariston
14	CE 53	208th	... of Stratoniceia
15	CE 65	211th	Xenodamus
16	CE 69	212th	Tiberius Claudius Artemidorus
17	CE 81	215th	Tiberius Claudius Rufus
18	CE 85	216th	Tiberius Flavius Artemidorus
19	CE 89	217th	Tiberius Flavius Artemidorus
20	CE 89	217th	Nicanor (boys)
21	CE 101	220th	Titus Flavius Archibius
22	CE 105	221st	Titus Flavius Archibius
23	CE 117	224th	Publius Aelius Aristomachus
24	CE 129	227th	Marcus Ulpius Domesticus
25	CE 149	232nd	Socrates
26	CE 153	233rd	Marcus Aurelius Demetrios
27	CE 173	238th	Marcus Aurelius Demostratus Damas
28	CE 177	239th	Marcus Aurelius Demostratus Damas
29	CE 181	240th	Marcus Aurelius Asclepiades (Hermodorus)
30	CE 189	242nd	Claudius Apollonius
31	CE 209	247th	Perelius Aurelius Alexander
32	CE 213	248th	Silicius Firmus Mandrogenes
33	CE 217	249th	Aurelius Aelix
34	CE 221	250th	Aurelius Phoibammon
35	CE 229	252nd	Claudius Rufus

---

614 Sakellarakis et al., *Oi Olympiakoi*, p. 297.

	Year	Olympics	Name
36	CE 233	253rd	Claudius Rufus
37	CE 237	254th	……………
38	CE 369	287th	Philumenus
	Disputed Olympic pankratiasts		
39	……..	……..	Rufus
40	……..	……..	Aurelius Toalius
41	……..	……..	Leucarus

The Isthmian Victors

Some of the athletes appearing here will already be familiar, as they had also won at the Olympian games; others were *periodonikēs*, while many of them were successful only at the Isthmian games.

Cimon, son of Campos of Ceos won the men's pankration sometime between 580 and 330 BCE.[615]

Here is a look at the inscription found at the Cyclades Islands which refers to him and a few of the subsequent victors:

IG XII, 5 608

1 [. . . . . ἀ]ν[δ(ρῶν)(?)]
   [. . . . . . .η]ς [Θ]ίβρων(ος) ἀν[δ(ρῶν)]
   [Λ]εο[κρ]έων Βώλεος ἀν[δρ(ῶν)]
   [Λ]ιπαρίων Λιπάρου ἀνδρῶ(ν)
5 [Λ]ιπαρίων Λιπά[ρ]ο[υ] [ἀ]νδρ[ῶν]
   [Λ]εοκρέων Βώλε[ο]ς ἀνδ[ρ(ῶν)]
   [Λεο]κ[ρέ]ων Βώλ[ε]ο[ς] ἀνδ[ρ(ῶν)]
   [Λι]παρίων Λιπάρου ἀνδρ[ῶ(ν)]
   [Φ]αιδιππίδης Λιπάρου ἀγ[ε(νείων)]
10 [ἀ]δελφοὶ τῆι αὐτῆι ἡμέραι.
   Κίμων Κάμπου ἀνδρῶν
   [Σ]μικυλ[ίν]ης(?) Τιμάρχο[υ] — —
   [Κρ]ῖνις Ἀξίλεω παίδων παγ(κράτιον)
   Πολύφ[α]ν[τ]ος Θεοφρά[δεο]ς ἀγεν(είων)
15 Ἀργεῖος Πανθ[εί]δ[ε]ω παίδω(ν)
   Λέων Λεωμέδοντος.
   οἵδε Νέμεια ἐνίκων — — —

---

615 Andrew Farrington, "Isthmionikai: A Catalog of Isthmian Victors," *Nikephoros* 21 (2012): p. 42.

    Λωκ[ίω]ν(?) Νεδ..τίου(?) ἀνδρῶ(ν)
    Ἔπακρος Ναυκύδεος ἀνδ[ρ(ῶν)]
20 Ἀλεξίδικος [Μ]ένητος ἀνδ(ρῶν)
    Κρινόλεως [Π]ρασέα ἀγε(νείων)
    Λιπαρίων Λι[π]άρου ἀνδρῶ(ν)
    Λαμπροκλῆς Ἀξίλεω ἀνδρ(ῶν)
    Κίμων Κάμπου ἀνδρῶν πα(γκράτιον)(?)
25 Πολύφαντος Θε[ο]φράδεος ἀγε(νείων)
    Ἀργεῖος Πανθείδεω ἀγενείω(ν)
    Λάχων Ἀριστομένεος παίδω(ν)
    Λάχων Ἀριστομένεος παίδω(ν)
    Λέων Λεωμέδοντος κῆρυξ.

Here is the translation:
    [...] in the men's category (?)
    [...] son of Thibron (in pankration, category) men's
    Leocreon son of Boleus, men's category
    Liparion son of Liparus, men's category
    Liparion son of Liparus, men's category
    Leocreon son of Boleus, men's category
    Leocreon son of Boleus, men's category
    Liparion son of Liparus, men's category
    Pheidippides son of Liparus, youth category

    [...] brothers (won) in one day
    Cimon son of Campus, men's category
    Smicylines, son of Timarchus ---
    Crinis son of Axileus, boys' pankration
    Polyphantus, son of Theophrades, youth category

    Argeios son of Pantheideus, boys' category
    Leon of Leomedon.
    The following won at the Nemean games
    Locion son of Ned [...]tius, men's category
    Epacrus, son of Naucydes, men's category

    Alexidicus, son of Menon, men's category
    Crinoleus, son of Praseas, youth category
    Liparion son of Liparus, men's category
    Lamprocles, son of Axileus, men's category
    Cimon, son of Campus, men's pankration category
    Polyphantus, son of Theophrades, youth category

> Argeios, son of Pantheideus, youth category
> Lachon, son of Aristomenes, boys' category
> Lachon, son of Aristomenes, boys' category
> Lachon, son of Aristomenes, boys' category
> Leon son of Leomedon (was) the herald.

Crinis, son of Axileus, won the boy's pankration between 580 and 330 BCE.[616] He was from Ceos.[617] He is referenced in the above inscription.

[S]micyl[i]nes, son of Timarchus, won the boy's pankration between 580 and 330 BCE.[618] He was also from Ceos[619] and is listed in the above inscription.

Leocreon, son of Voleus, won the men's pankration between 536 and 534 BCE.[620] He was also from Ceos.[621] His name is listed in the inscription above.

Euthymenes, who was from Aegina,[622] won the men's pankration between 500 and 482 BCE. Pindar mentions him in *Isthmian 6* (l. 60-62).

Hagias of Pharsalus, known from the Olympian games, was also successful at the Isthmian men's pankration between 494 and 480 BCE.[623]

Phylacidas won the men's pankration twice at the Isthmia between 490 and 478 BCE. He was from Aegina[624] and the youngest son of Lampon. Pindar dedicated the fifth and sixth *Isthmian* odes to him.[625]

The Athenian Olympic victor **Callias**, son of Didymias, won the men's pankration between 486 and 458 BCE.[626]

Liparion, son of Liparus, had two wins in men's boxing and one in men's pankration between 484 and 432 BCE.[627] He was from Ceos.[628] His name is included in the inscription above.

Pheidippides, son of Liparus, won the youth pankration between 483 and 330 BCE.[629, 630] His name is also included in the inscription above.

---

616 IG. XII, 5. 1.13.
617 Farrington, "Isthmionikai," p. 42.
618 IG XII 5. 1.12.
619 Farrington, "Isthmionikai," p. 42.
620 IG. XII. 5. 11, 6-7.
621 Farrington, "Isthmionikai," p. 43.
622 Farrington, "Isthmionikai," p. 44.
623 Farrington, "Isthmionikai," p. 44.
624 Farrington, "Isthmionikai," p. 45.
625 Kostouros, *Nemeōn* 2, p. 192.
626 Farrington, "Isthmionikai," p. 45.
627 IG. XII. 5.11.4-5, 8.
628 Farrington, "Isthmionikai," pp. 45, 46.
629 IG XII. 5.1.9.
630 Farrington, "Isthmionikai," p. 46.

Cleandrus, who was from Aegina,[631] won the men's pankration between 478 and 476 BCE. Pindar dedicated the eighth *Isthmian* ode to him.

Ephoudion from Maenalus won the men's pankration between 470 and 460 BCE.[632]

Strepsiadas of Thebes won the men's pankration between 456 and 448 BCE.[633] Pindar dedicated the seventh *Isthmian* ode to him.

The great pankratiast **Dorieus**, son of Diagoras of Rhodes, won the men's pankration between 438 and 422 BCE.[634]

The great **Promachus**, son of Dryon of Pellene, won the men's pankration between 410 and 395 BCE.[635]

Diophanes, son of Empedion of Athens, won the men's pankration between 400 and 350 BCE.[636] Inscription **IG II² 3125**, found in Attica, records his success:

1 Διοφάνης
  Ἐμπεδίωνος
  νίκη Ἰσθμοῖ.
  Ἐμπεδίωνος παῖδες Ἀθηναῖο[ι] δύ' ἐνίκων,
5 **Διοφάνης** ἀγένειος ἐ[ν] Ἰσθμῶι πανκρατι[αστής],
  κα[ὶ] πρόγονος Στέφ[ανος]· ῥώμην δὲ χερῶν ἐπ[έ]δ[ει]ξ[αν].

Translated:
  Diophanes, son of Empedion
  victory: Isthmia
  two sons of Empedion of Athens won,
  Diophanes, a youth, at Isthmia, pankratiast,
  and his older brother, Stephanos; they showed great strength in their hands

The well-known Olympic victor **Sostratus**, son of Sosistratus of Sicyon, won the men's pankration twelve times at the Isthmia and Nemea between 370 and 348 BCE.[637]

Euancritus of Thebes won the boys' pankration between 315 and 280 BCE.[638] A reference to him is featured in the following inscription. It was

---

631 Farrington, "Isthmionikai," p. 46.
632 Farrington, "Isthmionikai," p. 47.
633 Farrington, "Isthmionikai," p. 47.
634 Farrington, "Isthmionikai," p. 48.
635 Farrington, "Isthmionikai," p. 48.
636 Farrington, "Isthmionikai," p. 48.
637 Farrington, "Isthmionikai," p. 49.
638 Farrington, "Isthmionikai," p.51.

found at Thebes and is dated at between 320 and 284 BCE. It is interesting that here, pankration is referred to as *pammachon*, which was another name for it:

IG VII 2470

1 πάμμαχον, ᾦ Θήβα, κρατέοντά με παῖδα[ς ἀγῶνα]
   καὶ τὸ πάλιν μεσάταν ἁλικίαν τις ἐρεῖ
   τοίας ἐκ προβολᾶς **εὐάγκριτον·** ἁ δὲ Νέμειος
   νίκα μοι λεκτῶν ἦλθεν ἀπ' ἠϊθέων
5 πατρὸς δῶμα Τρίακος· ἆεθλα γὰρ οἱ παρὰ Δίρκαι
   ἀμφαδὸν Ἑλλάνων πλεῖστα φέροντι νέοι.
   vacat
7 Τεισικράτης ἐποίησε.

Here is the translation:
> In the *pammachon*, oh Thebes, **Euancritus** won the boys' category and again in the medium age group who can say anything about his force in battle; my victory at the Nemea was against selected opponents, unmarried men from the house of the father Triax.
> The young men brought back many prizes from competitions, showing them to the Greeks.
> Made by Teisicrates

Nicon had two victories in men's pankration between 310 and 284 BCE.[639]

The exceptional **Cleitomachus**, son of Hermocrates of Thebes, also had three wins here on the same day in wrestling, boxing and men's pankration between 220 and 216 BCE.[640]

Straton / Stratonicus, son of Corrhagus of Alexandria, was victorious in wrestling or pankration between 68 and 60 BCE.[641]

[**Dio[genes**, son of Sosibius, won the men's pankration. The date is not known, but he was from Aegium.[642]

Olympic victor **Heras** of Laodiceia won the men's pankration between 35 and 55 BCE.[643]

Titus Flavius Asclep[i---] of Miletus won in wrestling and men's pankration between 75 and 120 BCE.[644]

---

639 Farrington, "Isthmionikai," p.51.
640 Farrington, "Isthmionikai," p. 53.
641 Farrington, "Isthmionikai," p. 54.
642 Farrington, "Isthmionikai," p. 57.
643 Farrington, "Isthmionikai," p. 59.
644 Farrington, "Isthmionikai," p. 61.

Titus Flavius Artemidorus, son of Artemidorus of Adana, won the youth (*ageneioi*) pankration between 81 and possibly 94 CE.[645]

There was a winner at this point in time whose name has not been recovered. However, it is known that he was from Sparta. He won in wrestling and pankration between 95 and 130 CE.[646] Here is the inscription that refers to him:

IG V, 1 658

[τὴν ἐξ Ἄργους ἀ]-
1 [σ]πίδα, Ἴσθμι[α],
κοινοὺς Ἀσί-
ας καὶ ἄλλους
πενταετηρι-
5 κοὺς πλίστους
[ἀ]<γῶ>νας, Διο-
σκούροις Σω-
τῆρσι καὶ Ἑρ-
μᾷ Ἀγωνίῳ·
10 ἐστεφανω-
μένος καὶ Οὐ[ρ]-
άνια β καὶ Λε-
ωνίδεια πάλην,
πανκράτιον.

Translated:
> [...](won) the shield of Argos, at the Isthmia, at the League of Asia and many other quinquennial games, at the Saviors Dioscouroi and the Hermean games;
> he was crowned twice at the Urania and at the Leonideia, in wrestling and pankration.

Secundus, who was from Ephesus,[647] won the men's pankration between 100 and 250 CE.

Publius Aelius Aristomachus had two wins in boys' pankration and youth pankration in 117 and 119 CE.[648]

Publius Aelius Heliodorus of Seleucia won the men's pankration between 125 and 150 CE.[649]

---

645 Farrington, "Isthmionikai," p. 61.
646 Farrington, "Isthmionikai," p. 62.
647 Farrington, "Isthmionikai," p. 62.
648 Farrington, "Isthmionikai," p. 62.
649 Farrington, "Isthmionikai," p. 64.

The name of the winner from Stymphalus in the men's pankration between 131 and 135 CE is unknown.[650] The related inscription was found at Corinth and is dated to the mid-second century CE. It is included here:

Corinth 8, 3 223

face a [— — — — — — — — — — — — —]-
1 ριαν [ωι — — — — — — — — — —]
ὑπάτοις. vac. [ἐπὶ ἀγωνοθέτου]
Λ. Γελλίου Μυστικο[ῦ τοῦ Γελλίου]
Μενάνδρου· ἑλλη[νοδικῶν δὲ]
5 Μ. Ἀντωνίου Κλημ[εντείνου, Τιβ.]
Κλαυδίου Μαξίμο[υ, Γν. Κορνηλίου]
Πούλχρου, Τιβ. Ἀππ[αληνοῦ Ἀνα]-
ξιλάου, Γ. Ἀβιδίου Π[— —, Τιβ.]
Κλαυδίου Μαξίμου [νεωτέρου, — —]
10 [. . . . . .] Ἰκεσίου, Π. Μ[— — —]
[. . . . . . Σ]τ[α]τίου Ο[— — — — —]
[— — — — — — — — — — — — —]
face b [— — — — — — —]
1 [διαύ]λους
[ὁ δεῖνα Κ]ορίνθιος
[πεντ]άθλους
[ὁ δεῖνα — —]ειος
5 [πά]λη<ν>
[ὁ δεῖνα — —] vac.
[πυ]γμήν
[ὁ δεῖνα Ἀλ]εξανδρεύ[ς]
[πανκρά]τιον
10 [ὁ δεῖνα **Στ]υμ[φάλιος**(?)]
[— — — — — —]

Translated:

[...] with –[---] consuls.
With agonothetes Lucius Gellius Mysticus Menander;
With Hellanodikai Marcus Antonius Clementinus, Tiberius Claudius Maximus, Gnaeus Cornelius Pulchro, Tiberius Apallinos Anaxilas, G. Avidius P[...], Tiberius Claudius Maximus the younger, [...] Icesius, P.M[...], Statius O[...].
[...]

---

650 Farrington, "Isthmionikai," p. 64.

At Diaulos (?)
a Corinthian
in the Pentathlon
an [...]eios?
in wrestling
[a...]
in boxing
someone from Alexandria
in pankration
someone from Stymphalus (?)
[...]

T. Flavius won the men's pankration between 150 and 175 CE.[651] The inscription found at Corinth and dated at between 150 and 175 CE which refers to him is included here:

Corinth 8,3 228

```
face a [— — — — — — — — — —]
    1  παῖδας [ἡλι]κίας
       Θαυμαστὸς Ἐπικτήτου Τεν<ε>άτη[ς]
       πα[νκράτιο]ν
       T. Φλάβ[ιος — — — — — — —]
    5  [— — — — — — — — — —]
face b [— — — — — — — — — — —]
    1  [— — — — — —]ς Κορίνθ[ι]ος
       [— — — — — —]χον ἔξαθλον ἐγέν-
       [ετο — — — —] vac.
       [— — — — — Κορ]ίνθιος
    5  [— — — — — — — — —]
face c [— — — — — — — — — —]
    1  [— — — — — — —]ν[— — —]
       [Π. Αἴ]λιος Φορτο[υνᾶτος]
       [Λικ(?)]ινιανός
       [. Ἀ]ππουλήιο[ς]
    5  [. . . .]ανος
       [— — — — — — —]
```

Here is the translation:
[...]

---

651 Farrington, "Isthmionikai," p. 67.

In the boys' category
The admired son of Epictetus of Tenea in pankration
Titus Flavius [...]
[...]
[...] Corinthian
[...] in the exathlon became [...]
Corinthian[...]
[---]
[---]
[---]
Aelius Fortunatus
Licinianus
Apuleius
[...]anos

Titus Aelius Aurelius Menander was the winner of the youth pankration between 154 and 169 CE.[652]

Aurelius Hygianus of Smyntheion won the boys' pankration or wrestling between 161 and 250 CE.[653]

Marcus Aurelius Corus of Thyateira won the boys' pankration and the youth pankration between 164 and 166 CE.[654] Here is the inscription referring to him which was found at Cyzicus and dated as later than 166 CE:

IMT Kyz Kapu Dağ 1496

1 **Μ. Αὐρήλιος Κόρος** Θυατειρηνὸς καὶ Κυ-
ζικηνὸς καὶ Ἀθηναῖος καὶ Τραλλιανὸς
καὶ Βυζάντιος, νεικήσας κοινὸν
Ἀσίας ἐν Κυ‹ζ›ίκῳ παίδων παν-
5 κράτιον πενταετηρίδι ζ', νεικήσας καὶ Τράλλ‹ε›ις Ὀλύμπια παίδων πανκράτιον καὶ Ἀδριάνεια
Ἀθήνας ἀγενείων πανκράτιον
καὶ Ἴσθμια ἀγενείων παν-
10 κράτιον, καὶ Ῥώμην Καπετώλεια ἀγενείων πανκράτιον·
καὶ κατὰ τὸ ἑξῆς Ῥώμην
ἐπινείκια ἀγενείων παν-

---

652 Farrington, "Isthmionikai," p. 67.
653 Farrington, "Isthmionikai," p. 68.
654 Farrington, "Isthmionikai," p. 68.

κράτιον τιμηθείς,
15 χρυσείῳ βραβείῳ.

Translated:
Marcus Aurelius Corus, of Thyateira and Cyzicus and Athens and Tralles and Byzantium, won the boys' pankration at the League of Asia in Cyzicus, seven times at the quinquennials, he also won at the Olympia in Tralles in boys' pankration, and at the Hadrianeia in Athens in youth pankration, and at the Isthmia in youth pankration, and at the Capitoline games in Rome in the youth pankration; and then he was honored in Rome with a gold trophy for youth pankration.

Marcus Aurelius Asclepiades, also known as Hermadorus, of Alexandria, twice won the men's pankration, in 179 and 181 CE.[655]

Hermas, son of Ision of Antioch, won the men's pankration between 20 and 45 CE.[656]

Tiberius Claudius Artemidorus of Tralles won the men's pankration between 65 and 80 CE.[657]

Marcus Ulpius Domesticus of Ephesus won the men's pankration between 110 and 130 CE.[658]

Marcus Aurelius Demetrius of Hermopolis won the men's pankration between 140 and 170 CE.[659]

Gaius Perelius Aurelius Alexander of Thyateira won the men's pankration between 210 and 230 CE.[660]

Candidianus Aphrodisias won the men's boxing or pankration between 250 and 300 CE.[661]

Piseas of Aphrodisias won at men's boxing or pankration between 250 and 300 CE.[662]

Menodorus, son of Gnaeus, of Athens, won the men's pankration between 145 and 130 CE.[663]

Titus Flavius Archibius of Alexandria won the men's pankration between 90 and 110 CE.[664]

---

655 Farrington, "Isthmionikai," p. 69.
656 Farrington, "Isthmionikai," p. 72.
657 Farrington, "Isthmionikai," p. 73.
658 Farrington, "Isthmionikai," p. 74.
659 Farrington, "Isthmionikai," p. 75.
660 Farrington, "Isthmionikai," p. 79.
661 Farrington, "Isthmionikai," p. 80.
662 Farrington, "Isthmionikai," p. 80.
663 Farrington, "Isthmionikai," p. 81.
664 Farrington, "Isthmionikai," p. 82.

TABLE 4: Names of Isthmian pankratiasts

	Name
1	Cimon, son of Campos
2	Crinis, son of Axileus
3	Smicylines, son of Timarchus
4	Leocreon, son of Voleus
5	Euthymenes
6	Hgias
7	Phylacidas
8	Callias
9	Liparion
10	Pheidippides
11	Cleandros
12	Ephoudion
13	Strepsiadas
14	Dorieus
15	Promachus
16	Diophanes
17	Sostratus
18	Euancritus
19	Nicon
20	Cleitomachus
21	Straton or Stratonicus
22	Diogenes
23	Heras
24	Titus Flavius Asclep[i--]
25	Titus Flavius Artemidorus
26	... of Laconia
27	Secundus
28	Publius Aelius Aristomachus
29	Publius Aelius Heliodorus
30	... of Stymphalus
31	T. Flavius
32	Titus Aelius Aurelius Menander
33	Aurelius Hygianus
34	Marcus Aurelius Corus
35	Marcus Aurelius Asclepiades
36	Hermas
37	Tiberius Claudius Artemidorus
38	Marcus Ulpius Domesticus
39	Marcus Aurelius Demetrius

	Name
40	Perelius Aurelius Alexander
41	Candidianus Aphrodisias
42	Piseas
43	Menodorus
44	Titus Flavius Archibius

The Nemean Victors

Agestratus suffered from continuous headaches and turned to the Temple of Asclepius for some relief. Once there, he entered the inner sanctuary (*abaton*) and fell asleep, dreaming that the god, having cured him, stood him up and taught him pankration. The next day, he left the *abaton* in perfect health and sometime later, he won at pankration at the Nemean games. It is not known whether the athlete in question was Hegestratus, son of Philon, who apparently also won at Nemea, though the event is unknown.[665] The inscription below was found at Epidaurus and is dated to the fourth century BCE. It tells this same story, as it would have been told 2,500 years ago:

IG IV², 1 122

50 (XXIX) Ἀγέστρατος κεφαλᾶς [ἄ]λγος· οὗτος ἀγρυπνίαις συνεχόμενος διὰ
τὸμ πόνον τᾶς κεφαλᾶ[ς], ὡς ἐν τῶι ἀβάτωι ἐγένετο, καθύπνωσε καὶ ἐν[ύ]-
πνιον εἶδε· ἐδόκει αὐτὸν ὁ θεὸς ἰασάμενος τὸ τᾶς κεφαλᾶς ἄλγος ὀρ-
θὸν ἀστάσας γυμνὸν παγκρατίου προβολὰν διδάξαι· ἁμέρας δὲ γενη-
θείσας ὑγιὴς ἐξῆλθε καὶ οὐ μετὰ πολὺν χρόνον τὰ Νέμεα ἐνίκασε
55 παγκράτιον. vac.

Here it is in translation:

> **Agestratus** had a headache; he had gone without sleep for many days in a row because of it. As it happens at the sacred *abaton*, he fell asleep there and had a dream; he believed the god cured his headache and stood him opposite, nude, to show him how to strike with force in pankration; the day that he became well, he left and after a time he won at Nemea in pankration.

The Olympian victor **Hagias**, son of Acnonius Aparus of Pharsalus, won five times at Nemea.[666]

---
665 Kostouros, *Nemeōn* 2, p. 32.
666 Kostouros, *Nemeōn* 2, p. 33.

Antenor of Athens or Miletus won at Nemea between 330 and 320 BCE and was a *periodonikēs*.[667]

Aristes, son of Pheidon of Cleonae, won at pankration at Nemea four times. His victories are dated at about 550 BCE.[668]

Aristocleides, son of Aristophanes of Aegina, won in about the mid-fifth century BCE. Pindar's ode *Nemean 3* is dedicated to him and refers to his victories at Epidaurus and Megara.[669]

Astyanax, of Miletus, a *periodonikēs*, won four times at Nemea (323, 321, 319 and 317 BCE) at boxing and pankration.[670]

Aurelius Septimius Eirenaeus, son of Eutychus of Laodicea, was a boxer. He was victorious at Leucada, Chalcis and the Ionion in boxing and foot races, at Cition in boxing and pankration, and at Hierapolis three times in boxing, wrestling and pankration.[671]

The inscription that follows was found at Laodicea and is dated at 214 CE. It is included here in its entirety:

IGLSyr 4 1265

1 **Αὐρήλιος Σεπτίμιος**, Εὐτύχ[ου]
   υἱός, **Εἰρηναῖος**, κολὼν Λα<ο>[δι]-
   κεὺς μητροπολείτης κα[ὶ]
   ἄλλων πόλεων πολείτης, μ[ό]-
5 νος ἐγὼ ἐκ τῆς ἑαυτοῦ πατρίδ[ος]
   ἀπὸ πάσης κρίσεως ἀγωνισάμενος καὶ νεικήσας τοὺς ὑποτε-
   ταγμένους ἀγῶνας·
   ἐν Αὐγούστῃ Καισαρείᾳ, Σεουήρειον οἰκουμενικὸν Πυθικόν,
10 πυγμήν· Αὐγούστου Ἄκτια ἐν Νεικοπόλει τῆς περιόδου,
   παίδων πυγμὴν ἐν Καισαρείᾳ Ἰσάκτιον, παίδων πυγμὴν
   ἐν Τύρῳ Ἡράκλεια Κομμόδεια, παίδων πυγμήν· ἐν Τάρσῳ
   Ἰσολύμπιον οἰκουμενικὸν Κομμόδειον, ἀγενείων πυγμήν·
   ἐν Λαοδικείᾳ τῇ πατρίδι μου, Πυθιάδι πρώτῃ ἀχθείσῃ,
15 οἰκουμενικὸν Ἀντωνεινιανόν, ἀνδρῶν πυγμήν· καὶ
   ἠγωνισάμην ἐπὶ τὸν στέφανον ἀνδρῶν πυγμὴν τῆς ἀρ-
   χαίας περιόδου Σεβάσμια Νέμια τῇ πρὸ τριῶν καλανδῶν
   Ἰανουαρίων ἐπὶ τῆς πενταετηρίδος, Μεσσάλᾳ καὶ Σαβ[ε]ί-

---

667 Kostouros, *Nemeōn* 2, p. 43.
668 Kostouros, *Nemeōn* 2, p. 46.
669 Kostouros, *Nemeōn* 2, p. 47.
670 Kostouros, *Nemeōn* 2, p. 49.
671 Kostouros, *Nemeōn* 2, p. 52.

νῳ ὑπάτοις.
20 ταλαντιαῖοι· Ἀσκάλω(να)· Σκυ<θ>όπολ[ιν]· Σειδῶνα τρίς· Τρίπο-
λιν δίς· Λευκάδα γ', πυγμήν, δρόμον· ['Ιε]ράνπολιν τρίς, πυγμήν,
πάλην, πανκράτιον· Βέροιαν δίς· Ζεῦγμα δίς· Ἀπάμειαν τρίς· Χαλκίδα
πυγμήν, δρόμον· Σαλαμεῖνα τρίς· Κίτιν, πυγμήν, πανκράτιον· Μάζακα β'·
Εἰκόνιν, πυγμήν, δρόμον· Ἀντιόχειαν· Πάτρας, πυγμήν, δρόμον· Τάραντον,
πυγμήν·
25 Αἰγαίας β'· Ἄδανα β'· Μάμψαστον β' ἔτους νεσ' μηνὸς Ξαν-
δικοῦ, ὑπάτων Οὐετίου Γράτου καὶ Οὐε[ιτι]λίου Σελεύκου.

Here is the translation:
Aurelius Septimius, son of Eutychus, **Eirenaeus**, of Laodicea and honorary citizen of other cities, the only one from my native land to compete and succeed in all of the trials and evaluations and won at the following contests;
At Hisareia Augusta, at the Severan ecumenical Pythian (games), in boxing;
at the Augustan Actia in Nicopolis in the circuit, in boys' boxing, at the Isactian games in Caesarea in boys' boxing, at Tyros at the Commodean Heracleian games in boys' boxing; in Tarsus at the ecumenical Isolympian Commodean games in youth boxing;
in Laodicea, my native land, on the opening day of the Pythia, at the ecumenical Antonine games, in men's boxing; and I competed for the crown (*stephanitēs* games) in men's boxing of the ancient period at the Augustan Nemea three days before the January calends during the quinquennial, when Messalus and Sabinus were consuls.

In the *talantiaioi*[672] (non-sacred) games; at Ascalon; at Scythopolis; at Sidon three times; at Tripoli twice; at Leucada three times, in boxing and on the track; at Hierapolis three times, in boxing, in wrestling, in pankration; at Beroea twice; at Zeugma twice; at Apameia three times; at Chalcis, in boxing and track; at Salamis three times; at Cition, in boxing, in pankration; at Mazaka twice; at Eicon, in boxing and track; at Antioch; at Patras, in boxing and track; at Taranto in boxing; at Aegae, twice; at Adana twice; at Mopsuestia twice in the month of Xandicus, under the consulate of Vettius Gratus and Vetilius Seleucus.

According to the London papyrus[673], **Aurelius Phoibammon**, son of Poseidonius of Egypt, was a *periodonikēs*.[674]

---

672 Translator's note: games in which winners received monetary prizes.
673 The London Medical Papyrus (10059) is an ancient Egyptian papyrus containing medical and magical recipes and is housed at the British Museum. It is dated at the end of the eighteenth dynasty of Egypt, at about 1350 BCE.
674 Kostouros, *Nemeōn* 2, p. 54.

Autolycus was clearly a Nemean champion. An Athenian pankratiast was known by the name of Autolycus in the fifth century BCE, and symbolized the Athenians' resistance against Spartan domination during the era of the Thirty Tyrants. He is referred to by Pausanias (1.18.3 and 9.32.8), Plato (Lysis, 15) and Pliny (34.79). He was put to death by the rule of Thirty Tyrants in 403 BCE.[675] An inscription about Autolycus was found at Delphi and is dated at 331 BCE. It is included here:

Hommages L. Lerat 841
A.1 **[Αὐτ]όλυκο[ς Ἀθηναῖος]**
 [πα]γκ[ρ]ατ[ιαστής].

B.1 [Αὐτ]όλυκος Ἀθη[ναῖος]
 [παγ]κ[ρ]ατ[ι]αστής
 [Λε]ωχά[ρ]ης [ἐποήσε].

Translated:
 Autolycus of Athens
 pankratiast
 Autolycus of Athens
 pankratiast
 Erected by Leochares

Gaius Perelius Aurelius Alexander lived in the period of Emperor Caracalla (Marcus Aurelius Severus Antoninus Augustus) and was a *periodonikēs* in pankration. His Olympic victory is estimated to have been at the 247th Olympian games in 209 CE.[676] His victory at the Nemea must have been at about the same time.

With regard to **Demetrius the Hermopolitan**, of Alexandria, an inscription found in Rome (**IGUR I 239** is included in its entirety in the "Olympic Victors" chapter) and dated at the late second century CE indicates that Demetrius of Hermopolis and Alexandria had been crowned a *periodonikēs* in pankration, like the son of Marcus Aurelius Asclepiades, also known as Hermodorus.[677]

Dorieus, son of the famous Diagoras of Rhodes, was a seven-time winner at Nemea. He was victorious in 437, 435, 433, 431, 429, 427 and 425 BCE.[678]

---
675 Kostouros, *Nemeōn* 2, p. 54.
676 Kostouros, *Nemeōn* 2, p. 58.
677 Kostouros, *Nemeōn* 2, p. 64.
678 Kostouros, *Nemeōn* 2, p. 72.

Hermas, son of Ision, of Syrian Antioch, won at the Nemea, the Actia and the Heraea in Argos. Some believe he could be one and the same as Tiberius Claudius Hermas.[679]

Euthymenes of Aegina was an uncle from Phylacidas' mother's side of the family (fifth century) with victories at Nemea (possibly in pankration).[680]

Ephoudion of Maenalus won at Nemea in 465 BCE and was a *periodonikēs*.[681]

Heras of Laodicea of Phrygia was a victor at Argos.[682] It is believed that he may have won at the Heraea[683], while others claim[684] it was certainly at Nemea and that later Heras became a *periodonikēs*.

The great **Theagenes** (also Theogenes) of Thasos won nine times at Nemea.[685]

Callias, son of Didymius, of Athens, had four victories at Nemea (483, 481, 479 and 477 BCE).[686]

Callistratus, son of Philothaleus, was from Sicyon. He had five wins at Nemea (one in boxing, two in pankration, two in boxing and pankration).[687]

Cimon, son of Campos of Ceos, is included among the Nemean victors, probably with a win in pankration.[688]

Leon, son of Myonides, had numerous victories in youth wrestling, and wrestling and pankration at Nemea.[689]

Marcus Aelius Aurelius Menander was a *periodonikēs* in pankration, a three-time winner at Nemea, once in boys' competition and twice in men's competition.[690]

Marcus Aurelius Asclepiades of Alexandria was a two-time winner at Nemea.[691]

Marcus Aurelius Demetrius of Alexandria was a *periodonikēs* with a victory in 146 CE at Nemea.[692]

---

679 Kostouros, *Nemeōn* 2, p. 77.
680 Kostouros, *Nemeōn* 2, p. 79.
681 Kostouros, *Nemeōn* 2, p. 81.
682 Kostouros, *Nemeōn* 2, p. 83.
683 Games in honor of the goddess Hera, held at her sanctuary in the region of Mycenae at Prosymna, 5 miles north-east of Argos in late June-early July. After the middle of the third century BCE they were celebrated in Argos along with the Nemea and were called the *Heraea of Argos*.
684 Knab, *Die Periodoniken*, No 36.
685 Kostouros, *Nemeōn* 2, p. 84.
686 Kostouros, *Nemeōn* 2, p. 90.
687 Kostouros, *Nemeōn* 2, p. 92.
688 Kostouros, *Nemeōn* 2, p. 93.
689 Kostouros, *Nemeōn* 2, p. 101.
690 Kostouros, *Nemeōn* 2, p. 105.
691 Kostouros, *Nemeōn* 2, p. 112.
692 Knab, *Die Periodoniken*, No 47, p. 71.

Marcus Aurelius Demostratus Damas was a two-time *periodonikēs* and winner at Nemea.[693]

Marcus Ulpius Domesticus was from Ephesus. He was a *periodonikēs* in pankration.[694] He was a victor at Nemea in 150 CE.[695]

Melesias of Athens is the athlete to whom Pindar dedicated his ode, *Olympian 8*. He was a victor in both youth and men's competition, and a winner in pankration at Nemea. He was the most famous trainer of his time.[696] Melesias trained the Nemean champion wrestler Alcimidas of Aegina, the son of Theon. The ode *Nemean 6* is dedicated to him. Melesias also trained the Aeginite Timasarchus, a winner in boys' wrestling at Nemea, a reference to whom is included in the ode *Nemean 4*.[697]

The Athenian **Menodorus**, son of Gnaeus, won at Nemea in men's wrestling, youth wrestling and men's pankration.[698] An inscription referring to him was found at Delos and is dated at between 150 and 130 BCE. It is included here in its entirety and includes information on his victories:

---

693 Kostouros, *Nemeōn* 2, p. 115.
694 Kostouros, *Nemeōn* 2, p. 129.
695 Knab, *Die Periodoniken*, No 48, pp. 71-72.
696 Albanidis, *Istoria tēs athlēsēs*, p. 231.
697 Kostouros, *Nemeōn* 2, p. 133.
698 Kostouros, *Nemeōn* 2, p. 134.

ID 1957

a.1 **Μηνόδωρον** Γναίου Ἀθηναῖον, νικήσαντα τὴν περίοδον καὶ τοὺς ἄλλους ἱεροὺς ἀγῶνας, Δημήτριος Ἀπολλοδότου Ἀντιοχεύς, Ἀπόλλωνι.

b,1,cr 1.1 Ἐλευσίνια ἄνδρας παγκράτιον.
b,1,cr 2.1 [Πανα]θήναια] ἄνδρας παγκρά-
5 τιον.
b,1,cr 3.1 Ὀλύμπια [ἄνδρας] [πάλην].
b,1,cr 4.1 Σωτήρια ἄνδρας παγκράτιον.
b,1,cr 5.1 — — — ἄνδρας παγκράτιον.
b,1,cr 6.1 Νέμεα ἄνδρας πάλην.
b,1,cr 7.1 Ἐ[λε]υσίνια ἀγενείους πά-
5 λην.
b,1,cr 8.1 Νέμεα [ἄνδ]ρας παγκράτιον.
b,1,cr 9.1 Ἐλευσίνια ἄνδρας πάλην.
b,2,cr 10.1 Νέμεα ἀγενείους πάλην.
b,2,cr 11.1 Ἡράκλεια τὰ ἐν Θήβαις ἄνδρας
5 παγκράτιον.
b,2,cr 12.1 ΠαναΘήναια ἄνδρας παγκρά-
5 τιον.
b,2,cr 13.1 Δήλια τὰ ἐν Δήλωι ἄνδρας πάλην.
b,2,cr 14.1 Ῥωμαῖα τὰ ἐν Χαλκίδι ἄνδρας
5 παγκράτιον.
b,2,cr 15.1 Ἡραῖα τὰ ἐν Ἄργει ἄνδρας πάλην.
b,2,cr 16.1 Λύκαια ἄνδρας παγκράτιον.
b,2,cr 17.1 Ἡράκλεια τὰ ἐν Θήβαις

	ἄνδρας		Δωδώνη
5	παγκρά-		ἄνδρας
	τιον.		πάλην.
b,2,cr 18.1	Σωτήρια	b,3,cr 26.1	Τροφώνια
	τὰ ἐν		τὰ ἐν
	Δελφοῖς		Λεβαδείᾳ
	ἄνδρας		ἄνδρας
5	πάλην.	5	πάλην.
b,3,cr 19.1	Ῥωμαῖα	b,3,cr 27.1	Νυμφαῖα
	τὰ ἐν		τ[ὰ] ἐν
	Χαλκίδι		Ἀπολλω-
	ἄνδρας		[νίᾳ]
5	πάλην.	5	ἄνδρας
b,3,cr 20.1	Ἡραῖα τὰ		παγκρά-
	ἐν Ἄργει		τιον.
	ἄνδρας	b,4,cr 28.1	Νᾶα τὰ ἐν
	παγκρά-		Δωδώνη
5	τιον.		ἄνδρας
b,3,cr 21.1	Ἡράκλεια		παγκρά-
	τὰ ἐν	5	τιον.
	Θήβαις	b,4,cr 29.1	Τροφώνια
	ἄνδρας		τὰ ἐν
5	παγκρά-		Λεβαδείᾳ
	τιον.		ἄνδρας
b,3,cr 22.1	Ὀλύμπια	5	παγκρά-
	ἄνδρας		τιον.
	παγκρά-	b,4,cr 30.1	Ἡράκλεια
	τιον.		τὰ ἐν
b,3,cr 23.1	Ἡράκλεια		Θήβαις
	τὰ ἐν		ἄνδρας
	Θήβαις	5	παγκρά-
	ἄνδρας		τιον.
5	πάλην.	b,4,cr 31.1	Νυμφαῖα
b,3,cr 24.1	Σωτήρια		ἄνδρας
	τὰ ἐν		πάλην.
	Δελφοῖς	b,4,cr 32.1	Ἡράκλεια
	ἄνδρας		τὰ ἐν
5	παγκρά-		Θήβαις
	τιον.		ἄνδρας
b,3,cr 25.1	Νᾶα τὰ ἐν	5	πάλην.

b,4,cr 33.1 ὁ δῆμος
ὁ Ἀθη-
ναίων.
b,4,cr 34.1 ὁ δῆμος
ὁ Ῥοδίων
τῷ ξενίῳ.
b,4,cr 35.1 ὁ δῆμος
ὁ Θηβαίων
τῶν ἐν
Βοιωτίαι.
b,4,cr 36.1 βασιλεὺ[ς]
Ἀριαρά-
θης.

Translated:

Menodorus the Athenian, son of Gnaeus, who won the circuit and at other sacred games in honor of Apollo.
Demetrius, son of Apollodotus the Antiochian.
At the Eleusinia
in men's pankration
At the Panathenaea
in men's pankration
At the Olympia
in men's wrestling.
At the Soteria
in men's pankration.
[---]
in men's pankration
At the Nemea,
in men's wrestling.
At the Eleusinia
in youth wrestling.
At Nemea
in men's pankration.
At the Eleusinia
in men's wrestling.
At Nemea
in youth wrestling.
At the Heracleia in Thebes
in men's pankration.
At the Panathenaea
in men's pankration.
At the Deleia in Delos
in men's wrestling.
At the Romaea in Chalcis
in men's pankration.
At the Heraea in Argos
in men's wrestling.
at the Lycaea
in men's pankration.
At the Heracleia in Thebes
in men's pankration.
At the Soteria in Delphi
in men's wrestling.
At the Romaea in Chalcis
in men's wrestling.
At the Heraea in Argos
in men's pankration.
At the Heracleia in Thebes
in men's pankration.
At the Olympia
in men's pankration.
At the Heracleia in Thebes
in men's wrestling.
At the Soteria in Delphi
in men's pankration.
At the Naea in Dodona
in men's wrestling.
At the Trophonea in Lebadeia
in men's wrestling.
At the Nymphaea in Apollonia
in men's pankration.
At the Naea in Dodona
in men's pankration.
At the Trophonea in Lebadeia
in men's pankration.
At the Heracleia in Thebes
in men's pankration.
At the Nymphaea
in men's pankration.

> At the Heracleia in Thebes
> in men's wrestling.
> The citizens of Athens
> The citizens of Rhodes
> in honor of Xenios Zeus
> The citizens of Thebes in Boeotia
> King Ariarathes.

Nicon the Boeotian of Anthedon of Boeotia, won four times at Nemea, and was twice *periodonikēs*.[699]

Xenarches, son of Philandrides, was the first winner to emerge from Stratus in Acarnania (Pausanias 6.2.1). His statue was made by Lysippos. It is likely he had a victory at the 98th Olympics in 388 BCE.[700]

Publius Aelius Aristomachus had victories in boys' competition at Nemea.[701]

Promachus, son of Dryon, of Pellene, had two wins at Nemea (Pausanias 6.8.6).[702]

Pytheas, son of Lampon, of Aegina, won at Nemea in the youth category. He was the eldest son of Lampon, who, according to Herodotus (9.78-79), took part in the battle of Plataea. Pindar dedicated his ode *Nemean 5* to Pytheas in which we learn that his grandfather on his mother's side, Themistius, also had a double victory in boxing and pankration at Epidaurus and in fact had laid his bay laurel wreaths of victory at the shrine of Aeacus in Aegina. Pytheas also trained the younger brother of Phylacidas, also a victor at Nemea and Isthmus. Pytheas is described as a skilled boxer with exceptional strength in his hands. Like his brother and his uncle from his mother's side, Euthymenes, Pytheas also won at Isthmus in addition to Nemea. He was also victorious at his birthplace of Aegina and at Megara; his trainer was always Menander the Athenian. Pytheas' victory at Nemea was also memorialized by Bacchylides in his thirteenth epinicean victory song, in which he also refers to the particular care provided by the trainer Menander to his athlete.[703]

Straton or Stratonicus, son of Corrhagus, of Alexandria, won four times at Nemea - in wrestling and in boys' and youth pankration.[704]

---

699 Kostouros, *Nemeōn* 2, p. 144.
700 Kostouros, *Nemeōn* 2, p. 144.
701 Kostouros, *Nemeōn* 2, p. 158.
702 Kostouros, *Nemeōn* 2, p. 165.
703 Kostouros, *Nemeōn* 2, p. 167.
704 Kostouros, *Nemeōn* 2, p. 169.

Sostratus, son of Sosistratus, of Sicyon, was a *periodonikēs*. He collected a total of twelve victories at the Nemea and Isthmia.[705]

Tiberius Claudius Artemidorus was a two-time winner at Nemea.[706]

Timarchus, son of Demaenetus, won in pankration at the Nemea and the Isthmia.[707]

Timodemus, son of Timonous of Acharnae in Attica, a descendant of the Timodemus family, had won seven crowns at Nemea, where he earned his first victory. The ode Nemean 2 is dedicated to him.[708] Timodemus probably grew up in Salamis. Ajax and Timodemus are considered examples of the great fighters produced by Salamis. Ajax, the son of Telamon, was a famous strong man in antiquity. He could easily square off against a pankratiast. He was the strongest and best Achaean after Achilles.[709]

Titus Flavius Artemidorus had two wins in men's pankration at Nemea.[710]

Titus Flavius Archibius of Alexandria won three times in men's pankration at Nemea and was also a *periodonikēs*.[711]

Philippus Glycon, son of Asclepiades, of Pergamon, also won at Argos. It is not clear whether this victory was achieved at the Heraea or at the Nemea, which is more likely. He was also a *periodonikēs*.[712]

Phylacidas, son of Lampon, of Aegina, of the Psalychids family, was the youngest son of Lampon, with two wins at the Isthmia and one at Nemea. His older brother, Pytheas, was his teacher and trainer. Pindar dedicated the fifth and sixth *Isthmian* odes to him.[713]

An elegiac funerary inscription, Ephesos 2092, includes references to numerous wins of an unknown pankratiast at Olympia and Nemea.[714] It is included here:

---

705 Kostouros, *Nemeōn* 2, p. 172.
706 Moretti, *Olympionikai*, No 815, 820.
707 Kostouros, *Nemeōn* 2, p. 178.
708 Kostouros, *Nemeōn* 2, p. 180.
709 Stephen Instone, "Pindar's Enigmatic *Second Nemean*," *Bulletin of the Institute of Classical Studies* 36, no. 1 (December 1989): p. 115.
710 Kostouros, *Nemeōn* 2, p. 183.
711 Kostouros, *Nemeōn* 2, p. 184.
712 Kostouros, *Nemeōn* 2, p. 191.
713 Kostouros, *Nemeōn* 2, p. 192.
714 Kostouros, *Nemeōn* 2, p. 209.

Ephesos 2092

1 [—]νους Α[—]
  ἔνθα πάτρα μοι σῆμα
  τὸ λοίσθιον ἵνεκα δόξ[ης]
  ὤπασε τῷ Πίσας δισ[σά]-
5 κις ἀθλοφόρωι,
  ὅν ποτε καὶ Λερναῖα [πε]-
  ρὶ κροτάφοισι σέλ[ινα]
  ἔστεφε καὶ πολλῶ[ν]
  νίκεα πανκρατίω[ν·]
10 τὰς δὲ παρ' Ἀλφηῷ τ[ιμὰς]
  καὶ Ζηνὶ Νεμήωι
  οὗτος ὁ δυσπενθ[ὴς]
  τύνβος ἐνοσφίσα[το.]

Translated:
> [...]nus A[...](thenean?)
> here is the sign of my fatherland, the last in the name of glory, offered to the winner [...] of Pisa, whom at some point he crowned with a wreath of celery round his temple and with many other epinicea for pankration; these honors from Alpheus and Nemean Zeus, this mournful tomb took far away.

The athlete [-] **us** [-], **son of Aristeas Corazeus**, was a pankration athlete. The younger was a winner in the youth category at the Nemea and Actia games, at a competition of the Asian League, as well as the Olympian and Pythian games, and possibly at Isthmia. He was also a *periodonikēs*. This may have been the son of Stratoniceian wrestler Aristeas, who was twice an Olympic victor. Pausanias (5.21.10) included him among those athletes who came after Straton of Alexandria and managed to get a double victory in the same games.[715]

Titus Flavius Asclep[...] was a wrestler and pankratiast, winning three times at Nemea, twice at Isthmia and Great Actia as well as at a number of sacred games in Asia. He had also won the shield of Argos twice.[716]

There are also references to the victories of an unknown pankratiast in Lesvos, in many cities of Asia and at Nemea. The text referring to each location and the event (pankration) appears within relief wreaths.[717]

---

[715] Kostouros, *Nemeōn* 2, p. 214.
[716] Kostouros, *Nemeōn* 2, p. 219.
[717] Kostouros, *Nemeōn* 2, p. 224.

TABLE 5: Names of Nemean pankratiasts

	Name
1	Agestratus
2	Hagias
3	Antenor
4	Aristes
5	Aristocleides
6	Astyanax
7	Aurelius Septimius
8	Aurelius Phoibammon
9	Autolycus
10	Perelius Aurelius Alexander
11	Demetrius the Hermopolitan
12	Dorieus
13	Hermas
14	Euthymenes
15	Ephoudion
16	Heras
17	Theagenes
18	Callias
19	Callistratus
20	Cimon,
21	Leon,
22	Marcus Aelius Aurelius Menander
23	Marcus Aurelius Asclepiades
24	Marcus Aurelius Demetrius
25	Marcus Aurelius Demostratus Damas
26	Marcus Ulpius Domesticus
27	Melesias
28	Menodorus
29	Nicon
30	Xenarches
31	Publius Aelius Aristomachus
32	Promachus
33	Pytheas
34	Straton or Stratonicus
35	Sostratus
36	Tiberius Claudius Artemidorus
37	Timarchus
38	Timodemus
39	Titus Flavius Artemidorus

	Name
40	Titus Flavius Archibius
41	Philippus Glycon
42	Phylacidas
43	………..
44	[-] us [-] of Aristeas Corazeus
45	Titus Flavius Asclep[--]
46	………..

The Pythian Victors

Marcus Aelius Aurelius Menander of Caria was the pankration winner in 165 BCE. He is considered the most well-traveled athlete of his time and for good reason: he had competed almost everywhere. Count the places: Italy, Achaea, Lesvos, Bithynia, Mysia, Lydia, Ionia, Gaul, Phrygia, Cilicia, Syria, Phoenicia, Arabia and Mesopotamia.[718] He was also victorious at the Sebastan (or Augustan) Games at Naples, at the Balbilleia at Ephesus, at Smyrna, the Panathenaic and Olympian games at Athens, the Capitoline Games at Rome, at Lesvos, Nicomedia, Prusias, Claudiopolis, Ankara of Galatia, Pessinos, Damascus, Beirut, Tyrus, Caesarea Stratonis, Neapolis of Samaria, Scythopolis, Gaza, Paneas Caesarea, Hierapolis, Anazarbus, Mopsuestia, Tripolis of Syria, Philadelphia of Arabia, the city of Zeugma on the River Euphrates and at Cibyra.[719] Keep in mind that traveling from one city to another was no easy feat, as it is today. Roads were practically non-existent, animals were the usual mode of transport, and risks included thieves. Traveling by sea on ships of that era, mostly sailing ships, involved months-long journeys and was always under threats of pirates. In addition, the athletes had to find time to prepare for competition.

Aurelius Achilleus, of Ephesus, Ionia, won in pankration between 215 and 250 or 260 BCE. He had also appeared at games in Achaea.[720]

Marcus Aelius Asclepiades Hermodorus of Alexandria in Egypt was the pankration winner in 200 BCE. He had competed in Italy, Achaea, Mace-

---

718 Weir, *Roman Delphi*, p. 125.
719 Kostouros, *Nemeōn* 2, p. 105.
720 Weir, *Roman Delphi*, p. 126.

donia, Bithynia, Mysia, Lydia, Ionia, Egypt and Rhodes.[721] He also took part in many competitions in Italy, Greece and Asia. He was twice a Nemean victor.[722]

The outstanding **Marcus Aurelius Demostratus Damas** of Sardis was a two-time winner at Nemea in 180 BCE in pankration and boxing, while he also competed in Italy, Achaea, Macedonia, Bithynia, Mysia, Lydia, Ionia, Egypt and Rhodes.[723]

Marcus Aurelius Thelymetrus I and II, of Miletus in Ionia, were victors in the late second century in pankration, but they were apparently also present at the Achaean games.[724]

Tiberius Claudius Artemidorus won in pankration between 96 and 98 CE.[725]

Democrates of Magnesia in Ionia won in pankration, boxing and wrestling. He took part in competition at Achaea, Macedonia, Mysia, Ionia, Lydia, Lycia and Cappadocia in Syria.[726]

Titus Flavius Archibius of Alexandria in Egypt had victories in youth pankration, in wrestling and men's pankration at the Pythian games.[727]

Flavius Artemidorus of Adana, Cilicia, had two victories in men's pankration at the Pythian games.[728]

Menander, of Myra in Lycia, won in pankration in the second century, and was known to be present at the Achaean games.[729]

It is not clear whether the victory of **Philippus Glycon**, son of Asclepiades of Pergamon, at Argos was achieved at the Heraea or at the Nemea, which is more likely. He was also a *periodonikēs*.[730] He won in pankration and either in boxing or in wrestling in 125 CE.[731]

The Olympian **Hagias**, son of Acnonius, of Pharsalus, won three times at the Pythian Games. This was recorded in an inscription on the base of the Daochos II monument, as we saw earlier in the section on the Olympian victors.[732]

---

721 Weir, *Roman Delphi*, p. 126.
722 Kostouros, *Nemeōn 2*, p. 112.
723 Weir, *Roman Delphi*, p. 126.
724 Weir, *Roman Delphi*, p. 126.
725 Weir, *Roman Delphi*, p. 127.
726 Weir, *Roman Delphi*, p. 127.
727 Kostouros, *Nemeōn 2*, p. 184.
728 Kostouros, *Nemeōn 2*, p. 183.
729 Weir, *Roman Delphi*, p. 128.
730 Kostouros, *Nemeōn 2*, p. 191.
731 Weir, *Roman Delphi*, p. 128.
732 Kostouros, *Nemeōn 2*, p. 33.

Gaius Perelius Aurelius Alexander lived in the period of Emperor Caracalla (Marcus Aurelius Severus Antoninus Augustus) and was a *periodonikēs* in pankration. He most likely won at the 247th Olympian Games in 209 CE.[733]

Information about **Demetrius the Hermopolitan**, of Alexandria, is gleaned from an inscription found in Rome (**IGUR I 239**, which refers to the Olympian winners), dated to the late second century CE. It indicates that Demetrius of Hermopolis and Alexandria had been crowned a *periodonikēs* in pankration, just as the son of Marcus Aurelius Asclepiades, also known as Hermodorus.[734]

Ephoudion of Maenalus won at the Pythian games in 466 BCE as a *periodonikēs*.[735]

Heras of Laodicea of Phrygia was a winner at Pergamon, Smyrna, Actium, Delphi and Argos.[736]

The great **Theagenes** (also Theogenes) of Thasos won three times at the Pythian games.[737]

Callias the Athenian had two victories at the Pythian games.[738]

Leon, son of Myonides, had numerous victories in youth wrestling, and wrestling and pankration in the men's category. He was one of the most traveled athletes with participations at the Olympic, Isthmian, Nemean and Pythian games, the Heraea at Argos, the Hyacinthia at Cnidus, the Heracleia at Thebes, the Epiphaneia at Chios, the Dieia at Tralles and at the Romaea. He is believed to be from Elis or Rhodes.[739]

Marcus Ulpius Domesticus was a *periodonikēs* in pankration.[740]

The outstanding athlete **Nicon**, a two-time *periodonikēs* originally from Boeotia, also had two victories at the Pythian games.[741]

Sostratus, son of Sosistratus, of Sicyon, was a *periodonikēs* with two wins at the Pythian games.[742]

Timodemus, son of Timonous, of Acharnae, Athens, won four times at the Pythian games.[743]

---

733 Kostouros, *Nemeōn* 2, p. 58.
734 Kostouros, *Nemeōn* 2, p. 64.
735 Kostouros, *Nemeōn* 2, p. 81.
736 Kostouros, *Nemeōn* 2, p. 83.
737 Kostouros, *Nemeōn* 2, p. 84.
738 Kostouros, *Nemeōn* 2, p. 90.
739 Kostouros, *Nemeōn* 2, p. 101.
740 Kostouros, *Nemeōn* 2, p. 129.
741 Kostouros, *Nemeōn* 2, p. 144.
742 Kostouros, *Nemeōn* 2, p. 172.
743 Kostouros, *Nemeōn* 2, p. 180.

[-] us [-] of Aristeas Corazeus was a winner at the Pythian games, probably in the youth category.[744]

TABLE 6: Names of Pythian pankratiasts

	Name
1	Marcus Aelius Aurelius Menander
2	Aurelius Achilleus
3	Marcus Aurelius Asclepiades (Hermodorus)
4	Marcus Aurelius Demostratus Damas
5	Marcus Aurelius Thelymetrus I
6	Marcus Aurelius Thelymetrus II
7	Tiberius Claudius Artemidorus
8	Democrates
9	Titus Flavius Archibius
10	Flavius Artemidorus
11	Menander
12	Philippus Glycon
13	Hagias
14	Perelius Aurelius Alexander
15	Demetrius the Hermopolitan
16	Ephoudion or Ephotion
17	Heras
18	Theagenes
19	Callias
20	Leon, son of Myonides
21	Marcus Ulpius Domesticus
22	Nicon
23	Sostratus
24	Timodemus
25	[-] us [-] of Aristeas Corazeus

The Periodonikēs

A *periodonikēs* was someone who had won at all four sacred games (*hieroi agones*) - the Olympian, Isthmian, Nemean and Pythian games - in the circuit. The *periodos* was the four-year period between the Olympian games, which was also known as an Olympiad, during which the sacred games took place.

---

744 Kostouros, *Nemeōn* 2, p. 214.

Most *periodonikēs* were heavy event athletes and this may be due to the fact that a heavy athlete could stay in better shape longer than a track athlete.[745] One explanation may be that the heavy events were more complex. This meant that aside from their physical abilities, athletes also had to have good perception, imagination, tactics and strategy. With experience, these skills were developed and could be put to use even if the athletes were no longer in peak physical form. By comparison, the track events were based only on physical conditioning, which could not be maintained at peak level for an extended period of time.

There is information on twenty-two *periodonikēs* pankratiasts and one *periodonikēs* pankratiast in the boys' category. At this level of skill, it is exciting to count the number of wins for each athlete. They would literally sweep up the crowns, but they also had considerable staying power at this high level of competition. It is important to remember that there were no weight classes in pankration, and that the match would end either by withdrawal or by knock-out. This means that any reference to a victory implies that all losing participants had been defeated without question. We have already seen many of these great athletes winning at the sacred games, as mentioned earlier. It is possible to supplement information about them by cross-referencing details from other sources.

The first periodonikēs was the Athenian, **Callias**. He had won at Olympia in 472 BCE, at Nemea (483, 481, 479 and 475 BCE), at Isthmia (482, 480 and 474 BCE) and at the Pythian games (478 and 474 BCE).[746]

Ephotion of Maenalus in Arcadia had won at Olympia in 464 BCE, at Isthmia in 464, at Nemea in 465 and at the Pythian games in 466 BCE, rounding out the circuit.[747]

Hagias, of Pharsalus in Thessaly, had won at the 85th Olympian games in 440 BCE, at the Pythian games (450, 446 and 442 BCE), at Isthmia (450, 448, 446, 444, 442 and 440 BCE) and at Nemea (449, 447, 445, 443 and 441 BCE).[748]

Dorieus, the younger son of Diagoras of Rhodes, was also a great athlete, winning three times at Olympia (432, 428 and 424 BCE), eight times at Isthmia (438, 436, 434, 432, 430, 428, 426 and 424 BCE), four times at the Pythian games (438, 434, 430 and 426 BCE) and seven at Nemea (437, 435, 433, 431, 429, 427 and 425 BCE).[749]

Sostratus, son of Sosistratus, was a three-time Olympian victor (364, 360 and 356 BCE), a two-time winner at the Pythian games (362 and 358

---

745 Knab, *Die Periodoniken*, p. 6.
746 Knab, *Die Periodoniken*, No 5, pp. 53-55.
747 Knab, *Die Periodoniken*, No 10, pp. 55-56.
748 Knab, *Die Periodoniken*, No 11, 12, pp. 56-57.
749 Knab, *Die Periodoniken*, No 13, pp. 57-58.

BCE); he won six times at Isthmia (366, 364, 362, 360, 358 and 356 BCE) and six times at Nemea (367, 365, 363, 361, 359 and 357 BCE).[750]

Astyanax of Miletus was a three-time Olympian winner (324 and 320 and *akoniti* in 316 BCE) in boxing and pankration, a two-time winner at the Pythian games (322 and 318 BCE), five times at Isthmia (324, 322, 320, 318 and 316 BCE) and four times at Nemea (323, 321, 319 and 317 BCE). Each time, he won at both boxing and pankration.[751]

Antenor of Miletus had won at two Olympian games *akoniti* in 312 and 308 BCE, at the Pythian games in 314 in the boys' category and in 310 BCE in men's, at Isthmia in 314 in the boy's category, in 312 in the youth category, in 310 and 308 BCE in men's and at Nemea in 315 in the boys' category, in 313 in youth, and in 311 and 309 BCE in men's.[752]

Nicon the Boeotian had won at two Olympian games (300 and 296 BCE), at the Pythian games (302 and 298 BCE), at Isthmia (302, 300, 298 and 296 BCE) and at Nemea (303, 301, 299 and 297 BCE).[753]

Menodorus the Athenian won at the 155th Olympian games in 160 BCE and in 162 at the Pythian games, and at Isthmia and Nemea in 165 as a youth and in 163 and 161 BCE in the men's category.[754]

Straton of Alexandria had two Olympic wins in 68 BCE in wrestling and pankration, and in 64 BCE only in pankration. He had also won at the Pythian games in 66 BCE, at Isthmia (70, 68, 66 and 64 BCE) and at Nemea in 73 BCE in the boys' category. But in 71 BCE, he managed something that was unheard of: he had four victories in the boys' and youth categories in wrestling and pankration in a single day. He also won in 67 and 65 BCE. In all competitions, he took part in both events.[755]

Philippus Glycon of Pergamon won for the first time at the 189th Olympian games in 24 BCE in boys' pankration. His second win was in the men's category in 20 BCE. He also won at the Pythian games in 22 BCE, at Isthmia in 20 BCE and at Nemea in 23 and 21 BCE.[756]

Hermas of Antiochia won at the 191st and 192nd Olympian games in 16 and 12 BCE, at the Pythian games in 14 BCE, at Isthmia in 12 BCE, at Nemea in 15 and 13 BCE, and at the Actia and Heraea in 19, 18, 17 and 16 BCE.[757]

---

750 Knab, *Die Periodoniken*, No 15, p. 59.
751 Knab, *Die Periodoniken*, No 17, p. 60.
752 Knab, *Die Periodoniken*, No 18, pp. 60-61.
753 Knab, *Die Periodoniken*, No 21, pp. 61-62.
754 Knab, *Die Periodoniken*, No 29, p. 65.
755 Knab, *Die Periodoniken*, No 32, pp. 65-66.
756 Knab, *Die Periodoniken*, No 34, pp. 66-67.
757 Knab, *Die Periodoniken*, No 35, p. 67.

Heras of Laodicea of Phrygia won in 21 CE at the Olympic games in Smyrna and Pergamon, at Olympia in 25 CE, at the Pythian and Isthmian games in 23 and at Nemea in 22 and 24 CE.[758]

The **son of Aristeas** of Stratoniceia won in 35 CE at the Actian games in the youth category, in 39 CE at the Pythian and Isthmian games, in 41 CE at the 205th Olympian games and in 38 and 40 CE at Nemea.[759]

Titus Flavius Artemidorus of Adana, Cilicia, won twice at the Olympian games in 81 and 85 CE, twice at the Pythian games (79 and 83 CE), at Isthmia in 77 CE in the youth category and in 81 CE in wrestling and pankration and again in 83 CE. He also won twice at Nemea (82 and 84 CE) and once at the Capitoline games in Rome in 86 CE.[760]

Titus Flavius Archibius of Alexandria won at two Olympian games -the 220th and 221st in 101 and 105 CE, in 94 CE at Naples in the youth category, as a youth in 94 CE and in the men's category at the Capitolia in 98 and 106 CE, at the Pythian games in 94 CE in boys', in 99 CE in men's wrestling and pankration and in 103 CE in men's. He also won once at Isthmia (103 CE) and three times at Nemea (100, 102 and 104 CE).[761]

The only *periodonikēs* to achieve success at a young age was **Aristomachus**. He won at the Pythian and Isthmian games in 115 CE. He also won at Nemea in 116 CE in the boys' category, meaning before he was even sixteen years old. He also won at the Isthmian games in youth pankration in 117 CE and at Olympia in the men's category in the same year.[762]

Marcus Ulpius Domesticus of Ephesus won in 135 CE at the Pythian and Isthmian games, in 134 CE at Nemea and in 137 CE at Olympia.[763]

Marcus Aurelius Demetrius of Hermopolis completed the circuit by winning in 146 CE at Nemea, in 147 CE at the Pythian and Isthmian games and in 149 CE at the 232nd Olympics.[764]

Marcus Ulpius Firmus Domesticus won at Nemea in 150 CE, at the Pythian and Isthmian games in 151 CE and at Olympia in 153 CE.[765]

Marcus Aurelius Asclepiades won at Olympia in 181 CE, once at the Pythian games in 179 CE, twice at Isthmia, in 179 and 181 CE, and twice at Nemea, in 178 and 180 CE.[766]

---

758 Knab, *Die Periodoniken*, No 36, p. 67.
759 Knab, *Die Periodoniken*, No 38, p. 68.
760 Knab, *Die Periodoniken*, No 40, pp. 68-69.
761 Knab, *Die Periodoniken*, No 42, pp. 69-70.
762 Knab, *Die Periodoniken*, p. 70.
763 Knab, *Die Periodoniken*, No 45, p. 71.
764 Knab, *Die Periodoniken*, No 47, p. 71.
765 Knab, *Die Periodoniken*, No 48, pp. 71-72.
766 Knab, *Die Periodoniken*, No 51, p. 72.

Marcus Aurelius Demostratus Damas of Sardis won two times each at Olympia (189 and 193 CE), at the Pythian and Isthmian games (187 and 191 CE) and at Nemea (188 and 190 CE).[767]

Claudius Apollonius of Smyrna completed the circuit by winning in 285 CE at Olympia, in 283 at the Pythian and Isthmian games, and in 282 and 284 CE at Nemea.[768]

Claudius Rufus won at two Olympiads (301 and 305 CE), at the Pythian games (299 and 303 CE), at Isthmia (303 CE) and at Nemea (300 and 302 CE).[769]

TABLE 7: Names of periodonikes pankratiasts

	Name
1	Callias
2	Ephotion
3	Hagias
4	Dorieus
5	Sostratus
6	Astyanax
7	Antenor
8	Nicon
9	Menodorus
10	Straton
11	Philippus Glycon of Pergamon
12	Hermas
13	Heras
14	son of Aristeas of Stratoniceia
15	Titus Flavius Artemidorus
16	Titus Flavius Archibius
17	Aristomachus
18	Marcus Ulpius Domesticus
19	Marcus Aurelius Demetrius
20	Marcus Ulpius Firmus Domesticus
21	Marcus Aurelius Asclepiades
22	Marcus Aurelius Demostratus Damas
23	Claudius Apollonius
24	Claudius Rufus

---

767 Knab, *Die Periodoniken*, No 52, pp. 72-73.
768 Knab, *Die Periodoniken*, No 55, p. 74.
769 Knab, *Die Periodoniken*, p. 74.

The *aph' Hēracleous* athletes

These *aph' Hēracleous* athletes ("successors of Heracles") were by definition the super-athletes of the ancient world. They were the very few who managed to win in both wrestling and pankration at Olympia on the same day. Obviously, pankration comprised only half of this greatest sporting achievement. Of the 4,237 Olympian victors who must have won in all sports over the 293 Olympiads, the top ones were the *aph' Heracleous* athletes. The particularly small number of athletes with the title - only seven of them - testifies to the degree of difficulty of this feat. Perhaps the endurance and physical strength of the pankratiast combined with the agility and unique skills of the wrestler[770] resulted in a particularly rare set of abilities. According to legend, Heracles was the first to win both the wrestling and pankration events on a single day at the Olympics.[771] Thus, anyone who did the same thereafter earned the honorary title *aph' Heracleous*, designating them as Heracles' successors.

Though the term was known long before, the topic was first discussed by Friedrich Kindscher in 1845. The honorary title given these athletes was *paradoxos*[772] or *paradoxonikēs*.[773]

They were:[774]

- Caprus of Elis in 212 BCE
  Lucian (*Vera historia* II, 22) refers to him as Carus, writing:
  In wrestling, the winner was Carus (or Caranus), the descendant of Heracles, who defeated Odysseus for the championship.[775]
- Aristomenes of Rhodes in 156 BCE
- Protophanes of Magnesia in 92 BCE
- Straton of Alexandria in 68 BCE
- Marion of Alexandria in 52 BCE
- Aristeas of Stratoniceia in 13 CE
- Nicostratus of Cilicia in 37 CE

It should be noted that only in the tables of Olympian victors compiled by Eusebius Pamphili (*Chronicle*, Part 1, Ch. XXXIII) is there a reference to the second *aph' Heracleous* athlete at the 156th Olympian games in 156 BCE

---

770 Pavlinis, *Istoria tēs Gymnastikēs*, p. 77.
771 Yiannakis, *Archaiognōsia*, p. 146.
772 Note: extraordinary, against the odds.
773 Mouratidis, *Istoria physikēs agōgēs*, p. 372.
774 Yiannakis, *Archaiognōsia*, p. 146.
775 Clarence Forbes, "Oi Aph' Heracleous in Epictetus and Lucian," *The American Journal of Philology* 60, no. 4 (1939): p. 473.

as Aristoxenus of Rhodes,[776] and to the seventh Heracles successor as Stratus Argeates at the 204th Olympics in 37 CE.[777]

There was also another case of interest: at the 249th Olympian games in 217 BCE, the pankration winner was Aurelius Aelix. He wanted to compete in wrestling as well for a chance at earning the coveted title, but the *Hellanodikēs* did not allow him to. The reason given was that the athlete belonged to the circle of Roman emperor Elagabalus, and was equally malicious. The Eleans certainly did not want to bestow the honorary title of *aph' Heracleous* on an athlete with such a vicious character. Besides, it was forbidden by the Olympic philosophy of the games. And so they did not want to give him an opportunity to compete for the title of the eighth successor of Heracles. Others believe they did not want to violate the sanctity of the number "7."[778]

---

776 Kitriniaris, *Gymnasticus*, p. 134.
777 Kitriniaris, *Gymnasticus*, p. 136.
778 Yiannakis, *Archaiognōsia*, p. 146.

Chapter 5

HONORS FOR THE CHAMPIONS

Honors for winners at Olympia

The ancients believed that an Olympic victory was the result of the gods showing favor. The winner was their chosen one, and they helped the athlete to win the prize. The reputation that immortalized him in people's memory was his highest reward.

The day on which prizes were presented was the greatest moment of the victors' lives; it was the moment they had been hoping for throughout their training.

The games were over. On the fifth and final day, the day the victors were crowned; it was the day of the reception at the Prytaneion. The day for celebration had arrived. As the sun cast its early morning rays on the *Altis*, the sacred grove at Olympia, the victors would set off for the Temple of Zeus for the formal crowning ceremony. They had a red woolen band tied around their heads and held a palm branch in their right hand. These emblematic items had been given to them immediately after their victory by the *Hellanodikai* personally, while the *keryx*, or herald, called out their name, the name of their father and their native land as the crowd cheered excitedly *"tinella kallinike"* - "Hurray, glorious victor." All of these distinctions were associated with ancient cults and traditions. The woolen band, which was particularly widespread in worship, usually adorned sacred objects. Its power was intensified by the red color and was transferred to the one who wore it. The palm branch was directly linked to Theseus, who staged games at Delos upon returning from Crete in honor of Apollo. The winners there were crowned with palm leaves.

Decorated with the symbols of victory, the chosen ones proceeded towards the temple while the crowds showered them with leaves and flowers. The wreaths of wild olive branches waited on the gold and ivory (chryselephantine) altar inside the temple. A row of gods carved in relief decorated the three sides of the altar: Zeus, Hera (mother of the gods), Hermes, Apollo and

Artemis were along the front, Asclepius and Hygieia were along one side and Pluto, Dionysus, Persephone and the Nymphs were on the other. The order of the different Olympic sports, or *diathesis*, lined the back. The bronze tripod upon which the wreaths would be laid in the early days was stored in the grounds around the Temple of Zeus.

The victors would gather in front of the temple, as relatives, friends and the public crowded around them to watch the ceremony. One by one, the Olympic victors would enter the temple vestibule and receive their crown and honorary trophy. The crown symbolized the transfer of powers which acted on the one who wore it to help him flourish. The winner was considered to be favored by the gods, as it was only thanks to their help that he was able to achieve his victory.[779]

The festival ended with a celebratory feast put on by the Eleans in the Prytaneion to honor the victors. As night fell, the songs of the victors and their friends filled the valley of the River Alpheus.

The next day, everyone would set off on their return trip home. The names of all the Olympian victors would be recorded by the Elean *Hellanodikēs*. But the journey through time and space of these winners' names and achievements, starting in Olympia and the temples at the other sacred games, was just beginning.

Honors for winners returning home

An Olympian victory spread the winner's fame far and wide. A victorious athlete's name was closely linked to the name of his homeland, which became famous by association. Thus, the Olympian's return was greeted with great excitement. He would approach the city on a majestic chariot drawn by four horses, but would not enter through the gate. A section of the city wall would be torn down for his victory entrance. This custom grew out of the belief that the winner had acquired the status of a god, entering the city through a special gate as a god and not as a man. The meaning of this custom later changed: as human beings came to rely on their own strengths to succeed, they no longer needed divine intervention or help, and so the opening in the wall meant that the city that begot such a brave young man had no need of walls.[780] This honor was only paid to generals following a victory at war.[781]

---

779 Sakellarakis et al., *Oi Olympiakoi*, p. 134.
780 Plutarch, *Moralia*, 639e.
781 Albanidis, *Istoria tēs athlēsēs*, p. 81.

But material rewards were nothing to the Olympic champions compared to the immortality assured them by their fame. The wild olive branch, or *kotinos*, guaranteed them that. So it was not at all strange that kings and other rulers, as well as mere mortals, passionately sought to win the honorable crown that would entitle them to perpetuate their name by placing statues in the sacred *Altis*, which until then had only held statues of gods.[782]

The victor's immortality was also ensured by the epinicean odes the winners commissioned from poets. Meanwhile, many other Olympic winners gained immortality through the myths, legends and traditions that developed around their achievements.[783]

Many also received non-material recognition by being awarded responsibility for athletic events or honorary membership in the Council. In Athens, they were provided with free meals at the Prytaneion, which was considered a great honor indeed. They sometimes received monetary rewards; in Athens, an Olympic victor received 500 drachmas and an Isthmian winner got 100 drachmas, which were huge amounts for that time.[784] But aside from their pride of place at public celebrations and the prizes which also included money, they also received more tangible gifts such as olive oil, which was valued at several hundred drachmas.[785]

Fame beyond the *palaestrae*

The fact that pankration was particularly popular is also evident from the fame that followed its victors: recall the case of Dorieus, the third son of Diagoras, who was the best athlete in the family and a three-time Olympian winner in pankration. As we saw earlier, he took part in the Peloponnesian War. As he waged a naval attack on Athens in 408 BCE, he was captured and sentenced to death. But as the Athenians knew of his fame, they allowed him to go free.[786]

Polydamas was another of the better-known athletes in antiquity and an Olympic pankratiast in 408 BCE. He died when the cave in which he and his friends had sought shelter from the unbearable summer heat collapsed. Before it completely fell in, legend has it that Polydamas managed to hold it

---

782 Albanidis, *Istoria tēs athlēsēs*, p. 82.
783 Sakellarakis et al., *Oi Olympiakoi*, p. 140.
784 Albanidis, *Istoria tēs athlēsēs*, pp. 81, 82, 83.
785 Nicholas Kyriazis and Emmanouil M. L. Economou, "Macroculture, sports and democracy in classical Greece," European Journal of Law and Economics 40, no. 3 (December 2015): pp. 431-455, 444.
786 Pausanias, *VI* 7.4-7.

up long enough to allow his friends to get out and save themselves, though he was unable to escape.[787] On the strength of this legend, Polydamas remained in the memory of subsequent generations as a hero, extending his fame as an Olympic champion.

Professional associations – Guilds

The earliest professional associations appeared in the Hellenistic period and initially involved actors. Artists by the nature of their work fell under the aegis of Dionysus. Other theater specialties, poets and musicians joined these associations later. As a rule, only those talented enough to allow them to compete in the sacred games circuit could become full members of the Dionysian guilds.[788]

The growing number of competitions noted during the Hellenistic period provided a boost to these artists' groups. Their growing numbers led the authorities to recognize the existence of these unions and to provide them with certain benefits. A number of other guilds of this type emerged at about the same time in the Hellenic world.[789]

As for competitive sports, athletic associations were formed along the same lines as the professional artists' unions.[790] The first evidence of the existence of guilds is an inscription found at Erythrae in Asia Minor.[791] It mentions two guilds: those for athletes (*athlētēs*) from the inhabited world and those who were winners of the sacred games (*hieronikēs*) in the inhabited world. All athletes, whether victors or not, could join the first guild, but the second was open only to those who had been victorious at sacred games.[792] Essentially, they were the World Athletes Association and the World *Hieronikēs* Association.

Their purpose was achieved when the ruling Roman emperors granted them special privileges. The *hieronikēs* association from the start requested and received favorable treatment from Emperor Marcus Antonius (83-30 BCE), who saw it as an opportunity to generate some political capital for himself.[793] A letter he wrote in 33/32 BCE refers to the benefits granted to members of

---

787 Mouratidis, *Istoria physikēs agōgēs*, p. 362.
788 Boutet-Lanouette, «La vie agonistique,» p. 38-41.
789 Boutet-Lanouette, «La vie agonistique,» p. 38-41.
790 Boutet-Lanouette, «La vie agonistique,» p. 38-41.
791 Clarence Forbes, "Ancient Athletic Guilds," *Classical Philology* 50, no. 4 (October 1955): p. 239.
792 Mouratidis, *Istoria physikēs agōgēs*, p. 371.
793 Forbes, «Guilds,» p. 239.

the guild: exemptions from various functions, exemptions from military obligations, personal security and the right to wear royal purple.[794]

The president of the athletic guild was called the *xystarchēs*. The title is derived from the *xystos*. As we saw earlier, the *xystos* was the covered corridor, or portico, along the length of a stadium (less than 200 meters) where athletes could prepare for track competitions in bad weather.[795] These athletic guilds existed from the early Roman empire until almost the end of the fourth century CE, when the games ceased. The professional athletes and their guilds had Heracles as their patron and emblem.[796]

The *xystarchēs* was usually appointed by the emperor and held the office for life. The expression "once a *xystarchēs*, always a *xystarchēs*" held true.[797] There were also two officers in the guild (*synodos*): an *argyrotamias* (treasurer) and a *gramateus* (secretary), but the most important office was that of the *xystarchēs*. The *synodos* always had an *archiatros* (official physician), who was appointed by the emperor at his own expense. Those who became *xystarchēs* were usually well-known athletes of heavy sports.[798] And of these, most of them were pankratiasts. The position was quite an honorable one, and many cities also made the *xystarchai* legislators, generals, councilors, market regulators (*agoranomoi*) or heads of the *Hellanodikēs*.[799] During the reign of Claudius the Athenian, the youths, who always imitated the adult organizations and political appointments, chose their own *xystarchēs*.[800]

The *xystarchēs*' duties including managing major regular athletic meets and less often overseeing all of the other athletic competitions of the same *polis*, or all of the games in an entire province. He determined which athletes would participate in the various competitions, the amounts to be paid in monetary prizes to winners and the statues that had to be erected in their honor; he also represented the athletes when requesting various privileges from the emperor. In fact, in carrying out his duties, he would wear royal purple robes and a wreath on his head. Though the *gymnasiarchēs* and the *agonothetēs* continued to be elected by their communities, the *xystarchēs* was appointed by the emperor himself, which was not the case before the imperial era. Rome was interested in controlling Greek athletics, thereby influencing the people. It managed to do that to a large extent through the *xystarchēs*.[801]

---

794 Albanidis, *Istoria tēs athlēsēs*, p. 299; Mouratidis, *Istoria physikēs agōgēs*, p. 372.
795 Albanidis, *Istoria tēs athlēsēs*, p. 214; Mouratidis, *Istoria physikēs agōgēs*, p. 217.
796 Mouratidis, *Istoria physikēs agōgēs*, p. 373.
797 Forbes, «Guilds,» p. 247.
798 Mouratidis, *Istoria physikēs agōgēs*, p. 372.
799 Forbes, «Guilds,» p. 248.
800 Forbes, «Guilds,» p. 248.
801 Forbes, «Guilds,» p. 247.

Emperor Antoninus Pius (86-161 CE) gave them a headquarters in Rome in 143 CE next to the Baths of Trajan. The federation formed by the merger of the two original guilds was called the "sacred xystic guild." This enabled the emperor to more easily exert his influence over the Hellenic world through a centralized athletic association. Nevertheless, there are strong indications that the initiative to join the guilds originated with the athletes themselves, since they stood to gain more honors and privileges. One should also examine the possibility that the general xystic association was a type of super-managerial council of the combined guilds of athletes and *hieronikēs*. In this manner, the imperial era was a time of great advancement for the competitive life of the Hellenic world.[802]

But let's take a look at the establishment of professional associations from the point of view of the athletes. What reasons did they have to form them? The poorer athletes wanted to be able to make a living from athletic competition. That was one of the major reasons for founding the athletic guilds. Others included the fact that as the gymnasium grew, more members of the lower classes acquired access to athletics and contributed to the democratization of sports. This led to an expanded number of competitions and athletes who took part in them, to the development of a more systematic training system and better performance by more people. There was another reason of a social nature: the poverty that resulted from the Peloponnesian War led some to become mercenaries and others to become professional athletes.[803] There were also *hieronikēs* guilds in the cities of Ephesus, Tralles, Smyrna, Thyateira, Miletus and Hierapolis.[804] To cover their operating costs, these guilds received money from the various emperors and donations from private citizens. The guilds themselves did not sponsor athletes.

The emperors used the athletes who belonged to the guilds to entertain the people by becoming part of the "bread and entertainment." It was a means to cultivate the political apathy of the people and protect the interests of the emperors. The guilds were protected by the emperors, but offered little in the way of sporting ideals.[805] They were essentially a political tool. They proved to be a powerful weapon in imperial propaganda as they were ideal for encouraging worship of the emperors and a very effective means of maintaining their popularity at high levels.[806] However, the existence of these guilds alone attests

---

802 Boutet-Lanouette, «La vie agonistique,» p. 38-41.
803 H. W. Pleket, "Some aspects of the history of the athletic guilds," Zeitschrift für Papyrologie und Epigraphik 10 (1973): pp. 197, 198.
804 Forbes, «Guilds,» p. 241.
805 Mouratidis, *Istoria physikēs agōgēs*, pp. 372, 373.
806 Albanidis, *Istoria tēs athlēsēs*, p. 214; Mouratidis, *Istoria physikēs agōgēs*, p. 302.

to a significant change. Although they initially involved athletes who took part in sacred games, they had come to include professional athletes.

Here are some of them:
1. Tiberius Claudius Rufus of Smyrna
2. Marcus Aurelius Demetrius of Alexandria
3. Marcus Aurelius Asclepiades of Alexandria, son of Demetrius
4. Aelius Aurelius Menander of Aphrodisias
5. Publius Aelius Aristomachus of Magnesia
6. Lucius Silicius Firmus Mandrogenes of Magnesia
7. Marcus Ulpius Domesticus of Ephesus
8. Secundus of Ephesus, also a wrestler
9. Inventus of Smyrna, also a wrestler and boxer
10. Titus Flavius Artemidorus of Cyme, also a wrestler
11. Marcus Aurelius Demostratus Damas of Sardis, also a boxer[807]
12. P. Aelius Dioscorides of Philippoupolis[808]

The reason that the Roman emperors appointed mainly pankratiasts to the position of *xystarchēs* was that pankration was considered far more difficult and spectacular than the other sports. Olympic pankratiasts were also perceived to have better fighting skills, endurance, stamina and strength than other victors. Their selection is an acknowledgment of the superiority of pankration in the public perception as compared to the other sports in the Olympic lineup. This is borne out by Philostratus' opinion that pankration was the "sport of men."[809]

Paradoxos

Researchers claim that the *xystarchēs* was also called a *paradoxos*.[810] Others believe that not only the *xystarchēs*, but other leaders of the guild were called *paradoxoi* (plural) as well.[811] As we saw earlier, those members of the guild who managed to win at both pankration and wrestling on the same day at the Olympics were called *aph' Heracleous* (Heracles' successors) and also held the title of *paradoxos* or *paradoxonikēs* because such a feat was extremely difficult.

---

807 There are numerous references to the offices he held in the inscriptions found in the section on Olympic victors.
808 Forbes, "Guilds," p. 248.
809 Philostratus, *Imagines* 2.6.
810 Albanidis, *Istoria tēs athlēsēs,* p. 301.
811 Mouratidis, *Istoria physikēs agōgēs*, p. 372.

The terms *paradoxos* and *paradoxonikēs* actually refer to someone who achieves something contrary to expectations. The title originated with professional track athletes in the Roman Empire, though there were probably few such cases. It was used as a term to refer to competitors in music and theater. It appears in connection with the *hieron* and the ending -*ikēs*, as *periodon-ikēs*, or *pleiston*-ikēs ("victorious in several contests"), in combination with the name of the sport – *dolichos*, pankration, *palē* (wrestling) or pyx (boxing) – or the particular event (such as the Pythian games). Thus, athletes are variously referred to as a *dolichodromos hieronikēs*, a *Pythionikēs*, and an *Actionikēs paradoxos*. There are also references to distinguished artists with the title *periodonikēs paradoxos*, or *paradoxos kitharodos* (guitar player and singer), or *paradoxos tragodos* (performer of tragedy), *periodonikēs comodos* (comic singer or actor), *Capitolianikēs paradoxos, paradoxos comodos periodonikēs* and one *tragodos* and *poiitis* (poet) *paradoxos*.[812]

Money prizes for pankratiasts

The popularity of pankration is also demonstrated by the amounts of money paid to pankratiasts as prizes in *chrimatitēs* competitions.[813] Inscription **Roueché, PPAphr 52 (CIG 2758 A-G)**, found at Caria of Aphrodisias, notes that men pankratiasts received the largest amounts in dinars of all the other competitors. Here it is in its entirety:

   A [ἀγῶνος ... c.20 ... μου]-
      σικοῦ τῶν ἀπὸ τῆς συνόδου θέ[μ]α[τα τὰ]
      ὑπογεγραμμένα
I.4 σαλπικτῇ ✳ ρν
  5 κήρυκι ✳ ρν
      ἐνκωμιογράφῳ ✳ σ
      ποιητῇ ✳ σ
      παιδὶ κιθαρῳδῷ ✳ ρν
      πυθικῷ αὐλητῇ ✳ σ
10 κωμῳδῷ ✳ υ
      τ[ρα]γῳδῷ ✳ φ
      κυκλίῳ αὐλητῇ ✳ τν
      [...

---

812 K. Schneider, "Paradoxos," *RE* IXX$_3$ (1949): p. 1167.
813 Albanidis, *Istoria tēs athlēsēs*, p. 162.

II.4　ἀνδρὶ κιθαρῳδῷ ✻ φ
　5　διὰ πάντων ✻ σ
　　εἰς δὲ τὸν γυμνικὸν ✻ [. .]
　　τῶν πολειτῶν παί-
　　δων ἀγῶνα
　　σταδιαδρόμῳ ἀνδρὶ [✻] ,α
　10　παλαιστῇ ἀνδρὶ [✻] ,ασ
　　πανκρατιαστῇ ἀνδρὶ [✻] ,ασ
　　πύκτῃ ἀνδρὶ [✻] ,ασ

B.II　[. . .
　1　ἀνδρὶ κιθαρῳδῷ ✻ ,γϛν
　　δευτερείου ✻ ,α
　　ποιητῇ Ῥωμαικῷ [✻ . . .]
　　ποιητῇ [✻ . . .]
　5　διὰ πάντων ✻ ,α
　　γραμματεῖ . φν
　　πανηγυριάρχῃ [✻ . . .]
　8a　βήλων καὶ τῶν
　9/8b　διὰ θεάτρου ✻ ,α
　10　[. . .

DE.II　[—
　I.1　σαλπικτῇ ✻ φ
　　κήρυκι ✻ φ
　　πυθικῷ αὐλητῇ ✻ ,αυ
　　δευτερείου ✻ υ
　5　κυκλίῳ αὐλητῇ ✻ [,α]φ
　　δευτερείου ✻ φ
　　κωμῳδῷ ✻ ,αχ
　　δευτερείου ✻ φ
　　τριτείου ? τ
　10　τραγῳδῷ ✻ ,βψ
　　δευτερείου ✻ ω
　　τριτείου ✻ χ
　　[. . .
　　[. . .
　15　[. . .
　　[. . .
　　[. . .

[...]
[...]
20 [...]
[...]
[...]
[...]
[...]

II.1 ἀνδρὶ
δολιχαδρόμῳ ✳ ,β
ἀγενείοις
σταδιαδρόμῳ ✳ ,β
5 πεντάθλῳ . [,α]
παλαιστῇ ✳ ,γω
πύκτῃ [✳ ,γω]
πανκρατιαστ[ῇ] ✳ ,ε
ἀνδρὶ
10 πεντάθλῳ ✳ ,ατμ
παιδὶ
σταδιαδρόμῳ ✳ ,αυ

III.1 παισὶν
παλαιστ[ῇ ✳ ..]
πύκτῃ [✳ ..]
παγκρα[τιαστῇ ✳ ..]
5 ἀνδράσιν
παλαισ[τῇ ✳ ..]
πύκτῃ [✳ ..]
πανκρα[τιαστῇ ✳ ..]
ὁπλειτο[δρόμῳ ✳ ..]
10 κέλητι [τελείῳ ✳ ..]
κέλητι [πωλικῷ ✳ ..]
συνωρίδ[ι τελείᾳ ✳ ..]
συνωρίδ[ι πωλικῇ ✳ ..]
δευτερείου πωλικοῦ ✳ τν
15 ἅρματι τελείῳ ✳ ,αφ
ἅρματι πωλικῷ ✳ ,α
ἅρματος τελείου τὸ β' ✳ φ
18a ξυστάρχῃ [ε]ἰς ἀναπ[λή]-
19/18b [ρωσιν] ✳ ψμε
20 εἱμαντοπαρόχῳ ✳τα

      ἀφετηρίας μαγγάνων ✳ τ
      σκάμματος καὶ πηλώματος ✳ υ
      εἰς ἔλαιον ✳ ,β
      ἀγαλματοποιοῖς ✳ ,αφ
25
CF.III [—
  I.1 χοροκιθαρεῖ ✳ φ
      χοραύλῃ ✳ ψν
      κιθαρῳδῷ ✳ ,αφ
       δευτερείου ✳ υ
  5 πυρρίχῃ ✳ φ
      σατύρῳ ✳ ρν
      διὰ πάντων ✳ φ
      θέματα γυμνικά
       vacat
  10 παιδὶ δολιχαδρόμῳ ✳ φ[ ]
      παιδὶ σταδιαδρόμῳ ✳ φκε
      παιδὶ [δι]αυλ[ο]δρόμῳ ✳ φ
      παιδὶ πεντάθλῳ ✳ φ
      παιδὶ παλαιστῇ ✳ φ
  II.1 παιδὶ πύκτῃ ✳ ,α
      παιδὶ πανκρατιαστῇ ✳ ,αχν
      ἀγενείῳ σταδιαδρόμῳ ✳ ψν
      ἀγενείῳ πεντάθλῳ ✳ τπε
  5 ἀγενείῳ παλαιστῇ ✳ ,α
      ἀγενείῳ πύκτῃ ✳,αφ
      ἀγενείῳ πανκρατιαστῇ ✳ ,αφ
      ἀνδρὶ δολιχαδρόμῳ ✳ ψν
      vacat
  10 ἀνδρὶ σταδιαδρόμῳ ✳ ,ασν
      ἀνδρὶ διαυλαδρόμῳ ✳,α
      ἀνδρὶ πεντάθλῳ ✳ φ
      ἀνδρὶ παλαιστῇ ✳ ,β
      ἀνδρὶ πύκτῃ leaf ✳ ,β
  III.1 **ἀνδρὶ πανκρατιαστῇ ✳ ,γ**
      ὁπλειτοδρόμῳ ✳ φ
      ἀποβάτῃ ✳ σν
      ἱππικῷ ✳ ψν
  5 σκαμματος καὶ μαγγάνων
      εἰς τὸ στάδιον ✳ φ

       ἱμάντων μισθός ✶ σν
8a ξυστάρχῃ εἰς ἀναπλή-
9/8b ρωσιν ✶ χοδ
10 ἀνδριάντος scroll ✶ ,α
    vacat

Translated:
    For the music contest [...] those given by the guild and are listed below

for the trumpeter	150
for the *keryx* (crier)	150
for the panegyric writer	200
for the poet ..	200
for the young *kithara*-player	150
for the Pythian *aulos*[814]-player	200
for the comic singer	400
for the actor of tragedy	500
for the cyclic dance *aulos*-player[815]	350
for the adult *kithara*-player	500
for all citizens in the boys' gymnastic contest	200
for the adult *stadion* runner	1000
for the adult wrestler	1200
for the adult pankratiast	**1200**
for the adult boxer	1200
for the adult *kithara*-player	3250
for second place	1000
for the Roman poet	[...]
for the poet	[...]
for all	1000
for the secretary	550
for the festival president	[...]
(for the ushers and the)	
for the theater	1000

---

814 Translator's note: An aulos was an ancient Greek wind instrument.
815 Translator's note: the flute-player who accompanied the cyclic chorus.

[...]	
[...]	
for the trumpeter	500
for the *keryx* (crier)	500
for the Pythian *aulos*-player	1400
for second place	400
for the cyclic dance *aulos*-player	(1)500
for second place	500
for the comic singer	1600
for second place	500
for third place	300
for the actor of tragedy	2700
for second place	800
for third place	600
[...]	
[...]	
[...]	
for the adult *dolichos* runner	2000
of the youth (*ageneioi*)	
for the *stadion* runner	2000
for the pentathlete	[1000]
for the wrestler	3800
for boxer	[3800]
for the pankratiast	**5000**
for the adult pentathlete	1340
for the boy *stadion* runner	1400
of the boys	[...]
for the wrestler	[...]
for the boxer	[...]
for the pankratiast	**[...]**
for the men	[...]
for the wrestler	[...]
for boxer	[...]

for the pankratiast	[...]
for the full-grown *kelēs*[816]	[...]
for the young *kelēs*[817]	[...]
for the full-grown *synoris*[818]	[...]
for the young *synoris*[819]	[...]
second-place of the colt riders	350
for the chariot race with full-grown horses[820]	1500
for the chariot race with young horses[821]	1000
for second-place in the chariot race with full-grown horses	500
for the alternate *xystarchēs*	745
for the provider of *himantes* (leather strips)	301
of starting line *magano* mechanism[822]	300
of the sand and mud pit[823]	400
for the oil	2000
for the sculptors	1500
[---]	
for the chorus *kithara*-player	500
for the chorus *aulos*-player	750
for the *kithara*-player	1500
for second place	400
for the Pyrrhic dance	500
for the Satyric play	150
for all	500
(for) gymnastic prizes	
for the boy *dolichos* runner	500
for the boy *stadion* runner	525
for the boy running the *diaulos* (double *stadion*)	500
for the boy pentathlete	500
for the boy wrestler	500
for the boy boxer	1000
for the boy pankratiast	**1650**

for the youth *stadion* runner	750
for the youth pentathlete	385
for the youth wrestler	1000
for the youth boxer	1500
for the youth pankratiast	**1500**
for the adult *dolichos* runner	750
for the adult *stadion* runner	1250
for the adult running the *diaulos* (double stadion)	1000
for the adult pentathlete	500
for the adult wrestler	2000
for the adult boxer	2000
for the adult pankratiast	**3000**
for the runner racing in armor[824]	500
for the *apovatēs*[825]	250
for the horseman	750
of the pits and pulley system at the race course	500
expenses for *himantes*	250
for the alternate *xystarchēs*	674
for the statue	1000

Hero cults and deification of pankratiasts

One of the rare but important honors for mortals was to become the object of a *hero cult* after their death. There are references to hero cults of Olympic

---

816 Translator's note: Horse-racing.
817 Translator's note: Horse-race with colts or fillies.
818 Translator's note: horse-race with a pair of horses.
819 Translator's note: horse-race with a pair of colts or fillies.
820 Translator's note: race with a horse-drawn chariot.
821 Translator's note: race with a chariot drawn by colts or fillies.
822 Translator's note: the magano was part of the starting gate mechanism (hysplex) at horse-races.
823 Translator's note: part of the soil/mud.
824 Translator's note: the winner of a footrace run while wearing battle armor.
825 Translator's note: the one who was skilled at jumping from one horse or chariot to another in an equestrian race.

victors from the sixth and fifth centuries BCE, though it is believed it is mostly due to other unique characteristics or skills, and not just the fact they had won an Olympic event. In addition, they made sure to mention the fact that they had been victorious at the Olympic games on the funerary stone covering their mortal remains with a view to ensuring their immortality.[826]

Theagenes was the son of a priest, as his name attests: the son of the priest to the gods. But the outstanding achievements of his competitive career led his fellow citizens well beyond the kind of worship usually accorded an athlete. Instead, they honored him as a hero to a degree not often seen among athletes. He was worshiped as a hero well after his death with sacrifices, honors and offerings.[827] It was believed that his statue could cure one of a fever,[828] and there were cults of Theagenes in other Greek cities where they believed he had healing powers.[829] All of Greece acknowledged his abilities as a healer of fever. The escalation of the worship exhibited by the Thasians is an example of the significant expansion of hero cults in Greece and Asia Minor, particularly during the Hellenistic and Roman periods. In addition, Hippocrates, who stayed in Thasos for a long time to study the effects of fever, tells us that his presence had become endemic. To protect themselves from this illness, the Thasians sought help at the feet of the statue of Theagenes which had been erected in the sacred grounds of the Agora. During the first century BCE and perhaps even earlier, there was also an altar at which they offered sacrifices as their laws demanded and a box in which offerings were collected from followers, in addition to the statue.[830]

The great Cleitomachus of Thebes and Polydamas of Scotussa were also worshiped as heroes.[831]

Although the custom of worshiping great athletes as heroes did not extend past the classical years, their elevated status persisted into late antiquity.[832]

---

826 Sakellarakis et al., *Oi Olympiakoi*, p. 141.
827 Valavanis, *Athla*, p. 63.
828 Moretti, *Inscrizioni*, p. 51.
829 Lucian, *Dialogues of the Gods* 12.
830 Roland R. Martin, «Un nouveau règlement de culte thasien,» Bulletin de correspondance hellénique 64, no. 1 (1940): pp. 199, 200.
831 Mouratidis, *Istoria physikēs agōgēs*, p. 308.
832 Poliakoff, *Combat sports*, p. 129.

Chapter 6

THE SOCIAL BACKGROUND OF THE CHAMPIONS

Limited to aristocrats

During the Archaic and classical Greek period, only Greeks could take part in the Olympic games, a fact that gave the contest a national character.[833] In addition, only members of the aristocracy were able avoid doing manual labor and have access to appropriate training, which was expensive. They also needed funds to travel to Olympia and cover the costs of staying there for a month previous to the games. Although in theory, social position, occupation and financial status did not affect participation in the games, the fact is that up until the sixth century BCE, only the wealthy and members of the aristocracy had the capacity to take part. There was no express prohibition, but the opportunities offered to less well-off members of society were very limited.[834]

The fact remains that training and athletic success, even for a boy athlete, was an expensive proposition. In fifth century BCE Athens, the young victors came from the aristocracy, while in the fourth century BCE, the aristocracy continued to be identified with athletic achievement, despite the exceptions that prove the rule.[835] Initially, then, the Olympic games were intended to be an activity for wealthy aristocrats.

But why did aristocrats actually take part? The creation of the hoplite phalanx with soldiers from the lower classes in the early eighth century BCE left the nobility with few opportunities to demonstrate its superiority. Their

---

833 Philostratus, *Gymnasticus*, 25.
834 Evangelos Albanidis and Vassiliki Nikolakaki, "The Social Origin of Ancient Olympic Victors" (Paper presented at the International Olympic Academy, 7th International Session for Educators and officials of higher institutes of physical education, 20-27 July 2006, Athens 2007): p. 176.
835 Samara and Albanidis, "Ē agōnistikē parousia," p. 8.

competing in the Olympic games could have been an acceptable way for them to prove their bravery.[836]

Their incentive was not the prospect of material profit from an athletic victory, since they were already wealthy, but the acquisition of certain social capital and respect on a nationwide level.[837]

As religious gatherings, the panhellenic games also attracted a number of street vendors and merry-makers, but the games themselves were aristocratic. They only matured and flourished once they acquired their national form.[838]

Restricted participation

Aside from the practical reasons for limiting participation, there were also express rules as to who could take part. Slaves were not even allowed to use the *palaestrae* or *gymnasia* for exercise nor could they attend the games as spectators.[839] Competitors who had been declared cheaters or had been found guilty of disrespect were also not allowed to compete.[840] Athletes who had not spent the ten months preceding the games training were also excluded.[841] This prerequisite left out anyone who could not fund ten months of training. Solon's laws indicate that anyone who was not a slave could train at a gymnasium in Athens, although in practice only those with free time could take part in athletics for the better part of the sixth century BCE.[842]

Famous aristocrat pankratiasts

One such participant was Athenian politician **Phrynon**, who won in pankration at the Olympics of 636 BCE.[843]

Timasitheus of Delphi, a two-time pankration winner at the Olympics and three times a victor at the Pythian games, later played a significant role

---

836 Albanidis and Nikolakaki, "The Social Origin," p. 176.
837 Hubbard, "Contemporary," p. 385.
838 Drivas: *Askiseis*, p. 158.
839 Pavlinis, *Istoria tēs Gymnastikēs*, p. 153.
840 Pavlinis, *Istoria tēs Gymnastikēs*, p. 153.
841 Pavlinis, *Istoria tēs Gymnastikēs*, p. 154.
842 Hubbard, "Contemporary," p. 381.
843 Mouratidis, *Istoria physikēs agōgēs*, p. 314.

in an attempt by an oligarchic faction of aristocrats to seize control of Athens. Their abortive coup was punished with the death penalty.[844]

Hagias was the great-grandfather of Daochos, a well-to-do Thessalian from Pharsalus and an *hieromnēmon*, meaning he represented Thessaly at the Delphic Amphictyony in 338-334 BCE.[845]

Aelius Aurelius Menander was also from an aristocratic and illustrious family.

Stomios of Elis was the commander of the Elean cavalry in the Battle of Leuctra in 371 BCE.[846]

Aristes of Cleonae was a four-time pankration winner at Nemea and was active through about half of the sixth century. He was the brother of Leocedes, son of Pheidon. Since we know that the name of Leocedes' father was Pheidon, we can conclude that the father was the son of the famous tyrant of Argos.[847]

Damagetus and **Dorieus** were sons of the great Diagoras of Rhodes, who was the great-grandson of the king of the ancient city of **Ialysus** in Rhodes and the daughter of Messenian hero **Aristomenes**.[848]

Pindar

Pindar has been an important source of information. Four of the Nemean odes and five of the Isthmian odes are dedicated to aristocrat pankratiasts.

Nemean 2 (written at about 470 BCE) is dedicated to **Timodemus**, son of Timonous of Acharnae, who achieved his first victory at Nemea.[849] The family of Timodemus had won four trophies at the Pythian games, eight crowns at Corinth and another seven at Nemea.

Here is the ode in its entirety:

ΤΙΜΟΔΗΜῼ ΑΧΑΡΝΕΙ ΠΑΓΚΡΑΤΙΑΣΤῌ

ὅθεν περ καὶ Ὁμηρίδαι
ῥαπτῶν ἐπέων τὰ πόλλ' ἀοιδοὶ
ἄρχονται, Διὸς ἐκ προοιμίου· καὶ ὅδ' ἀνὴρ

---

844 Poliakoff, Combat sports, p. 130.
845 Valavanis, *Athla*, p. 37.
846 Moretti, *Olympionikai*, p.119.
847 Moretti, *Inscrizioni*, p. 6.
848 Pavlinis, *Istoria tēs Gymnastikēs*, p. 70.
849 Pindar, *Nemean* 2, 13.

καταβολὰν ἱερῶν ἀγώνων νικαφορίας δέδεκται πρῶτον Νεμεαίου
ἐν πολυυμνήτῳ Διὸς ἄλσει.
ὀφείλει δ' ἔτι, πατρίαν
[10] εἴπερ καθ' ὁδόν νιν εὐθυπομπὸς
αἰὼν ταῖς μεγάλαις δέδωκε κόσμον Ἀθάναις,
θαμὰ μὲν Ἰσθμιάδων δρέπεσθαι κάλλιστον ἄωτον, ἐν Πυθίοισί τε νικᾶν
Τιμονόου παῖδ': ἔστι δ' ἐοικὸς
ὀρειᾶν γε Πελειάδων
μὴ τηλόθεν Ὠαρίωνα νεῖσθαι.
[20] καὶ μὰν ἁ Σαλαμίς γε θρέψαι φῶτα μαχατὰν
δυνατός. ἐν Τρωΐᾳ μὲν Ἕκτωρ Αἴαντος ἄκουσεν: ὦ Τιμόδημε, σὲ δ' ἀλκὰ
παγκρατίου τλάθυμος ἀέξει.
Ἀχάρναι δὲ παλαίφατοι
εὐάνορες: ὅσσα δ' ἀμφ' ἀέθλοις,
Τιμοδημίδαι ἐξοχώτατοι προλέγονται.
[30] παρὰ μὲν ὑψιμέδοντι Παρνασῷ τέσσαρας ἐξ ἀέθλων νίκας ἐκόμιξαν:
ἀλλὰ Κορινθίων ὑπὸ φωτῶν
ἐν ἐσλοῦ Πέλοπος πτυχαῖς
ὀκτὼ στεφάνοις ἔμιχθεν ἤδη:
ἑπτὰ δ' ἐν Νεμέᾳ τὰ δ' οἴκοι μάσσον' ἀριθμοῦ
Διὸς ἀγῶνι. τόν, ὦ πολῖται, κωμάξατε Τιμοδήμῳ σὺν εὐκλέϊ νόστῳ:
[40] ἀδυμελεῖ δ' ἐξάρχετε φωνᾷ.

And translated:

FOR TIMODEMUS OF ACHARNAE PANCRATIUM

Just as the Homeridae, the singers of woven verses, most often begin with Zeus as their prelude, so this man has received a first down-payment of victory in the sacred games by winning [5] in the grove of Nemean Zeus, which is celebrated in many hymns. And if the life that guides him straight along the path of his fathers has given him as an adornment to great Athens, it must be that the son of Timonous will often reap the finest bloom of the Isthmian games, and be victorious in the Pythian contests. [10] It is right for Orion to travel not far from the mountain Pleiades. And certainly Salamis can raise a warrior. In Troy Hector heard of Aias. And you, Timodemus, are exalted [15] by your enduring spirit of valor in the pancratium. Acharnae has long been famous for fine men. And in everything that has to do with contests, the sons of Timodemus are proclaimed the most outstanding. Beside Parnassus, ruling on high, they carried off four victories in the games, [20] while the men of Corinth have already given them eight garlands in the glades of noble Pelops; in the Nemean contest of Zeus they have won seven times, and at home their victories are countless. Citizens, praise Zeus in a victory procession for Timodemus' glorious homecoming. [25] Begin with a sweet-singing voice![850]

The third Nemean ode (475 BCE) is dedicated to **Aristocleides** of Aegina,[851] son of Aristophanes. He was a descendant of the Myrmidons and Aeacidae, the early inhabitants of the island of Aegina, named for the mythical sister of the Asopide nymph, Nemea.

ΑΡΙΣΤΟΚΛΕΙΔῌ ΑΙΓΙΝΗΤῌ ΠΑΓΚΡΑΤΙΑΣΤῌ

ὦ πότνια Μοῖσα, μᾶτερ ἁμετέρα, λίσσομαι,
τὰν πολυξέναν ἐν ἱερομηνίᾳ Νεμεάδι
ἵκεο Δωρίδα νᾶσον Αἴγιναν· ὕδατι γὰρ
μένοντ᾽ ἐπ᾽ Ἀσωπίῳ μελιγαρύων τέκτονες
κώμων νεανίαι, σέθεν ὄπα μαιόμενοι.
[10] διψῇ δὲ πρᾶγος ἄλλο μὲν ἄλλου·
ἀεθλονικία δὲ μάλιστ᾽ ἀοιδὰν φιλεῖ,
στεφάνων ἀρετᾶν τε δεξιωτάταν ὀπαδόν·
τᾶς ἀφθονίαν ὄπαζε μήτιος ἁμᾶς ἄπο·
ἄρχε δ᾽ οὐρανοῦ πολυνεφέλα κρέοντι, θύγατερ,
δόκιμον ὕμνον· ἐγὼ δὲ κείνων τέ νιν ὀάροις
[20] λύρᾳ τε κοινάσομαι. χαρίεντα δ᾽ ἕξει πόνον
χώρας ἄγαλμα, Μυρμιδόνες ἵνα πρότεροι
ᾤκησαν, ὧν παλαίφατον ἀγορὰν
οὐκ ἐλεγχέεσσιν Ἀριστοκλείδας τεὰν
ἐμίανε κατ᾽ αἶσαν ἐν περισθενεῖ μαλαχθεὶς
παγκρατίου στόλῳ· καματωδέων δὲ πλαγᾶν
[30] ἄκος ὑγιηρὸν ἐν βαθυπεδίῳ Νεμέᾳ τὸ καλλίνικον φέρει.
εἰ δ᾽ ἐὼν καλὸς ἔρδων τ᾽ ἐοικότα μορφᾷ
ἀνορέαις ὑπερτάταις ἐπέβα παῖς Ἀριστοφάνεος· οὐκέτι πρόσω
ἀβάταν ἅλα κιόνων ὑπὲρ Ἡρακλέος περᾶν εὐμαρές,
ἥρως θεὸς ἃς ἔθηκε ναυτιλίας ἐσχάτας

---

850 Pindar, *Nemean 2*, trans. Diane Arnson Svarlien, 1990, http://www.perseus.tufts.edu/hopper/text?doc=Perseus%3Atext%3A1999.01.0162%3Abook%3DN.%3Apoem%3D2, retrieved Sept. 30, 2016.
851 Pindar, *Nemean* 3, 23.

[40] μάρτυρας κλυτάς· δάμασε δὲ θῆρας ἐν πελάγεσιν
ὑπέροχος, διά τ' ἐξερεύνασε τεναγέων
ῥοάς, ὅπα πόμπιμον κατέβαινε νόστου τέλος,
καὶ γᾶν φράδασσε. θυμέ, τίνα πρὸς ἀλλοδαπὰν
ἄκραν ἐμὸν πλόον παραμείβεαι;
Αἰακῷ σε φαμὶ γένει τε Μοῖσαν φέρειν,

[50] ἕπεται δὲ λόγῳ δίκας ἄωτος, "ἐσλὸς αἰνεῖν·"
οὐδ' ἀλλοτρίων ἔρωτες ἀνδρὶ φέρειν κρέσσονες·
οἴκοθεν μάτευε. ποτίφορον δὲ κόσμον ἔλαβες
γλυκύ τι γαρυέμεν. παλαιαῖσι δ' ἐν ἀρεταῖς
γέγαθε Πηλεὺς ἄναξ ὑπέραλλον αἰχμὰν ταμών·
ὃς καὶ Ἰωλκὸν εἷλε μόνος ἄνευ στρατιᾶς,

[60] καὶ ποντίαν Θέτιν κατέμαρψεν
ἐγκονητί. Λαομέδοντα δ' εὐρυσθενὴς
Τελαμὼν Ἰόλα παραστάτας ἐὼν ἔπερσεν·
καί ποτε χαλκότοξον Ἀμαζόνων μετ' ἀλκὰν
ἕπετό οἱ· οὐδέ νίν ποτε φόβος ἀνδροδάμας ἔπαυσεν ἀκμὰν φρενῶν.

[70] συγγενεῖ δέ τις εὐδοξίᾳ μέγα βρίθει·
ὃς δὲ διδάκτ' ἔχει, ψεφηνὸς ἀνὴρ ἄλλοτ' ἄλλα πνέων οὔ ποτ' ἀτρεκεῖ
κατέβα ποδί, μυριᾶν δ' ἀρετᾶν ἀτελεῖ νόῳ γεύεται.
ξανθὸς δ' Ἀχιλεὺς τὰ μὲν μένων Φιλύρας ἐν δόμοις
παῖς ἐὼν ἄθυρε μεγάλα ἔργα, χερσὶ θαμινὰ

[80] βραχυσίδαρον ἄκοντα πάλλων, ἴσα τ' ἀνέμοις
μάχᾳ λεόντεσσιν ἀγροτέροις ἔπρασσεν φόνον,
κάπρους τ' ἔναιρε, σώματα δὲ παρὰ Κρονίδαν
Κένταυρον ἀσθμαίνοντα κόμιζεν,
ἑξέτης τὸ πρῶτον, ὅλον δ' ἔπειτ' ἂν χρόνον·
τὸν ἐθάμβεον Ἄρτεμίς τε καὶ θρασεῖ' Ἀθάνα,
κτείνοντ' ἐλάφους ἄνευ κυνῶν δολίων θ' ἑρκέων·

[90] ποσσὶ γὰρ κράτεσκε. λεγόμενον δὲ τοῦτο προτέρων
ἔπος ἔχω· βαθυμῆτα Χείρων τράφε λιθίνῳ
Ἰάσον' ἔνδον τέγει, καὶ ἔπειτεν Ἀσκλήπιον,
τὸν φαρμάκων δίδαξε μαλακόχειρα νόμον·
νύμφευσε δ' αὖτις ἀγλαόκαρπον
Νηρέος θύγατρα, γόνον τέ οἱ φέρτατον

[100] ἀτίταλλεν, ἀρμένοισι πᾶσι θυμὸν αὔξων·
ὄφρα θαλασσίαις ἀνέμων ῥιπαῖσι πεμφθεὶς
ὑπὸ Τρωΐαν, δορίκτυπον ἀλαλὰν Λυκίων τε προσμένοι καὶ Φρυγῶν
Δαρδάνων τε, καὶ ἐγχεσφόροις ἐπιμίξαις
Αἰθιόπεσσι χεῖρας, ἐν φρασὶ πάξαιθ', ὅπως σφίσι μὴ κοίρανος ὀπίσω

[110] πάλιν οἴκαδ' ἀνεψιὸς ζαμενὴς Ἑλένοιο Μέμνων μόλοι.
τηλαυγὲς ἄραρε φέγγος Αἰακιδᾶν αὐτόθεν:
Ζεῦ, τεὸν γὰρ αἷμα, σέο δ' ἀγών, τὸν ὕμνος ἔβαλεν
ὀπὶ νέων ἐπιχώριον χάρμα κελαδέων.
βοὰ δὲ νικαφόρῳ σὺν Ἀριστοκλείδᾳ πρέπει,
[120] ὃς τάνδε νᾶσον εὐκλέϊ προσέθηκε λόγῳ
καὶ σεμνὸν ἀγλααῖσι μερίμναις
Πυθίου Θεάριον. ἐν δὲ πείρᾳ τέλος
διαφαίνεται, ὦν τις ἐξοχώτερος γένηται,
ἐν παισὶ νέοισι παῖς, ἐν ἀνδράσιν ἀνήρ, τρίτον
ἐν παλαιτέροισι, μέρος ἕκαστον οἷον ἔχομεν
[130] βρότεον ἔθνος. ἐλᾷ δὲ καὶ τέσσαρας ἀρετὰς
θνατὸς αἰών, φρονεῖν δ' ἐνέπει τὸ παρκείμενον.
τῶν οὐκ ἄπεσσι. χαῖρε, φίλος. ἐγὼ τόδε τοι
πέμπω μεμιγμένον μέλι λευκῷ
σὺν γάλακτι, κιρναμένα δ' ἔερσ' ἀμφέπει,
πόμ' ἀοίδιμον Αἰολῇσιν ἐν πνοαῖσιν αὐλῶν,
[140] ὀψέ περ. ἔστι δ' αἰετὸς ὠκὺς ἐν ποτανοῖς,
ὃς ἔλαβεν αἶψα, τηλόθε μεταμαιόμενος, δαφοινὸν ἄγραν ποσίν:
κραγέται δὲ κολοιοὶ ταπεινὰ νέμονται.
τίν γε μέν, εὐθρόνου Κλεοῦς ἐθελοίσας, ἀεθλοφόρου λήματος ἕνεκεν
Νεμέας Ἐπιδαυρόθεν τ' ἄπο καὶ Μεγάρων δέδορκεν φάος.

Here it is in translation:

FOR ARISTOCLEIDES OF AEGINA PANCRATIUM

Queenly Muse, our mother! I entreat you, come in the sacred month of Nemea to the much-visited Dorian island of Aegina. For beside the waters of the Asopus young men are waiting, craftsmen of honey-voiced [5] victory-songs, seeking your voice. Various deeds thirst for various things; but victory in the games loves song most of all, the most auspicious attendant of garlands and of excellence. Send an abundance of it, from my wisdom; [10] begin, divine daughter, an acceptable hymn to the ruler of the cloud-filled sky, and I will communicate it by the voices of those singers and by the lyre. The hymn will have a pleasant toil, to be the glory of the land where the ancient Myrmidons lived, whose marketplace, famous long ago, [15] Aristocleides, through your ordinance, did not stain with dishonor by proving himself too weak in the strenuous course of the pancratium. But in the deep plain of Nemea, his triumph-song brings a healing cure for wearying blows. Still, if the son of Aristophanes, who is beautiful, and whose deeds match his looks, [20] embarked on the highest achievements of manliness, it is not easy to cross the trackless sea beyond the pillars of Heracles, which that hero and god set up as famous witnesses to the furthest limits of seafaring. He subdued the monstrous beasts in the sea, and tracked to the very end the streams of the shallows, [25] where he reached the goal that sent him back home again, and he made the land known. My spirit, towards what foreign headland are you turning my voyage? I bid you to summon the Muse in honor of Aeacus and his race; consummate justice attends the precept, "praise the noble." [30] And no man should prefer to desire what is alien. Search at home; you have won a suitable adornment for singing something sweet. Among old examples of excellence is king Peleus, who rejoiced when he cut a matchless spear, and who alone, without an army, captured Iolcus, [35] and caught the sea-nymph Thetis after many struggles. And powerful Telamon, the comrade of Iolaus, sacked the city of Laomedon; and once he followed him to meet the bronze-bowed strength of the Amazons. And fear, the subduer of men, never dulled the edge of his mind. [40] A man with inborn glory has great weight; but he who has only learned is a man in darkness, breathing changeful purposes, never taking an unwavering step, but trying his hand at countless forms of excellence with his ineffectual thought. But golden-haired Achilles, staying in the home of Philyra as a child, played at great deeds, often [45] brandishing in his hands a javelin with a short blade; swift as the wind, he dealt death to wild lions in battle, and he slew wild boars and carried their panting bodies to the Centaur, son of Cronus, first when he was six years old, and afterwards for all the time he spent there. [50] Artemis and bold Athena gazed at him with wonder, as he slew deer without the help of dogs and crafty nets; for he excelled with his feet. I have this story as it was told by earlier generations. Deep-thinking Cheiron reared Jason under his stone roof, and later Asclepius, [55] whom he taught the gentle-handed laws of remedies. And he arranged a marriage for Peleus with the lovely-bosomed1 daughter of Nereus, and brought up for her their incomparable child, nurturing his spirit with all fitting things, so that when the blasts of the sea-winds sent him [60] to Troy, he might withstand the spear-clashing war-shout of the Lycians and Phrygians and Dardanians; and when he came into close conflict with the spear-bearing Ethiopians, he might fix it in his mind that their leader, powerful Memnon the kinsman of Helenus, should not return to his home. From that point the light of the Aeacids has been fixed to shine far. [65] Zeus, it is your blood and your contest at which my song aimed its shot, shouting the joy of this land with the voices of young men. Their cry is well-suited to victorious Aristocleides, who linked this island with glorious praise and the sacred [70] Theoric temple of the Pythian god with splendid ambitions. By trial the accomplishment is made manifest, of that in which a man proves himself preeminent, as a boy among young boys, a man among men, or, thirdly, among elders, according to each stage which we, the race of men, possess. [75] And mortal life sets in motion four excellences, and bids us to think of what is at hand. You are not without these excellences. Farewell, my friend! I am sending this to you, honey mixed with white milk, crested with foam from mixing, a draught of song accompanied by the Aeolian breathings of flutes, [80] although it is late. The eagle is swift among birds: he swoops down from afar, and suddenly seizes with his talons his blood-stained quarry; but chattering daws stay closer to the ground. By the grace of Clio on her lovely throne and because of your victorious spirit, the light has shone on you from Nemea and Epidaurus and Megara.[852]

The fifth Nemean ode (after 480 BCE) is dedicated to **Pytheas** of Aegina,[853] who won the youth pankration at Aegina and Megara under the tutelage of his trainer, Menander. He was the son of Lampon and also trained the younger brother of Phylacidas, a pankration victor at the Nemean and Isthmian games. Pytheas and Phylacidas were of the Psalychids family.

ΠΥΘΕᾼ ΑΙΓΙΝΗΤῌ ΑΓΕΝΕΙῼ ΠΑΓΚΡΑΤΙΑΣΤῌ

οὐκ ἀνδριαντοποιός εἰμ', ὥστ' ἐλινύσοντα ἐργάζεσθαι ἀγάλματ' ἐπ' αὐτᾶς βαθμίδος
ἑσταότ': ἀλλ' ἐπὶ πάσας ὁλκάδος ἔν τ' ἀκάτῳ, γλυκεῖ' ἀοιδά,
στεῖχ' ἀπ' Αἰγίνας, διαγγέλλοισ', ὅτι
Λάμπωνος υἱὸς Πυθέας εὐρυσθενὴς
νίκη Νεμείοις παγκρατίου στέφανον,
[10] οὔπω γένυσι φαίνων τέρειναν ματέρ' οἰνάνθας ὀπώραν,
ἐκ δὲ Κρόνου καὶ Ζηνὸς ἥρωας αἰχματὰς φυτευθέντας καὶ ἀπὸ χρυσεᾶν Νηρηΐδων
Αἰακίδας ἐγέραιρεν ματρόπολίν τε, φίλαν ξένων ἄρουραν:
τάν ποτ' εὔανδρόν τε καὶ ναυσικλυτὰν
θέσσαντο πὰρ βωμὸν πατέρος Ἑλλανίου
[20] στάντες, πίτναν τ' εἰς αἰθέρα χεῖρας ἁμᾶ
Ἐνδαΐδος ἀριγνῶτες υἱοὶ καὶ βία Φώκου κρέοντος,
ὁ τᾶς θεοῦ, ὃν Ψαμάθεια τίκτ' ἐπὶ ῥηγμῖνι πόντου.
αἰδέομαι μέγα εἰπεῖν ἐν δίκᾳ τε μὴ κεκινδυνευμένον,
πῶς δὴ λίπον εὐκλέα νᾶσον, καὶ τίς ἄνδρας ἀλκίμους
[30] δαίμων ἀπ' Οἰνώνας ἔλασεν. στάσομαι: οὔ τοι ἅπασα κερδίων
φαίνοισα πρόσωπον ἀλάθει' ἀτρεκής:
καὶ τὸ σιγᾶν πολλάκις ἐστὶ σοφώτατον ἀνθρώπῳ νοῆσαι.
εἰ δ' ὄλβον ἢ χειρῶν βίαν ἢ σιδαρίταν ἐπαινῆσαι πόλεμον δεδόκηται, μακρά μοι
αὐτόθεν ἅλμαθ' ὑποσκάπτοι τις: ἔχω γονάτων ἐλαφρὸν ὁρμάν:

---

852 Pindar, *Nemean 3*, trans. Diane Arnson Svarlien, 1990, http://www.perseus.tufts.edu/hopper/text?doc=Perseus%3Atext%3A1999.01.0162%3Abook%3DN.%3Apoem%3D3, retrieved Sept. 30, 2016.
853 Pindar, *Nemean* 5, 4.

[40] καὶ πέραν πόντοιο πάλλοντ' αἰετοί.
πρόφρων δὲ καὶ κείνοις ἄειδ᾽ ἐν Παλίῳ
Μοισᾶν ὁ κάλλιστος χορός, ἐν δὲ μέσαις
φόρμιγγ᾽ Ἀπόλλων ἑπτάγλωσσον χρυσέῳ πλάκτρῳ διώκων
ἀγεῖτο παντοίων νόμων· αἱ δὲ πρώτιστον μὲν ὕμνησαν Διὸς ἀρχόμεναι σεμνὰν
Θέτιν
Πηλέα θ᾽, ὥς τέ νιν ἁβρὰ Κρηθεῒς Ἱππολύτα δόλῳ πεδᾶσαι
[50] ἤθελε ξυνᾶνα Μαγνήτων σκοπὸν
πείσαισ᾽ ἀκοίταν ποικίλοις βουλεύμασιν,
ψεύσταν δὲ ποιητὸν συνέπαξε λόγον,
ὡς ἄρα νυμφείας ἐπείρα κεῖνος ἐν λέκτροις Ἀκάστου
εὐνᾶς. τὸ δ᾽ ἐναντίον ἔσκεν· πολλὰ γάρ νιν παντὶ θυμῷ
παρφαμένα λιτάνευεν· τοῦ δὲ ὀργὰν κνίζον αἰπεινοὶ λόγοι·
[60] εὐθὺς δ' ἀπανάνατο νύμφαν, ξεινίου πατρὸς χόλον
δείσαις· ὁ δ᾽ ἐφράσθη κατένευσέν τέ οἱ ὀρσινεφὴς ἐξ οὐρανοῦ
Ζεὺς ἀθανάτων βασιλεύς, ὥστ᾽ ἐν τάχει
ποντίαν χρυσαλακάτων τινὰ Νηρεΐδων πράξειν ἄκοιτιν,
γαμβρὸν Ποσειδάωνα πείσαις, ὃς Αἰγᾶθεν ποτὶ κλειτὰν θαμὰ νίσσεται Ἰσθμὸν
Δωρίαν·
[70] ἔνθα μιν εὔφρονες ἶλαι σὺν καλάμοιο βοᾷ θεὸν δέκονται,
καὶ σθένει γυίων ἐρίζοντι θρασεῖ
πότμος δὲ κρίνει συγγενὴς ἔργων περὶ
πάντων. τὺ δ᾽ Αἰγίναθε δίς, Εὐθύμενες,
Νίκας ἐν ἀγκώνεσσι πίτνων ποικίλων ἔψαυσας ὕμνων.
[80] ἤτοι μεταΐξαντα καὶ νῦν τεὸς μάτρως ἀγάλλει κείνου ὁμόσπορον ἔθνος, Πυθέα.
ἁ Νεμέα μὲν ἄραρεν μείς τ᾽ ἐπιχώριος, ὃν φίλησ᾽ Ἀπόλλων·
ἅλικας δ᾽ ἐλθόντας οἴκοι τ᾽ ἐκράτεις
Νίσου τ᾽ ἐν εὐαγκεῖ λόφῳ. χαίρω δ᾽, ὅτι
ἐσλοῖσι μάρναται πέρι πᾶσα πόλις.
ἴσθι, γλυκεῖάν τοι Μενάνδρου σὺν τύχᾳ μόχθων ἀμοιβὰν
[90] ἐπαύρεο· χρὴ δ᾽ ἀπ᾽ Ἀθανᾶν τέκτον᾽ ἀθληταῖσιν ἔμμεν.
εἰ δὲ Θεμίστιον ἵκεις, ὥστ᾽ ἀείδειν, μηκέτι ῥίγει· δίδοι
φωνάν, ἀνὰ δ᾽ ἱστία τεῖνον πρὸς ζυγὸν καρχασίου,
πύκταν τέ νιν καὶ παγκρατίῳ φθέγξαι ἑλεῖν Ἐπιδαύρῳ διπλόαν
νικῶντ᾽ ἀρετάν, προθύροισιν δ᾽ Αἰακοῦ
ἀνθέων ποιάεντα φέρε στεφανώματα σὺν ξανθαῖς Χάρισσιν

The translation follows:
FOR PYTHEAS OF AEGINA BOYS' PANCRATIUM

I am not a sculptor, to make statues that stand motionless on the same pedestal. Sweet song, go on every merchant-ship and rowboat that leaves Aegina, and announce that Lampon's powerful son Pytheas [5] won the victory garland for the pancratium at the Nemean games, a boy whose cheeks do not yet show the tender season that is mother to the dark blossom. He has brought honor to the Aeacids, the heroic spearmen descended from Cronus and Zeus and the golden Nereids, and to his mother city, a land friendly to guests. [10] Once by the altar of father Zeus Hellenius the illustrious sons of Endais and the strong, mighty Phocus stood and prayed, stretching their hands to the sky, that the city would one day be famous for men and ships. Phocus was the son of the goddess Psamatheia; he was born by the shore of the sea. Reverence restrains me from speaking of an enormous and unjust venture, [15] how indeed they left the glorious island, and what divine power drove the brave men from Oenone. I will stop: it is not always beneficial for the precise truth to show her face, and silence is often the wisest thing for a man to heed. But if it is resolved to praise wealth, or the strength of hands, or iron war, [20] let someone mark off a long jump for me from this point. I have a light spring in my knees, and eagles swoop over the sea. The most beautiful chorus of Muses sang gladly for the Aeacids on Mt. Pelion, and among them Apollo, sweeping the seven-tongued lyre with a golden plectrum, [25] led all types of strains. And the Muses began with a prelude to Zeus, then sang first of divine Thetis and of Peleus; how Hippolyte, the opulent daughter of Cretheus, wanted to trap him with deceit. With elaborate planning she persuaded her husband, the watcher of the Magnesians, to be a partner in her plot, and she forged a false story; [30] that Peleus had made an attempt on her in Acastus' own bed. But the opposite was true; for she often begged him and coaxed him with all her heart, but her reckless words provoked his temper. Without hesitating he refused Acastus' bride, fearing the anger of father Zeus, the god of hospitality. And from the sky Zeus who rouses the clouds noticed, [35] Zeus the king of the immortals, and he promised that soon he would make one of the Nereids of the golden distaff the sea-dwelling wife of Peleus, after gaining the consent of their brother-in-law Poseidon, who often comes from Aegae to the famous Dorian Isthmus. There joyful bands welcome the god with the cry of reed-pipes, and contend with the bold strength of their limbs. [40] The fortune that is born along with a man decides in every deed. And you, Euthymenes from Aegina, have twice fallen into the arms of Victory and attained embroidered hymns. Truly even now, Pytheas, your mother's brother honors the kindred race of that hero following after you. Nemea is linked to him, and Aegina's festival month which belongs to Apollo. [45] And he was victorious over his peers both at home and in the lovely hollows of the hill of Nisus. I rejoice, because every state strives for noble deeds. Know that through the help of Menander's good fortune you won sweet requital for your toils. It is fitting that a trainer of athletes should come from Athens. [50] But if you come to Themistius, let there be no more coldness! Lift up your voice, and hoist the sails to the top-most yard; proclaim him as a boxer, and tell how he claimed double excellence with his victory in the pancratium atEpidaurus. Bring to the porch of Aeacus green garlands of flowers, in company with the golden-haired Graces.[854]

The eleventh Nemean ode (446 BCE) is dedicated to **Aristagoras** of Tenedos,[855] son of Hagesilas, to commemorate his installation at the Prytaneion. Aristagoras had garnered twelve wins at local games in wrestling and pankration. His parents would not allow him to take part in the Delphic and Olympian games. This would indicate two things: the games at Olympia were of a different level and one had to be determined to take part; secondly, the mentality of Greek parents has not changed over the last 2,500 years. Despite the existence of the Nemean ode, no victory is known nor has been recorded in connection to him at the Nemean games.[856]

ΑΡΙΣΤΑΓΟΡᾼ ΤΕΝΕΔΙῼ ΠΡΥΤΑΝΕΙ

παῖ Ῥέας, ἅ τε πρυτανεῖα λέλογχας, Ἑστία,
Ζηνὸς ὑψίστου κασιγνήτα καὶ ὁμοθρόνου Ἥρας,
εὖ μὲν Ἀρισταγόραν δέξαι τεὸν ἐς θάλαμον,
εὖ δ' ἑταίρους ἀγλαῷ σκάπτῳ πέλας,
οἵ σε γεραίροντες ὀρθὰν φυλάσσοισιν Τένεδον,
πολλὰ μὲν λοιβαῖσιν ἀγαζόμενοι πρώταν θεῶν,
πολλὰ δὲ κνίσσᾳ· λύρα δέ σφι βρέμεται καὶ ἀοιδά·
καὶ ξενίου Διὸς ἀσκεῖται Θέμις ἀενάοις
[10] ἐν τραπέζαις. ἀλλὰ σὺν δόξᾳ τέλος
δωδεκάμηνον περᾶσαι σὺν ἀτρώτῳ κραδίᾳ,
ἄνδρα δ' ἐγὼ μακαρίζω μὲν πατέρ' Ἁγησίλαν,
καὶ τὸ θαητὸν δέμας ἀτρεμίαν τε ξύγγονον.
εἰ δέ τις ὄλβον ἔχων μορφᾷ παραμεύσεται ἄλλους,
ἔν τ' ἀέθλοισιν ἀριστεύων ἐπέδειξεν βίαν,

---

854 Pindar, *Nemean 5*, trans. Diane Arnson Svarlien, 1990, http://www.perseus.tufts.edu/hopper/text?doc=Perseus%3Atext%3A1999.01.0162%3Abook%3DN.%3Apoem%3D5, retrieved Sept. 30, 2016.
855 Pindar, *Nemean* 11.3.
856 Giorgos P. Kostouros, *Nemeōn Athlōn Diēgēsis* [Record of Nemean feats], Vol. 1 (Athens, Nisos, 2008) pp. 293-295.

[20] θνατὰ μεμνάσθω περιστέλλων μέλη,
καὶ τελευτὰν ἁπάντων γᾶν ἐπιεσσόμενος·
ἐν λόγοις δ᾽ ἀστῶν ἀγαθοῖσί νιν αἰνεῖσθαι χρεών,
καὶ μελιγδούποισι δαιδαλθέντα μελιζέμεν ἀοιδαῖς.
ἐκ δὲ περικτιόνων ἑκκαίδεκ᾽ Ἀρισταγόραν
ἀγλααὶ νῖκαι πάτραν τ᾽ εὐώνυμον
ἐστεφάνωσαν πάλᾳ καὶ μεγαυχεῖ παγκρατίῳ.
ἐλπίδες δ᾽ ὀκνηρότεραι γονέων παιδὸς βίαν
ἔσχον ἐν Πυθῶνι πειρᾶσθαι καὶ Ὀλυμπίᾳ ἄθλων.

[30] ναὶ μὰ γὰρ ὅρκον, ἐμὰν δόξαν παρὰ Κασταλίᾳ
καὶ παρ᾽ εὐδένδρῳ μολὼν ὄχθῳ Κρόνου
κάλλιον ἂν δηριώντων ἐνόστησ᾽ ἀντιπάλων,
πενταετηρίδ᾽ ἑορτὰν Ἡρακλέος τέθμιον
κωμάσαις ἀνδησάμενός τε κόμαν ἐν πορφυρέοις
ἔρνεσιν. ἀλλὰ βροτῶν τὸν μὲν κενεόφρονες αὖχαι
ἐξ ἀγαθῶν ἔβαλον· τὸν δ᾽ αὖ καταμεμφθέντ᾽ ἄγαν

[41] ἰσχὺν οἰκείων παρέσφαλεν καλῶν
χειρὸς ἕλκων ὀπίσσω θυμὸς ἄτολμος ἐών.
συμβαλεῖν μὰν εὐμαρὲς ἦν τό τε Πεισάνδρου πάλαι
αἷμ᾽ ἀπὸ Σπάρτας· Ἀμύκλαθεν γὰρ ἔβα σὺν Ὀρέστᾳ,
Αἰολέων στρατιὰν χαλκεντέα δεῦρ᾽ ἀνάγων·
καὶ παρ᾽ Ἰσμηνοῦ ῥοὰν κεκραμένον
ἐκ Μελανίπποιο μάτρωος. ἀρχαῖαι δ᾽ ἀρεταὶ
ἀμφέροντ᾽ ἀλλασσόμεναι γενεαῖς ἀνδρῶν σθένος·

[50] ἐν σχερῷ δ᾽ οὔτ᾽ ὦν μέλαιναι καρπὸν ἔδωκαν ἄρουραι,
δένδρεά τ᾽ οὐκ ἐθέλει πάσαις ἐτέων περόδοις
ἄνθος εὐῶδες φέρειν πλούτῳ ἴσον,
ἀλλ᾽ ἐν ἀμείβοντι. καὶ θνατὸν οὕτως ἔθνος ἄγει
μοῖρα. τὸ δ᾽ ἐκ Διὸς ἀνθρώποις σαφὲς οὐχ ἕπεται
τέκμαρ· ἀλλ᾽ ἔμπαν μεγαλανορίαις ἐμβαίνομεν,
ἔργα τε πολλὰ μενοινῶντες· δέδεται γὰρ ἀναιδεῖ

[60] ἐλπίδι γυῖα· προμαθείας δ᾽ ἀπόκεινται ῥοαί.
κερδέων δὲ χρὴ μέτρον θηρευέμεν·
ἀπροσίκτων δ᾽ ἐρώτων ὀξύτεραι μανίαι.

Here is the translation:

FOR ARISTAGORAS OF TENEDOS ON HIS INSTALLATION AS PRESIDENT OF THE COUNCIL

Daughter of Rhea, you who have received the town hall under your protection, Hestia, sister of Zeus the highest and of Hera who shares his throne, welcome

Aristagoras to your dwelling, and welcome to a place near your splendid scepter his companions, [5] who, in honoring you, guard Tenedos and keep her on a straight course; often they worship you, first of the gods, with libations, and often with the savor of burnt sacrifice. Lyres and songs peal among them, and Themis, who belongs to Zeus the god of hospitality, is honored with everlasting feasts. With glory to the end [10] may he fulfill his twelve-month office, with his heart unwounded. I call that man blessed in his father Hagesilas, in his marvellous body, and in his inborn steadiness. But if any man who has prosperity surpasses others in beauty, and displays his strength by being best in the games, [15] let him remember that his robes are thrown around mortal limbs, and that he will clothe himself with earth, the end of all. Yet it is right for him to be praised in the good words of his fellow-citizens, and for us to adorn him with the honeyed sound of songs. For in contests of those who live around him, sixteen [20] splendid victories crowned Aristagoras and his illustrious fatherland, in wrestling and in the proud pancratium. But the too hesitant hopes of his parents restrained the boy's strength from attempting the contests at Pytho and Olympia. For I swear by the power of Oath: in my judgment, whether he went to Castalia [25] or to the well-wooded hill of Cronus, he would have returned home in finer fashion than the opponents who strove against him, having celebrated the four years' festival ordained by Heracles, and having crowned his hair with purple wreaths. But, among mortals, empty-headed pride [30] casts one man out of his goods; and a timid spirit foils another man of the fine achievements that should be his, dragging him back by the hand as he disparages his own strength too much. Truly, it was easy to recognize in him the ancient blood of Peisander of Sparta, who came from Amyclae with Orestes, [35] leading here a bronze-armored host of Aetolians, and also the blending of his blood with that of his mother's ancestor Melanippus, beside the stream of the Ismenus. But ancient excellence yields strength in alternate generations of men; the dark fields do not give fruit continuously, [40] nor are trees accustomed to bear an equal wealth of fragrant flowers in every circling year, but in alternation. And thus the race of mortal men is led by Fate. But no clear sign comes to mortals from Zeus. Nevertheless we embark on bold endeavors, [45] longing for many deeds, for our limbs are bound by shameless hope, while the streams of foresight lie far away. But we must hunt for due measure in our love of gain. The madness of unattainable desires is too sharp.[857]

Of the Isthmian odes, the fourth (477/6 BCE) is dedicated to **Melissus of Thebes**.[858]

---

[857] Pindar, *Nemean 11*, trans. Diane Arnson Svarlien, 1990, http://www.perseus.tufts.edu/hopper/text?doc=urn:cts:greekLit:tlg0033.tlg003.perseus-eng1:11, retrieved Sept. 30, 2016.
[858] Pindar, *Isthmian* 4.2.

ΜΕΛΙΣΣῼ ΘΗΒΑΙῼ ΠΑΓΚΡΑΤΙῼ

ἔστι μοι θεῶν ἕκατι μυρία παντᾷ κέλευθος:
ὦ Μέλισσ᾽, εὐμαχανίαν γὰρ ἔφανας Ἰσθμίοις
ὑμετέρας ἀρετὰς ὕμνῳ διώκειν:
αἷσι Κλεωνυμίδαι θάλλοντες αἰεὶ
σὺν θεῷ θνατὸν διέρχονται βιότου τέλος. ἄλλοτε δ᾽ ἀλλοῖος οὖρος

[10] πάντας ἀνθρώπους ἐπαΐσσων ἐλαύνει.
τοὶ μὲν ὦν Θήβαισι τιμάεντες ἀρχᾶθεν λέγονται
πρόξενοί τ᾽ ἀμφικτιόνων κελαδεννᾶς τ᾽ ὀρφανοὶ
ὕβριος: ὅσσα δ᾽ ἐπ᾽ ἀνθρώπους ἄηται
μαρτύρια φθιμένων ζωῶν τε φωτῶν
ἀπλέτου δόξας, ἐπέψαυσαν κατὰ πᾶν τέλος: ἀνορέαις δ᾽ ἐσχάταισιν

[20] οἴκοθεν στάλαισιν ἅπτονθ᾽ Ἡρακλείαις:
καὶ μηκέτι μακροτέραν σπεύδειν ἀρετάν.
ἱπποτρόφοι τ᾽ ἐγένοντο,
χαλκέῳ τ᾽ Ἄρει ἅδον.
ἀλλ᾽ ἀμέρᾳ γὰρ ἐν μιᾷ
τραχεῖα νιφὰς πολέμοιο τεσσάρων
ἀνδρῶν ἐρήμωσεν μάκαιραν ἑστίαν:
νῦν δ᾽ αὖ μετὰ χειμέριον ποικίλων μηνῶν ζόφον

[30] χθὼν ὥτε φοινικέοισιν ἄνθησεν ῥόδοις
δαιμόνων βουλαῖς. ὁ κινητὴρ δὲ γᾶς Ὀγχηστὸν οἰκέων
καὶ γέφυραν ποντιάδα πρὸ Κορίνθου τειχέων,
τόνδε πορὼν γενεᾷ θαυμαστὸν ὕμνον
ἐκ λεχέων ἀνάγει φάμαν παλαιὰν

[40] εὐκλέων ἔργων: ἐν ὕπνῳ γὰρ πέσεν: ἀλλ᾽ ἀνεγειρομένα χρῶτα λάμπει,
Ἀωσφόρος θαητὸς ὣς ἄστροις ἐν ἄλλοις:
ἅ τε κἀν γουνοῖς Ἀθανᾶν ἅρμα καρύξαισα νικᾶν
ἔν τ᾽ Ἀδραστείοις ἀέθλοις Σικυῶνος ὤπασεν
τοιάδε τῶν τότ᾽ ἐόντων φύλλ᾽ ἀοιδᾶν.
οὐδὲ πανηγυρίων ξυνᾶν ἀπεῖχον

[50] καμπύλον δίφρον, Πανελλάνεσσι δ᾽ ἐριζόμενοι δαπάνᾳ χαῖρον ἵππων.
τῶν ἀπειράτων γὰρ ἄγνωστοι σιωπαί,
ἔστιν δ᾽ ἀφάνεια τύχας καὶ μαρναμένων,
πρὶν τέλος ἄκρον ἱκέσθαι:
τῶν τε γὰρ καὶ τῶν διδοῖ:
καὶ κρέσσον᾽ ἀνδρῶν χειρόνων

[59] ἔσφαλε τέχνα καταμάρψαισ'. ἴστε μὰν Αἴαντος ἀλκὰν φοίνιον, τὰν ὀψίᾳ
ἐν νυκτὶ ταμὼν περὶ ᾧ φασγάνῳ, μομφὰν ἔχει παίδεσσιν Ἑλλάνων ὅσοι Τρῴανδ᾽
ἔβαν.
ἀλλ᾽ Ὅμηρός τοι τετίμακεν δι᾽ ἀνθρώπων, ὅς αὑτοῦ
~ πᾶσαν ὀρθώσαις ἀρετὰν κατὰ ῥάβδον ἔφρασεν
θεσπεσίων ἐπέων λοιποῖς ἀθύρειν.
τοῦτο γὰρ ἀθάνατον φωνᾶεν ἕρπει,
[70] εἴ τις εὖ εἴπῃ τι: καὶ πάγκαρπον ἐπὶ χθόνα καὶ διὰ πόντον βέβακεν
ἐργμάτων ἀκτὶς καλῶν ἄσβεστος αἰεί.
προφρόνων Μοισᾶν τύχοιμεν, κεῖνον ἅψαι πυρσὸν ὕμνων
καὶ Μελίσσῳ, παγκρατίου στεφάνωμ᾽ ἐπάξιον,
ἔρνεϊ Τελεσιάδα. τόλμᾳ γὰρ εἰκὼς
θυμὸν ἐριβρεμετᾶν θηρῶν λεόντων
[80] ἐν πόνῳ, μῆτιν δ᾽ ἀλώπηξ, αἰετοῦ ἅ τ᾽ ἀναπιτναμένα ῥόμβον ἴσχει.
χρὴ δὲ πᾶν ἔρδοντα μαυρῶσαι τὸν ἐχθρόν.
οὐ γὰρ φύσιν Ὠαριωνείαν ἔλαχεν:
ἀλλ᾽ ὀνοτὸς μὲν ἰδέσθαι,
συμπεσεῖν δ᾽ ἀκμᾷ βαρύς.
καίτοι ποτ᾽ Ἀνταίου δόμους
[90] Θηβᾶν ἄπο Καδμεϊᾶν μορφὰν βραχύς, ψυχὰν δ᾽ ἄκαμπτος, προσπαλαίσων ἦλθ᾽
ἀνήρ
τὰν πυροφόρον Λιβύαν, κρανίοις ὄφρα ξένων ναὸν Ποσειδάωνος ἐρέφοντα
σχέθοι,
υἱὸς Ἀλκμήνας: ὃς Οὐλυμπόνδ᾽ ἔβα, γαίας τε πάσας
καὶ βαθύκρημνον πολιᾶς ἁλὸς ἐξευρὼν θέναρ,
ναυτιλίαισί τε πορθμὸν ἀμερώσαις.
νῦν δὲ παρ᾽ Αἰγιόχῳ κάλλιστον ὄλβον
[100] ἀμφέπων ναίει, τετίματαί τε πρὸς ἀθανάτων φίλος, Ἥβαν τ᾽ ὀπυίει,
χρυσέων οἴκων ἄναξ καὶ γαμβρὸς Ἥρας.
τῷ μὲν Ἀλέκτρᾶν ὕπερθεν δαῖτα πορσύνοντες ἀστοὶ
καὶ νεόδματα στεφανώματα βωμῶν αὔξομεν
ἔμπυρα χαλκοαρᾶν ὀκτὼ θανόντων,
τοὺς Μεγάρα τέκε οἱ Κρειοντὶς υἱούς: 65
[110] τοῖσιν ἐν δυθμαῖσιν αὐγᾶν φλὸξ ἀνατελλομένα συνεχὲς παννυχίζει
αἰθέρα κνισάεντι λακτίζοισα καπνῷ,
καὶ δεύτερον ἆμαρ ἐτείων τέρμ᾽ ἀέθλων
γίνεται, ἰσχύος ἔργον.
ἔνθα λευκωθεὶς κάρα 70
μύρτοις ὅδ᾽ ἀνὴρ διπλόαν
[120] νίκαν ἀνεφάνατο παίδων τρίταν πρόσθεν, κυβερνατῆρος οἰακοστρόφου
γνώμᾳ πεπιθὼν πολυβούλῳ. σὺν Ὀρσέᾳ δέ νιν κωμάξομαι, τερπνὰν ἐπιστάζων
χάριν.

Here it is in translation:

FOR MELISSUS OF THEBES PANCRATIUM

Thanks to the gods, I have countless paths opening on every side; Melissus, at the Isthmian games you revealed abundant resources for celebrating in song the excellence of your family, in which the sons of Cleonymus flourish perpetually, [5] with a god's favor, as they progress towards the mortal end of life. But a changeable wind sweeps down and drives all men at different times. These men truly are spoken of as honored in Thebes from the beginning; they have good relations with the neighboring towns, and are bereft of loud arrogance. And as for the memorials that fly through all the world, [10] memorials of boundless fame for living and dead men, they have attained all of these in full. Through their manly deeds they reached from home to touch the farthest limit, the pillars of Heracles— do not pursue excellence any farther than that! And they became breeders of horses [15] and were pleasing to bronze-clad Ares. But on a single day the rough storm of war robbed their blessed hearth of four men. Now, after the wintry gloom of the changing months, the ground has blossomed as if with crimson roses by the will of the gods. The shaker of the earth who dwells at Onchestus [20] and at the sea-bridge before the walls of Corinth, by offering to that family this marvellous song, wakes from her bed their ancient fame for glorious deeds. For she had fallen asleep, but now she has awakened and her body shines, marvellous to see, like the morning-star among other stars. [25] She proclaimed their chariot victorious on the high ground of Athens and also in Sicyon at the games of Adrastus, and thus gave them leaves of song, like these, from the singers of their time. Nor did they keep their curved chariot from competing in the general contests; striving against all of Greece, they rejoiced in spending their wealth on their horses. [30] Those who attempt nothing face silence and obscurity, and fortune remains hidden even to those who contend, until they reach the final goal. For she dispenses from this side and from that, and the skill of weaker men [35] can overtake and trip up a stronger man. Indeed, you know of the bloodstained might of Aias, which late at night he pierced by falling on his own sword, thus bringing blame on all the sons of the Greeks who went to Troy. But he is honored throughout the world by Homer, who set the record right concerning all his excellence and told it with the staff of his divine words, for posterity to play. [40] For if one says something well, that saying goes forth speaking with an immortal voice. And the radiance of fine deeds, forever unquenchable, has crossed the fruitful earth and the sea. May we win the favor of the Muses and kindle that torch of song, a worthy garland from the pancratium [45] for Melissus, too, the scion of the race of Telesias. For in the toil of conflict he resembles the spirit of loud-roaring lions in boldness, while in wisdom he is like the fox, who forestalls the swoop of the eagle by falling on her back. And it is right to do anything to blot out one's enemy. For Melissus was not allotted the nature of Orion; [50] he is negligible to look at, though heavy to grapple with in his strength. And yet once there went from Thebes, Cadmus' city, a hero short in stature but unflinching in spirit. This hero went to the house of Antaeus in grain-bearing Libya, to keep him from roofing Poseidon's temple with the skulls of strangers, [55] Alcmena's son. He went to Olympus, after he had explored all lands and the high-cliffed hollow of the gray sea, and had tamed the straits for sailors. Now he dwells beside aegis-bearing Zeus, and has the most beautiful prosperity. He is honored as a friend by the immortals and is married to Hebe; [60] he is lord of a golden house, and son-in-law to Hera. For him, above the Electran gates, we Thebans, busily preparing the feast and the circle of newly-built altars, pile up burnt offerings in honor of the eight bronze-clad men, now dead, the sons whom Megara, Creon's daughter, bore him. [65] For them the flame rises in the rays of the setting sun and blazes all night long, prodding the air with fragrant smoke. And on the second day is that struggle of strength, the final event of the annual games. And there, his head wreathed with white [70] myrtle, this man showed forth a double victory, having won before in the boy's contest by heeding the wise advice of his helmsman and trainer, Orseas. I will honor him together with Orseas in my victory-song, pouring delightful grace on both.[859]

The fifth (477/6 BCE) and sixth (after 476 BCE) Isthmian odes are dedicated to **Phylacidas** of Aegina.[860]

ΦΥΛΑΚΙΔΑ ΑΙΓΙΝΗΤῌ ΠΑΓΚΡΑΤΙῼ

μᾶτερ Ἀλίου πολυώνυμε Θεία,
σέο ἕκατι καὶ μεγασθενῆ νόμισαν
χρυσὸν ἄνθρωποι περιώσιον ἄλλων:
καὶ γὰρ ἐριζόμεναι
νᾶες ἐν πόντῳ καὶ ἅρμασιν ἵπποι
διὰ τεάν, ὤνασσα, τιμὰν ὠκυδινάτοις ἐν ἁμίλλαισι θαυμασταὶ πέλονται:
ἔν τ' ἀγωνίοις ἀέθλοισι ποθεινὸν
[10] κλέος ἔπραξεν, ὅντιν' ἀθρόοι στέφανοι
χερσὶ νικάσαντ' ἀνέδησαν ἔθειραν
ἢ ταχυτᾶτι ποδῶν.
κρίνεται δ' ἀλκὰ διὰ δαίμονας ἀνδρῶν.
δύο δέ τοι ζωᾶς ἄωτον μοῦνα ποιμαίνοντι τὸν ἄλπνιστον εὐανθεῖ σὺν ὄλβῳ,
εἴ τις εὖ πάσχων λόγον ἐσλὸν ἀκούῃ.
μὴ μάτευε Ζεὺς γενέσθαι: πάντ' ἔχεις,
εἴ σε τούτων μοῖρ' ἐφίκοιτο καλῶν.

---

859 Pindar, *Isthmian 4*, trans. Diane Arnson Svarlien, 1990, http://www.perseus.tufts.edu/hopper/text?doc=urn:cts:greekLit:tlg0033.tlg004.perseus-eng1:4, retrieved 9/26/2016.
860 Pindar, *Isthmian* 5.22, 6.10.

[20] θνατὰ θνατοῖσι πρέπει.
  τὶν δ᾽ ἐν Ἰσθμῷ διπλόα θάλλοισ᾽ ἀρετά,
  Φυλακίδα, κεῖται, Νεμέᾳ δὲ καὶ ἀμφοῖν,
  Πυθέᾳ τε παγκρατίου. τὸ δ᾽ ἐμὸν
  οὐκ ἄτερ Αἰακιδᾶν κέαρ ὕμνων γεύεται:
  σὺν Χάρισιν δ᾽ ἔμολον Λάμπωνος υἱοῖς
  τάνδ᾽ ἐς εὔνομον πόλιν. εἰ δὲ τέτραπται
  θεοδότων ἔργων κέλευθον ἂν καθαράν,
[30] μὴ φθόνει κόμπον τὸν ἐοικότ᾽ ἀοιδᾷ
  κιρνάμεν ἀντὶ πόνων.
  καὶ γὰρ ἡρώων ἀγαθοὶ πολεμισταὶ
  λόγον ἐκέρδαναν, κλέονται δ᾽ ἔν τε φορμίγγεσσιν ἐν αὐλῶν τε παμφώνοις
  ὁμοκλαῖς μυρίον χρόνον: μελέταν δὲ σοφισταῖς
  Διὸς ἕκατι πρόσβαλον σεβιζόμενοι:
  ἐν μὲν Αἰτωλῶν θυσίαισι φαενναῖς
  Οἰνεΐδαι κρατεροί,
[40] ἐν δὲ Θήβαις ἱπποσόας Ἰόλαος
  γέρας ἔχει, Περσεὺς δ᾽ ἐν Ἄργει, Κάστορος δ᾽ αἰχμὰ Πολυδεύκεος τ᾽ ἐπ᾽ Εὐρώτα
  ῥεέθροις.
  ἀλλ᾽ ἐν Οἰνώνᾳ μεγαλήτορες ὀργαὶ
  Αἰακοῦ παίδων τε: τοὶ καὶ σὺν μάχαις
  δὶς πόλιν Τρώων πράθον ἑσπόμενοι
  Ἡρακλῆϊ πρότερον,
  καὶ σὺν Ἀτρείδαις. ἔλα νῦν μοι πεδόθεν:
  λέγε, τίνες Κύκνον, τίνες Ἕκτορα πέφνον,
[50] καὶ στράταρχον Αἰθιόπων ἄφοβον
  Μέμνονα χαλκοάραν: τίς ἄρ᾽ ἐϋλὸν Τήλεφον
  τρῶσεν ἑῷ δορὶ Καΐκου παρ᾽ ὄχθαις;
  τοῖσιν Αἴγιναν προφέρει στόμα πάτραν
  διαπρεπέα νᾶσον: τετείχισται δὲ πάλαι
  πύργος ὑψηλαῖς ἀρεταῖς ἀναβαίνειν.
  πολλὰ μὲν ἀρτιεπὴς
  γλῶσσά μοι τοξεύματ᾽ ἔχει περὶ κείνων
[60] κελαδέσαι: καὶ νῦν ἐν Ἄρει μαρτυρήσαι κεν πόλις Αἴαντος ὀρθωθεῖσα ναύταις
  ἐν πολυφθόρῳ Σαλαμὶς Διὸς ὄμβρῳ
  ἀναρίθμων ἀνδρῶν χαλαζάεντι φόνῳ.
  ἀλλ᾽ ὅμως καύχημα κατάβρεχε σιγᾷ:
  Ζεὺς τά τε καὶ τὰ νέμει,
  Ζεὺς ὁ πάντων κύριος. ἐν δ᾽ ἐρατεινῷ

[70] μέλιτι καὶ τοιαίδε τιμαὶ καλλίνικον χάρμ' ἀγαπάζοντι. μαρνάσθω τις ἔρδων
ἀμφ' ἀέθλοισιν γενεὰν Κλεονίκου
ἐκμαθών: οὔτοι τετύφλωται μακρὸς
μόχθος ἀνδρῶν: οὐδ' ὁπόσαι δαπάναι
ἐλπίδων ἔκνισ' ὄπιν.
αἰνέω καὶ Πυθέαν ἐν γυιοδάμαις
Φυλακίδᾳ πλαγᾶν δρόμον εὐθυπορῆσαι
χερσὶ δεξιόν, νόῳ ἀντίπαλον.
λάμβανέ οἱ στέφανον, φέρε δ' εὔμαλλον μίτραν,
[80] καὶ πτερόεντα νέον σύμπεμψον ὕμνον.

Translated:

FOR PHYLACIDAS OF AEGINA PANCRATIUM

Mother of the Sun, Theia of many names, for your sake men honor gold as more powerful than anything else; [5] and through the value you bestow on them, o queen, ships contending on the sea and yoked teams of horses in swift-whirling contests become marvels. And in athletic contests, someone who has wreathed his hair with many garlands has achieved longed-for fame, when he has been victorious with his hands [10] or with the swiftness of his feet. But the valor of men is judged by gods, and there are only two things that cultivate the sweetest flower of life in blossoming prosperity: to have good fortune and a noble reputation. Do not seek to become Zeus; you have everything, [15] if a share of these fine things comes to you. Mortal aims befit mortal men. But for you, Phylacidas, flourishing twofold excellence is recorded at the Isthmus, and at Nemea for both you and Pytheas in the pancratium. But my heart [20] cannot taste songs without telling of the race of Aeacus. I have come with the Graces for the sons of Lampon to this well-governed city. If Aegina turns her steps to the clear road of god-given deeds, then do not grudge [25] to mix for her in song a boast that is fitting recompense for toils. In heroic times, too, fine warriors gained fame, and they are celebrated with lyres and flutes in full-voiced harmonies for time beyond reckoning. Heroes who are honored by the grace of Zeus provide a theme for skilled poets: [30] among the Aetolians the brave sons of Oeneus are worshipped with shining sacrifices; in Thebes the horseman Iolaus has his honor, and Perseus in Argos, and the spearman Castor together with Polydeuces by the streams of Eurotas. But in Oenone the honors belong to the great-hearted spirits [35] of Aeacus and his sons. Twice in battles they sacked the city of the Trojans: the first time following Heracles, the second time the sons of Atreus. Now, drive me into the air! Tell me, who killed Cycnus, and who Hector, [40] and the fearless commander of the Ethiopians, bronze-armed Memnon? Who wounded noble Telephus with his spear by the banks of Caïcus? Men whose voices name the outstanding island of Aegina as their fatherland, built long ago [45] as a tower for lofty excellence to ascend. My swift tongue has many arrows, to shout the praises of these heroes. And now the city of Aias, Salamis, could testify that she was saved by her sailors in Ares' confrontation in the destructive storm sent by Zeus, [50] when slaughter poured like hail on countless men. Nevertheless, quench this boast in silence. Zeus dispenses both good and bad, Zeus the master of all. But such honors as these also welcome the joy of triumph, covered with the delicious honey of song. Let a man strive and contend [55] in the games when he has learned from the race of Cleonicus. The long toil of their men is not hidden in blind darkness, nor has thought of the expense fretted away their devotion to their hopes. I praise Pytheas also among limb-subduing pancratiasts, [60] skillful with his hands in guiding straight the course of Phylacidas' blows, and with a mind to match. Take a garland for him, and bring him a fillet of fine wool, and send along this winged new song.[861]

ΦΥΛΑΚΙΔΑ ΑΙΓΙΝΗΤΗ ΠΑΓΚΡΑΤΙΩ

θάλλοντος ἀνδρῶν ὡς ὅτε συμποσίου
δεύτερον κρητῆρα Μοισαίων μελέων
κίρναμεν Λάμπωνος εὐάθλου γενεᾶς ὕπερ, ἐν Νεμέᾳ μὲν πρῶτον, ὦ Ζεῦ,
τίν γ› ἄωτον δεξάμενοι στεφάνων,
νῦν αὖτε Ἰσθμοῦ δεσπότα
Νηρεΐδεσσί τε πεντήκοντα, παίδων ὁπλοτάτου
[10] Φυλακίδα νικῶντος. εἴη δὲ τρίτον
σωτῆρι πορσαίνοντας Ὀλυμπίῳ Αἴγιναν κάτα
σπένδειν μελιφθόγγοις ἀοιδαῖς.
εἰ γάρ τις ἀνθρώπων δαπάνᾳ τε χαρείς
καὶ πόνῳ πράσσει θεοδμάτους ἀρετάς,
σύν τέ οἱ δαίμων φυτεύει δόξαν ἐπήρατον, ἐσχατιαῖς ἤδη πρὸς ὄλβου
βάλλετ› ἄγκυραν θεότιμος ἐών.
[20] τοίαισιν ὀργαῖς εὔχεται
ἀντιάσαις Ἀΐδαν γῆράς τε δέξασθαι πολιὸν
ὁ Κλεονίκου παῖς: ἐγὼ δ› ὑψίθρονον
Κλωθὼ κασιγνήτας τε προσεννέπω ἑσπέσθαι κλυταῖς
ἀνδρὸς φίλου Μοίρας ἐφετμαῖς.
ὔμμε τ›, ὦ χρυσάρματοι Αἰακίδαι,
τέθμιόν μοι φαμὶ σαφέστατον ἔμμεν

---

861 Pindar, *Isthmian 5*, trans. Diane Arnson Svarlien, 1990, http://www.perseus.tufts.edu/hopper/text?doc=urn:cts:greekLit:tlg0033.tlg004.perseus-eng1:5, retrieved Sept. 30, 2016.

[30] τάνδ' ἐπιστείχοντα νᾶσον ῥαινέμεν εὐλογίαις.
μυρίαι δ' ἔργων καλῶν τέτμηνθ' ἑκατόμπεδοι ἐν σχερῷ κέλευθοι,
καὶ πέραν Νείλοιο παγᾶν καὶ δι' Ὑπερβορέους·
οὐδ' ἔστιν οὕτω βάρβαρος οὔτε παλίγγλωσσος πόλις,
ἅτις οὐ Πηλέος ἀίει κλέος ἥρωος, εὐδαίμονος γαμβροῦ θεῶν, οὐδ' ἅτις Αἴαντος
Τελαμωνιάδα καὶ πατρός· τὸν χαλκοχάρμαν ἐς πόλεμον

[40] ἆγε σὺν Τιρυνθίοισι πρόφρονα σύμμαχον ἐς Τροΐαν, ἥρωσι μόχθον,
Λαομεδοντίαν ὑπὲρ ἀμπλακίαν
ἐν ναυσὶν Ἀλκμήνας τέκος.
εἷλε δὲ Περγαμίαν, πέφνεν δὲ σὺν κείνῳ Μερόπων
ἔθνεα καὶ τὸν βουβόταν οὔρεϊ ἴσον
Φλέγραισιν εὑρὼν Ἀλκυονῆ, σφετέρας δ' οὐ φείσατο

[50] χερσὶν βαρυφθόγγοιο νευρᾶς
Ἡρακλέης. ἀλλ' Αἰακίδαν καλέων
ἐς πλόον κύρησε δαινυμένων.
τὸν μὲν ἐν ῥινῷ λέοντος στάντα κελήσατο νεκταρέαις σπονδαῖσιν ἄρξαι
καρτεραίχμαν Ἀμφιτρυωνιάδαν,
ἄνδωκε δ' αὐτῷ φέρτατος
οἰνοδόκον φιάλαν χρυσῷ πεφρικυῖαν Τελαμών,

[60] ὁ δ' ἀνατείναις οὐρανῷ χεῖρας ἀμάχους
αὔδασε τοιοῦτον ἔπος· "εἴ ποτ' ἐμάν, ὦ Ζεῦ πάτερ,
θυμῷ ἐθέλων ἀρὰν ἄκουσας,
νῦν σε, νῦν εὐχαῖς ὑπὸ θεσπεσίαις
λίσσομαι παῖδα θρασὺν ἐξ Ἐριβοίας
ἀνδρὶ τῷδε, ξεῖνον ἁμὸν μοιρίδιον τελέσαι,
τὸν μὲν ἄρρηκτον φυάν, ὥσπερ τόδε δέρμα με νῦν περιπλανᾶται

[70] θηρός, ὃν πάμπρωτον ἄθλων κτεῖνά ποτ' ἐν Νεμέᾳ·
θυμὸς δ' ἑπέσθω." ταῦτ' ἄρα οἱ φαμένῳ πέμψεν θεὸς
ἀρχὸν οἰωνῶν μέγαν αἰετόν· ἀδεῖα δ' ἔνδον νιν ἔκνιξεν χάρις,
εἶπέν τε φωνήσαις ἅτε μάντις ἀνήρ·
"ἔσσεταί τοι παῖς, ὃν αἰτεῖς, ὦ Τελαμών·
καί νιν ὄρνιχος φανέντος κέκλε' ἐπώνυμον εὐρυβίαν Αἴαντα, λαῶν

[80] ἐν πόνοις ἔκπαγλον Ἐνυαλίου."
ὣς ἄρα εἰπὼν αὐτίκα
ἕζετ'. ἐμοὶ δὲ μακρὸν πάσας ἀγήσασθ' ἀρετάς·
Φυλακίδᾳ γὰρ ἦλθον, ὦ Μοῖσα, ταμίας
Πυθέᾳ τε κώμων Εὐθυμένει τε. τὸν Ἀργείων τρόπον
εἰρήσεταί που κἀν βραχίστοις.
ἄραντο γὰρ νίκας ἀπὸ παγκρατίου
τρεῖς ἀπ' Ἰσθμοῦ, τὰς δ' ἀπ' εὐφύλλου Νεμέας,

[90] ἀγλαοὶ παῖδές τε καὶ μάτρως· ἀνὰ δ' ἄγαγον ἐς φάος οἵαν μοῖραν ὕμνων·
τὰν Ψαλυχιδᾶν δὲ πάτραν Χαρίτων
ἄρδοντι καλλίστᾳ δρόσῳ,
τόν τε Θεμιστίου ὀρθώσαντες οἶκον τάνδε πόλιν
θεοφιλῆ ναίοισι. Λάμπων δὲ μελέταν
ἔργοις ὀπάζων Ἡσιόδου μάλα τιμᾷ τοῦτ' ἔπος,
[100] υἱοῖσί τε φράζων παραινεῖ,
ξυνὸν ἄστει κόσμον ἑῷ προσάγων,
καὶ ξένων εὐεργεσίαις ἀγαπᾶται,
μέτρα μὲν γνώμᾳ διώκων, μέτρα δὲ καὶ κατέχων·
γλῶσσα δ' οὐκ ἔξω φρενῶν· φαίης κέ νιν ἀνδράσιν ἀθληταῖσιν ἔμμεν
Ναξίαν πέτραις ἐν ἄλλαις χαλκοδάμαντ' ἀκόναν.
πίσω σφε Δίρκας ἁγνὸν ὕδωρ, τὸ βαθύζωνοι κόραι
[110] χρυσοπέπλου Μναμοσύνας ἀνέτειλαν παρ' εὐτειχέσιν Κάδμου πύλαις.

Translated:

FOR PHYLACIDAS OF AEGINA PANCRATIUM

Just as we mix the second bowl of wine when the men's symposium is flourishing, here is the second song of the Muses for Lampon's children and their athletic victories: first in Nemea, Zeus, in your honor they received the choicest of garlands, [5] and now in honor of the lord of the Isthmus and the fifty Nereids, for the victory of the youngest son, Phylacidas. May there be a third libation of honey-voiced songs to pour over Aegina in honor of Zeus Soter of Olympia. [10] For if a man, rejoicing in expense and toil, achieves godly excellence, and a divinity sows the seed of lovely fame in him, then he already casts his anchor on the farthest shore of prosperity, since he is honored by the gods. The son of Cleonicus prays that with such feelings [15] he will meet death and welcome gray old age. And I entreat Clotho, throned on high, and her sister Fates, to hear my friend's prayers for fame. And as for you, sons of Aeacus with your golden chariots, [20] I say that it is my clearest law to sprinkle you with praises whenever I set foot on this island. Countless continuous roads have been cut a hundred feet wide for your fine deeds, both beyond the springs of the Nile and through the land of the Hyperboreans. There is no city so barbarous or so strange in its speech [25] that it does not know the fame of the hero Peleus, the fortunate in-law of gods, or of Aias and his father Telamon. The son of Alcmena led him in ships to Troy, the toil of heroes, for war that delights in bronze, as an eager ally along with the men of Tiryns because of Laomedon's wrongdoing. [30] He took Pergamos, and with Telamon's help he slew the tribes of Meropes, and the herdsman Alcyoneus, huge as a mountain, whom he found at Phlegrae, and he did not keep his hands off the deep-voiced bow-string, not [35] Heracles. But when he came to summon the son of Aeacus to that expedition, he found them feasting. Standing in a lion's skin, the strong warrior, son of Amphitryon, was asked to pour the first libation of nectar by incomparable Telamon, who lifted up to him [40] the wine-bearing goblet bristling with gold. And Heracles stretched his invincible hands up to heaven and said, "Father Zeus, if you have ever heard my prayers with a willing heart, now, now with divine prayers [45] I entreat you to grant this man a brave son from Eriboea, a son fated to be my guest-friend. May he have a body as invulnerable as this skin that is now wrapped around me, from the beast whom I killed that day in Nemea as the very first of my labors. And may he have spirit to match." When he had spoken, the god sent to him [50] the king of birds, a great eagle. He felt thrilled inside with sweet joy, and he spoke like a prophet: "Telamon, you will have the son that you ask for. Name him after the bird that appeared: wide-ruling Aias, awesome in the war-toils of the people."[1] [55] He spoke, and immediately sat down. But for me it would take a long time to tell the story of all their excellence. For I came, Muse, a steward of victory-songs to Phylacidas and Pytheas and Euthymenes. The story will be told in the Argive manner, very briefly. [60] For those splendid boys and their uncle won three victories in the pancratium—at the Isthmus, and others at Nemea with its fine trees, and they brought to light a great share of praises. With the lovely dew of the Graces they refresh the family of the Psalychids; [65] they have kept upright the house of Themistius, and they live in a city which the gods love. Lampon, "taking care with his work," honors these words of Hesiod, and he advises his sons with them too, thus bringing a shared adornment to his city. [70] He is loved for his kindness to his guest-friends; he pursues with moderation in his thoughts and restrains with moderation. He does not say one thing and think another. You might say that for athletes he is like the bronze-mastering Naxian whetstone among other stones. I shall give him to drink the pure water of Dirce, which the deep-waisted daughters of [75] golden-robed Mnemosyne brought forth beside the fine-walled gates of Cadmus.[862]

The seventh Isthmian ode (454 BCE) is dedicated to **Strepsiades** of Thebes.[863]

---

862 Pindar, *Isthmian 6*, trans. Diane Arnson Svarlien, 1990,. http://data.perseus.org/citations/urn:cts:greekLit:tlg0033.tlg004.perseus-eng1:6, retrieved Sept. 30, 2016.
863 Pindar, *Isthmian* 7.29.

ΣΤΡΕΨΙΑΔῌ ΘΗΒΑΙῼ ΠΑΓΚΡΑΤΙῼ

τίνι τῶν πάρος, ὦ μάκαιρα Θήβα,
καλῶν ἐπιχωρίων μάλιστα θυμὸν τεὸν
εὔφρανας; ἦ ῥα χαλκοκρότου πάρεδρον
Δαμάτερος ἁνίκ' εὐρυχαίταν
ἄντειλας Διόνυσον; ἢ χρυσῷ μεσονύκτιον νίφοντα δεξαμένα τὸν φέρτατον θεῶν,
ὁπότ' Ἀμφιτρύωνος ἐν θυρέτροις
[10] σταθεὶς ἄλοχον μετῆλθεν Ἡρακλείοις γοναῖς;
ἢ ὅτ' ἀμφὶ πυκναῖς Τειρεσίαο βουλαῖς;
ἢ ὅτ' ἀμφ' Ἰόλαον ἱππόμητιν;
ἢ Σπαρτῶν ἀκαμαντολογχᾶν; ἢ ὅτε καρτερᾶς Ἄδραστον ἐξ ἀλαλᾶς ἄμπεμψας ὀρφανὸν
μυρίων ἑτάρων ἐς Ἄργος ἵππιον;
ἢ Δωρίδ' ἀποικίαν οὕνεκεν ὀρθῷ
ἔστασας ἐπὶ σφυρῷ
[20] Λακεδαιμονίων, ἕλον δ' Ἀμύκλας 15
Αἰγεῖδαι σέθεν ἔκγονοι, μαντεύμασι Πυθίοις;
ἀλλὰ παλαιὰ γὰρ
εὕδει χάρις, ἀμνάμονες δὲ βροτοί,
ὅ τι μὴ σοφίας ἄωτον ἄκρον
κλυταῖς ἐπέων ῥοαῖσιν ἐξίκηται ζυγέν. 20
κώμαζ' ἔπειτεν ἁδυμελεῖ σὺν ὕμνῳ
καὶ Στρεψιάδᾳ· φέρει γὰρ Ἰσθμοῖ
[30] νίκαν παγκρατίου· σθένει τ' ἔκπαγλος ἰδεῖν τε μορφάεις· ἄγει τ' ἀρετὰν οὐκ αἴσχιον φυᾶς.
φλέγεται δὲ ἰοπλόκοισι Μοίσαις,
μάτρωΐ θ' ὁμωνύμῳ δέδωκε κοινὸν θάλος, 25
χάλκασπις ᾧ πότμον μὲν Ἄρης ἔμιξεν,
τιμὰ δ' ἀγαθοῖσιν ἀντίκειται.
[40] ἴστω γὰρ σαφὲς ὅστις ἐν ταύτᾳ νεφέλᾳ χάλαζαν αἵματος πρὸ φίλας πάτρας ἀμύνεται,
λοιγὸν ἄντα φέρων ἐναντίῳ στρατῷ,
ἀστῶν γενεᾷ μέγιστον κλέος αὔξων 30
ζώων τ' ἀπὸ καὶ θανών.
τὺ δέ, Διοδότοιο παῖ, μαχατὰν
αἰνέων Μελέαγρον, αἰνέων δὲ καὶ Ἕκτορα
Ἀμφιάρηόν τε,
εὐανθέ' ἀπέπνευσας ἁλικίαν 35
προμάχων ἀν' ὅμιλον, ἔνθ' ἄριστοι

[50] ἔσχον πολέμοιο νεῖκος ἐσχάταις ἐλπίσιν.
ἔτλαν δὲ πένθος οὐ φατόν: ἀλλὰ νῦν μοι
Γαιάοχος εὐδίαν ὄπασσεν
ἐκ χειμῶνος. ἀείσομαι χαίταν στεφάνοισιν ἁρμόσαις. ὁ δ᾽ ἀθανάτων μὴ
θρασσέτω φθόνος, 40
ὅ τι τερπνὸν ἐφάμερον διώκων
ἕκαλος ἔπειμι γῆρας ἔς τε τὸν μόρσιμον
αἰῶνα. θνάσκομεν γὰρ ὁμῶς ἅπαντες:
[60] δαίμων δ᾽ ἄϊσος: τὰ μακρὰ δ᾽ εἴ τις
παπταίνει, βραχὺς ἐξικέσθαι χαλκόπεδον θεῶν ἕδραν: ὅτι πτερόεις ἔρριψε
Πάγασος 45
δεσπόταν ἐθέλοντ᾽ ἐς οὐρανοῦ σταθμοὺς
ἐλθεῖν μεθ᾽ ὁμάγυριν Βελλεροφόνταν
Ζηνός: τὸ δὲ πὰρ δίκαν
γλυκὺ πικροτάτα μένει τελευτά.
[70] ἄμμι δ᾽, ὦ χρυσέα κόμα θάλλων, πόρε, Λοξία, 50
τεαῖσιν ἁμίλλαισιν
εὐανθέα καὶ Πυθόϊ στέφανον.

And the translation:

FOR STREPSIADES OF THEBES PANCRATIUM

In which of the local glories of the past, divinely blessed Thebe, did you most delight your spirit? Was it when you raised to eminence the one seated beside Demeter of the clashing bronze cymbals, flowing-haired [5] Dionysus? Or when you received, as a snow-shower of gold in the middle of the night, the greatest of the gods, when he stood in the doorway of Amphitryon, and then went in to the wife to beget Heracles? Or did you delight most in the shrewd counsels of Teiresias? Or in the wise horseman Iolaus? [10] Or in the Sown Men, untiring with the spear? Or when you sent Adrastus back from the mighty war-shout, bereft of countless companions, to Argos, home of horses? Or because you stood upright on its feet the Dorian colony of the men of Lacedaemon, and your descendants, [15] the Aegeids, captured Amyclae according to the Pythian oracles? But since ancient grace sleeps, and mortals are forgetful of whatever does not reach the highest bloom of skillful song, joined to glorious streams of words, [20] then begin the victory procession with a sweet-singing hymn for Strepsiades; for he is the victor in the pancratium at the Isthmus, both awesome in his strength and handsome to look at; and he treats excellence as no worse a possession than beauty. He is made radiant by the violet-haired Muses, and he has given a share in his flowering garland to his uncle and namesake, [25] for whom Ares of the bronze shield mixed the cup of destiny; but honor is laid up as recompense for good men. For let him know clearly, whoever, in this cloud of war, wards off the hailstorm of blood in defense of his dear fatherland by bringing destruction to the enemy host, that he is causing the greatest glory to grow for the race of his fellow-citizens, [30] in both his life and his death. And you, son of Diodotus, emulating the warrior Meleager, emulating Hector and Amphiaraus, breathed out your blossoming youth [35] in the front ranks, where the best men sustained the strife of war at the limit of their hopes. They endured unspeakable sorrow; but now the holder of the earth has sent me calm after the storm. I shall sing entwining my hair with garlands. May the envy of the immortals not disturb [40] whatever delight I pursue from day to day as I peacefully make my way towards old age and the allotted span of my life. For we die all alike, but our fates are diverse. If a man looks to things far away, he is too short to reach the bronze-floored home of the gods; winged Pegasus threw his master Bellerophon, who wanted to go to the dwelling-places of heaven and the company of Zeus. A thing that is sweet beyond measure is awaited by a most bitter end. But grant to us, Loxias, luxuriant with your golden hair, [50] a blossoming garland also from your contests at Pytho.[864]

The eighth Isthmian ode (478 BCE) is dedicated to **Cleandrus** of Aegina.[865]

ΚΛΕΑΝΔΡῼ ΑΙΓΙΝΗΤῌ ΠΑΓΚΡΑΤΙῼ

Κλεάνδρῳ τις ἁλικίᾳ τε λύτρον
εὔδοξον, ὦ νέοι, καμάτων
πατρὸς ἀγλαὸν Τελεσάρχου παρὰ πρόθυρον ἰὼν ἀνεγειρέτω
κῶμον, Ἰσθμιάδος τε νίκας ἄποινα, καὶ Νεμέᾳ
[10] ἀέθλων ὅτι κράτος ἐξεῦρε. τῷ καὶ ἐγώ, καίπερ ἀχνύμενος θυμόν, αἰτέομαι
χρυσέαν καλέσαι Μοῖσαν. ἐκ μεγάλων δὲ πενθέων λυθέντες
μήτ᾽ ἐν ὀρφανίᾳ πέσωμεν στεφάνων,
μήτε κάδεα θεράπευε: παυσάμενοι δ᾽ ἀπρήκτων κακῶν
γλυκύ τι δαμωσόμεθα καὶ μετὰ πόνον:
[20] ἐπειδὴ τὸν ὑπὲρ κεφαλᾶς
τὸν Ταντάλου λίθον παρά τις ἔτρεψεν ἄμμι θεός,
ἀτόλματον Ἑλλάδι μόχθον. ἀλλά
μοι δεῖμα μὲν παροιχόμενον
καρτερὰν ἔπαυσε μέριμναν: τὸ δὲ πρὸ ποδὸς ἄρειον ἀεὶ <σκοπεῖν>
χρῆμα πᾶν. δόλιος γὰρ αἰὼν ἐπ᾽ ἀνδράσι κρέμαται,

---

864 Pindar, *Isthmian* 7, trans. Diane Arnson Svarlien, 1990, http://data.perseus.org/citations/urn:cts:greekLit:tlg0033.tlg004.perseus-eng1:7, retrieved Sept. 30, 2016.
865 Pindar, *Isthmian* 8.1

[30] ἑλίσσων βίου πόρον· ἰατὰ δ' ἔστι βροτοῖς σύν γ' ἐλευθερίᾳ καὶ τά. χρὴ δ' ἀγαθὰν ἐλπίδ' ἀνδρὶ
μέλειν· χρὴ δ' ἐν ἑπταπύλοισι Θήβαις τραφέντα
Αἰγίνᾳ Χαρίτων ἄωτον προνέμειν,
πατρὸς οὕνεκα δίδυμαι γένοντο θύγατρες Ἀσωπίδων
[40] ὁπλόταται, Ζηνί τε ἅδον βασιλέϊ.
ὃ τὰν μὲν παρὰ καλλιρόῳ
Δίρκᾳ φιλαρμάτου πόλιος ᾤκισσεν ἁγεμόνα·
σὲ δ' ἐς νᾶσον Οἰνοπίαν ἐνεγκὼν
κοιμᾶτο, δῖον ἔνθα τέκες
Αἰακὸν βαρυσφαράγῳ πατρὶ κεδνότατον ἐπιχθονίων· ὃ καὶ
[50] δαιμόνεσσι δίκας ἐπείραινε· τοῦ μὲν ἀντίθεοι
ἀρίστευον υἱέες υἱέων τ' ἀρηΐφιλοι παῖδες ἀνορέᾳ χάλκεον στονόεντ' ἀμφέπειν
ὅμαδον· σώφρονές τ' ἐγένοντο πινυτοί τε θυμόν.
ταῦτα καὶ μακάρων ἐμέμναντ' ἀγοραί,
[60] Ζεὺς ὅτ' ἀμφὶ Θέτιος ἀγλαός τ' ἔρισαν Ποσειδᾶν γάμῳ,
ἄλοχον εὐειδέ' ἐθέλων ἑκάτερος
ἑὰν ἔμμεν· ἔρως γὰρ ἔχεν.
ἀλλ' οὔ σφιν ἄμβροτοι τέλεσαν εὐνὰν θεῶν πραπίδες,
ἐπεὶ θεσφάτων ἐπάκουσαν· εἶπε δ'
εὔβουλος ἐν μέσοισι Θέμις,
[70] οὕνεκεν πεπρωμένον ἦν φέρτερον γόνον ἄνακτα πατρὸς τεκεῖν
ποντίαν θεόν, ὃς κεραυνοῦ τε κρέσσον ἄλλο βέλος
διώξει χερὶ τριόδοντός τ' ἀμαιμακέτου, Δί τε μισγομέναν ἢ Διὸς παρ'
ἀδελφεοῖσιν.--"ἀλλὰ τὰ μὲν παύσατε· βροτέων δὲ λεχέων τυχοῖσα
[80] υἱὸν εἰσιδέτω θανόντ' ἐν πολέμῳ,
χεῖρας Ἄρεΐ ἀκμάν ποδῶν.
τὸ μὲν ἐμὸν Πηλέϊ γάμου θεόμορον
ὀπάσσαι γέρας Αἰακίδᾳ,
ὄντ' εὐσεβέστατον φάτις Ἰωλκοῦ τράφειν πεδίον·
ἰόντων δ' ἐς ἄφθιτον ἄντρον εὐθὺς
[90] Χείρωνος αὐτίκ' ἀγγελίαι·
μηδὲ Νηρέος θυγάτηρ νεικέων πέταλα δὶς ἐγγυαλιζέτω
ἄμμιν· ἐν διχομηνίδεσσιν δὲ ἑσπέραις ἐρατὸν
[100] λύοι κεν χαλινὸν ὑφ' ἥρωϊ παρθενίας." ὣς φάτο Κρονίδαις ἐννέποισα θεά· τοὶ
δ' ἐπὶ γλεφάροις νεῦσαν ἀθανάτοισιν· ἐπέων δὲ καρπὸς οὐ κατέφθινε. φαντὶ
γὰρ ξύν' ἀλέγειν καὶ γάμον Θέτιος ἄνακτα. καὶ νεαρὰν ἔδειξαν σοφῶν στόματ'
ἀπείροισιν ἀρετὰν Ἀχιλέος· ὃ καὶ Μύσιον ἀμπελόεν
[110] αἵμαξε Τηλέφου μέλανι ῥαίνων φόνῳ πεδίον, γεφύρωσέ τ' Ἀτρεΐδαισι νόστον,
Ἑλέναν τ' ἐλύσατο, Τρωΐας ἶνας ἐκταμὼν δορί, ταί νιν ῥύοντό ποτε μάχας
ἐναριμβρότου ἔργον ἐν πεδίῳ κορύσσοντα, Μέμνονός τε βίαν

[120] ὑπέρθυμον Ἕκτορά τ' ἄλλους τ' ἀριστέας: οἷς δῶμα Φερσεφόνας μανύων Ἀχιλεύς,
οὖρος Αἰακιδᾶν, Αἴγιναν σφετέραν τε ῥίζαν πρόφαινεν.
τὸν μὲν οὐδὲ θανόντ᾽ ἀοιδαὶ ἔλιπον,
ἀλλά οἱ παρά τε πυρὰν τάφον θ᾽ Ἑλικώνιαι παρθένοι
στάν, ἐπὶ θρῆνόν τε πολύφαμον ἔχεαν.
[130] ἔδοξ᾽ ἄρα τόδ᾽ ἀθανάτοις,
ἐσλόν γε φῶτα καὶ φθίμενον ὕμνοις θεᾶν διδόμεν.
τὸ καὶ νῦν φέρει λόγον, ἔσσυταί τε
Μοισαῖον ἅρμα Νικοκλέος
μνᾶμα πυγμάχου κελαδῆσαι. γεραίρετέ νιν, ὅς Ἴσθμιον ἂν νάπος
Δωρίων ἔλαχεν σελίνων: ἐπεὶ περικτίονας
[140] ἐνίκασε δή ποτε καὶ κεῖνος ἄνδρας ἀφύκτῳ χερὶ κλονέων. τὸν μὲν οὐ κατελέγχει
κριτοῦ γενεὰ πατραδελφεοῦ: ἁλίκων τῷ τις ἁβρὸν
ἀμφὶ παγκρατίου Κλεάνδρῳ πλεκέτω
μυρσίνας στέφανον, ἐπεί νιν Ἀλκαθόου τ᾽ ἀγὼν σὺν τύχᾳ
[150] ἐν Ἐπιδαύρῳ τε νεότας δέκετο πρίν:
τὸν αἰνεῖν ἀγαθῷ παρέχει:
ἥβαν γὰρ οὐκ ἄπειρον ὑπὸ χειᾷ καλῶν δάμασεν.

Translated:

FOR CLEANDROS OF AEGINA PANCRATIUM

Young men! One of you go, in honor of Cleandros and his youth, to the splendid doorway of his father Telesarchus, and awake the victory-song, glorious recompense for his troubles, as a reward for his victory at the Isthmus, and [5] because he found strength in the Nemean games. Therefore I too, though grieving in my heart, am asked to invoke the golden Muse. Released from great sorrows, let us not fall into bereavement of garlands; do not nurse your pain. Having ceased from insurmountable troubles, we will sing something sweet for the people, even after toil. Since [10] one of the gods has turned aside for us the stone of Tantalus above our heads, an unbearable hardship for Greece. But as for me, the passing away of terror has stopped my mighty worry. It is always better to look at what lies before one's foot, in every case. For a treacherous lifetime hangs over men's heads, [15] twisting around the path of life. Yet even this may be healed for mortals, if only they have freedom. It is right for a man to take to heart good hope; and it is right for a man raised in seven-gated Thebes to offer the choicest bloom of the Graces to Aegina. For as twin daughters they were born to the same father, the youngest of Asopus' children, and they were pleasing to Zeus the king. He caused one of them to dwell beside the beautiful stream [20] of Dirce, to lead a chariot-loving city; but he carried you to the island Oenopia and slept with you there, where you bore Aeacus, the dearest of all men on earth to the loud-thundering father. Aeacus settled disputes even for the gods. His god-like [25] sons and their sons, devoted to war, were the best in manliness, engaged in the brazen battle-throng that causes groans, and they were wise and prudent in spirit. All this was remembered even by the assembly of the blessed gods, when Zeus and splendid Poseidon contended for marriage with Thetis, each of them wanting her to be his lovely bride; for desire possessed them. [30] But the immortal minds of the gods did not accomplish that marriage for them, when they heard the divine prophecies. Wise Themis spoke in their midst and said that it was fated that the sea-goddess should bear a princely son, stronger than his father, who would wield another weapon in his hand more powerful than the thunderbolt [35] or the irresistible trident, if she lay with Zeus or one of his brothers. "No, cease from this. Let her accept a mortal's bed, and see her son die in battle, a son who is like Ares in the strength of his hands and like lightning in the swift prime of his feet. My counsel is to bestow this god-granted honor of marriage on Peleus son of Aeacus, [40] who is said to be the most pious man living on the plain of Iolcus. Let the message be sent at once to Cheiron's immortal cave, right away, and let the daughter of Nereus never again place the leaves of strife in our hands. On the evening of the full moon [45] let her loosen the lovely bridle of her virginity for that hero." So the goddess spoke, addressing the sons of Cronus, and they nodded assent with their immortal brows. The fruit of her words did not perish, for they say that Zeus shared the common concern even for the marriage of Thetis. And the voices of poets made known the youthful excellence of Achilles to those who had been unaware of it—Achilles, who [50] stained the vine-covered plain of Mysia, spattering it with the dark blood of Telephus, and bridged a homecoming for the Atreids, and freed Helen, cutting with his spear the sinews of Troy, which had once tried to keep him from marshalling on the plain the work of man-slaying war—he cut down [55] the high-spirited strength of Memnon, and Hector, and other excellent heroes. Achilles, champion of the sons of Aeacus, showed them the way to the house of Persephone, and thus brought fame to Aegina and to his race. Even when he was dead songs did not forsake him; beside his pyre and tomb the Muses of Helicon stood, and poured over him the many-voiced dirge. It proved to be the will of the immortals [60] to make a noble man, even when dead, a theme for the hymns of goddesses; and even now this brings up a subject for words, and the Muses' chariot rushes forward to shout praises in memory of Nicocles the boxer. Honor him, who won the garland of wild Dorian celery in the Isthmian valley; since [65] he too was once victorious over all that lived around him, battering them with his inescapable hands. He is not dishonored by the offspring of his father's distinguished brother. Therefore let another young man weave for Cleandros a garland of tender myrtle in honor of the pancratium, since the contest of Alcathous and the young men of Epidaurus welcomed him before in his success. A good man may praise him, [70] for he did not restrain his youth, keeping it hidden in his pocket and ignorant of fine deeds.[866]

The change in social class of the participants

The true weapon of the warrior was his physical strength and skills, and the only effective preparation for battle, even indirectly, was to engage in athletics and in exercise generally. The democratization and popularity of physical education is largely due to this belief, as physical training continued to hold pride of place in education.[867]

Once democracy was established during the sixth century and more so during the fifth century BCE, with the wider acceptance of the gymnasium as a public education institutions, the middle and lower classes began to gain access to athletic competition. As a result, athletes from the lower classes were able to take part in local and national sporting events and ultimately came to compete in the Olympic games.[868] Opinions differ as to the exact timeline, the extent of and the causes behind this development, but most agree that by the end of the fifth century BCE and certainly by the end of the fourth century, there is enough evidence to indicate that athletes from both privileged and non-privileged classes stood side by side, without being obliged to show respect for each athlete on the basis of his ancestry or social position.[869]

Some researchers have interpreted this development as an indicator of democratization, but one could also say that in reality it was a continuation of the hegemony of the upper classes which earned credit with merchants and craftsmen. Along with the broadening of the talent pool, pressure to produce better athletes for transnational competition led to more professionalized sports and an expansion of athletic training. The extension of privileges inherent among the higher classes to those few successful athletes ultimately served to reaffirm the nationwide status and thus the domestic power of the ruling class of every city.[870] The athletic arena was not on its own a tool for changing social class; it functioned more as a means to be used by those who had recently risen socially to acquire symbolic ornaments of privilege. This

---

866 Pindar, *Isthmian 8*, trans. Diane Arnson Svarlien, 1990, http://data.perseus.org/citations/urn:cts:greekLit:tlg0033.tlg004.perseus-eng1:8, retrieved Sept. 30, 2016.
867 Marrou, *Istoria tēs ekpaideusēs*, p. 102.
868 Albanidis and Nikolakaki, "The Social Origin," p. 176.
869 Hubbard, "Contemporary," p. 381.
870 Hubbard, "Contemporary," p. 379.

assimilation of aristocratic customs did not so much challenge the status of the aristocratic leadership as it manifested the attempt of successful athletes to join its ranks and be included in the upper classes.[871] In one respect, it is possible that this assimilation into the next highest social class of the city made possible by the games served as one of the incentives for competitors.[872]

We have seen that at some point between 600 and 400 BCE, young athletes from the wealthier classes united with athletes from lower classes. The emergence of urban *gymnasia* may have facilitated the training of these young athletes, and success at local games and monetary prizes may have helped the more talented young athletes to hire a private trainer and devote more time to their training and ultimately reach an Olympian level. The fact that the ability of poor youths and adult athletes reached an Olympic level shortly after 600 BCE is not in doubt, but their chance of winning would have been slight. The monetary prizes could not have been large enough to finance the training required for the ten months leading up to the start of the games and the one month's stay at Elis. A typical example is that of the very wealthy and powerful Athenian politician Alcibiades in the late fifth century BCE who complained that some of the athletes arriving at Olympia were from small, insignificant towns with a low birth rate and level of training.[873]

But why did athletes from the lower classes compete at all? What was their incentive? Possibly it was the honors, both moral and material, that Olympic victors and generally all winners of athletic contests enjoyed, including money, special statues, social recognition and a powerful influence over public opinion. These aspects would have served as a strong incentive for more athletes of a non-aristocratic background to take part in athletic contests.[874]

Funding for athletes from lower classes

Aside from athletes receiving financial support from their families, there was another way for less well-off athletes to pay for the expenses involved in a high level of training on their own. That was to try to win at a smaller local contest offering monetary prizes, or *chrēmatitēs* games. The money from a first win may not have been enough to start a career, but subsequent victories could finance their career as they progressed. There is also the opinion that access

---

[871] Hubbard, "Contemporary," pp. 385, 386.
[872] Hubbard, "Contemporary," p. 385.
[873] Pleket, "The Olympic Games," p. 406.
[874] Albanidis and Nikolakaki, "The Social Origin," p. 177.

to public *gymnasia* and the *ephēbeia* reserved for training youths, which were paid for my most *poleis*, was a major help to poorer athletes seeking quality training.[875] On the other hand, an ambitious athlete who lacked the resources to train properly could very well find himself badly injured.[876]

After the fourth century BCE, it is easier to see that people without family wealth could still succeed in sports through sponsorships provided by their *poleis* for their training.[877] It is possible there was funding available for what we would call sponsorship for very talented young athletes from their own *polis*, which would have made a difference in the democratic era. The oldest known evidence of such practices is from an inscription at Ephesus dated at 300 BCE, according to which the trainer of a talented young athlete who was not from a privileged class but had won at Nemea asked the city's popular assembly to fund the athlete's training and trips abroad, particularly throughout the Aegean.[878] A papyrus from 257 BCE tells us that the wealthy Zenon of Alexandria hired Ptolemaeus as a coach for the young athlete Pyrrhus and assumed all expenses for his training.[879]

How the ruling class saw athletics

A paradox was discernible in classical Athens: though more opportunities were made available to all of the civic classes of Athenian society to take part in games, it actually had a limited effect on athletic participation. The athletes of the city continued to emerge mainly from the upper classes. It is then surprising that lower-class Athenians who were very popular athletes were honored generously by the city rulers and even more so than other groups which were also popular. This paradox may be due to the cultural overlap between athletics and war in Athenian democracy. The practical and ideological democratization of war during the classical era in Athens was legitimized and supported by the upper classes associated with sports.[880]

But something else was also happening. The upper class of Athens, and perhaps in other cities as well, supported and, where necessary, was called

---

875 Albanidis and Nikolakaki, "The Social Origin," p. 179.
876 Poliakoff, *Combat sports*, p. 131.
877 Poliakoff, *Combat sports*, p. 131.
878 Pleket, "The Olympic Games," p. 406; Nigel B. Crowther, "Athlete and State: Qualifying for the Olympic Games in Ancient Greece," Journal of Sport History 23, no. 1 (Spring 1996): p. 35; Poliakoff, Combat sports, p. 131.
879 Poliakoff, *Combat sports,* p. 32.
880 Pritchard, "Sport, War and Democracy," p. 212.

upon to pay for the training of athletic teams and other activities related to competitive games. Through this generous funding, members of the social elite earned the gratitude of the people and this often translated into political support or leniency if they ever had to come up before a popular committee. For example, after 350 BCE, the ruling class in the city of Athens undertook the staging of about 100 athletic events a year. In fact, there were reports of Athenians who spent more on notable athletic festivals than on military forces and clearly much more money than for all other public activities. This led Aristophanes to refer to the "union of wealth aimed at exploiting musical and athletic games."[881]

By sponsoring these agonistic festivals, the benefactors endeavored to keep Greek civilization alive. A donation to help a city acquire a new building or to create an athletic competition turned out to be an excellent way for a benefactor to leave behind a permanent record of his life there.[882]

Democracy in classical Athens had paid much attention to keeping the athletic venues of the city in good condition, and leading politicians contributed to developing these public assets. In the fifth century BCE, for example, Cimon followed the precedent of previous tyrants and provided private funds to renovate the Academy, while Pericles used public funds to do likewise for the Lyceum and Alcibiades introduced a law to modify the Cynosarges gymnasium. Later on, during the fourth century BCE, Lycurgus not only completed the construction of the Theater of Dionysus, but also supervised the construction of the Panathenaic Stadium and further renovation of the Lyceum.[883]

During the Hellenistic and Roman periods, the cultural convergence of the Hellenistic era with new customs had a major impact on the Olympic games. *Gymnasia* were established in all *poleis*, while after 337 BCE most of them had been incorporated into the institution of the *ephēbeia*. Competitions also became more frequent, while members of the middle and lower classes were certainly afforded more opportunities to take part in the Olympics.

During the Roman imperial period, the athletic arena was characterized by spectacle, costly benefits for athletes and a growing participation by the lower classes at athletic meetings. One characteristic of the era was the less well-off athletes who were associated with the economic support they received. In 300 BCE, the city of Ephesus sponsored two young athletes (Athenodorus and Timonax) so they could take part in the panhellenic games.[884]

---

881 Pritchard, "Sport, War and Democracy," p. 213.
882 Boutet-Lanouette, «La vie agonistique,» pp. 1-4.
883 Pritchard, "Sport, War and Democracy," p. 213.
884 Albanidis and Nikolakaki, "The Social Origin," p. 178.

Inscriptions inform us that during the Roman years, professional athletes, such as members of athletic guilds, took part in the Olympic games. The members of these guilds originated mainly from the middle and lower classes. Many were often illiterate. Numerous writers of the Roman period, such as Galen, Philostratus, Plutarch, Lucian and Epictetus, were highly critical of these athletic practices and of the low level of education of those involved. Their criticism further reveals the lower social status of participating athletes.[885]

MARBLE BASE OF STATUE OF OLYMPIC PANKRATIAST KALLIAS OF ATHENS.
AFTER 472 BCE. THE WORK OF ATHENIAN SCULPTOR MICON.
OLYMPIA ARCHAEOLOGICAL MUSEUM
(photo from the author's collection)

---

885 Albanidis and Nikolakaki, "The Social Origin," p. 179.

Chapter 7

PANKRATION IN EDUCATION

Organization of the education system

Education is a collective method through which every society initiates its youth into the values and ways of its cultural life. This process obviously is a lengthy one, since a particular culture must first solidify the unique form which will then be reflected in its education system.[886]

In the Hellenistic period, the educational process took twelve years: from the age of seven to nineteen.[887]

In Athens, about which more information is available, education was neither compulsory nor public. The state did not determine how long this process had to be; however, it did supervise and regulate the proper function of the individual schools through various laws.[888] Physical training began at the age of seven and continued at the *gymnasia* and *palaestrae* under the supervision of the state.[889] Once the youths reached the age of eighteen and began attending the *ephēbeia*, they continued their training until they were twenty-one years old.[890] In general, physical training was of primary importance throughout Greece and, along with music, contributed to the balanced development of young people. Physical exercise was such an important part of education for the ancient Greeks that those who did not engage in it were considered uneducated.[891] Athletics were one of three areas of traditional male education in classical Athens. The other two were music and grammar. Moreover, we know that during the fifth century BCE in Athens and other Greek city-states, physical education was an established subject for children and was offered at public primary schools from the age of six through fourteen.[892]

---

886 Marrou, *Istoria tēs ekpaideusēs*, p. 13.
887 Marrou, *Istoria tēs ekpaideusēs*, p. 227.
888 Mouratidis, *Istoria physikēs agōgēs*, p. 138.
889 Marrou, *Istoria tēs ekpaideusēs*, p. 228.
890 Aristotle, *Politics*, 1336b, 38-40.
891 Mouratidis, *Istoria physikēs agōgēs*, p. 164.
892 Kyriazis and Economou, "Macroculture," pp. 431-455, 444.

In more detail:

In the early stages, up to the age of seven, children could enjoy their childhood as they stayed with their families. The mother oversaw the child's education, with the help of nannies, female teachers or the father.[893]

From the age of seven to eleven, the children were sent to schools where they were taught privately by teachers, or they could learn a craft.[894] At this age, the children studied reading, writing, arithmetic, poetry, gymnastics and music with the help of a music teacher or *kithara* player.

Between the ages of eleven and fourteen, the child had to learn to use the language properly, develop his vocabulary, perfect his accent and enunciation, and interpret poetry and historical writings under the guidance of a man of letters or a scholar.[895] At fifteen, a young boy would have finished his general studies.[896]

Secondary education (fourteen to eighteen years of age) was apparently a privilege enjoyed by the affluent classes who could afford the cost of further education. This phase lasted until the youths were of an age to enter the *ephēbeia*.[897]

Before proceeding with the *ephēbeia*, however, let us take a look at what the philosophers of the time believed about the relationship between education and gymnastics.

Athletic exercise held a very significant place in what the Greeks called *agōgē*, or "training." It was not, however, an end in itself, since one-sided physical training was considered savage and brutal. The term *paideia* meant educating citizens in excellence and goodness. The ultimate goal of such an education was to create the ideal human to rule and be ruled justly.

In discussing the training of *Phylakes*, the guardians who, in *The Republic*, were charged with the highest duty of protecting the fatherland, Plato claimed that their training should include gymnastics for the body and music for the soul. In fact, music - together with poetry - should take precedence over gymnastics.[898] Athletic training functioned to supplement their musical training, starting at a young age and continuing without interruption.[899]

---

893 George Bitros and Anastassios Karayiannis, "Character, knowledge and skills in ancient Greek education: Lessons for today's policy makers," Munich Personal RePEc Archive 18012 (Oct. 20, 2009): p. 8.
894 Aristotle, *Politics*, 1337a, 1-5.
895 Goodwin F. Berquist, Jr., "Isocrates of Athens: foremost speech teacher of the ancient world," The Speech Teacher 8, no. 3 (1959): p. 251.
896 Berquist, "Isocrates of Athens," p. 251.
897 Kyriazis and Economou, "Macroculture," pp. 431-455, 445.
898 Plato, *The Republic*, 376 e.
899 Gogaki, *Oi antilipseis*, p. 136.

He distinguished two types of gymnastics: *orchēsis* (dance) and *palē* (wrestling). *Orchēsis* would play the role of teaching gymnastics and dance movement for the choral dance performances held during religious public ceremonies and would include any form of repetitive rhythmic movement of the feet, hands, head, eyes or the entire body.[900] The other type of exercise, *palē*, would represent competitive gymnastics and military preparations for battle. It was an exercise for the hands, the sides of the body and the neck which aimed to develop physical strength and health in combination with a desire to win, which was believed to be most appropriate for military conflict. According to Plato, the techniques that Antaeus and Cercyon developed in wrestling, or Epeius and Amycus in boxing were of no value since they were not useful in military battles. Plato insisted that movements in wrestling were very similar to those in battle and young men should learn them mainly for military purposes and not just to become better wrestlers.[901] He also believed that citizens should eagerly send their children to the *paidotribēs* (physical trainers) so they would not appear cowardly at war.[902]

Plato detailed the movements that he called the *choros*, and further broke down the two types of dance mentioned earlier. He called the first *polemikos*, with beautiful bodies in solemn movement that emanated nobility, while the second involved the movement of ugly bodies which he called *favlos*, a more inferior, debauched type. Both types had two sub-types. Of the *spoudaioi* - the two virtuous forms - one was warlike and contained movements of handsome and brave soldiers who are giving their all in battle, and the other contained movements depicting more temperate souls enjoying their prosperous lives with moderation. The first was called the *Pyrrhic* dance and featured movements intended to evade blows of all kinds by swerving, ducking, jumping in the air and crouching. The second he called "pacific," since it imitated the peaceful life of modest pleasures.[903] He also suggested contests with or without weapons as an additional weight, and training in wrestling, boxing, pankration and warfare in all age classes: for boys seven to sixteen years of age; for ephebes (youths) aged seventeen to twenty; and men, from age twenty on.[904]

Aristotle believed that in order for gymnastics to fulfill its logical purpose, the young boys should be turned over to the *paidotribēs* and *gymnastēs*

---

900 Plato, Laws, 655d, 795d.
901 Gogaki, *Oi antilipseis*, pp. 129, 130, 131.
902 Plato, *Gorgias*, 518a.
903 Gogaki, *Oi antilipseis*, pp. 132, 133.
904 Plato, *Laws*, 833c.

(coaches and trainers) so they could be taught certain habits.[905] He also believed that the pentathlon was a sport best adapted to warfare, as it provided all-round benefits, superior strength, enhanced stature and increased swiftness of foot.[906] Aristotle had contempt for professional athletes because he believed they followed a training regimen that was inappropriate for citizens; they developed disproportionately and adhered to excessive dieting.[907]

Philostratus, on the other hand, was a supporter of the pankration: firstly, because it was the most difficult and spectacular sport and thus he believed it was the most worthy for the men of Olympia.[908] Moreover, it highlighted the complex demands to which pankratiasts would have to respond; they would have to be more skilled as wrestlers compared to boxers, and possess better boxing skills than wrestlers.[909] He wondered why it took so long to add boys' pankration to the Olympic program, even though it had already acquired quite a reputation in other places.[910] He noted that athletes in heavy events, including pankratiasts, were trained by the Eleans in the month leading up to the games, and this was a time of year when the sun was at its hottest and the mud in the Arcadian valley burned. The athletes tolerated the dust, which was hotter than the Ethiopian sand, sticking to their bodies and suffered through training starting at midday, under the burning sky.[911]

The institution of the *ephēbeia*

It is important to take a look at the institution of the *ephēbeia*, why it was so important and how it was related to pankration.

Although before the fourth century BCE, the Greeks were divided but powerful, they were now even more divided and very weak. The lengthy wars had exhausted the larger *poleis* so that there was no major power within Greece able to deter hostilities.[912] To get a sense of how likely the outbreak of conflict between cities was, it is sufficient to consider that though in the Mycenaean era there were no more than one hundred city-states, during the Archaic and classical period, there were more than one thousand.[913] In Athens particularly,

---

905 Aristotle, *Politics*, 1338b.
906 Aristotle, *Rhetoric*, 1361b.
907 Aristotle, *Politics*, 1335b 6-12.
908 Philostratus, *Imagines* 2.6.
909 Philostratus, *Gymnasticus*, 36.
910 Philostratus, *Gymnasticus*, 13.24.
911 Philostratus, *Gymnasticus*, 11.18.
912 Mouratidis, *Istoria physikēs agōgēs*, p. 157.
913 Nicholas Kyriazis and Xenophon Paparrigopoulos, "War and democracy in ancient Greece," Eu-

the situation was not good at all after the Battle of Chaeronea in 338 BCE, when its army proved too weak to defend itself against the well-organized Macedonia phalanx. At one time, Athenian citizens were eager to spill their blood to protect their homeland, but in this period many were unwilling to enter into military service. This forced the state to pay mercenaries to defend it, filling the gap left by the indifference of its citizens. The Athenian state was thus forced, especially after its defeat at Chaeronea, to introduce a compulsory draft in order to enlist young men. Athens was willing to pay all expenses for their training and armor, which was presented to them at a public ceremony before the city rulers.[914]

We learn from Aristotle that young men were registered at these schools, called *ephēbeia*, after they reached the age of eighteen. The training period lasted through their nineteenth and twentieth years,[915] and was similar to the modern-day compulsory military service in Greece. After these two years, the *ephēboi* were recognized as proper citizens. The *ephēbeia* was completely controlled by the *polis*.[916]

It is believed that the institution of the *ephēbeia* came into being in 335 BCE, after Athens lost the Battle of Chaeronea in 338 BC. In fact, the instigator of the idea was Epicrates, a fourth century, wealthy rhetorician and demagogue who even financed the institution for a time. Some, however, believe that military training existed in both the pre-classical and classical periods and that Epicrates merely expanded it.[917]

Information on the institution of the *ephēbeia* is only available with regard to the two major cities of Athens and Sparta. But they were more or less the same in other Greek cities as well.[918] As we saw earlier, every Greek city had a gymnasium and a *palaestra*. The importance ascribed to the training of youths is demonstrated by the fact that in cities with more than one gymnasium, one was used exclusively to train the *ephēboi*.[919]

In Athens, the parents of eighteen-year-old citizens elected at a popular assembly three men over the age of forty to organize the *ephēboi* and train them throughout Attica. The three served as ephors (guardians), one of whom was the *sophronistēs* (superintendent) and another was the *epimelitēs*

---

ropean Journal of Law and Economics 38 (2014): pp. 167, 168.
914 Mouratidis, *Istoria physikēs agōgēs*, pp. 157, 158.
915 Aristotle, *Athenian Constitution*, 42.1.
916 Farantos, *Philosophia 1*, pp. 96, 97.
917 Anastasios Giannikopoulos, "Pote archise o thesmos tēs ephēveias [When did the institution of ephebeia begin]?" Archaeologia 35 (1993): p. 65.
918 Marrou, *Istoria tēs ekpaideusēs*, pp. 232, 233.
919 Albanidis, *Istoria tēs athlēsēs*, p. 222.

(manager). The same popular assembly also elected two *paidotribēs* and other instructors who trained the youths in weapons-handling.[920]

In the first year, the ephebes were posted to a camp in Piraeus and underwent physical training and military instruction. Their particular assignment was to guard the coast and engage in athletic activities (games, footraces, throwing, jumping, boxing, pankration, hunting and dancing). In the second year, they focused on military field exercises and joined garrisons at fortified border positions where they served as national guardsmen.[921] Their main military training requirement was to patrol the area and they were sometimes called *peripoloi*, from the word for patrolling. The food was the same for everyone. In the second year, the young men put on a public demonstration and continued with their military training.[922] The *ephēboi* put on three demonstrations of what they had learned - one each year and one upon graduating, which was the most important and was held before the Council and sometimes, if not always, at the Panathenaic Stadium.[923]

Nevertheless, after the mid-fourth century BCE, the physical training provided at the *ephēbeia*, initially taking place in the first year of the program, was extended to the second year at the expense of weapons training. The reason for this was that the *ephēbeia* had already become more of a cultural institution and were considered an extension of the general education system of the Athenians.[924] The *ephēboi* still enjoyed physical exercise as the mainstay of their program, but they also took part in footraces, torch relays, wrestling, boxing, pankration, rowing and equestrian competitions.[925] These contests were held at the local deme level for the entertaining of the city's youth, and not at the panhellenic level of competition. The *palaestrae* at these training facilities were intended for use only by professional athletes, already specialized since childhood and held for the benefit of all Greeks.[926]

One could serve in the cavalry, providing his own horse and equipment, or as a soldier without full armor (*psilos*), or as a sailor. The *ephēbeia* of Attica is described as an adapted version of the Spartan training, or indoctrination, of the heavily armed soldier in ethics and democracy. The military exercises in which the *ephēboi* took part were not merely ceremonial, but were aimed

---

920 Farantos, *Philosophia 1*, p. 96.
921 Marrou, *Istoria tēs ekpaideusēs*, p. 234.
922 Farantos, *Philosophia 1*, p. 96.
923 Chrysis Pelekidis, *Histoire de l'éphébie attique des origines à 31 avant Jésus-Chris* (E. de Boccard, Paris, 1962), pp. 272, 273.
924 Papakyriakou, «Ē koinonikē sēmasia,» pp. 140, 141.
925 Marrou, *Istoria tēs ekpaideusēs*, p. 257.
926 Marrou, *Istoria tēs ekpaideusēs*, p. 257.

at preparing young men for war.[927] It was a system of political and military training for the soldier-citizen.[928] This training system was less rigorous than that of Sparta, while literacy was considered more important and music was an integral part of their *agōgē*.[929]

Before continuing, here is a look at an inscription referring to the role of heavy sports in the training of *ephēboi*. Here, too, each *ephēbos* is listed first by name, then his family name and his city:

IG II2 956; SIG 3, 667

51 παῖδας πάλην τῆ[ς π]ρώτης ἡλικία[ς]·
   Νίκων Νικογένου Αἰγεῖδος φυλῆς.
   παῖδας πάλην τῆς δευτέρας ἡλικία[ς]·
   Μελέτων Στρομβυλίωνος Αἰγεῖδος φυλ[ῆς].
55 παῖδας πάλην τῆς τρίτης ἡλικίας·
   Ἀπολλώνιος Ἀπολλωνίου Αἰγεῖδος φυλ[ῆς].
   παῖδας ἐκ πάντων πάλην·
   Ἡραγόρας Διονυσοδώρου Ἀθην[αῖος].
   ἄνδρας πάλην· Εὔδημος Σωκ[ράτους Ἀθη]-
60 ναῖος. παῖδας πυγμὴν τῆς πρώ[της ἡλικίας]·
   Εὐφρέας Εὐφρέου Ἀκαμαντίδο[ς φυλῆς].
   παῖδας πυγμὴν τῆς δευτέρας ἡλ[ικίας]·
   Παυσανίας Παυσανίου Οἰνεῖδος φυ[λῆς].
   παῖδας πυγμὴν τῆς τρίτης ἡλικί[ας]·
65 Ἡρακῶν Πείθωνος Ἱπποθωντίδος φυ[λῆς].
   παῖδας ἐκ πάντων πυγμήν· Δωρό[θεος]
   Χαρμίδου Ἀθηναῖος. ἄνδρας πυγ[μήν]·
   Σωσικράτης Δημονόμου Ἀθηνα[ῖος].
   παῖδας **παγκράτιον** τῆς πρώτη[ς ἡλικίας]·
70 Φιλέας Φιλέου Ἀκαμαντίδος φυλ[ῆς].
   παῖδας **παγκράτιον** τῆς δευτέρα[ς] ἡλι[κίας]·
   Ἄβρων Καλλίου [Α]ἰγ[ε] παῖδαςἶδος φυλῆς.
   παγκράτιον τῆς τρίτης ἡλικίας·
   Ἀπολλώνιος Ἀπ{π}ολλωνίου {²⁶Ἀπολλωνίου}²⁶ Ἀτταλίδος φυλῆ[ς].
75 παῖδας ἐκ πάντων **παγκράτιον**· Σάμος Σάμο[υ]
   Ἀθηναῖος. ἄνδρας **παγκράτιον**· Θεοδωρίδ[ης] 15

---

927 Pelekidis, *Histoire*, p. 270.
928 Marrou, *Istoria tēs ekpaideusēs*, p. 233.
929 Pavlinis, *Istoria tēs Gymnastikēs*, p. 281.

Translated:
- Boys' wrestling, first age group: Nicon, son of Nicogenes, of the Aigeis tribe
- Boys' wrestling, second age group: Meleton, son of Strombylion, of the Aigeis tribe
- Boys' wrestling, third age group: Apollonius, son of Apollonius, of the Aegeis tribe
- Boys' wrestling, all ages: Heragoras, son of Dionysodorus, of Athens
- Men's wrestling: Eudemus, son of Socrates, of Athens
- Boys' boxing, first age category: Euphreas, son of Euphreas, of the Acamantis tribe
- Boys' boxing, second age group: Pausanius, son of Pausanius, of the Oineis tribe
- Boys' boxing, third age group: Heracon, son of Peithon, of the Hippothontis tribe
- Boys boxing, all ages: Dorotheos, son of Charmides, of Athens
- Men's boxing: Sosicrates, son of Demonomos, of Athens
- Boys' **pankration**, first age group: Phileas, son of Phileas, of the Acamantis tribe
- Boys' **pankration**, second age group: Habron, son of Callias, of the Aegeis tribe
- Boys' **pankration**, third age group: Apollonius, son of Appolonius, of the Attalis tribe
- Boys' **pankration**, all ages: Samos, son of Samos, of Athens
- Men's **pankration**: Theodorides, son of Pausanias, of Athens

Participating in the institution of the *ephēbeia* was an essential prerequisite for acquiring civic rights. For this reason, there was provision for a special class for youths with a physical disability, such as poor eyesight, that prevented them from taking part in athletic activities.[930]

The institution of *ephēbeia* was also developed at the three major *gymnasia* in Athens: the Academy, the Lyceum and the Cynosarges.[931] At these schools, the city's youth engaged in sports, military training and general studies.[932] It was not unusual to see foreign career athletes who wanted to take part in games to be training in the same space as the young *ephēboi*.[933] The Lyceum in Athens was no exception, and there is a reference to two competitive age classes - youth and men - who competed at the Theseian games.[934]

The *ephēbeia* were considered to be institutions of higher education. The Athenians ascribed great importance to the well-rounded education of youth with prestigious positions in society. This institution lasted for more than six hundred years (335 BCE - 266 CE).[935]

---

930 Marrou, *Istoria tēs ekpaideusēs*, p. 243.
931 Pelekidis, *Histoire*, p. 260.
932 Tyler Jo Smith, *A Companion to Greek Art* (Blackwell, Oxford 2012), pp. 547, 548.
933 Théophile Homolle, «Le gymnase de Delphes,» *Bulletin de correspondance hellénique* 23 (1899): p. 575.
934 Pelekidis, *Histoire*, p. 261.
935 Mouratidis, Istoria physikēs agōgēs, p. 157.

In Sparta, the young men were called *eirens* and they attended *ephēbeia* at the same age as the Athenian youths.[936] Their curriculum included additional exercises, such as outdoor camping, hiking and excursions, both at day- and nighttime, swimming, ship navigation and the equestrian arts in all their variations. As for their basic education in the first year, rhetoric and philosophy were added, along with nature studies and civic education. Thus, the *ephēbeia* was a higher civic institution which shaped ideal citizens who could defend their homeland in both war and peace.[937] Spartans were fighters above all and their lives belonged completely to the state. There could be no hesitation when receiving an order. Moreover, when there was hard work to be done or they were subjected to hardship, they had to be physically robust enough to endure it.[938] Training was brutal. What Aristotle has to say is interesting: an athletic approach was largely avoided, and they did not take part in special training; they did not allow themselves to rest or sleep for long periods and they avoided the mandatory diet of athletes. As to the rules governing pankration, there were no restrictions. Competitors could strike any target in any manner they wished. It was the ultimate form of man-to-man combat. They were killing machines.

In the early stages of Spartan education, the youths had to achieve their maximum physical abilities without a careful diet, without rest or overeating.[939] Boxing and pankration were used as exercise in Sparta, while competing in these events was forbidden to Spartans because they were strictly forbidden from surrendering during the contest. For their training, they used everything that the rest of the Greeks did, with additional violent and dangerous games.[940] In Sparta, once a boy reached the age of seven, his care was taken over by the state and he was placed in groups, or "herds." At age twelve, the groups became more organized and training more vigorous until the age of fourteen. The boys were then considered *ephēboi* and training continued at the same rigorous pace until they reached the age of twenty. The Spartans then would stop their training program, but were obliged to keep their physical strength up through activities like hunting.[941]

It is interesting to note that the Spartans did not have lessons in weaponry even though their country was perhaps the most warlike of all time. They endeavored to create hardy and invincible fighters and weapons han-

---

936 Pavlinis, *Istoria tēs Gymnastikēs*, p. 273.
937 Chrysafis: *Ē gymnastikē*, p. 220.
938 Pavlinis, *Istoria tēs Gymnastikēs*, p. 276.
939 Pavlinis, *Istoria tēs Gymnastikēs*, p. 278.
940 Pavlinis, *Istoria tēs Gymnastikēs*, p. 281.
941 Plutarch, *Lycurgus*, 16-24.

dlers without weapons training.[942] It is rather hard to imagine that the military corps of *ephēboi* and *eirens* did not train regularly or receive some instruction in the use of weapons. However, regular exercise and weapons training were not part of the boys' gymnasium, nor did the *ephēboi* engage in these during their training. And they certainly did not rely on these exercises to develop good fighters. The essence was this: at that time, fighting was hand-to-hand and the Spartans realized that a good fighter had to be strong in body and spirit. This was achieved through wrestling, boxing and pankration and not with the superfluous arts of weaponry. They also knew that the art of piercing an enemy with a spear or sword, or defending oneself with a shield did not require much time to master. The negligible benefit to be derived would have disastrous results, since a more cowardly soldier would become bolder and thus become more vulnerable. That is why Plato said that no one knowledgeable in weaponry was very courageous and the reason why the Spartans did not teach weapons handling and instead practiced contact sports.[943]

The training regimen at the *ephēbeia* changed significantly during the Roman era. The *ephēboi* trained in track sports, such as the single-course *stadion*, the double-course *diaulos* and in the longer *dolichos*. They also practiced wrestling, boxing and pankration, as they did in the Hellenistic period. Competition in archery, javelin throwing and weaponry all but disappeared, even though these activities were more closely related to military training. Meanwhile, training in the use of the catapult had become redundant.[944]

Nevertheless, the *ephēbeia* played a much larger role: aside from its purely military purpose, the *ephēbeia* served needs for socialization, discipline,[945] and initiation into the Greek way of life, with the key element being the cultivation of an aptitude for athletics. The *ephēboi* took part with their weapons in processions at both the Eleusinian and Great Panathenaic games. Through this institution, individuals were converted into citizens who became members of a society with rights and obligations. They also learned to obey their laws and rulers.[946]

The institution of the ephebeia evolved considerably over its lifetime. During the Roman imperial era, the initial two-year, compulsory and publicly funded matriculation had become a rather aristocratic, prestigious school

---

942 Pavlinis, *Istoria tēs Gymnastikēs*, p. 283.
943 Pavlinis, *Istoria tēs Gymnastikēs*, p. 284.
944 Nigel Kennell, "The Greek Ephebate in the Roman Period," The International Journal of the History of Sport 26, no. 2 (February 2009): p. 332.
945 Evangelos Albanidis, "The Ephebia in the Ancient Hellenic World and its Role in the Making of Masculinity," The European Sports History Review 2 (2000): p. 17.
946 Albanidis, *Istoria tēs athlēsēs*, p. 225.

whose high tuition was covered by the students themselves.[947] After 119-118 BCE, the corps of *ephēboi* also accepted foreigners.[948] In numbers, its development looks like this: between 335 and 325 BCE, about 380 *ephēboi* were recruited, but as the population grew, the number of recruits rose to between 650 and 700.[949] In the imperial period (after 30 CE), Athens and Rome had equivalent populations (Rome: 440,000, Athens: 431,000). In Rome, *ephēboi* made up about a quarter of inhabitants, while in Athens, they were somewhat less than 20 percent, or about 86,200.[950] Of these thousands of *ephēboi*, just a few hundred were privileged to attend the *ephēbeia*. Attendance led to a certain conceit on the part of the youths, since the institute was seen as a symbol of luxury in the city.[951] It is clear, then, that pankration was essential in this important and, as it turned out, elitist institution.

The institution of the *ephēbeia* is believed to have been the Greek institution with the greatest assimilative power and which extensively contributed to the Hellenization of other peoples. Ephebeia were to be found in 124 Greek cities throughout the Hellenic world at that time[952] - from Marseilles to the Black Sea - and they resembled those of Athens in character.[953] The gymnasium and the *ephēbeia* functioned as a pole of attraction for the local inhabitants who aspired to learn about and to follow the Greek way of life.[954]

Spartan athletic festivals

The **Gymnopaediae** annual festival, held in honor of Apollo and the fallen Spartans at Thyrea, was of particular interest. All Spartans took part in the Gymnopaediae, divided into groups. The principal part of the festival involved the three dances of the elders, the men and the children, which they danced while chanting songs and paeans. It is possible that the children competed in the morning, the Spartan warriors in the oppressive midday heat, and the elders in the afternoon. Athenaeus reported that at the Gymnopaediae, nude children mimicked the movements of wrestling and pankration. In *Laws*, Plato described the entire festival as a process to toughen up the youngsters and

---

947 Albanidis, *Istoria tēs athlēsēs*, p. 225.
948 Marrou, *Istoria tēs ekpaideusēs*, p. 238.
949 Marrou, *Istoria tēs ekpaideusēs*, p. 237.
950 Yiannakis, Istoria physikēs agōgēs kai tou athlētismou, p. 9.
951 Marrou, *Istoria tēs ekpaideusēs*, p. 238.
952 Albanidis, Istoria tēs athlēsēs, p. 224.
953 Marrou, *Istoria tēs ekpaideusēs*, p. 240.
954 Albanidis, *Istoria tēs athlēsēs*, p. 293.

promote endurance. It is easy to imagine that this was indeed the case, considering the event was held in extremely hot conditions and would have been tested the endurance and fortitude of Sparta's youth.[955]

The Gymnopaediae lasted several days and was an important festival that included both athletic competition and contests in music and dance. Nothing could stop or interfere with this great event, not even Sparta's defeat at the Battle of Leuctra. Although the ephors had been informed of their army's loss at the hands of the Thebans, they allowed the festival to continue until every last event had been completed.

In general, athletic events were sacred for the Spartans and it is widely known that they refused to interrupt one of their annual events to offer military support to their allies during the Peloponnesian War. It is possible that the Gymnopaediae began in 668 BCE, one year after Sparta's loss to Argos, as a way of boosting the morale of the Spartan citizens so they could fight to recover their occupied land (which they did in 544 BCE).[956]

Another athletic festival held in Sparta which included competition was the **Leonidea**, staged to honor those who had fallen at Thermopylae. This celebration was held every year, but only Spartan citizens could take part. It is noteworthy that the Leonidea schedule included pankration, in which the Spartans did not take part when they were to compete against other Greeks.[957] Sparta's athletic festivals continued until the early part of the Common Era.[958]

---

[955] Albanidis, *Istoria tēs athlēsēs*, p. 206.
[956] Mouratidis, *Istoria physikēs agōgēs*, p. 135.
[957] Mouratidis, *Istoria physikēs agōgēs*, p. 135.
[958] Mouratidis, *Istoria physikēs agōgēs*, p. 555.

Chapter 8

PANKRATION AFTER 393 CE

Olympism

At Olympia, under the protection of the divine, the phenomenon of ruthless, bloody and deadly warfare between primitive people changed form and over time was replaced by peaceful, sacred contests; enmity was transformed into noble competition, enemies became friends and fellow athletes, and human beings established their society and created civilization.[959] Instead of battling their fellow humans in hatred, they began to compete with grace, purity, love and good will. Olympism and Hellenism changed the course of humanity. From the chaos and anxiety of primitive life, humans took the road of living in a society, seeking education and humanist values.[960] Thus, Olympism was not merely a means for physical development of the human body, but a higher form of cultivating and developing all those traits that instill substance in human beings.[961] The athletic spirit that grew out of the authentic Olympic spirit is a free spirit, devoid of national, political, economic or other constraints.[962]

The Roman period

Rome conquered Greece in 146 CE, and the Romans' differing concept of competition led to the decline of athletics.[963] Of course, there were some philhellene emperors who attempted to revive the panhellenic games and athletics

---

959 Papakyriakou: *Philosophia*, p. 154.
960 Papakyriakou: *Philosophia*, p. 155.
961 Papakyriakou: *Philosophia*, p. 155.
962 Papakyriakou: *Philosophia*, p. 155.
963 Yiannakis, *Istoria tēs physikēs agōgēs kai tou athlētismou*, p. 9.

in general. But they failed because they themselves were not able to consciously embrace the concept.⁹⁶⁴

While the Romans saw Greeks as models of education, they did not follow their example. The Romans saw athletes not as free citizens, but as slaves, criminals and thugs. They were people from the lower social strata and rarely came from the higher classes. This was quite the opposite of what we have seen at Olympia, where athletes were free, proud and rebellious: they were personalities. Roman athletes did not seek to win the victor's crown; their goal was to earn privileges, payments and favors. The Romans built stadiums, hippodromes and amphitheaters with the aim of asserting themselves. They never glorified the games; it never occurred to them to convince the Roman people that the games were imposed by the gods and that the patrons and architects of the contests were gods, goddesses and demigods.⁹⁶⁵ The Romans wanted to prevail through sheer quantity and ferocity of the spectacle. One such example was Caesar's wish to impress by presenting 320 pairs of gladiators. Aside from gladiators, Caligula also presented an actual military battle as spectacle. Pompey had 500 lions killed in five days. Charity towards the defeated gladiator in the Roman Empire was humiliating. The Roman games were bloody spectacles highlighting the vicious instincts of the competing gladiators. There were no noble, refined or human sentiments.⁹⁶⁶

Cassius makes reference to pankration as being part of the Roman games. The event was apparently part of the games staged by Caligula for the Roman people, and it is featured as a popular sport. Roman pankratiasts belonged to professional association and their goal was to solidify and advance their professional interests.⁹⁶⁷

Christianity

Aside from the impact of the Romans, the spread of Christianity that followed proved to be an enemy to all things ancient Greek, including athletics which constituted a strong aspect of Greek culture. For Christians, the development of physical skills represented a type of idolatry, since the body was the prison of the soul.⁹⁶⁸ Athletic activity had to be fought against - and it was. In-

---

964 Yiannakis, *Istoria tēs physikēs agōgēs kai tou athlētismou*, pp. 9, 10.
965 Yiannakis, *Istoria tis physikēs agogēs kai tou athlētismou*, p. 10.
966 Yiannakis, *Istoria tis physikēs agogēs kai tou athlētismou*, pp. 11, 12.
967 Yiannakis, *Istoria tis physikēs agogēs kai tou athlētismou*, p. 28.
968 Papakyriakou, *Philosophia*, p. 97.

stead, life took on an ascetic and monastic character. The physical body was neglected and no attention was paid to the earthly existence.[969] The new religion played havoc with physical training. The preachers of Christian religion declared that the body was material and perishable while also the prison of the soul; it is subject to stimuli and excites humans and it must be punished, left untended and immovable.[970] Competitive games conflicted with the Christian conscience and were seen as spectacle rather than as part of an educational system.[971]

At that time, the wealth of knowledge and the eloquence of the learned impressed young people, creating a model which they endeavored to emulate. Thus, the glory of the learned acquired a status akin to that of the Olympic victor, and naturally this gave way to new ideas and beliefs.[972]

But there is no single reason for the end of the ancient games. Their decline came slowly, partly as a result of social and economic circumstances. External factors such as Christianity and new philosophies that believed in life after death clashed with the paganistic worship at Olympia, but they alone were not enough to bring about the games' ultimate fall.[973]

The internal breakdown of the games

There were also obvious signs of deterioration. A lack of respect for competitive traditions, the ability to buy victory, the intervention of professional athletics, extravagant displays of popular worship of winners, the exclusive and unilateral devotion to training and games, the insatiable greed of athletes resulting in overfed and overdeveloped bodies, speculation by trainers and poor training practices, inferior techniques which had lowered athletic ethics and harmed the athletes' status in the eyes of the people, neglect of their intellectual and moral development - these are just some of the factors that played a decisive role in the downfall of the institution.[974] Overall, however, the professionalization of athletics and Christianity were the leading factors.[975] The institution of the games had worn itself out and come full circle.[976]

---

969 Papakyriakou, *Philosophia*, p. 98.
970 Yiannakis, *Istoria tis physikēs agogēs kai tou athlētismou*, pp. 12, 13.
971 Marrou, *Istoria tēs ekpaideusēs*, p. 287.
972 Papakyriakou, *Philosophia*, p. 98.
973 Crowther, *Sport*, p. 54.
974 Papakyriakou, *Philosophia*, p. 98.
975 Yiannakis, *Istoria tis physikēs agogēs kai tou athlētismou*, pp. 9, 10.
976 Papakyriakou: *Philosophia*, p. 99.

Thus, the 293rd and final Olympic games were held in 393 CE, and the following year, emperor Theodosius abolished them in an effort to strengthen Christianity. His decree was the Olympic spirit's swan song, but also effectively put an end to the worldwide spirit of athleticism.[977] Immediately after the Olympian games were abolished, the gold and ivory statue of Olympian Zeus created by Phidias was looted out of its temple and taken to Constantinople. It ceased to be the object of awe and respect for the Greeks at Olympia and was taken to Byzantium as a museum exhibit. Olympia, abandoned, fell into ruin.[978] The historian, Paparigopoulos, wrote: "Theodosius forbade any sacrifices conducted during the day or night on pain of death... The angry mobs in the provinces were not content to just abolish the cult; they wanted to destroy the very structures. Some of the bishops and most of the monks were eager to help with the desecration. This was the way that Christianity triumphed under Theodosius."[979]

Nevertheless, the memory of the Olympian games was not lost; it was kept alive in the collective conscience through art and by reading the Greek poets and writers of prose, long after the sites of the games had fallen into ruin.[980]

The ancient Greek gymnastic and agonistic tradition must have been very strong to endure through the centuries, despite the persistent and systematic war waged by the church and its followers.[981]

Byzantium

Despite opposition to sports by the priesthood, Byzantine athletics did exist. The games held after 394 CE were merely a display of physical skill by professional athletes, and pankration was among the events that endured during this period.[982]

Nevertheless, sports such as wrestling, boxing and pankration were considered unacceptable at this time because, by their nature, they injured and deformed the body, and especially the face that was made "in the image of

---

977 Thomas Yiannakis, Ē physikē agōgē apo to 394 m.Ch. [Physical education after 394 CE], Athens 1981, p. 7.
978 Yiannakis, Ē physikē agōgē, p. 8.
979 Yiannakis, Ē physikē agōgē, p. 7.
980 Louis Callebat, "The Modern Olympic Games and their Model in Antiquity," International Journal of the Classical Tradition 4, no. 4 (Spring 1998): p. 555.
981 Yiannakis, Ē physikē agōgē, p. 11.
982 Yiannakis, Ē physikē agōgē, p. 10.

the Creator." The ideal Byzantine Christian was thin, weak and pale.[983] In fact, because pankratiasts used only their hands to achieve victory up to the time of Chrysostomos, the *agonothetēs* did not place the crown on the victor's head, but first crowned his right hand.[984] The Byzantine Christians also considered it highly inappropriate that the athletes appeared at the stadiums nude.[985]

Death and injury among athletes at competitions was not a rare occurrence during the Byzantine era. However, the judges would examine the motives behind a death or injury before arriving at a ruling. The competition categories were either public or private, with the former recognized by the state. Based on this distinction, penalties for accidents were less severe at public events and more severe at private contests. According to the Pandects, a compendium of Roman law, when a wrestler, pankratiast or boxer killed his opponent at public games or while training, the *Lex Aquilia* (Aquilian law, named for the Roman consul) was not applied, because the accident was considered to have been committed in the "name of glory and bravery, and was not in violation of the law." (Clement, *Stromateis* 2, Ch. 13; Pandect 9.2.3). If an athlete harmed his opponent after the match, he was then held responsible under Aquilian law.[986]

Other tough games included the Byzantine *klōtsata*, *klōtsies* or kicks. This competitive game was played by two opponents. They would start off at some distance from one another and advance in leaps to the accompaniment of Byzantine music as they tried to kick each other in the face or body. It was quite a dangerous game and was rarely played.[987] According to Cretan satirical poet Stephanos Sachlikis of Crete (1331-1403): "Some prefer wrestling and others like singing, while others like kicking and hair-pulling instead."[988] There is no proof, but it may have bore some relation to pankration, since it was the only sport involving kicking.

---

983 Yiannakis, *Istoria tis physikēs agogēs kai tou athlētismou*, p. 58.
984 Yiannakis, *Istoria tis physikēs agogēs kai tou athlētismou*, p. 71.
985 Yiannakis, *Istoria tis physikēs agogēs kai tou athlētismou*, p. 57.
986 Yiannakis, *Istoria tis physikēs agogēs kai tou athlētismou*, p. 88.
987 Yiannakis, *Istoria tis physikēs agogēs kai tou athlētismou*, p. 108.
988 Yiannakis, Ē physikē agōgē, pp. 39, 40.

Middle Ages - Renaissance

In the Middle Ages, a training system devised by Italian physician and philologist Girolamo Mercuriale (1530-1606), which was based on ancient Greek gymnastics,[989] was very influential.

Then came the Philanthropinists, who were educators and philosophers concerned about the one-sided intellectual and spiritual education in Europe. They came up against the teachings of those who preached the divine word and were influenced by the classical system that promoted a balanced body and soul.[990]

The work of German Guts Muths (1759-1839) was based on the ancient classical writers, the book by Mercuriale, and the knowledge, experience and shortcomings of the European educational systems that he sought to correct.[991]

It is worth taking a look at how the athletic systems developed in Europe immediately following, which all shared elements taken from Greek athletics.

In Germany, the gymnastics system was developed by Friedrich Ludwig Jahn (1778-1852)[992] and Adolf Spiess (1810-1858)[993]; the Swedish system was developed by Pehr Henrik Ling (1776-1839);[994] in England, the system was introduced by Thomas Arnold (1795-1842); and in France, by Georges Hébert, who developed a system of physical education there. Hébert was an officer in the French Navy and director of a number of military schools. In 1913, he presented his proposed method in Paris, drawing admiration and respect from the intellectual world of France. He divided the natural movements of primitive humans that corresponded to modern needs into ten categories of natural exercises. One of these involved defensive moves that included methods of defense and offense based on boxing, wrestling and pankration, which he incorporated into his system.[995] Thus, pankration continued to influence athletics in Europe even into the twentieth century.

---

989 Yiannakis, Ē physikē agōgē, pp. 40, 41, 42.
990 Yiannakis, Ē physikē agōgē, pp. 42, 43.
991 Yiannakis, Ē physikē agōgē, pp. 43, 44.
992 Yiannakis, Ē physikē agōgē, p. 45.
993 Yiannakis, Ē physikē agōgē, p. 51.
994 Yiannakis, Ē physikē agōgē, p. 53.
995 Yiannakis, Ē physikē agōgē, pp. 58, 59, 60.

Chapter 9

PANKRATION IN THE EAST

The course of pankration in the East was far more interesting. Through the conquests of Alexander the Great and the possessions of his successors for more than 300 years in Central Asia and the north-western section of present-day India, education at the *gymnasia* was adopted by local populations and military as a place of training in martial sports and warfare.[996]

The establishment of contests in bare-handed combat at a professional level, which appeared in ancient Greece, required a systematic methodology if the fighter was to be effective against a trained opponent.[997] The idea of a professional athlete who could distinguish himself at athletic competitions was of vital importance to continuing the science of unarmed combat, as cultivated at the various gymnasiums that flourished throughout the Seleucid Empire and the Greco-Bactrian Kingdom.[998] It was typical for the Roman and Parthian royalty to retain Greek personal bodyguards and athletes who had been trained mainly by Greeks, known to excel in combat sports.[999] But even the Tamil kings in India had hired Greco-Roman *Yavanas* as palace guards.[1000]

There are few sources regarding Greek athletics in the Parthian era.[1001] It is known that local Asian populations took part in Greek athletic events, and even in sacred games. In fact, a text found in Delos refers to two Phoenician champions, a boxer and an athlete from Sidon (modern-day Lebanon). The latter was crowned victor in pankration at the Panathenaic games in 142

---

[996] Lucas Christopoulos, "Greek Combat Sports and Their Transmission to Central and East Asia," 106 *Classical World* 106, no. 3 (Spring 2013): p. 432.
[997] Christopoulos, "Greek Combat Sports," 431-459, p. 431.
[998] Christopoulos, "Greek Combat Sports," p. 432.
[999] Christopoulos, "Greek Combat Sports," p. 440.
[1000] Christopoulos, "Greek Combat Sports," p. 440.
[1001] Note: located in the region of modern-day Iran.

BCE.[1002] This would indicate the degree to which Greek athletics and military training had been adapted to non-Greek conditions at Asian gymnasiums. Besides, the infiltration of Greek civilization is evident from the fact that Greek was the official language in imperial Parthia.[1003]

The Kushan Empire[1004] that followed (100-300 CE) continued to emulate Greek combat sports through a Hellenized Buddhist warlike dynasty which worshiped the deity of Heracles, known as Vajrapani, as the god of strength.[1005] The dynasty mainly consisted of itinerant knights, including Parthians, Sakas and Greeks (*Yavanas*).[1006]

The spread of combat sports to Eastern Asia continued through the Greco-Buddhist tradition, which incorporated training at a gymnasium and was considered the center for education for both war and philosophy. In Thailand, Burma (now Myanmar), Japan, Vietnam, Tibet and China, combat sports evolved further over the years into a number of schools influenced by local customs and traditions.[1007]

In the chapter on pankration, we saw that the Greeks also used breathing as a method of recovery after practice, calling it an exercise of the *pneuma*, which meant "spirit" as well as "breath," among other things. Two thousand years after Oribasius had written his ideas, the parallels between the ancient Greek combat sports and the claims of experts in Chinese combat sports are evident; they acknowledged the importance of vital energy (*Qi*) while engaging in them just as the *pneuma* was important in ancient Greek training.[1008] It is believed in Chinese martial arts that the inhalation and exhalation must be used properly because as the air returns to the stomach, it becomes food to be absorbed. The internal organs of the body move in concert with the breath and thus, if breathing is not correct, these organs will suffer. If the breath is perfect, the internal body will be in harmony.[1009]

Moreover, when athletes practicing Chinese, Japanese or Korean martial arts strike a blow, it is sometimes accompanied by a cry in an attempt to unify the internal power of will and the *pneuma*, or breath. They endeavor to strike

---

1002 Christopoulos, "Greek Combat Sports," p. 443.
1003 Christopoulos, "Greek Combat Sports," p. 434.
1004 Its territory included sections that now belong to Afghanistan, China, Kyrgyzstan, India, Nepal, Pakistan, Tajikistan, Uzbekistan and Turkmenistan.
1005 Christopoulos, "Greek Combat Sports," p. 432.
1006 Christopoulos, "Greek Combat Sports," p. 435.
1007 Christopoulos, "Greek Combat Sports," p. 437.
1008 Christopoulos, "Greek Combat Sports," p. 443.
1009 Christopoulos, "Greek Combat Sports," p. 443.

with the entire body, exhaling from the lower part of the abdomen in order to momentarily externalize the whole of their mental and physical strength.[1010]

Thus, after the death of Alexander the Great, it would appear that while the authentic characteristics of the Greek combat sports gradually dissipated in the Hellenic world, they have been retained and now survive in diverse forms in Central and East Asia.[1011]

PANATHENAIC PRIZE AMPHORA, 5th CENTURY BCE.
METROPOLITAN MUSEUM OF ART, NEW YORK.

1010 Christopoulos, "Greek Combat Sports," p. 447.
1011 Christopoulos, "Greek Combat Sports," p. 456.

EPILOGUE

As we saw in the preceding pages, wars in ancient times were everyday occurrences, so it was particularly desirable to have citizens who well prepared to fight. The city-states invested in gymnasiums, *palaestrae*, stadiums and trainers to meet that need. As such, aside from the overall benefit and ideological and intellectual dimensions attributed to athletics, they could ensure their citizens would be ready to defend their homeland. As methods of warfare evolved and came to rely more on weapons and the formation of the phalanx, pankration as a method of unarmed combat was downgraded. Nevertheless, it still remained an important means of military training, helping soldiers to enhance their strength, discipline and endurance during the hardship of battle.

As a sport, pankration was the most popular at the Olympic and other major games. But pankratiasts were also particularly well-loved. The people deified the great victors and ascribed supernatural abilities to them. The sacred games were of such a high level that only professional athletes were capable of winning honors. They managed this either through their own financial resources, or through cash prizes they won at *chrēmatitēs* (money-earning) games, or by being sponsored by individuals or cities, or through a combination of more than one source. With the development of *gymnasia*, the democratization of society and the establishment of the *ephēbeia*, members of the lower social classes were able to achieve Olympic champion status.

Pankration also played a political role. As competitive games were Romanized, the athletes took advantage of their popularity to organize themselves into guilds, through which they were able to secure more privileges. On the other hand, emperors who wanted to leverage the reputations of pankratiasts appointed them to serve as *xystarchēs* and provided benefits for the purpose of giving the people "bread and spectacle." Athletic guilds cashed in on the reputation of the great athletes, though they added little to the athletic ideal. Nevertheless, they proved to be an important means of expanding and maintaining the popularity of the emperors at high levels.

Aside from the narrow confines of the athletic context, however, the meaning of the Greek word *agon*, or contest, in the classical period was becoming more and more diversified. In addition to athletic games, the competitive spirit began to infiltrate every aspect of Greek social life. The most significant change was that the Greek *agon* was broadened from the external and natural sphere to the internal, spiritual and intellectual sphere. This internalization of the competitive spirit was mainly embodied by philosophical debate, legal disputes, political discourse, theatrical contests and other areas.[1012]

Ancient Greece was not the only place where contests were held. But only in Greece did a system of *agones* and an agonistic spirit take hold and affect almost all aspects of life in the *polis*. From this perspective, the *agon* was a uniquely Greek creation in the ancient world. In all types of contests, the Greeks showed a fearless spirit of competitiveness which they legitimized, rationalized and formalized. When the era of Greek civilization drew to a close, the agonistic spirit did not disappear; it continued to play an important role in Roman and subsequent Western civilization.[1013]

But something else was also happening. The theory of Macroculture, which originates as a conceptual tool from organizational theory, asserts that out of the operation and form of activity of a business, an organization or a society in general, a system may gradually take shape that will incorporate a number of common values, norms, beliefs and customs which are shared or are accessible to its members. In other words, an effective coordination of activity takes place between independent economically active entities in a way that makes it possible to provide a widely understood set of rules of behavior and action. The context and the way in which the values and norms developed over a long period of time through athletics in ancient Greece from the Mycenaean period onward were ultimately transferred to the field of politics, and acted to precipitate the emergence of democracy during classical antiquity. The case of ancient Athens is the most typical manifestation.

A system of values, such as equality, honesty, integrity, altruism, virtue, fairness, *homonoia* (same-mindedness), friendship and others was developed among competitors taking part in athletic activities. The ancient athletes operated as a unified organism, according to the theory of Macroculture, based on a mesh of values that functioned interactively for all athletes. These athletic values and norms were diffused from the field of athletics into the field of politics, decisively contributing to the formation of new standards, such as patriotism, mutual trust, self-sacrifice, bravery in defending the city-state

---

1012 Daqing, "On the Ancient Greek αγών [agon]," pp. 6807-6808.
1013 Daqing, "On the Ancient Greek αγών [agon]," p. 6806.

from outside threats, and in developing the right to free expression - all values which were essential in establishing democracy.[1014] The notion of aesthetics in athletics was the unity of Good, Pure, True, Just and Free during the athletic productive process.[1015]

All of these values had been incorporated into ancient Greece education. However, the history of ancient education is of interest to those living in the modern Western world provided it reveals the immediate sources of its educational tradition. The essence of the intellectual civilization of the West is a creation of Greek civilization, which is also true to an extent in the educational system itself.[1016]

As we saw, the sanctity of the victor was linked to the oldest function of the games, of which we are reminded by the crowning of the winner. This sanctity of the ancient seasonal king followed the victors of the sacred games into the classical period. Aside from sanctifying the winner, a victory was also an indication that the *polis* had achieved its ideal in shaping a youth marked by excellence, which served to best guarantee its future. A victory reflected on the athlete's home city and was shared by both.[1017] In other words, a victory was living proof that the *polis* included fighting men, warning away anyone who may have had their sights on the native land of the victor. The glorious victory of its athletes was the greatest advertisement for a nation beyond its borders. Such reputations acted as natural protection, since the victors were seen as the city's human fortification. That was the implication of demolishing a section of the walls upon the return of the victor.[1018]

The ancient Greeks were able to substitute the Olympian and other sacred games for any large-scale violence, so that the games functioned as a mechanism to resolve conflicts by creating more realistic expectations of the relative strength of each *polis*. Individually, the athletes, though they received a prize without particular material value at the games, were richly rewarded by their city and provided with an incentive that was in line with their *polis*. The increased expectations in relation to the strength of the city meant fewer feuds, thus lowering the cost of disputes and saving on the expense of maintaining armies. This allowed the ancient Greeks to stem the dispersal of wealth associated with violence. By holding on to their resources and continuing the

---

[1014] Emmanouil Economou, Nicholas Kyriazis and D. Economou, "Ē theoria tēs makrokoultouras kai ē anadeixē tōn dēmokratikōn ideōdōn mesō tou athlētismou stēn archaia Ellada [Macroculture, sports and democracy in classical Greece]," paper presented at 20th International Congress on Physical Education & Sport, May 18-20, 2012, Komotini 2012: p. 8.
[1015] Farantos, *Philosophia 1*, p. 43.
[1016] Marrou, *Istoria tēs ekpaideusēs*, p. 10.
[1017] Gogaki, *Oi antilipseis*, pp. 177-179.
[1018] Gogaki, *Oi antilipseis*, p. 236.

ancient games, the Greeks were able to amass not just economic wealth, but an intangible richness of art, philosophy, history, justice and political theory - the institutional and cultural heritage that ultimately became the foundation of Western civilization.[1019]

As the most popular and powerful representative of the agonistic structure, pankration participated more than any other sport in this important contribution by ancient Greek athletics to the world. With pankration as its focus, this book examined an era and delved into a world that no longer exists, at least not in the form that it did once. That period in history was no more than the beginning of a journey that has not reached its destination and may never will. If in doubt, you can seek out the beginnings of your own culture and your education and you may find that you are more Greek than you can imagine, and more of a pankratiast than you think.

[1019] Douglas W. Allen and Vera Lantinova, "The ancient olympics as a signal of city-state strength," *Economics of Governance* 14 (October 2013): pp. 42, 43.

BIBLIOGRAPHY

Original sources:

Athenaeus, Deipnosophistae
    [Dinner-table philosophers]
Apollonius of Rhodes, Argonautica
Aristotle, Athenian Constitution
Aristotle, Politics
Aristotle, Rhetoric
Diodorus of Sicily, 17,100,2-6.
Lucian, Dialogues of the Gods
Xenophon, Symposium
Pausanias, Description of Greece, I
Pausanias, Description of Greece, V
Pausanias, Description of Greece, VI
Pausanias, Description of Greece, VII
Pausanias, Description of Greece, VIII
Pausanias, Description of Greece, X
Pindar, Isthmian Odes
Pindar, Nemean Odes
Plato, Gorgias
Plato, Laws
Plato, The Republic
Plutarch, Moralia
Plutarch, Lycurgus
Plutarch, Alexander
Philostratus, Gymnasticus
Philostratus, Imagines

BCH 10 (1886) 233, 13
BCH 68/69 (1944/5) 125, 37
Corinth 8, 3 223
Corinth 8, 3 228
Ephesos 1134
Ephesos 2092
Ephesos 3581
Ephesos 756
FD III 1:556
FD III 4:460
Hommages L. Lerat 841
I. Ephesos 1612

I.Napoli I 50
I.Napoli I 51
ID 1957
IG I³ 1473
IG I³ 893
IG II² 3125
IG IV², 1 122
IG IX, 2 249
IG V, 1 658
IG V, 1 669
IG VII 2470
IG XI, 4 1216
IG XII, 5 608
IG XII, 6 2:640

IG XII, 6 IG. II2, 956-62,964.SIG 3, 667
IGLSyr 4 1265
IGUR I 235
IGUR I 236
IGUR I 239
IGUR I 240
IGUR I 243
IGUR I 250
IGUR I 26
III 1178
IMT Kyz Kapu Dağ 1496
IvO 152
IvO 153
IvO 231
IvP II 534
IvP II 535
Magnesia 220
Miletos 104 Ionia
Roueché, PPAphr 52 (CIG 2758 A-G)
Sardis 7, 1 79
SEG39, 1292
Syll.³ 36A
Syll.³ 82

Secondary sources:

Albanidis, Evangelos. (2000). "The Ephebia in the Ancient Hellenic World and its Role in the Making of Masculinity." *The European Sports History Review* 2 (2000): 4-22.

Albanidis, Evangelos. *Istoria tēs athlēsēs ston archaio Ellēniko kosmo* [History of sport in the ancient Greek world]. Salto, Thessaloniki, 2004.

Albanidis, Evangelos and Vassiliki Nikolakaki. "The Social Origin of Ancient OlympicVictors" Paper presented at the International Olympic Academy: 7th International Session for Educators and officials of higher institutes of physical education, 20-27 July 2006, Athens, 2007: 174-182.

Allen, Douglas W. and Vera Lantinova. "The ancient Olympics as a signal of city-state strength." *Economics of Governance* 14 (October 2013): 23-44.

Andersen, Wayne. "Chasing shadows: lives of ancient Greek statues as lived by writers." *The European Legacy* 9, no. 4 (2004): 503-513.

Bartels, M. E., Judith Swaddling and Adrian P. Harrison, "An Ancient Greek Pain Remedy for Athletes," *Pain Practice* 6, no. 3 (2006): 212-218.

Berquist, Jr., Goodwin F. "Isocrates of Athens: foremost speech teacher of the ancient world." *The Speech Teacher* 8, no. 3 (1959): 251-255.

Bitros, George, and Anastassios Karayiannis. "Character, knowledge and skills in ancient Greek education: Lessons for today's policy makers." *Munich Personal RePEc Archive* 18012 (Oct. 20, 2009): 1-29.

Boutet-Lanouette, Matthieu. «La vie agonistique dans les cites Grecques d' époque imperiale analyse de l' Αγών des Balbilleia d' Ephese (IER-III^{E}siecle p.C.).» Master's thesis, Quebec, 2007.

Burleson, Cindy. "The ancient Olympic Truce in modern-day peacekeeping: revisiting Ekecheiria." *Sport in Society* 15, no. 6 (August 2012): 798-813.

Callebat, Louis. "The Modern Olympic Games and their Model in Antiquity." *International Journal of the Classical Tradition* 4, no. 4 (Spring 1998): 555-566.

Christopoulos, Lucas. "Greek Combat Sports and their Transmission to Central and East Asia," *Classical World: A Quarterly Journal on Antiquity* 106, no. 3 (2013): 431-459.

Chrysafis, Ioannis E. Ē *Gymnastikē ton archaiōn [The fitness training of the ancients]*. National Academy of Physical Education, Athens, 1965.

Crowther, Nigel B. "Numbers of Contestants in Greek Athletic Contests." *Nikephoros* 6 (1993): 39-52.

Crowther, Nigel B. "Athlete and State: Qualifying for the Olympic Games Ancient Greece." *Journal of Sport History* 23, no. 1 (Spring 1996): 34-43.

Crowther, Nigel B. "Visiting the Olympic Games in Ancient Greece: Travel and Conditions for Athletes and Spectators." *The International Journal of the History of Sport* 18, no. 4 (December 2001): 37-52.

Crowther, Nigel B. "Athletics and Literature in the Roman Empire (review)." *Mouseion: Journal of the Classical Association of Canada* 7, no. 3 (2007): 267-270.

Crowther, Nigel B. *Sport in Ancient Times*. Praeger, Westport, 2007.

Daqing, Wang. "On the Ancient Greek αγών [agon]." *Procedia Social and Behavioral Sciences* 2, no. 5 (2010): 6805–6812.

Drivas, Achilleas. *Oi sōmatikes askēseis stēn proistorikē Ellada* (Physical exercise in prehistoric Greece). Athens, 1965.

Duvinage, Cedric. "The Ancient History of Sports Referees." In *Referees in Sports Contests*. Gabler Verlag, Wiesbaden, 2012: 17-21.

Economou, Emmanouil, Nicholas Kyriazis and D. Economou. "Ē theoria tēs makrokoultouras kai ē anadeixē tōn dēmokratikōn ideōdōn mesō tou athlētismou stēn archaia Ellada [Macroculture, sports and democracy in classical Greece]." Paper presented at 20th International Congress on Physical Education & Sport, May 18-20, 2012, Komotini (2012): 1-8.

Farantos, Georgios. *Philosophia 1: Theōria tou ellēnikou Athlētismou* [Philosophy 1: Theory of Greek Athletics]. Telethrion, Athens 1992

Farrington, Andrew. "Isthmionikai: A catalogue of Isthmian Victors." *Nikephoros* 21. Weidmann, 2012.

Forbes, Clarence. "*Oi Aph Heracleous* in Epictetus and Lucian." *The American Journal of Philology* 60, no. 4 (1939): 473-474.

Forbes, Clarence. "Ancient Athletic Guilds." *Classical Philology* 50, no. 4 (October 1955): 238-252.

Gardiner, E. Norman. "The Pankration and Wrestling. III." *The Journal of Hellenic Studies* 26 (1906): 4-22.

Giannaki, Sotiria, Nikitas Nomikos and Thomas Yiannakis. "Ē ypervasē tōn koinōnikōn kai thrēskeutikōn oriōn ōs genesiourgos aitia tōn archaiōn Ellēnikōn Agōnōn [The transgression of social and religious norms as a trigger for the ancient Greek games." Paper presented at 14th International Congress on Physical Education & Sport, Komotini, Greece, May 19-21, 2006.

Giannikopoulos, Anstasios."Pote archise o thesmos tēs ephēveias [When did the institution of ephebeia begin]?" *Archaeologia* 35 (1993): 64-73.

Gogaki, Konstantina. *Oi antilēpseis tōn archaiōn Ellēnōn gia ton athlētismo* [The perceptions of the ancient Greeks about athletics]. Tipothito-Giorgos Dardanos. Athens, 2005.

Golden, Mark. *Sport in the ancient world from A to Z*. London: Routledge, 2004.

Harris, H.A. *Sport in Greece and Rome*. Thames and Hudson, London, 1972.

Homolle, Théophile. «Le gymnase de Delphes.» *Bulletin de correspondance hellénique* 23 (1899): 560-583.

Hubbard, Thomas."Contemporary sport sociology and ancient Greek athletics." *Leisure Studies* 27, no. 4 (October 2008): 379-393.

Instone, Stephen. "Pindar's Enigmatic *Second Nemean*." *Bulletin of the Institute of Classical Studies* 36, no. 1 (December 1989): 109-116.

Ioannidis, Andreas. "Via kai athlēmata," *Archaiologia* (quarterly periodical) 1, no. 4, Athens, 1982.

Karyotakis, Iakovos. *Istoria ton vareon agonismaton* [History of heavy sports]. Self-published, Athens, 1974.

Kennell, Nigel. "The Greek Ephebate in the Roman Period." *The International Journal of the History of Sport* 26, no. 2 (February 2009): 323-342.

Kidd, Bruce. "The myth of the ancient Games." *Sport in Society* 16, no. 4 (2013): 416-424.

Kissoudi, Penelope. "Closing the Circle: Sponsorship and the Greek Olympic Games from Ancient Times to the Present Day." *The International Journal of the History of Sport* 22, no. 4 (July 2005): 618-638.

Kitriniaris, K.S. *Gymnasticus by Philostratus,* Patsilinakos, Athens, 1961.

Knab, Rudolf. *Die Periodoniken*. Ares Publishers, Chicago, 1934.

Komitoudis, Dimitris. "Ē proponētikē tōn Archaiōn Ellēnōn (Athletic training of the ancient Greeks). PhD diss., University of Crete, 1997.

Konsolaki, Eleni. "Trauma kefalēs kai trachēlou stēn Archaia Ellada [Head and neck trauma in Ancient Greece]." PhD diss., Univeristy of Crete, Herakleio, 2011.

Kosmetatou, Elizabeth. "Constructing Legitimacy: The Ptolemaic *Familiengruppe* as a Means of Self-Definition in Posidippus' *Hippika*." In *Labored in Papyrus Leaves: Perspectives on an Epigram Collection Attributed to Posidippus (P.Mil.Vogl. VIII 309)*, edited by Benjamin Acosta-Hughes, Elizabeth Kosmetatou and Manuel Baumach, Center for Hellenic Studies, Washington, D.C., 2004.

Kostouros, Giorgos P. *Nemeōn Athlōn Diēgēsis* [Record of Nemean feats], Vol. 1. Athens, Nisos, 2008.

Kostouros, Giorgos P. *Nemeōn Athlōn Diēgēsis* [Record of Nemean feats], Vol. 2. Athens, Nisos, 2008.

Kyle, Donald G. "Pan-Hellenism and Particularism: Herodotus on Sport, Greekness, Piety and War." *The International Journal of the History of Sport* 26 (2) (February 2009): 183-211.

Kyle, Donald G. (2013). "Greek Athletic Competitions: The Ancient Olympics and More," in *A Companion to Sport and Spectacle in Greek and Roman Antiquity*, edited by Paul Christensen and Donald G. Kyle. Wiley-Blackwell, Hoboken, 2013: 21-35.

Kyriazis, Nicholas and Emmanouil M. L. Economou. "Macroculture, sports and democracy in classical Greece." *European Journal of Law and Economics* 40, no. 3 (December 2015): 431-455.

Kyriazis, Nicholas and Xenophon Paparrigopoulos. "War and democracy in ancient Greece." *European Journal of Law and Economics* 38 (2014): 163–183.

Liddell, Henry G., and Scott, Robert. A Greek-English Lexicon. Oxford. Clarendon Press. 1940. http://www.perseus.tufts.edu

Liddell, Henry George and Robert Scott, *A Greek-English Lexicon*. Retrieved Oct. 20, 2015. http://www.perseus.tufts.edu/hopper/text?doc=Perseus%3atext%3a1999.04.0057

Marrou, Henri-Irénée. *Istoria tēs ekpaideusēs kata tēn archaiotētas: O ellēnikos kosmos* [A history of education in antiquity]. Translated by Valia Sereti. Daidalus I. Zacharopoulos. Athens, 2009.

Martin, Roland R. «Un nouveau règlement de culte thasien.» *Bulletin de correspondance hellénique* 64, no. 1 (1940): 163-200.

Masterson, D. W. "The ancient Greek origins of sports medicine." *British Journal of sport Medicine* 10, no. 4 (1976): 196-202.

Menenakos, Evangelos, Nicholas Alexakis, Emmanuel Leandros, Gerasimos Laskaratos, Nikolaos Nikiteas, John Bramis and Abe Fingerhut. "Fatal Chest Injury with Lung Evisceration During Athletic Games in Ancient Greece. *World Journal of Surgery* 29, no. 10 (2009): 1348-1351.

Milavic, Anthony. "Pankration and Greek Coins." *The International Journal of the History of Sport* 18, no.2 (2001): 179-192.

Miller, Stephen G. *Arete: Greek Sports from Ancient Sources.* University of California Press, 2012.

Moretti, Luigi. *Inscrizioni Agonistiche Crèche.* Angelo Signorelli, Rome, 1953.

Moretti, Luigi. *Olympionikai, I vincitori negli antichi Agoni Olimpici.* Academia Nazionale dei Lincei, Rome, 1957.

Mouratidis, Ioannis. *Istoria physikēs agōgēs me stoicheia philosophias* [The History of Physical Education (with Elements of Philosophy)]. Christodoulidis. Thessaloniki, 2009.

Nomikos, Nikitas N., George N. Nomikos and Demetrios S. Kores. "The use of deep friction massage with olive oil as a means of prevention and treatment of sports injuries in ancient times." *Archives of Medical Science* 6, no. 5 (2010): 642-645.

Packard Humanities Institute, Project Centers, Cornell University, Ohio State University, Project History, Searchable Greek Inscriptions. Retrieved Aug. 10-11-12, 2015. http://epigraphy.packhum.org/inscriptions/main

Papakonstantinou, Zinon. "Prologue: Sport in the Cultures of the Ancient World." *The International Journal of the History of Sport* 26, no. 2 (February 2009): 141–148.

Papakyriakou, Evangelos P. *Philosophia physikēs agōgēs kai athlitismou* [Philosophy of physical education and sports], Thessaloniki 1985.

Papakyriakou, Evangelos. "Ē koinonikē sēmasia tēs fysikēs agōgēs kai tou athlētismou stēn Athēna tou 5ou aiōna [The social significance of physical education and athletics in 5th century Athens]." PhD diss., University of Thessaloniki, 1988.

Papantoniou, Georgios. "Oi epidraseis tēs ēthikēs stous Olympiakous agōnes tēs archaiotētas: apo tēn enarxē tōn agōnōn eōs to telos tēs klasikēs epochēs [The effects of ethics on the Olympic games of antiquity: from the beginning of the games to the late classical period] (776-336 BCE)." PhD. diss. University of Thessaly, Trikala, 2003.

Papantoniou, Georgios. "Religiosity as a main element in the ancient Olympic Games." *Sport in Society* 11, no. 1 (January 2008): 32-43.

Patrucco, Roberto. *Lo sport nella Grecia Antica.* Firenze: L. S. Olschki, 1972.

Pavlinis, Evangelos. *Istoria tēs Gymnastikēs [History of Athletics].* G. Ē. Kallergi, Athens, 1927.

Pelekidis, Chrysis. *Histoire de l'éphébie attique des origins à 31 avant Jesus-Christ.* E. de Boccard, Paris, 1962.

Pleket, H. W. "Some aspects of the history of the athletic guilds." *Zeitschrift für Papyrologie und Epigraphik* 10 (1973): 197-227.

Pleket, H. W. "The Olympic Games in antiquity." *European Review* 12, no.3, (2004): 401-413.

Poliakoff, Michael B. *Studies in the Terminology of Greek Combat Sports.* Hain, Frankfurt, 1986.

Poliakoff, Michael B. *Combat Sports in the Ancient World: Competition, Violence and Culture (Sports and History Series),* Yale University Press, New Heaven, 1987.

Pritchard, David M. "Sport, War and Democracy in Classical Athens." *The International Journal of the History of Sport* 26, no. 2 (February 2009): 212–245.

Sakellarakis G., M. Andronikos, N. Gialouris N., K. Palaiologou and M. Pentazou. *Oi Olympiakoi Agōnes stēn archaia Ellada* [The Olympic Games in ancient Greece]. Ekdotiki Athinon, Athens, 1982.

Samara, Aikaterini and Evangelos Albanidis. "Ē agōnistikē parousia and ē athlētikē proetoimasia tōn paidōn stēn Ellinikē and Romaikē archaiotēta [The competitive presence and athletic preparation of youths in Greek and Roman antiquity." Paper presented at the 19th International Congress on Physical Education & Sport, Komotini, Greece, May 20-22, 2011.

Savidis, Lazaros E. *Pankration: to olympiakon agōnisma* [Pankration: the Olympic sport], Eleftheri Skepsis, Athens, 2004.

Schneider K. "Paradoxos." *RE* IXX$_3$ (1949): 1166-1167.

Simopoulos, A. P. "Nutrition and fitness from the first Olympiad in 776 BC to 393 AD and the concept of positive health." *The American Journal of Clinical Nutrition* 49, no. 5 (1989): 921-6.

Smith, Tyler J. *A Companion to Greek Art*. Blackwell, Oxford, 2012.

Strasser, Jean-Yves. «La carrière du pancratiaste Markos Aurèlios Dèmostratos Damas. *Bulletin de correspondance hellénique* 127, no. 1, (2003): 254-299.

Thurston, Alan J. "Art of preserving health: Studies on the medical supervision of physical exercise." *ANZ Journal of Surgery* 79, no. 12 (2009): 941–945.

Valavanis, Panos. *Athla, Athlētes kai Epathla* [Events, Athletes and Prizes]. Erevenites, Athens, 1996.

Weir, Robert G. A. *Roman Delphi and its Pythian Games*. Archeopress, Oxford, 2004.

Yiannakis, Thomas, *Istoria tēs physikēs agōgēs kai tou athlētismou kata tēn Romaikē kai Vyzantinē Epochē* [History of physical education and athletics in the Roman and Byzantine Period]. Athens, 1978.

Yiannakis, Thomas. *Archaiognōsia – Philosophia tēs Agōnistikēs* (Philosophy of Competition). Athens, 1979.

Yiannakis, Thomas. Ē physikē agōgē apo to 394 m.Ch [Physical education after 394 CE]. Athens, 1981.

Yiannakis, Thomas. *Istoria physikēs agōgēs: apo tous prōtogonous laous mechri sēmera* [History of physical education from primitive peoples to the present]. University of Athens Faculty of Physical Education and Sport Science, Athens, 1989.

Yiannakis, Thomas. *Ieroi-Panellēnioi agōnes* [Sacred-Panhellenic games]. Athens, 1998.

Yiannakis, Thomas B., and Sylvia T. Yiannaki, "The Meaning of Names in Greek Antiquity, with Special Reference to Olympic Athletes." *The International Journal of the History of Sport* 15 no. 3 (December 1998): 103-114.

INDEX

[Dio[genes 166
[S]micyl[i]nes 164

A

Academy 54, 61, 62, 212, 245, 254, 274
Adolf Spiess 264
Aelius Aurelius Menander 170, 172, 177, 185, 186, 189, 202, 214
ageneioi 89, 121, 167, 208
Agesidamus 125, 128
Agestratus 173, 185
agōgē 248, 253, 262, 263, 264, 278
agon 37, 67, 69, 86, 269, 274
agonothetēs 160, 200, 263
agoranomoi 200
akroatērion 62
akrocheiria 53
akrochersitēs 119
aleiptērion 62, 64
aleiptēs 11, 55, 57, 62
alindēsis 44
Altis 84, 118, 196, 198
alytai 72
alytarchēs 72
Amyntas 127, 128
anathēmata 33
Androsthenes 116, 126, 127
anephedros 11, 51
Antenor 121, 124, 128, 174, 185, 191, 193
Antiochus 118, 124, 127
archiatros 200
argyrotamias 200
Aristeas 130, 161, 184, 189, 192, 193, 194
Aristeas Corazeus 131, 189
Aristes 174, 185, 214
aristeuein 29
aristeus 29
Aristocleides 174, 185, 216, 218, 219
Aristomachus 136, 137, 161, 172, 182, 185, 192, 193, 202
Aristomenes 127, 128, 164, 194, 214
Aristophon 121, 128

aristos 29
Aristotle 39, 62, 69, 73, 80, 97, 247, 248, 249, 250, 251, 255, 272
Arrachion 59, 100, 106
Arrichion 100
asphaltodēs 57
Astyanax 121, 128, 174, 185, 191, 193
athla 29
Athleō 29
athlētēs 29, 199
athlon 29
athlos 29
Aurelius Achilleus 186, 189
Aurelius Aelix 158, 161, 195
Aurelius Hygianus 170, 172
Aurelius Phoibammon 158, 161, 175, 185
Aurelius Septimius Eirenaeus 174
Aurelius Toalius 159, 160, 162
Autolycus 176, 185

B

Bia 38
Bouleuterion 84
boxing 26, 27, 30, 36, 39, 40, 43, 44, 45, 46, 50, 52, 54, 56, 60, 62, 64, 74, 77, 86, 101, 105, 108, 110, 111, 112, 115, 125, 129, 130, 136, 143, 149, 153, 158, 159, 164, 166, 169, 171, 174, 175, 177, 182, 187, 191, 203, 249, 250, 252, 254, 256, 262, 264

C

Calas 129, 161
Callias 112, 113, 127, 164, 172, 177, 185, 188, 189, 190, 193, 254
Callistratus 177, 185
Candidianus Aphrodisias 171, 173
Caprus 125, 128, 194
choros 249
chrimatites 65
chryseon genos 77
Cimon 162, 163, 172, 177, 185, 245
Claudius Apollonius 133, 157, 158, 161, 193
Claudius Rufus 52, 133, 157, 158, 161, 162, 193, 202
Cleandrus 165, 238
Cleisthenes 68, 70, 93
Cleitomachus 54, 125, 128, 166, 172, 211
coryceum 62
Crinis 163, 164, 172
Cynosarges 61, 245, 254

D

Damagetus 114, 127, 214
Delphi 64, 66, 67, 68, 76, 92, 93, 94, 101, 102, 103, 104, 105, 109, 111, 115, 129, 130, 131, 132, 135, 144, 148, 149, 153, 154, 157, 176, 181, 186, 187, 188, 213, 278
Demetrius the Hermopolitan 143, 176, 185, 188, 189
Democrates 126, 187, 189
Diallos 125, 126, 128
diathesis 197
didaktērion 63
Diophanes 165, 172
Dioxippus 119, 120, 121, 128
disolympios 111
dolichos 54, 108, 111, 203, 208, 209, 210, 256
Dorieus 54, 114, 115, 116, 127, 165, 172, 176, 185, 190, 193, 198, 214
drachmas 58, 198
Dromeas 105, 106

E

eirens 255, 256
ekecheiria 68, 69
elaiothesion 62, 64
Elis 40, 60, 65, 68, 69, 70, 71, 72, 73, 75, 76, 77, 79, 84, 86, 98, 125, 129, 131, 148, 153, 157, 188, 194, 214, 243
enagonioi nomoi 50
ephēbeia 12, 244, 245, 247, 248, 250, 251, 252, 254, 255, 256, 257, 268
ephebeion 62, 64
ephēboi 251, 252, 253, 254, 255, 256, 257
ephedros 51
Ephodion 113
Ephotion 113, 127, 189, 190, 193
Ephoudion 113, 165, 172, 177, 185, 188, 189
Epicrates 251
epimelitēs 251
Epitimadas 113, 127
Epitimidas 113
eu agōnizesthai 60
Euancritus 165, 166, 172
Eurymenes 101, 106
Euthymenes 164, 172, 177, 182, 185, 222, 235
exedra 62

F

fair play 60, 105
favlos 249
Flavius Artemidorus 133, 161, 167, 172, 183, 185, 187, 189, 192, 193, 202
Friedrich Ludwig Jahn 264

G

Gaius Perelius Aurelius Alexander 171, 176, 188
Georges Hébert 264
gloios 57
Golden Age 77
gramateus 200
Great Panathenaic 94, 256
Greek Dark Ages 28, 32
Guilds 12, 199, 200, 201, 202, 275
Guts Muths 264
gymnasia 16, 61, 62, 63, 71, 213, 243, 244, 247, 254, 265, 268
gymnasiarchēs 200
gymnasion 61, 62
gymnastēs 11, 55, 56
Gymnopaediae 257, 258
gymnos 61

H

Hagias 101, 103, 104, 106, 164, 173, 185, 187, 189, 190, 193, 214
haltēres 53
Heironomia 53
Hekatombaion 85
Hellanodikeio 71
Heras 131, 161, 166, 172, 177, 185, 188, 189, 192, 193
Hermas 130, 131, 161, 171, 172, 177, 185, 191, 193
Hermodorus 142, 143, 154, 155, 156, 161, 176, 186, 188, 189
hieronikēs 199, 201
himantes 44, 45, 209, 210
homonoia 269
Hyperboreans 78, 234

I

Idaean Dactyls 78
Idaean Heracles 25, 79
iera 33, 52
ieromēnia 69
Iphitos 68
isopalia 52
Isthmus 66, 67, 103, 130, 144, 149, 182, 222, 231, 234, 235, 237, 240

J

judo 45
ju-jitsu 45

K

Karate 54
Kata 54
klōtsata 263
klōtsies 263
konistērion 62
kōrykos 45, 53
kotinos 79, 87, 198
Kung fu 54
kylisis 44, 45

L

Leocreon 163, 164, 172
Leonidea 258
Leon, son of Myonides 124, 163, 164, 177, 185, 188, 189
Liparion 163, 164, 172
Lucius Silicius Firmus Mandrogenes 158, 202
Lyceum 61, 62, 245, 254
Lygdamis 99, 100, 106

M

Macroculture 198, 247, 248, 269, 270, 275, 276
Marcus Aurelius Asclepiades 75, 142, 143, 154, 155, 156, 161, 171, 172, 176, 177, 185, 188, 189, 192, 193, 202
Marcus Aurelius Corus 170, 171, 172
Marcus Aurelius Demetrius 142, 154, 171, 172, 177, 185, 192, 193, 202
Marcus Aurelius Demostratus Damas 143, 144, 145, 148, 150, 161, 178, 185, 187, 189, 193, 202
Marcus Aurelius Thelymetrus I and II 187
Marcus Ulpius Domesticus 138, 139, 140, 141, 142, 161, 171, 172, 178, 185, 188, 189, 192, 193, 202
Marcus Ulpius Firmus Domesticus 192, 193
Marion 129, 161, 194
mastigophorous 72
Melesias 56, 178, 185
Menander 56, 130, 168, 170, 172, 177, 182, 185, 186, 187, 189, 202, 214, 220, 222
Menodorus 171, 173, 178, 181, 185, 191, 193
Mercuriale 264
mina 58
mna 58
myriaethlos 111

N

Nemea 64, 66, 67, 91, 92, 103, 104, 108, 110, 111, 113, 115, 116, 117, 118, 119, 130, 131, 144, 148, 154, 157, 165, 166, 173, 174, 175, 176, 177, 178, 181, 182, 183, 184, 187, 190, 191,

192, 193, 214, 216, 218, 220, 222, 231, 234, 235, 244
Nicanor 134, 161
Nicon 124, 128, 166, 172, 182, 185, 188, 189, 191, 193, 254
Nicostratus 131, 161, 194
Niki akoniti 51
nomophylakes 71

O

Oenomaus 79
Olympia 12, 16, 24, 25, 26, 27, 29, 50, 51, 52, 54, 60, 61, 63, 65, 66, 67, 68, 69, 70, 71, 72, 73, 74, 75, 76, 77, 78, 79, 80, 81, 82, 83, 84, 85, 86, 87, 94, 98, 99, 101, 104, 107, 110, 111, 112, 113, 114, 115, 116, 117, 118, 121, 127, 129, 130, 131, 132, 134, 144, 148, 154, 157, 158, 159, 160, 171, 181, 183, 190, 192, 193, 194, 196, 197, 212, 223, 225, 234, 243, 250, 259, 260, 261, 262
orchēsis 249
orthopalē 44
orthostandēn 44, 45
ostrakōdēs 57
Oxylus 68

P

paideia 248
paidotribēs 11, 55, 56, 58, 63
palaestrae 12, 16, 58, 62, 63, 107, 198, 213, 247, 252, 268
Palē 44
pammachia 43
pammachon 43, 166
pankratiasts 7, 12, 16, 38, 39, 45, 46, 49, 51, 53, 54, 56, 64, 75, 98, 99, 100, 162, 172, 185, 189, 190, 193, 200, 202, 203, 210, 213, 214, 250, 260, 263, 268
pankration 15, 16, 17, 27, 30, 38, 39, 40, 42, 43, 44, 45, 50, 52, 53, 54, 55, 56, 59, 60, 61, 62, 64, 71, 74, 75, 86, 87, 89, 92, 94, 95, 97, 98, 99, 100, 101, 103, 104, 105, 108, 110, 112, 115, 116, 125, 127, 128, 129, 130, 131, 132, 134, 135, 136, 137, 138, 142, 143, 154, 157, 158, 159, 160, 162, 163, 164, 165, 166, 167, 168, 169, 170, 171, 173, 174, 175, 176, 177, 178, 181, 182, 183, 184, 186, 187, 188, 190, 191, 192, 194, 195, 198, 202, 203, 213, 214, 220, 223, 249, 250, 252, 254, 255, 256, 257, 258, 260, 262, 263, 264, 265, 266, 268, 271
paradoxonikēs 133, 194, 202, 203
paradoxos 194, 202, 203
paradromis 62
Pehr Henrik Ling 264
pēlodēs 57
Perelius Aurelius Alexander 158, 161, 171, 173, 176, 185, 188, 189
perichōroi 65
periodonikēs 66, 104, 124, 131, 133, 137, 138, 142, 143, 144, 145, 150, 151, 152, 154, 155, 156, 158, 162, 174, 175, 176, 177, 178, 182, 183, 184, 187, 188, 189, 190, 192, 203
periodos 66, 113, 189
perioikoi 65

peripoloi 252
Phaedimus 125, 128
Pheidippides 163, 164, 172
Philandrides 118, 182
Philippus Glycon of Pergamon 191, 193
Philostratus 38, 39, 43, 44, 46, 50, 51, 53, 54, 55, 56, 57, 59, 92, 100, 101, 117, 125, 158, 202, 212, 246, 250, 272, 275
Philumenus 159, 162
Phrynon 100, 106, 213
Phylacidas 164, 172, 177, 182, 183, 186, 220, 229, 231, 232, 234, 235
Phylakes 248
Pisa 68, 79, 148, 153, 157, 184
Piseas 171, 173
Plato 23, 27, 39, 40, 43, 54, 62, 63, 73, 80, 97, 176, 248, 249, 256, 257, 272
plethrion 72
pneuma 57, 58, 266
polemikos 249
polis 25, 33, 34, 40, 41, 60, 67, 76, 84, 105, 200, 244, 251, 269, 270
Polydamas 116, 117, 118, 127, 198, 199, 211
Poomsae 54
Promachus 117, 127, 165, 172, 182, 185
Pronaia 64
prorrhesis 11, 72
Protophanes 128, 161, 194
Prytaneion 24, 196, 197, 198, 223
psilos 252
Publius Aelius Aristomachus 136, 137, 161, 167, 172, 182, 185, 202
Publius Aelius Heliodorus 167, 172
Publius Cornelius Ariston 131, 161
Pulydamas 116
Pygmē 44
pyrrichē 54
pyrrichios 54
Pytheas 182, 183, 185, 220, 221, 222, 231, 232, 235

R

rabdouchous 72
referee 39, 72
religiosity 34, 37, 107
Rexibius 101, 106
Rufus 52, 133, 158, 159, 161, 162, 193, 202

S

sacred xystic guild 201
Savate 45
Secundus 167, 172, 202
shadowboxing 45, 53

Socrates 63, 126, 142, 161, 254
sophronistēs 58, 251
Sostratus 118, 127, 165, 172, 183, 185, 188, 189, 190, 193
sphairistērion 62, 64
Sphodrias 129, 161
spondophoroi 70, 99
stadion 26, 86, 103, 104, 207, 208, 209, 210, 256
stēsas tous antagōnistas 74
Stomios 118, 127, 214
Straton 129, 161, 166, 172, 182, 184, 185, 191, 193, 194
Stratonicus 166, 172, 182, 185
Strepsiadas 165, 172
Stymphalus 168, 169, 172
synodos 200

T

Taekwondo 54
T. Flavius 169, 172
Theagenes 105, 108, 109, 111, 112, 127, 177, 185, 188, 189, 211
The Iliad 29, 31, 35, 36, 81
thematikoi 65, 149, 153, 154, 157
The Odyssey 29, 31, 35, 36
Thomas Arnold 264
Tiberius Claudius Artemidorus 132, 133, 161, 171, 172, 183, 185, 187, 189
Tiberius Claudius Rufus 52, 133, 157, 161, 202
Timanthes 114, 127
Timarchus 163, 164, 172, 183, 185
Timasitheus 101, 106, 213
Timodemus 113, 114, 127, 183, 185, 188, 189, 214, 215, 216
tinella kallinike 196
Titus Aelius Aurelius Menander 170, 172
Titus Flavius Archibius 134, 161, 171, 173, 183, 186, 187, 189, 192, 193
Titus Flavius Artemidorus 133, 167, 172, 183, 185, 192, 193, 202
Titus Flavius Asclep 166, 184
topikoi 65
trauma 36, 59, 276

W

wrestling 26, 27, 29, 30, 36, 38, 42, 43, 44, 45, 52, 53, 54, 55, 60, 62, 63, 64, 72, 74, 77, 86, 101, 103, 104, 116, 119, 125, 127, 128, 129, 130, 131, 134, 135, 136, 158, 159, 166, 167, 169, 170, 174, 175, 177, 178, 181, 182, 187, 188, 191, 192, 194, 195, 202, 203, 223, 225, 249, 252, 254, 256, 257, 262, 263, 264

X

Xenarches 182, 185
Xenodamus 132, 161

Xenophon 50, 63, 82, 118, 127, 250, 272, 276
xystarchēs 133, 200, 202, 209, 210
xystos 62, 133, 200

Y

Yavanas 265, 266
ypopaidotribēs 56

Z

Zanes 60
Zeus 25, 27, 29, 52, 60, 64, 76, 77, 78, 79, 80, 83, 84, 87, 88, 92, 105, 106, 123, 124, 131, 182, 184, 196, 197, 215, 216, 219, 222, 224, 225, 229, 231, 232, 234, 235, 238, 240, 241, 262

The Author

Spyros Loumanis was born in Athens. He has been practicing Chung do Kwan Taekwondo for 40 years with Grand Master Choi Dukkyu 8th Dan from Kukkiwon. He has worked as a professional instructor for the last 20 years.

He holds the 6th Dan. He has also practiced Muay Thai, Kickboxing, Judo (1st Dan) and Tai Chi Chuan. He holds a Master of Science degree from Democritus University of Thrace in Maximizing Athletic Performance and degrees in Business Administration from the University of Piraeus and the Technological Educational Institute of Athens.

He lives in Athens with his wife.

www.spyrosloumanis.com

www.ingramcontent.com/pod-product-compliance
Lightning Source LLC
Chambersburg PA
CBHW080636170426
43200CB00015B/2862